# COMING
# ON STRONG

# COMING ON STRONG

## GENDER AND SEXUALITY IN
## TWENTIETH-CENTURY WOMEN'S SPORT

## Susan K. Cahn

HARVARD UNIVERSITY PRESS
*Cambridge, Massachusetts*
*London, England*

*To my parents,*
*Gretchen and James Cahn*

This Harvard University Press paperback edition is published by
arrangement with The Free Press, a division of Macmillan, Inc.

First Harvard University Press paperback edition, 1995

*Library of Congress Cataloging-in-Publication Data*

Cahn, Susan K.
Coming on strong : gender and sexuality in twentieth-century
women's sport / Susan K. Cahn.
p. cm.
Includes bibliographical references.
ISBN 0-674-14434-1 (pbk.)
1. Sports for women—history—20th century. 2. Sexual
discrimination against women—history—20th century.
3. Gender identity. I. Title.
GV709.C34 1994
796'.0194—dc20
93-29348
CIP

# Contents

# Preface

As a sports-minded teenager of the 1970s, I marveled at the courage and skill of the pioneer female athletes of my generation. Prompted by new federal legislation against sex discrimination and, more generally, by feminist demands for female access to traditionally male realms of society, the sports world seemed to undergo a rapid, almost instant transformation. Within a few short years, girls' and women's athletic leagues, tournaments, sports camps, and city, state, and national championships sprouted to serve women at the high school, college, and professional levels. The media took note as well, giving extensive coverage to such female tennis and gymnastic stars as Billie Jean King, Chris Evert, Kathy Rigby, and Olga Korbut. As one of the grateful beneficiaries of these changes, I eagerly joined my high school basketball team and thrilled at my good fortune—the chance to be involved in what I assumed was the first-ever interscholastic sporting opportunity for girls.

Delighting as I did in the chance to play in organized competition, I was not concerned with the blatantly second-class status of women's sport in budget matters and the media; it did not occur to me that it could be otherwise. And though I had ached to play Little League baseball as a young girl, I never wondered why baseball remained off limits to girls. My concerns were personal and immediate, mostly about jump shots and playing time. I did suffer twinges of embarrassment knowing that I still harbored a secret wish to play halfback on my high school football team. And though I suspected that what made me "right" in "jock" circles might be making me all "wrong" in the nonathletic social scene, I assumed these were the private dilemmas of a girl born on the cusp of a new era. I had some vague images of women athletes of the past, like the amazing Babe Didrikson or the lithe Althea Gibson. But if I thought of them at all, it was as anomalies of an earlier age—athletes who had miraculously done it on their own in an age when women didn't play sports. As far as I knew, no tradition of women's competitive sport paved the way for my pioneering generation.

Years later my training in women's history and feminist studies has led me to reconsider those suppositions. I know now that histories get buried. Questions deemed insignificant may be worth asking. And interpretations oblivious to gender are most likely misguided and incomplete. As a graduate student I began to wonder about the tradition of women's athletics in the United States. Was it a linear story, a steady climb from exclusion to inclusion? Or had specific time periods, classes, or cultures supported women's athletics before the 1970s? Which women played sports, and what had doing so meant for them? If women had participated in the past, why had sports remained such a bastion of male activity and identity?

This book, which began as my Ph.D. dissertation for the University of Minnesota, addresses these and other questions designed to recover, and gain insight from, a history that for the most part has been ignored by both popular and scholarly writers. It is not a comprehensive history of women's athletics. Rather, it is a study of how gender and sexuality have been culturally constructed within and through twentieth-century U.S. women's sport. Precisely because women in sport crossed into a "male" realm, both critics and advocates articulated their beliefs about femininity, the female body, and the meaning of womanhood, leaving a rich body of historical evidence on how common-sense beliefs about womanhood and manhood are made and altered over time. By looking at how athletes, educators, sporting officials, promoters, and journalists have clashed and compromised over gender issues in sport, we can learn something about how ordinary and influential people create society's gender and sexual arrangements, and how their actions are conditioned by the circumstances and beliefs of their time.

As I worked on my dissertation and then this book, several institutions and many individuals provided financial, intellectual, and personal support. I am grateful to the Graduate School and the History Department of the University of Minnesota for assisting me financially at the dissertation level. A University of Minnesota dissertation fellowship, a dissertation special research grant, and a grant from the McMillan Travel fund provided extremely helpful support. Subsequently I have received financial assistance from a Clemson University Faculty Development Grant and a Julian Park Publication Fund Grant from the State University of New York at Buffalo.

The financial support I received enabled me to travel in several regions of the country collecting oral histories from athletes who competed in high-level competition from as early as the 1930s and as late as the 1970s. A few of these women had been famous athletes of their day. The vast majority, however, received little recognition during their playing days and have received even less attention from historians or other scholars. I owe them a great debt for sharing their time, stories, and knowledge with me. They provided me with a level of detail about women's athletic participation that is unavailable in written sources. More important, they gave me critical insights into the experience and perspectives of women athletes, information that transformed my own thinking about women's sport history. I would like to thank them for their great intellectual contribution to this project and at the same time acknowledge that their interpretations and mine were not the same in every instance, and that my own questions and interests have taken this study in directions that may not reflect their priorities. I would also like to thank them for their hospitality and for the thoroughly enjoyable experience of getting to meet them and listen to their life stories, which collectively paved the way for athletes of my and future generations.

I am also grateful for the generous help of archivists, friends, colleagues, and editors. As I worked with a variety of historical collections, I benefited from the knowledge and assistance of archivists, especially those at the University of Wisconsin, Tennessee State University, Smith College, Radcliffe College, and the Chicago Historical Society. My adviser at the University of Minnesota, Sara Evans, encouraged me throughout and after my years in graduate school, offering her unwavering support in all phases of the research and writing of this project. Professors Mary Jo Maynes and Janet Spector also generously shared their time and ideas and offered insightful criticisms and challenging questions as well as personal support along the way. Members of my dissertation writing group read numerous essays, conference papers, and chapter drafts from the project's inception to its completion. I would like to thank Davida Alperin, Greta Gaard, Priscilla Pratt, and Diana Swanson for their advice and comradeship. In revising the manuscript for publication, several colleagues have read chapters and made valuable suggestions. Pamela Mack, George Chauncey, Jr., Kath Weston, Don Sabo, Wanda Wakefield, Tamara Thornton, and Liz Kennedy have all given generously of their time and ideas. Cindy Himes Gissendanner and Mary Jo Festle, scholars who also study U.S. women's sport history, have been especially helpful and gracious in their willingness to share ideas and sources. Thanks also to Scott Henderson, who provided invaluable help in the final stages. Finally, I am grateful to Joyce Seltzer, my editor at The Free Press, who went to bat for this project early on and then offered her constant encouragement and support. Her high standards and excellent advice have made this a better book.

In addition numerous friends and family members read chapters and/or offered encouragement, helpful criticisms, and laughter in just the right doses. I owe many thanks to Maureen Honish, Nan Enstad, Sharon Doherty, Linda Silber, Barbara Appleby, Betsy Scholl, Robin McDuff, Elizabeth Martín-García, Lotus Cirilo, Lisa Cahn, Kathleen Duffy, Shelly, Ellen Mamer, my brothers, Steven and Peter Cahn, and my parents, Gretchen Cahn and James Cahn. Finally, I would like to thank Birgitte Soland, who doesn't even like sports. Her powerful intellect, generous heart, easy laughter, and abiding love have made this a better book and enriched my life immeasurably.

# INTRODUCTION

In the early 1980s a talented young Czech immigrant to the United States took the women's tennis world by storm. Martina Navratilova lost only six matches from 1982 to 1984, and by 1985 had accumulated 8.5 million dollars in winnings, more than any other player in the sport's history.[1] The refreshingly candid, lithe, muscular Navratilova symbolized the advances women had made in the athletic world and, more broadly, in traditionally male activities involving money and power. As an outspoken critic of sexual inequality in sport, she represented both the ongoing struggle and the impressive gains women had made in more than a decade of challenges to the historic barriers to women's participation in sport.

As Navratilova and other female athletes gained celebrity status, many observers heralded their accomplishments as proof that modern women had finally cast off the physical and psychological shackles of past centuries. Yet others looked less favorably on these developments, perceiving women's entrance into sport as an unsettling and unwelcome intrusion into the realm of masculinity. In the tennis world Navratilova's mounting victory toll invited subtle condemnation and not-so-subtle ridicule from tennis experts, fans, and the press.

Some wondered whether Navratilova even belonged on the women's tour anymore, given her apparent invincibility. Noting her high-tech, precision-oriented training methods, they characterized her as a "bionic sci-fi creation" of her training team—a kind of unnatural, even monstrous "Amazon" who "has the women's game pinned to the mat."[2] Rather than bask in hard-earned glory, therefore, Navratilova felt continually pressed to

1

counter her public image as some kind of hulking predator who kept "beating up all those innocent girls."[3] This image, reflected in media comments like "She's simply *too good*," placed her at odds with, and not within, the women's tennis circuit.[4]

By implication these representations also suggested that she was at odds with her sex; "the bleached blonde Czech bisexual defector" who "bludgeoned" and "teased" her hopelessly inferior opponents appeared to be something other than a "natural" female.[5] One of her frustrated "victims" suggested to a reporter that for Navratilova to play that well, she "must have a chromosomic screw loose somewhere."[6] Navratilova's stunning accomplishments could have been construed as an example of one athlete's successful attempt to use her natural talents, hard work, and state-of-the-art training regimen to reach new levels of athletic excellence.[7] Yet many Americans simply could not separate the concept of athletic superiority from its cultural affiliation with masculine sport and the male body. Her startlingly "masculine" accomplishments generated farfetched explanations; contemporaries portrayed her as an extraordinary product of science, technology, or—worse—chromosomal defect.

Martina Navratilova's tarnished reputation suggests that even in this age of apparent progress, the historic association between athletic prowess and masculinity has endured. Highly skilled female athletes continue to meet with profound skepticism. At times, not only their femininity but their biological sex comes into question. Several enthusiastic young athletes from Lewisville, Texas, found this out during a girls' soccer match in the fall of 1990. On watching their daughters' team go down to defeat, two irate fathers stomped onto the field and demanded that the opposing side send its three best players to the bathroom so that an officially designated parent could verify their sex. These men could not fathom the fact that girls were capable of such talented play. After the game one of the aggrieved fathers belligerently "complimented" the winning team's nine-year-old star, goalie Natasha Dennis, by saying "Nice game, boy!" and "Good game, son." Nonplussed by the implication that her athletic ability derived from what might be between her legs, Dennis pluckily suggested that someone should instead take her accusers "and check and see if they have anything between their ears."[8]

Experiences like those of Martina Navratilova and Natasha Dennis are as old as women's attempts to break into the male sporting tradition. Athletics have long been the province of men. In the Western world, not only have men dominated the playing fields, but athletic qualities such as aggression, competitiveness, strength, speed, power, and teamwork have been associated with masculinity. For many men sport has provided an arena in which to cultivate masculinity and achieve manhood.

Consequently women's very participation in sport has posed a conundrum that Americans have grappled with for more than a century. Beginning in the late nineteenth century, American women made determined collective efforts to break down the barriers to female athletic involvement. They claimed sport as a right, a joy, and a signal aspect of women's emancipation. These attempts elicited both approval and scorn, generating a series of controversies that spanned the century. The matter went far beyond the issue of decorum—which kinds of behavior were deemed appropriate for the female sex. The controversies surrounding female athleticism broached fundamental questions about the content and definition of American woman- and manhood. Would women engaging in a traditionally male activity become more manlike? What exactly were "manly" and "womanly" qualities, and did they have to be limited to men and women, respectively? And if athleticism was not *essentially* masculine, did this mean that all gender differences were mutable and not ordained by, and permanently ensconced in, nature?

When women athletes insisted on their right to sport, alarmed and intrigued observers wrestled publicly with these very questions. In 1912 the *Ladies Home Journal* published an article titled "Are Athletics Making Girls Masculine?" Author Dudley Sargent, prominent physical educator and director of Harvard University's Hemenway Gymnasium, wondered along with many of his contemporaries whether female athleticism would make women into masculine facsimiles of the "opposite" sex.[9] Or, conversely, they worried that women could "feminize" sport, diluting its masculine content and eroding the boundary between male and female spheres of activity.

Sargent gave voice to the central, underlying tension in American women's sport—the contradictory relationship between athleticism and womanhood. In subsequent years others examined the same question, often in a harsher light than the relatively sympathetic Sargent. Journalists responded to Mildred ("Babe") Didrikson Zaharias's stunning athletic accomplishments of the 1930s through the 1950s by mocking her "mannish" appearance. They described her face as hawkish and hairy, her body as a whipcord, and her personality as a "conqueror type" that included "an unusual amount of male dominance."[10] Under the weight of such allegations, even supporters of women's sport felt pressed to concede that some female athletes excelled because of their genetically constituted "android tendencies."[11]

The apprehensions of skeptics did not go unanswered. Over the course of the century, advocates of women's sport developed numerous and often competing strategies to cope with the dissonance between masculine sport and feminine womanhood. The boldest among them accepted the charge of masculinization but claimed its positive value. They contended that women's athleticism would indeed endow women with masculine attributes, but that these qualities would benefit women as well as men, contributing to female emancipation and eliminating needless sexual distinctions.

Female physical educators responded more cautiously. Several generations of professionals sought to protect the reputation and health of female athletes by devising separate, less physically taxing versions of women's sport. In effect educators created a respectable "feminine" brand of athletics designed to maximize female participation while averting controversy. By contrast, popular promoters of community and commercial sport attempted to feminize the athlete more than the activity. They touted the feminine and sexual charms of female competitors, making sporting events into combination beauty-athletic contests. These and other sport advocates engaged in protracted battles for the control of women's sport, each side promising that under its authority women's athletics would gain respect and acceptance.

Individual athletes developed personal strategies to resolve the tension between their love of sport and the cultural condemnation of "mannish" or "tomboyish" athletes. Some made special efforts to demonstrate femininity through their dress, demeanor, and off-field interests. Other, more defiant types refused the compromise. With their "tough" manners and aggressive play, they embraced a style that critics called "mannish" but that they themselves saw as perfectly consistent with womanhood. Still others opted for a middle course, claiming allegiance to conventional definitions of femininity while at the same time trying to stretch their boundaries to include athletic activities.

Ironically, many of the collective and individual strategies athletes and their advocates employed to defuse the tension between sport and womanhood actually deepened the gender divide in athletic culture. Efforts to create a separate, distinct women's brand of sport effectively defined "feminine" sport as a lesser version of male sport: less competitive, less demanding, and less skillful. Commercial promoters were far more willing to commend top-notch athletes for their "masculine" excellence. But by going to great lengths to highlight the feminine attractiveness and sexual charms of female competitors, promoters implied that by itself, athleticism remained a manly trait, one that must be compensated for by proof of femininity.

Forced to deal with a constant barrage of criticism from diehard defenders of a male sporting tradition, generations of twentieth-century female athletes and their advocates successfully carved a niche for women in a sporting culture whose deep identification with masculinity nevertheless remained unyielding. With "real" sport and "real" athletes defined as masculine, women of this century have occupied only a marginal space in the sports world and an even more tenuous position in athletic governance.

Consequently many, perhaps even most, women have until recently been profoundly alienated from sport, and thus from the physical competence, confidence, and pleasures that sport makes available. However, those women who persisted in athletics found in sport a positive, even life-transforming experience. While dismissing, defying, or simply putting up with the societal hostility toward women athletes, they created a vibrant female sporting tradition. Generations of women athletes have promoted physical competence, celebrated the joy of play, developed a deep appreciation for athletic competition and excellence, and forged loving, supportive bonds among women in a nontraditional setting.

The persistent but unsteady tension between female athleticism and male-defined sport forms a central thread in the history of women's sport, illuminating not only women's complicated standing in the athletic world but the vital interplay between sport and the surrounding culture. From early-twentieth-century controversies over the intrepid "athletic girl," to midcentury racial politics surrounding African American women track stars, to more recent legislative struggles over gender equity in school athletics, women's athletic history offers a lens through which to understand both the complicated gender dynamics of sport and the social experience of women athletes. A century of women's efforts to obtain a meaningful place in the sporting world provides critical insights into the history of gender relations in American society.

# CHAPTER 1

# THE NEW TYPE OF ATHLETIC GIRL

⊃○⊂

In the fall of 1911 *Lippincott's Monthly* described the modern athletic woman: "She loves to walk, to row, to ride, to motor, to jump and run . . . as Man walks, jumps, rows, rides, motors, and runs."[1] To many early-twentieth-century observers, the female athlete represented the bold and energetic modern woman, breaking free from Victorian constraints, and tossing aside old-fashioned ideas about separate spheres for men and women. Popular magazines celebrated this transformation, issuing favorable notice that the "hardy sun-tanned girl" who spent the summer in outdoor games was fast replacing her predecessors, the prototypical "Lydia Languish" and the "soggy matron" of old.[2]

With the dawning of the new century, interest in sport had burgeoned. More and more Americans were participating as spectators or competitors in football, baseball, track and field, and a variety of other events. At the same time women were streaming into education, the paid labor force, and political reform movements in unprecedented numbers. Women's social and political activism sparked a reconsideration of their nature and place in society, voiced through vigorous debates on a wide range of issues, from the vote to skirt lengths. Popular interest in sport and concern over women's changing status converged in the growing attention paid to the "athletic girl," a striking symbol of modern womanhood.

The female athlete's entrance into a male-defined sphere made

her not only a popular figure but an ambiguous, potentially dis-
ruptive character as well. Sport had developed as a male preserve,
a domain in which men expressed and cultivated masculinity
through athletic competition. Yet, along with other "New
Women" who demanded access to such traditional male realms
as business and politics, women athletes of the early twentieth
century claimed the right to share in sport. They stood on the
borderline between new feminine ideals and customary notions
of manly sport, symbolizing both the possibilities and the dangers
of the New Woman's daring disregard for traditional gender
arrangements.[3]

The female athlete's ambiguity created a dilemma for her advocates. Given women's evident enjoyment of such "masculine"
pursuits, could the "athletic girl" (and thus, the modern woman)
reap the benefits of sport (and modernity) without becoming less
womanly? The *Lippincott's Monthly* article was titled "The
Masculinization of Girls." And while it concluded positively that
"with muscles tense and blood aflame, she plays the manly role,"
women's assumption of "the manly role" generated deep hostility
and anxiety among those who feared that women's athletic activity would damage female reproductive capacity, promote sexual
licentiousness, and blur "natural" gender differences.[4]

The perceived "mannishness" of the female athlete complicated her reception, making the "athletic girl" a cause for concern
as well as celebration. Controversy did not dampen women's
enthusiasm, but it did lead some advocates of women's sport to
take a cautious approach, one designed specifically to avert
charges of masculinization. Women physical educators took an
especially prudent stance, articulating a unique philosophy of
women's athletics that differed substantially from popular ideals
of "manly sport."

The tension between sport and femininity led, paradoxically,
to educators' insistence on women's equal right to sport and on
inherent differences between female and male athletes. Balancing
claims of equality and difference, physical educators articulated a
woman-centered philosophy of sport that proposed "moderation" as the watchword of women's physical activity. Moderation
provided the critical point of difference between women's and

men's sport, a preventive against the masculine effects of sport. It was this philosophy, with its calculated effort to resolve the issue of "mannishness," which guided the early years of twentieth-century women's athletics.

Interest in women's athletics reflected the growing popularity of sport in industrial America. In a society in which the division between leisure and labor was increasingly distinct, many Americans filled their free time with modern exercise regimens and organized sport. It was in the middle and latter decades of the nineteenth century that two pivotal traditions developed— that of "manly sport" and that of female exercise. Each would influence the turn-of-the-century boom in women's sport and shape the views of female physical educators.

Traditions of "manly sport" developed over the course of the nineteenth century as large-scale transformations in the American economy, class relations, and leisure habits helped spawn new forms of athletic culture. In an antebellum society destabilized by rapid commercialization and the first stages of industrial revolution, the emerging middle class took an inordinate interest in cultivating self-discipline and a strictly regulated body. Not only did they perceive the growing numbers of poor, immigrant, urban workers as an unruly mass in need of disciplined activity, they also worried about their own capacity to subdue momentary passions for the controlled, regulated habits of body deemed necessary for climbing the ladder of success. Exercise—as well as diet, health, and sexual reforms—offered a means to these ends.

Guided by a Victorian philosophy of "rational recreation" and a religious ideal of "muscular Christianity," male sport and exercise began to flourish in the years before the Civil War. Physical culture specialists prescribed rigorous routines designed to improve both body and mind. A strict regimen of physical exercise was expected to contain sexual energy, breed self-control, and strengthen a man's moral and religious fiber through muscular development. The physically fit Victorian man could then channel his mental and physical energies into a life of productive labor and moral rectitude.

By contrast, a much-less-respectable sporting life developed outside the middle class. Bachelor clerks, artisans, and shopkeepers joined other adventurous men in an informal sporting fraternity. They created a rich social and athletic life by organizing baseball clubs and frequenting prizefights, boat races, footraces, and gambling dens. Their ranks included men from the "lower orders" as well as men of higher social standing, who—chafing at the restrictions of polite society—enjoyed a rough-and-tumble life-style in which gambling, drinking, and hard living mixed with athletics.[5] Together these activities made up the "sporting life." In rejecting the dominant ethos of self-discipline and delayed gratification, it presented a rebellious underside to proper Victorian culture.

In both its rough and respectable forms, male sport cultivated an ideal of virile, athletic manhood. This ideal took deeper root after the Civil War, when industrialization, urban concentration, immigrant-community formation, and the expansion of education made sport accessible to a greater number and variety of men. Organized athletics of the late nineteenth century spanned class and ethnic differences. German Turnverein gymnastic societies, Scottish Caledonian track clubs, and Irish, German, and Italian baseball clubs allowed immigrants to join the American sporting scene while cultivating ethnic solidarity. Upper-class Americans cultivated their own sporting tradition in elite, exclusive metropolitan athletic clubs like the New York Athletic Club. For recreation outside the city, they turned to country clubs that offered cricket, tennis, golf, and yachting.[6]

The expansion of higher education spurred the growth of sport on college campuses as well. By the century's end, informal student sport had developed into highly organized collegiate athletic programs under the control of paid administrators and professional coaches. Crew, track, and football played an important role in schools' institutional growth, generating revenue and publicity while attracting students and a loyal alumni. Competitive intercollegiate sport was complemented by physical education programs in which exercise specialists introduced young males to military drill and European systems of gymnastic exercise.[7]

By the turn of the century, the advent of commercial sport

media, especially the new sporting sections of daily newspapers, further popularized both professional and amateur athletics. The press attracted nationwide fan interest and granted a new respectability to professional prizefighting and baseball. At the amateur level the media promoted athletic contests sponsored by the newly founded Amateur Athletic Union (AAU).[8] Press coverage also helped generate interest at the grass-roots level. Between 1900 and 1915 neighborhood and working-class associations began to form athletic clubs, industrial teams, and church-sponsored leagues, providing the first organized athletic opportunities for urban laboring men.[9]

Significantly, this apparent democratization of sport occurred at a time when the lives of impoverished workers and immigrants seemed further and further removed from the comfortable ones of white-collar workers and businessmen. The tensions spawned by class injustices and other social inequities nurtured turn-of-the-century protest movements in which industrial workers, farmers, women's rights advocates, and radicals seriously challenged the social order. Under these circumstances the dramatic increase in the popularity of men's sport coincided with a concerted effort among men of the upper ranks to protect their social position and authority.

Athletic life offered one method of reinforcement. The image of virile athletic manhood proved reassuring, especially for professionals, merchants, and white-collar workers whose work in the new corporate economy no longer required physical labor.[10] Fortified by rigorous exercise, well-to-do men could cultivate their physical superiority, restore their confidence, and regain the "hard" edge required for effective leadership. Earlier, more personal Victorian concerns about individual masculine character now shaded into a public interest in restoring the collective manliness of a beleaguered Anglo-Saxon elite.

Political thinkers extended this logic to their concerns over the creation of a mighty and powerful nation. Worried that the middle- and upper-class American male was losing his virility and that the nation as a whole would soon endure the weak leadership of soft, effeminate men, turn-of-the-century politicians like Theodore Roosevelt looked to "the strenuous life" for a remedy.

Those who no longer toiled at physical labor could forge their masculinity on the ball fields and gridirons. Through arduous sport they would acquire the health benefits of vigorous exercise and, more important, valuable training for war and the moral and physical traits of commanding leadership. Faced by what they viewed as the artificiality and effeteness of urban industrial existence, "strenuous life" devotees drew on a nostalgic image of a simpler, pastoral life of physical rigor and unchallenged male dominance that they hoped to re-create in the realm of sport.

While proponents of manly sport hoped that sport could renew middle-class manhood, Progressive Era reformers of the early 1900s argued that sport and recreation could serve as a training ground for working-class and immigrant youth as well. Reformers perceived an excess of energy in working-class boys who, left to their own devices, might turn their fervor toward sexual and criminal delinquency. Through school athletics, settlement houses, Young Men's Christian Associations (YMCAs), church leagues, and playgrounds, welfare workers reached out to underprivileged youth through sport. They speculated that if athletic training could reinvigorate pampered boys, it could also provide safe outlets for the passions of working-class youth.[11]

Thus, as organized sport gained in popularity, it intensified the association between athleticism and masculinity. American men confronting the changes wrought by industrialization, urbanization, and mass immigration looked to sport as a crucial avenue for defining and expressing their manhood. It is not surprising, then, that women who tried to carve out a place in the athletic world met with some resistance.

⌒○⌒

Turn-of-the-century women, when confronted with deeply entrenched notions of manly sport, turned to their own traditions of female exercise and athletic participation. Disturbed by evidence of female frailty, proponents of women's health had begun advocating moderate exercise for women as early as the 1830s. Antebellum advice columnists, educators, feminists, and health reformers called for improved female health through "physical culture." Subsequently members of two late nineteenth-century professions, medicine and physical education, further developed these arguments and became strong advocates of female exercise.

Nineteenth-century medical science characterized women as the physiologically inferior sex, weakened and ruled by their reproductive systems. Given evidence of women's poor health— chronic fatigue, pain and illness, mood swings, and menstrual irregularities—experts theorized that the cyclical fluctuations of female physiology caused physical, emotional, and moral vulnerability and debilitation. Formally educated doctors eager to secure their professional status took a special interest in women's health problems. In the name of medical science, they claimed to be authorities on the female body, capable of diagnosing and treating woman's condition. One such treatment was moderate exercise, designed to strengthen and regulate the female body.[12]

Medical rationales for female exercise interested women educators, who found them useful in their efforts to justify women's pursuit of higher education. As the number of women in college jumped from 11,000 in 1870 to 85,000 in 1900, educators had to counter widespread assertions that mental strain would cause nervous disorder and reproductive dysfunction in female students.[13] Based on "vitalist" scientific theories, which posited that bodies had a finite amount of circulating energy that was drawn to different parts of the body by activity, conservatives warned that education presented a serious danger by pulling necessary energy from the female reproductive system to the brain.[14] Educators found an antidote in the claim that physical education would prevent these potential traumas. An exercise regimen would theoretically return energy to the body and strike a proper balance between physical and mental activity.

The concern over college women's health cracked open the doors of academe to women physical educators. In the 1880s physical culture specialists founded the Sargent School and Boston Normal School of Gymnastics to train women as instructors of physical education. A decade later graduates began to fan out around the country in newly established college P.E. departments. Soon these departments created degree-granting majors, so that in addition to instructing every female student in a course of mandatory physical exercise, physical educators trained the next generation of professionals.[15] Thus, buttressed by institutional support, scientific theories, and a newly formed organization of male and female professionals—the American Association for the Advancement of Physical Education (later changed to the American Physical Education Association, or APEA)—women physical educators approached the new century with optimism.[16]

Interest in physical education found its complement in the growing popularity of women's competitive sport inside and outside of academic institutions. While physical culture experts had been promoting controlled, regimented exercise, others had begun to encourage women to take up more active, competitive athletic games. As with men's sport, these activities split along the divide between rough and respectable.

Nineteenth-century newspapers occasionally reported on highly unconventional women ballplayers and runners who competed for prize money before a paying public. In the 1880s New Orleans promoter Harry H. Freeman put together a touring women's baseball team, which folded under rumors of illicit sexual activities.[17] Other women entered the boxing or wrestling ring in events that combined spectacle, sport, and gambling. In 1876, for example, Hill's Theater in New York City featured a contest between two pugilists, Nell Saunders and Rose Harland, with the victor to receive a silver butter dish.[18] These athletes violated every Victorian standard of proper feminine behavior. Brazenly to occupy male athletic space, to engage in physical competition, and to parade the female body before the public prompted not only allegations of "unladylike" behavior but charges of prostitution—the ultimate public female degradation.[19]

Women's sport gained credibility more readily among the wealthier classes, where it took root in an established tradition of upper-class leisure. Outdoor amusements like croquet, horseback riding, archery, swimming, golf, and tennis allowed well-to-do women of the post–Civil War era to display the latest styles in outdoor apparel along with the abundant free time of the rich. When women with money and time to spare gathered to play fashionable games, they entered a culture of conspicuous leisure that also included dining, bathing, and drinking at the nation's most exclusive resorts and clubs. For these women sport was both a liberating, adventurous pastime and an enjoyable way to display their wealth and to strengthen elite social ties.[20]

When clubs began opening tournament play to women in the 1870s, several sports moved beyond the recreational level to more serious levels of competition. Sporting organizations like the National Archery Association, the United States National Lawn Tennis Association, and the United States Golf Association sponsored the first women's national championships in archery, tennis and golf in 1879, 1887, and 1895 respectively.[21] While tournament competition allowed a few athletes to train vigorously and pursue athletic excellence, most women continued to enjoy leisurely paced games played for fun and fresh air. These activities formed a socially acceptable pastime consistent with the refinement expected of "proper ladies." When Alfred B. Starey wrote that "archery, like tennis, is too refined a sport to offer any attractions to the more vulgar elements of society," he expressed a common class attitude. The notion that "refined" women played suitably "refined" games protected elite sportswomen from violating the boundary between proper womanhood and "vulgar" women of other classes.[22]

The bicycle craze of the late 1880s and 1890s opened up athleticism to middle-class as well as elite women. Cycling won widespread acceptance and broke new ground for women's right to public outdoor exercise. Frances Willard, leader of the Woman's Christian Temperance Union, was one of an estimated thirty thousand women who took up cycling in the 1890s. She was unusual, however, in that she learned to ride at the age of fifty-three and then proceeded to write an extended essay, "A Wheel Within a Wheel; How I Learned to Ride the Bicycle." She explained that although the first women to ride publicly were "thought by some to be a sort of semi-monster," severe criticism had abated by the 1890s, and she "could see no reason in the world why a woman should not ride the silent steed so swift and blithesome." In recommending the virtues of "the silent steed," Willard also expounded on the broad social import of women's new pursuit. The bicycle, according to Willard, was not merely a "vehicle of so much harmless pleasure." Rather, it promised to lay to rest the "old fables, myths, and follies associated with the idea of woman's incompetence" in athletic activities, at the same time augmenting the "good fellowship and mutual understanding between men and women who take the road together . . . rejoicing in the poetry of motion."[23]

However, while feminists like Willard, medical experts, and the ordinary cyclist sang the praises of cycling, critics claimed that excess riding caused women serious physiological damage. They cautioned against the risk of uterine displacement, spinal shock, pelvic damage, and hardened abdominal muscles. Avid cycling reputedly could also harden the facial muscles into a hideous "bicycle face," notable for its protruding jaw, wild staring eyes, and strained expression.[24] The same athletic activity that spelled liberation to women like Willard signaled danger to more conservative observers.

Despite such warnings, the bicycle merely whetted the appetite of many young women for more competitive activities. They brought their keen athletic interest to the high schools and colleges they attended in rapidly expanding numbers. Students formed baseball and crew teams and enjoyed a variety of other sports either informally or through organized intramural play. In 1891 Bryn Mawr students further formalized these arrangements by founding the first college Women's Athletic Association (WAA).[25] The same year the invention of basketball by YMCA worker James Naismith provided women with a game that would soon change the tenor of college women's sport. The game was instantly and immensely popular among female students. Their spirited play ushered in a new period in women's sport—years in which concerns about the masculine character of sport enlivened the debate over the healthful versus harmful effects of athletics on women.

As the United States entered the new century, women across the nation secured greater access to athletics. Concurrent developments in elite sport, school athletics, and public recreation gave female athletes a foothold in the early-twentieth-century world of sport. These advancements would gradually bring the "athletic girl" into sharper cultural focus.

Sport for wealthy women entered a new era when prominent society women founded the Chicago Women's Athletic Club in 1903. Designed as a lavish setting for exercise and leisure, the club featured a gymnasium, a swimming pool, bowling alleys, fencing rooms, a Turkish bath, and various sitting and dining rooms.[26] Soon thereafter, women organized a New York and an Illinois Women's Athletic Club, followed by similar ventures in major cities around the country. Like their nineteenth-century predecessors, most club members continued to participate in sport as an enjoyable and carefree form of elite sociability. Yet a smaller group of women began to assert the value of more serious athletic training. They ambitiously pursued competitive opportunities, especially through tournament play in the popular sports of golf and tennis.

Some rebels further flouted convention when they dared to pursue such "men's" sports as auto racing, polo, shooting, and long-distance walking. Eleonora Sears, a Boston Brahmin and descendant of Thomas Jefferson, made a name for herself in these sports, as well as in tennis, squash, and equestrian events. She was one of the first well-known women publicly to appear in pants and short hair, confidently donning slacks, boots, and a riding hat. As a polo player she had the audacity to ride astride and wear jodhpurs. Attending a 1909 International Women's Conference in London, Sears wandered over to the polo club, where—finding the American and English teams competing for the International Cup—she caused a public outcry by requesting (and being denied) a place on the U.S. team. Sears had not only unusual athletic ability but the privilege, the means, and the attendant confidence to ignore the constraints that confined most women to a much narrower sphere of athletic activity.[27]

Similar opportunities did not exist for working-class girls and women, whose long workday usually precluded leisure activities beyond nighttime neighborhood strolls and occasional movies or dancing. However, as part of a broader series of "child-saving" measures being urged on the nation—reforms such as child labor laws, compulsory education, and public health regulations—middle-class urban reformers began providing recreational activities for working-class youth. The Playground Association of America was formed in 1906 to organize play groups and athletic activities for city boys and girls. It aimed not only to provide an alternative to the dangerous life of the street but to instill physical and moral discipline, instructing poor immigrant youth in "American" concepts of cooperation, democracy, achievement, and subordination to the group.[28] As a result of Progressive Era activism, young working-class women obtained their first organized athletic opportunities. As schoolgirls they could take part in activities offered by settlement houses, Young Women's Christian Associations (YWCAs), city playgrounds, and public schools.[29] After leaving school, women occasionally found opportunities in workplace recreation programs that offered annual outings and field days featuring games and races for female employees.[30]

For young middle-class women college campuses provided a crucial site for athletic experimentation, a place away from home where athletic ventures were one of the numerous ways in which young women explored their independence and charted a new generational course. Student social life at some schools thrived around active women's sport programs. In 1904 the student newspaper at the University of Minnesota extolled the "Athletic Girl" as "the truest type of all American Co-eds."[31] And at Radcliffe and Smith, campus life reached a pitched frenzy during the annual class basketball tournaments, which matched the best players from each year's class in a highly ritualized, intense series of games. With songs, pranks, and banners, the entire student body turned out to exhort their classmates on to victory.[32]

Tournaments and other campus-based athletic competitions were the mainstay of extensive intramural programs initiated and coordinated by students. The most avid competitors also joined intercollegiate varsity clubs, which—though fewer in number—provided athletes the additional benefits of travel, off-campus socializing, and the prestige of representing one's school in public. To celebrate female athletic achievement, WAAs devised an elaborate system of awards, culminating in the varsity letter. College yearbooks of the time featured striking photographs of formally posed women's varsity teams, looking proudly into the camera with college letter sweaters in full display.

With her exuberant physicality, disregard for Victorian notions of female restraint, and her intrepid incursion into a male cultural domain, the athletic woman captured the spirit of modern womanhood. But her unorthodox behavior also subverted the commonly accepted view of sport as a fundamentally masculine pursuit. The complex set of meanings surrounding women's participation in sport led observers alternately to praise and damn the "athletic girl."

Some physical educators and women's advocates saw sport as an avenue toward female self-reliance and independence, applauding the aggressive, unremitting quality of play that left women "hot, breathless and disheveled" by game's end.[33] Like feminists of the time, they reasoned that crossing barriers into "male" spheres contributed to a fuller realization of womanliness, free from the debilitating, restrictive femininity of old. They argued that athletics imbued women with such "human" (rather than "feminine") attributes as loyalty, teamwork, and a democratic ethos while "allowing them to forget, for the time being, that they are girls."[34]

Against a background of expanding consumerism, others emphasized the benefits of sport for female health and beauty. Advertisers, the popular press, and health and beauty experts increasingly characterized health by the body beautiful.[35] Exercise columns in popular magazines instructed women on the need to exercise, claiming that both beauty and improved health would follow. In "To Reduce Flesh" Marie Montaigne explained: "The charm of a well proportioned figure is not to be overestimated, and it is one which almost any woman can possess by the expenditure of systematic effort, acquiring incidentally good health with her good figure."[36] Beauty expert J. Parmley Paret echoed this reasoning, urging all women to exercise because "feminine beauty, in both face and figure, is largely dependent on it."[37]

Some extended this argument by linking athletic beauty to evolutionary gains for the species. Dudley Sargent, founder of the prestigious Sargent School for women's physical education, claimed that both "good form in figure and good form in motion

. . . tend to inspire admiration in the opposite sex and therefore play an important part in what is termed 'sexual selection.' "[38] By this reasoning the quest to continue the species would condition a man to select a fit, athletic woman as a mate.

Despite their confident claims for a new feminine beauty, sport advocates had to answer criticisms that athletics would masculinize the female body and character. They took time to assure skeptics that the modern athlete would not be "the loud, masculinely dressed, man-aping individual, but the whole-hearted, rosy-cheeked healthy girl . . . happy, smiling and simply radiating good health."[39] They also cultivated allies among well-respected health officials who could help refute opponents' claims. In one show of support, the editor of *Nation's Health* dismissed fears of mannishness as a groundless absurdity: "There is no reason why in games of speed and skill girls should not be the equal of boys . . . and there is no more reason why athletics should coarsen their fibre than that equitation should make them 'horsey.' "[40]

Try as they might, though, health and physical education experts failed to persuade the skeptics who were convinced that sport would turn the female body into a facsimile of the male. Such corporeal suspicions were often rooted in deeper concerns about the social implications of female athleticism. The female athlete kindled acute anxieties about the erosion of men's physical supremacy and the loss of distinct male and female preserves. With her physical daring and spirited temperament, she took her place alongside politically minded suffragists and feminists, young working women known for their cheap finery and bold manners, and more staid but powerful professional women. Together they formed a threatening cadre of New Women whose public presence prompted shrill calls for a return to more familiar patriarchal arrangements.[41]

Disturbed by the upset of a traditional gender order, conservatives voiced their fears in somatic terms as they discussed the predicted consequences of female muscular development. Even a strong supporter like Dudley Sargent admitted: "It is only by taking on masculine attributes that success in certain forms of athletics can be won."[42] Similarly Dr. G. L. Meylan concluded that women's small shoulders and large hips disqualified them from

gymnastic expertise. While acknowledging that gymnastic training might overcome such limitations, he nevertheless advised
against it because, "of course, we should not care to see our
women teachers of physical training . . . approach the masculine
type."[43] Few observers could loose the concept of athleticism
from its locus in the male body.

Critics believed that sport posed other dangers to the female
body as well, predicting both reproductive damage and the loss
of sexual control. The nineteenth-century medical belief in
women's biological weakness and instability due to menstruation
survived the turn of the century, leading many "modern" doctors
and exercise specialists to reiterate earlier warnings against strenuous sport. They walked a fine line, on the one side promoting
mild exercise as a way to curb mental strain and regulate the
"fluctuations of the functional wave," yet at the same time pro-
hibiting vigorous competition on the grounds that "emotional
stimulation must be avoided, and decided concessions must be
made to the depression, physical and psychical, the lessened inhibitions and physiological control during the fluctuations of
puberty and menstruation."[44]

References to psychic ailments, lessened inhibitions, and loss
of control hinted at emotional and sexual dangers that awaited
the overenthusiastic athlete. Medical experts and educators perceived the female psyche as naturally prone to stress and nervous
illness. Many warned that the nerve-straining violence of unmodified sport was a proven cause of neurosis. Citing the sudden
death of an overzealous high school ballplayer and the "uncom-
monly fat" condition of many retired athletes, they peppered
their articles with horror stories of the harmful and "possibly
fatal" consequences of unregulated physical competition.[45]

In the figure of the "overzealous girl," so incited by competition that she could not stop, experts focused on the "powerful
impulses" roused by competition, impulses that would cause her
to all too easily succumb to the "pitfall of over-indulgence."[46]
Cheered on by the "wild huzzahs," the "adoration" and
"applause of the multitude," she was likely to give in to "the
intoxication of outstripping her competitors."[47] The exact nature
of the "powerful impulses" or "over-indulgence" remained

unstated, yet the language suggests a thinly veiled reference to female sexuality.

Perceptions of sexual danger in sport were fueled by widespread societal fears about female passion, unleashed and out of control. Alarmed observers throughout the country commented on the eroticism of the New Woman. Magazine articles like the 1913 piece titled "Sex O'Clock in America" rang the death knell for the image of the passionless Victorian lady, fading quickly before the figure of the passionate, explicitly erotic modern woman.[48] Certainly by 1914 an exuberant sexual energy, clearly independent of maternal function, divorced the New Woman from nineteenth-century purity and propriety. Young working-class women who shocked observers with their colorful dress, street smarts, and audacious manners attracted the most notice. But the changing habits and sexual mores of the sports-loving middle-class female athlete also evoked concern.

Discussions about sexuality in athletics typically concentrated on the uncontrolled passions of adolescent females who competed in high school and college sport, a constituency comprised overwhelmingly of middle- and upper-middle-class girls and women.[49] Working-class women, whose sexual habits received constant attention in other realms, formed too small a constituency within women's sport to merit significant comment. By contrast, the privilege and privacy of wealth seemed to protect upper-class athletic women from sexual scrutiny. Middle-class female students, however, were already at the center of more general debates on women's education. The nervousness produced by their academic presence readily spilled over into veiled discussions of the sexual hazards of female athleticism.

Critics claimed that women students risked their modesty, mental health, and maternal capacity when they abandoned self-restraint for the exhilaration of competition. Dr. Angenette Parry advised special caution for "college girls," who "are the ones who chiefly go in for athletics in excess."[50] Even those who supported women's sport advised that because adolescent girls were "temperamentally more inclined to overdo," they required careful supervision.[51] Concerned educators and medical experts painted a portrait of the frenzied coed for whom "the temptation to excess is apt to be overwhelming."[52] They concluded that if left unregulated, these conditions made "moderation an impossibility."[53]

⟨⟩○⟨⟩

Criticisms of the collegiate athletes' morals and muscles posed a distinct challenge to the limited authority and marginal position of women physical educators, who were just beginning to lay claim to professional status in the academic world.[54] With a substantial increase in female college enrollment in both single-sex and coed institutions, jumping from 85,000 in 1900 to 283,000 in 1920, physical educators found a ready-made constituency for athletic training.[55] But they also faced the unenviable task of defending women's physical activity and their own expertise in academically oriented, male-dominated schools. Confident of their abilities to instruct women in good habits of exercise but somewhat fearful of the "masculine" reputation of sporting competitions, women in P.E. tempered their support for competitive sport.

Between 1890 and World War I they gradually articulated an athletic philosophy captured in the word *moderation*. On the assumption that zealous competition threatened female health and morality, they sought to replace it with moderate competition based on "the smallest amount of exercise which will call out a vigorous response."[56] With this approach physical educators endeavored to protect their own professional interests and shield young women from the supposed physical and moral dangers of uncontrolled "masculine" athletic games.

Intellectual guidance and confirmation were sought from the more prestigious professions of science and medicine. Since the mid-nineteenth century, physicians had championed moderate exercise as both prevention and cure for physical and mental deterioration caused by natural weakness, menstrual havoc, cultural confinement, and intellectual strain.[57] Slightly modified versions of this medical doctrine were introduced directly into the P.E. curriculum when several colleges hired women physicians to head their physical education departments. Early-twentieth-century physical training directors like Dr. Eliza Mosher at the

University of Michigan, her cousin Dr. Clelia Duel Mosher at Stanford, and Dr. J. Anna Norris at the University of Minnesota added the weight of medical authority to the fledgling field of women's P.E. Although they committed themselves to improving female health and, in some cases, to challenging the notion that menstruation was a disabling or pathological condition, they tended to abide by medical concepts of pervasive female illness and the dangers of excessive physical activity.[58]

Strengthened by their intellectual and institutional ties to medical science, physical educators confidently set forth to implement their philosophy of moderation. However, they faced an obstacle in students who found "masculine" competitive sport more appealing than repetitive, formalized exercise regimens. Women educators devised a solution based in female separatism. By establishing separate women's departments that offered specially modified "female" versions of "male" games, educators differentiated women's activities from more strenuous male versions of sport. They carved out a separate realm of play in which women could gain the traditional benefits of sport—health, fun, "sportsmanship," and a cooperative ethos—without fear of sexual harm or the taint of masculinity.

The separatist strategy and cautious, protective approach to female health and sexuality were shared by a generation of women active in turn-of-the-century educational and reform circles. While not necessarily advocates of women's political rights, female physical educators often viewed their mission as consistent with a broad-based "woman movement," dedicated to raising the status of women and expanding the realm of female activity and influence. Many women active in Progressive Era reform and women's organizations accepted the prevailing view that natural differences in biology and sensibility divided men and women. They scorned "masculine" aggressiveness and competitiveness and sought to protect women from the dangers of public life as well as to empower them. They introduced protective legislation for women workers, founded women's schools and refuges, and relied on extensive female political and social networks to push their agenda.

Physical educators expressed a similar commitment to building female networks and protecting vulnerable women. They viewed sport positively but feared the possible exploitation of women athletes who competed without benefit of trained female supervision. In particular, female professionals worried that male promoters would make a sexual spectacle of the female athlete, forcing her to reveal and overexert her body in the interest of commercial profit and male entertainment. Their suspicions were not unfounded. The media frequently reduced the young female athlete or sports fan to no more than her sexual attributes. Two stanzas—whose double entendre metaphors can't have been lost on contemporary male readers—of a poem by prominent sportswriter Grantland Rice (an advocate of women's sport) on the woman baseball fan capture the lurid aura surrounding women's appearance on the sporting scene:

> The type of girl which keeps each head cavorting in a whirl,
> Is the nectarine of nature which we dub "The Baseball Girl."
>
> She's got "proper curves," you know, well rounded out and neat,
> She has the "speed"—nor do we refer unto her feet.
> She always "makes a hit" to boot, and, what is very nice,
> She's ready at the proper time to "make a sacrifice."[59]

This type of treatment appalled physical educators. They, too, celebrated women's physical freedom and athletic enjoyment. But their interest went hand in hand with a commitment to improve women's health, to preserve gender differences, and to protect a female sexual sensibility believed to be more delicate and vulnerable than men's.

Motivated by these concerns, women educators took aggressive steps to institutionalize their belief in moderation and to extend their professional control. Within the APEA concerns about unregulated female competition led to the formation of the National Women's Basketball Committee (which became the Committee on Women's Athletics, or CWA, in 1917). College P.E. directors formed regional organizations and later a national association, the National Society for College Directors of Physical Education for Women (later the National Association of Physical Education for College Women, or NAPECW).[60] With a unified voice, these regional and national networks affirmed the importance of moderation in extracurricular sport and in the core curriculum.

Based in a view of women as naturally inferior and weak, the P.E. curriculum became a mechanism for monitoring and guiding student physical performance and well-being. Aimed at strengthening the vulnerable female body, health exams; follow-up consultations; lectures on "parenthood training"; posture inspections; special classes for the "defective student"; and hygiene cards on which students reported on their daily diet, exercise, sleep, and dress habits became the norm on many campuses.[61] Through such techniques of measurement, supervised training, and inspection, well-intentioned physical educators developed a regime of student surveillance. Even as they worked to free their female charges from the corsets and imposed frailty of an earlier time, these women helped to create new forms of discipline and control for the modern female body.[62]

Beyond overseeing the curriculum, women physical educators took command of student athletic life, making the prohibition of varsity sports a central item on their professional agenda. Because of the perceived health dangers of aggressive competition, professional leaders urged P.E. staff members to monitor student-run Women's Athletic Associations (WAAs) and set strict policies on competition.[63] The question of competition remained open to debate, but by 1920 the tide of opinion had swung decisively against varsity intercollegiate competition for women. Educators restricted competition to on-campus, intramural activities designed to limit physical strain, competitive zeal, and public spectatorship while appealing to students of all ability levels and not just a talented few.

Students did not necessarily agree with these policies and persisted in questioning the ban on intercollegiate sport.[64] Yet in the end they had little choice but to comply. The most fervent athletes were often physical education majors who were under additional pressure to accept the status quo. The instructors who laid down the law against competition were their teachers, mentors, and future employers. Students respected professors' opinions, or, if not, could oppose them only at their own risk. They never mounted a serious protest, especially since thriving intramural programs offered substantial athletic opportunities that seemed to satisfy the majority of interested students.

The P.E. profession's commitment to athletic moderation reflected not only a shared female perspective but a particular set of class values. The medical notion of the frail, nonphysical female with a delicate sensibility could only describe middle- and upper-class women who did not have to work at hard physical labor or contend with the harsh life of the streets.[65] Physical educators took leisure time and advanced schooling for granted. Their protective creed of moderation emerged out of middle-class institutions and affected primarily middle-class women.

Exercise specialists made their class assumptions explicit when they advanced the idea that athletics substituted for the physical labor of earlier housewives. Writing for *Good Housekeeping*, Sarah Comstock advocated sport as a "substitute for those invigorating forms of work and play that filled the days of primitive women." Because the contemporary woman envisioned by Comstock no longer toiled over the wash, she needed "some outdoor sport that will make up for the exhilaration she misses by sending that blouse to the laundry. It isn't fair that the laundress should monopolize the benefits."[66]

In concentrating on the leisured modern housewife or, more typically, her school-age daughter, physical educators idealized an image of womanliness rooted in notions of refinement, self-restraint, and efficiency—core attributes of "respectable" middle-class culture. Smith College P.E. Director Dorothy Ainsworth impressed on her students an ideal of "greater womanliness, fair play and self control." And Wisconsin's Blanche Trilling expressed a similar belief that athletic training would contribute to American womanhood "not only in building up sound bodies, but also in bringing the girls to a realization of true dignity in manners."[67]

Aiming for the "best type of well-developed, controlled and efficient womanhood" did not absolutely exclude the poor, immigrants, or women of color.[68] But calls for self-restraint, refinement, and efficiency celebrated a "womanliness" rooted in the privileged position of the "lady." It depended for contrast on a view of women of color and the working class as robust, unruly, insensitive to pain or exhaustion, and rough in manners.[69]

The class contrast was especially evident when physical educators commented on the few working women who came under their purview in industrial training schools or business recreation programs. They suspected the working girl of poor hygiene and unseemly interests fostered by the pernicious amusements and nightlife of the modern city. The physical training director of the Manhattan Trade School for Girls described her wish "to create a love for simple, wholesome pleasures that will take the place of the strenuous and unwise recreations that are so alluring to the young business girl." Once involved in "joyous, active exercise," the working girl would develop "judgment, accuracy, self-control, and harmonious working with others."[70]

Such lofty ambitions formed a veneer over more coercive methods and objectives. Trade-school recreational instructors used physical exams and strictly supervised exercise routines to inspect students for physical, mental, or moral defects that could then be "checked or forcefully corrected" through alterations in dress, posture, hygiene, and comportment.[71] They aimed to inculcate habits of "bodily efficiency" and "hygienic living" that would enable young women "to adjust themselves to their new environment of the work room."[72]

While using supervised exercise to adjust the shopgirl to her work environment and prepare the female collegian for her role as a proper bourgeois woman, physical educators also attempted to strengthen educated women for motherhood. By the early twentieth century, decades of declining birthrates and poor health among middle- and upper-class white women caused serious alarm among wealthy Americans of Anglo-Saxon Protestant descent. With cries of "Race Suicide," they predicted that immigrant populations and the "prolific poor" would soon overwhelm white, native-born "racial stock." Fears of population decline among the "better classes" called attention to the low maternity rates of educated women. While many scientists continued to dwell on the dangers athleticism posed to the female reproductive system, some eugenicists looked to sport as a way to increase the fertility and improve the physical vigor of middle- and upper-class American women. A reinvigorated motherhood would allow the "fittest" race to expunge weaker strains and take its natural place atop the social order.

Under the banner of eugenics, physical educators negotiated the tension between fit motherhood and masculine athleticism. While they warned that lack of exercise left women unfit for motherhood, they also counseled that overexertion would dissipate female reproductive resources and, as a result, the race.[73] Arabella Kenealy, a British doctor widely read in the United States, claimed that women who acquired masculine attributes through competitive sport purchased them at the cost of a future generation's manhood: "A woman who wins golf and hockey matches may be said . . . to energize her muscles with the potential manhood of possible sons . . . since over-strenuous pursuits [could] sterilize women as regards male offspring."[74] Under a program of supervised moderate exercise, however, physical educators championed the abilities of fit women to produce strong, healthy sons, and thus a mighty nation.

In their formulation of policies and philosophies, physical educators held to a definition of womanhood particular to their late-Victorian middle-class upbringings. Because of the biases they themselves encountered as women in male-dominated schools, they deemed it specially important to project the dominant image of "respectable" womanhood. Strict adherence to middle-class standards of feminine behavior would smooth the road to a secure position within academe, at the same time producing a generation of physically fit, socially acceptable young women who had been spared the harmful effects of masculine sport.

Between 1900 and 1920 women's sporting pursuits accounted for only a tiny fraction of all athletic opportunities. Yet, in the context of the growing popularity of sport, athletic women of every class confronted the contradiction inherent in being both "woman" and "athlete." For them the gender tension proved both limiting and fruitful. It cast suspicion on the femininity of women in sport, yet it also contributed to the dynamic image of the "athletic girl" who refused to be excluded from a domain of masculine privilege and pleasure. The female athlete embodied the New Woman, in bold motion, treading fearlessly into forbidden realms and discovering her unique character. Noting that "no sport is too reckless, too daring, or too strenuous" for the experienced female athlete, author and amateur athlete Anna de Koven pronounced that the tomboy had moved from disgrace to honor as the symbol of a "new type of American girl, new not only physically, but mentally and morally."[75]

This image of the modern female athlete embraced women of all classes, but assumed different meanings in different settings. Physical educators successfully limited competition for middle-class college students while providing a significant degree of athletic opportunity through intramural sport programs founded on the principle of moderation. Women active in exclusive sports like golf, tennis, and equestrianism participated with fewer restrictions. Insulated from public reproach by wealth and status, they competed vigorously in private athletic and country clubs. The freedom from scrutiny that elite women gained from privilege, working-class women derived from neglect. Before 1920 only a smattering of neighborhood athletic clubs and social welfare institutions offered athletic programs for women. However, the few organized activities open to working-class girls and women rarely insisted on modified rules or restricted competition.

Until World War I these class-specific sport milieus coexisted peacefully, encouraged by the growing popularity of sport and the mixed but often warm reception accorded the modern woman's athletic interest. The "athletic girl" won acceptance in part because she seemed to epitomize the spirit of New Womanhood, but also because as long as the numbers of women participating in sport remained small, the female athlete did not yet jeopardize men's actual control of the sporting world. This situation was a temporary one, however. The expansion of women's sport in the late teens and early 1920s fostered a highly competitive style of play that threatened many men's sense of superiority and clashed head-on with physical educators' carefully constructed philosophy of moderation.

# CHAPTER 2

# GRASS-ROOTS GROWTH AND SEXUAL SENSATION IN THE FLAPPER ERA

—⊃○⊂—

In 1927 American tennis sensation Helen Wills won the first of her eight women's singles championships at England's prestigious Wimbledon tennis tournament. That year marked the beginning of Wills's absolute reign in the world of tennis. Combining "man-like strokes" with "feminine grace," she began a streak of uninterrupted victories that lasted until 1933.[1]

The young star from Berkeley had begun her tennis career on the private courts of northern California. As the daughter of a physician father and doting mother, she received all the educational and athletic benefits of an upper-middle-class upbringing. Yet, when she burst upon the national scene in 1923, winning the first of her seven U.S. singles titles at Forest Hills, New York, she won instant popularity as a "commoner" who had broken into the snobbish upper-class world of championship tennis. Her fresh face, girlish beauty, and trademark plain white visor enhanced her reputation as a simple yet poised and graceful young champion. Within a few short years she achieved the status of a national hero, revered by the public as "the American girl" or simply "our Helen."

Wills's success and popularity in the late 1920s capped a decade of tremendous growth in women's sports. While stars of tennis, golf, and swimming gained national celebrity status, in communities across the country ordinary female athletes took to the playing fields with less fanfare but an equal amount of enthu-

31

siasm.[2] As interest and participation levels rose, so too did women's skill level. When Helen Wills racked up victory after victory against female challengers, the caliber of her play so impressed observers that some suggested she should begin entering men's tournaments. Wills seemed uninterested in pursuing this option and stated that men were still the superior tennis players. However, she did acknowledge the possibility that some day the best women might defeat top-ranked male tennis players.[3]

In a decade of extraordinary progress for women athletes, Wills's prediction did not seem farfetched. After all, in 1924 a twenty-year-old backstroker from Chicago, Sybil Bauer, shocked the sportsworld by breaking the world (men's) record in the backstroke. Two years later teenage phenomenon Gertrude Ederle, an Olympic medal winner from New York, gained international renown by becoming only the sixth person to swim the English Channel—two hours faster than the five men who preceded her.[4]

The energy and skill of female athletes held Americans in thrall. Most striking was the sportswoman's expressed love of competition and her dedication to victory. In 1920 French tennis star Suzanne Lenglen, who reigned supreme in European tennis and would soon tour the United States to take on the best American women, informed the readers of *Collier's* magazine that serious female players "are out to win. No mercy is shown." In sport, she added, "There is no such thing as 'ladies first.' "[5] Helen Wills apparently heeded Lenglen's advice, using her steely resolve and legendary powers of concentration to cut down opponents "without even a pretense of mercy."[6]

A fascinated public observed the phenomenon with one part admiration and one part consternation. When figures like Wills, Lenglen, or Ederle pursued and achieved athletic excellence, they incorporated masculine qualities of strength, speed, and agility into a new standard of womanhood. Feminists heralded female athletic success as an advance for all women. But traditionalists looked on in anxious wonder, suspecting that the changes might also signal a loss of masculine privilege and superiority. If women were no longer a fragile, timid group in need of protection, men could not be assured of their own role as powerful protectors, and consequently relations between the sexes would have to be reconsidered.

The resulting unease found expression in media reactions to Helen Wills as she extended her remarkable string of victories. Her performance began to strike some observers as more disturbing than pleasing. Reporters who had earlier lauded the "American girl's" charm, now described Wills's winning streak as a product of cold, relentless play; she was a "heartless crusher of lesser talents" and a "killer type of fighter" whose "austere and inexorable" style had "all the warmth and animation of a deceased codfish."[7]

Whether praised or panned, Wills and other women athletes occupied a central place in a popular discourse preoccupied with assessing the meaning and relative power of womanhood and manhood. As athletic opportunities spread rapidly at the grass-roots level and women made new inroads into national and international sport, the female athlete exceeded the bounds of "moderation" proposed by cautious experts, earning a reputation for physical excellence and sexual appeal—qualities that stirred not only excitement but fierce debate. Sport in the 1920s became an important site, symbolic as well as actual, for reflecting on and negotiating contemporary gender relations. Observers witnessed increasing numbers of fun-loving women competing against each other and, indirectly, against men as well. Frequently they interpreted the spectacle not only in athletic terms but as part of a larger contest between modern women and men struggling over resources and power.

The popularity of sport in the 1920s reflected far-reaching changes in American society. With the expansion of corporate capitalism, enterprising businesses realized that leisure could be commercialized on a larger scale and sold to working- and middle-class consumers in the form of recreational equipment, sportswear, and public entertainment. As the economy shifted toward mass-marketed consumer products and commercial entertainment aimed at a broadly based middle-class clientele, more and more Americans began to look for personal fulfillment through consumption and leisure.[8]

Athletics in particular captured the imagination of this newly prosperous, fun-seeking public. Professional baseball and boxing, amateur track and field, swimming, golf, tennis, college football, and auto and horse racing thrived in the 1920s. Athletic attendance surpassed all previous totals, as sport, along with the movies, attracted mass audiences from diverse class and ethnic backgrounds.[9]

While the popularity of big-time sport helped produce a national sporting culture, sports organized at the community level contributed to the forging of ethnic, racial, or local identities that resisted the development of a "mass" consumer society or a homogeneous American "melting pot." The years before and during World War I were marked by rapid industrialization, urbanization, immigration, and accompanying labor, ethnic, and racial conflict. In the postwar period a quieter process of ethnic and racial community consolidation ensued. Urban immigrant communities—whether African Americans from the rural south or newly arrived Mexican or European immigrants—continued the work of establishing businesses, churches, welfare groups, social clubs, and recreation centers. These institutions facilitated the transition to American city life and strengthened community identity.

As part of this process, neighborhood recreation agencies, churches, and businesses sponsored athletic activities for adults and youth.[10] These community-based activities were supplemented by recreational sports sponsored by reformers, educators, municipal officials, and industrial leaders. Under their guidance burgeoning school and work athletic programs, city park programs, and semipublic recreation agencies like YMCAs offered a wide range of youth and adult sports to local community members. Women's sports, while never the main attraction, flowered in all these settings.[11]

The transformations in population, consumption, and leisure made the 1920s a "golden age" of sport. While more and more Americans participated in neighborhood sporting events, national athletic celebrities like New York Yankee slugger Babe Ruth, boxer Jack Dempsey, golfer Bobby Jones, and football halfback Red Grange captured the hearts of star-struck fans. Restless under the increasingly bureaucratic, impersonal nature of economic and political life, audiences responded to heroic figures like Ruth, with his immense appetite for life and relentless pursuit of pleasure, profit, and individual glory.[12]

These conditions also opened the door to women athletes of the 1920s. They benefited not only from the new interest in sport but from the wider set of cultural changes that gave birth to the flapper era. It was in this period that middle-class women shed the vestiges of Victorian reserve to explore new social behaviors in the cafés, clubs, and dancehalls that made up urban nightlife.[13] Particularly important were the changes in sexual morals and manners that accompanied the expansion of consumer culture. Middle-class Americans of the post–World War I era joined working-class youth in a pleasure-filled world of commercial recreation and nightlife, in the process making a decisive break with the sexual values of an earlier era.

Victorians had viewed male sexuality as an almost bestial force in need of constant containment less it overwhelm the delicate sensibilities of "good" women, who were thought either to lack sexual impulses or to feel them only in relation to maternal instincts. By contrast, modern sexual doctrine recognized both female and male sexual desire as a positive life force and necessary ingredient for marital happiness. The positive view of female sexuality encouraged women's broader participation in the realm of public leisure, an arena traditionally associated with the bawdiness of vaudeville theater and the illicit sexuality of taverns, dance clubs, and gambling joints. In the altered atmosphere of the late teens and twenties, both female eroticism and female public leisure gained a measure of respectability, even as they provoked heated cultural debates. Eagerly consuming the latest fashions in dance, music, and clothing, young women joined with men to create modern forms of public courtship and heterosexual companionship that placed a high value on sexual intimacy.

While the slim, boyish, and flirtatious women known as flappers symbolized women's dramatic break with tradition, women athletes shared many of the flapper's characteristics. The female athlete resembled the flapper in her boyish athleticism, independence, and willful, adventurous spirit. Frequently applauded for their physical beauty and modern charm, each also presented an image of youthful sexual appeal. Both athletes and flappers flourished in an age when commercial entertainment boomed, when female fashions allowed for freer movement and greater exposure, when dance styles as well as sports were becoming more physically demanding, and when the greater acceptance of female sexuality had broken men's exclusive hold on public physicality, leisure, and sport.[14]

Behind the image of the flapper and celebrity athletes like Helen Wills and Gertrude Ederle stood the masses of ordinary women who turned to sport, as well as dance, for a pleasurable form of physical activity. Young black and white women of small or average means for the first time found significant opportunities to engage in athletic activities, from basketball and baseball to tennis and track and field.

A well-established pattern of racial segregation and exclusion set the parameters for African American women's athletic participation. Although in the earliest years of men's professional baseball and football a few African Americans had been permitted to play, as league governance structures were formalized, so too were strict policies of racial exclusion. Even in sports like horseracing, boxing, and cycling, which had a history of African American participation and success, explicit and de facto exclusionary policies had effectively ended most mixed-race athletic competition by the 1920s.

Excluded on the basis of race from segregated national competitions and organized white sports, African American athletes, whether female or male, most often pursued sport in the community setting—in church leagues, YWCAs and YMCAs, settlement-house recreation programs, and independent African American clubs. In the teens and early twenties the black press reported a smattering of women's contests, but in the middle and later years of the decade, such events seemed to catch fire in both Northern and Southern black communities.

Women's track and field gained an immediate following, in part because it seemed to hold the greatest possibility for affirming black athletic excellence through head-to-head competition with white athletes. In 1919 Thomas Anderson of the *New York News* described track as "the gateway to the field of open competition between white and colored teams in all branches of amateur sport."[15] Unlike baseball and football, in which little interracial competition occurred, Northern track meets often pitted black and white athletes against one another in face-to-face competition with at least the semblance of fairness and equal opportunity. In addition it was a relatively inexpensive sport that didn't require the organizing and financing of large teams or leagues. African American newspapers frequently reported the success of local "race girls" in playground, press, and school meets from around the country.[16] In 1923, the *St. Louis Argus* heralded young women of the Philadelphia Meadowbrook Club for making "track history for the race . . . in an unusual manner" by shattering a record in the quarter-mile relay.[17]

Even more popular than track, the sport of basketball sprouted in black communities throughout the country. In Chicago the Roamer Girls thrilled local sports fans by remaining undefeated for six seasons. The team, made up of local talent from Chicago's South Side neighborhood, was coached by Sol Butler, a celebrated war hero who won track-and-field honors at the post–World War I Inter-Allied Games in Europe and then came home to star in Chicago's African American men's basketball league and coach in the women's. The Roamer Girls did not lack for challengers, vying in league competition against the Lincoln Settlement, Olivet Sunday School, and Joan of Arc teams. They took on occasional "Nordic" or "lily" (white) opponents as well.[18] Chicago's claim to basketball excellence was matched on the east coast by the Blue Belts and the Mysterious Five, vaunted women's teams from the New York City–New Jersey area.[19]

By the late 1920s colleges, industrial training schools, and normal schools throughout the southern and mid-Atlantic states also regularly reported game scores to the black press. They arranged to play against nearby schools, traveling clubs, and local Y or community teams. Several regions created more formal interscholastic leagues, such as the Georgia-Carolina College League and the Inter-State Athletic Association of Kansas and Missouri girls' teams.[20]

Along with basketball, baseball and tennis gained a foothold in black communities. The small number of women's baseball teams precluded the development of league play. Instead independent promoters organized barnstorming teams like Madame J. H. Caldwell's Chicago Bloomer Girls. Little evidence about Madame Caldwell survives, leaving no clues to the origin of her title or the source of her baseball expertise and enthusiasm. The record does show, however, that she promoted her team aggressively, using boldness, wit, and perseverance to drum up both players and fans. In 1920 she submitted a notice to the *Chicago Defender* that read, "Wanted—Ladies to Play Ball." Caldwell stated that her team would meet all challengers, white or black, male or female, and issued a provocative summons that asked: "Our women are voting now, so why not be able to play a real game of baseball?"

Apparently Caldwell received no shortage of responses. Within a single two-week period, her Bloomer Girls played a Sunday school team from Grace Presbyterian, a local boys' team, and the "Hebrew Maidens" from Chicago's Hebrew Institute. In a three-game series against a Chicago boys' team, she created excitement by substituting a white pitcher and catcher for her usual black battery. The admission charge of twenty-five cents helped raise money for travel to Michigan and other nearby states, where the Bloomer Girls took on opponents of both genders and different ages and races.[21]

While women's baseball attracted attention as a novelty event, tennis had a more genteel reputation and was popular among the small black middle class. Private clubs like Chicago's Prairie Tennis Club hosted citywide tournaments and developed local talent for the national African American women's championship established in 1917 by the Amateur Tennis Association (ATA).[22] Though nurtured in "society circles," African American tennis appears to have welcomed talented players from any background. Ora Washington of Philadelphia and Isadore Channels of Chicago, the dominant women players in ATA tennis, moved back and forth between the summer tennis circuit and winter basketball teams situated in a more working-class milieu.

Women's sport, like men's, helped to develop cohesive black communities in the wake of the wartime and post–World War I northern and urban migrations. Athletic contests became community social events that could enhance racial pride and neighborhood identity.[23] Women's basketball games, for instance, often played to packed audiences in local churches or recreation centers. Sometimes curtain raisers for men's games, other times the main features following younger girls' or boys' openers, women's games drew hundreds of spectators, or even thousands in gymnasiums like the Manhattan Casino—an arena known for its freezing temperatures and seating capacity of more than three-thousand.[24] Dances and live music frequently followed the games. For ten cents, a quarter, or free of charge, community members enjoyed a long evening's entertainment.

As black communities developed their own commercial institutions, entertainment forms, and newspapers, women's athletics came to occupy a subordinate but well-accepted position among black sport followers.[25] The African American press never granted women's sport the coverage or respect that it devoted to male athletics. Yet prominent papers like the *Chicago Defender*, the *Pittsburgh Courier*, the *Philadelphia Tribune*, and the *Baltimore Afro-American* did report regularly on women's events, with a respectful tone that only rarely hinted of condescension.[26] Once a team gained name recognition and community support, editors dropped gender signifiers like "Girls" or "Lassies," assuming that readers were familiar with the team.

By reporting on women's sport the press contributed to its growing popularity, helping top female athletes to become well-known personalities. In a 1927 *Chicago Defender* reader poll to name the city's most popular black athlete, women were five of the seventeen vote getters. Leading the roster were tennis player Mrs. C. O. Seames and basketball wizard Virginia Willis.[27] Mrs. Seames was a fixture in Chicago's tennis and society circles. Having played and taught tennis since the turn of the century, "Mother" Seames managed to maintain her popularity even after her tennis talents were surpassed by those of younger champions.[28] Virginia Willis, who brought her skillful ball-han-dling and sharpshooting abilities to the Roamer Girls and Olivet teams, was celebrated by the black press for her ability to "do more with a basketball than a Baptist preacher can do with a chicken bone."[29] Popular figures like Seames and Willis formed the top layer of a much broader base of African American women whose athletic efforts received a generally warm recep-tion in black communities of the 1920s.

The lighthearted, celebratory tone of some press reports should not obscure the deeper and more political ramifications of sport in black communities. Segregation and discrimination forced African Americans to develop their own sporting institutions; interracial competition was the exception in a sports world that was every bit as segregated as other public arenas. However, when black athletes did challenge white opponents, athletic com-petition became an important symbol of early-twentieth-century racial problems and progress.

Members of the press and community looked to athletes to prove that when given the chance in fair competition, African Americans could equal or surpass white achievements. When a 1914 University of Michigan student named Phyllis Wheatley Waters led her otherwise white freshman team over the junior basketball team, the *Indianapolis Freeman* commended her for "measuring arms day by day with the scions of America's noblest families and holding her own with the best of them." Similarly, a 1926 *Pittsburgh Courier* headline announced, "Race Girl Is Star in Press Meet." The article reported that a black high school stu-dent, Ernestine Gloster, won five medals at a predominantly white track meet sponsored by another local newspaper. In com-mending efforts like Waters's and Gloster's, the press suggested that African American athletes could solve the race problem through "sheer merit."[30]

More often the symbolic importance remained understated, expressed in the routine signifiers of sports-page accounts of "Race Girls" versus a "Nordic team." Despite the casual tone, remarks such as, "The sable passers, however, feel that they will be able to cope with these 'lily' ball tossers," suggest that interracial competition heightened the stakes and expressed aspirations that went beyond those involved in a single athletic encounter.[31] Although interracial matches were far from the norm, their very rareness amplified the significance of sporting events that brought black and white athletes into direct competition.

In the few instances when African American women competed internationally or in white-dominated sports like endurance swimming, the political implications of their endeavor became more obvious. The *Pittsburgh Courier* rallied behind long-distance swimmer Ellen Ray as she trained for a 1927 Hudson River swim, a formidable event in which the solitary athlete competed against the elements and the clock. While Ray solicited advice from "anyone who would like to see a colored woman bring fame and honor to her race and sex in the world of sports," the *Courier* reporter expressed his general "faith in the athletic ability of the colored womanhood of America."[32]

Even though they rarely received attention in the white press, these events accomplished at the local level what national figures like black heavyweight boxing champion Jack Johnson achieved at the national level when he defeated successive "white hopes." In an era marked by racial tension and racist violence, athletes dramatized profound social struggles in a structured, contained arena. When black and white women went head to head in physical competition at a track meet or a basketball game, crowds gathered to watch an athletic battle that symbolized the larger possibility of a black challenge to white power.

Overshadowed in large metropolitan areas by coverage of local and national men's sports, white women involved in grass-roots athletic activities garnered less media attention.[33] Nevertheless the growth of popular sports did provide young white women with a realm of physical freedom and social possibility. The years when they could participate in athletics occupied a short interlude between childhood restrictions and adult family and financial obligations. Athletically inclined adolescents and young working women grasped the opportunity to develop their physical capabilities, cultivate new social bonds among peers, and explore more physical and energetic models of womanhood.

White working-class women, like black women, took up sports through a variety of community-based athletic activities funded by local businesses, neighborhood clubs, and municipal and social welfare agencies. Commercial sponsors often generated interest by promoting events as novelties or glamour exhibitions, touting them as spectacles of fantastic skill and youthful beauty. Recreation and social service agencies disapproved of these ventures and committed resources to developing noncommercial forms of sport free from promotional hype. They designed urban recreation programs as a "constructive leisure" alternative, hoping to substitute "wholesome" athletics for the coarser atmosphere of the dancehall and sporting extravaganza.[34]

Another opportunity developed through industrial sports. Healthy corporate profits and management fears of labor unrest led industries of the 1920s to offer employee recreation as one strategy for obtaining an efficient and faithful work force. New "industrial relations" experts were concerned not only with employees' work lives but also with their off-hours pursuits. By 1920, 75 percent of the labor force worked less than a fifty-four-hour week, and almost 50 percent of American workers put in less than forty-eight hours per week, compared to a mere 8 percent of the labor force ten years earlier.[35] Corporate executives hoped that by filling employees' leisure hours with sporting activities, industrial recreation programs would inspire company loyalty and inhibit union organizing. Carnegie Steel's welfare director, A. H. Wyman, explained that industrial sports improved worker efficiency and fostered "a stronger feeling of loyalty to their bosses."[36] He was echoed by a Pittsburgh steel company executive who believed that recreation trained workers to cooperate with the company "in non-controversial subjects, so that these leaders are likely to be anchors to windward when outside leaders attempt to gather a following."[37]

In the 1920s businesses across the country constructed recreation facilities and sponsored teams that competed in intramural company events, in local industrial and municipal leagues, and occasionally in national competition.[38] Bowling, baseball, and basketball were the most common activities, but some industries sponsored football and track teams as well. Heavy manufacturing industries typically geared their offerings to male laborers. But financial enterprises like banks, insurance companies, and business schools, with their high percentages of female employees, were ardent backers of women's sports, especially basketball and bowling.[39]

The Travelers Insurance Company of Hartford, Connecticut, sponsored a women's basketball team that met a variety of challengers from across New England. In 1922, for example, the Travelers squad matched up against alumnae teams from regional colleges, industrial teams like the Winsted Nutmegs and the Connecticut state-champion American Thread team, and other financial enterprises like Aetna Life and Chase National Bank of New York.[40] In New Jersey the Prudential Insurance Company Athletic Association of Newark reported in 1930 that it had recently completed its ninth season of year-round sports for women. With an air of self-satisfaction, the author noted that since "nary a physical blot has been charged against an enviable competitive record," the Prudential girls had definitely refuted the charge that sports were detrimental to women.[41]

Financial and industrial centers of the Midwest and West offered women similar opportunities, including a full slate of bowling, swimming, track, tennis, golf, basketball, and riflery at the Western Electric Hawthorne Plant in Illinois.[42] By 1925 Chicago hosted a city basketball championship that attracted the best local teams sponsored by urban and suburban area businesses.[43] In the West, Dallas was a hotbed of women's industrial sports. Basketball teams from the area dominated AAU national tournaments of the late 1920s and early 1930s. The Employers' Casualty Company of Dallas boasted national championships— led by future Olympian Babe Didrikson—in both basketball and track and field.

Industrial and municipal athletic programs offered rural and urban communities a lively, inexpensive form of entertainment. More important, they furnished teenage girls and young working women a recreational outlet and a chance to develop skills and achieve public recognition. Although by 1930 the percentage of married workers had climbed to just under 30 percent of women in the labor force, the great majority of female wageworkers continued to be young, single women for whom paid work was an interlude between school and marriage.[44] Monotony and drudgery characterized most jobs. Young workers looked forward to the end of their shift, when they could join their peers in a satisfying, expressive realm of leisure.

Yet many young working women continued to ignore organized sports, preferring the dancehall and nickelodeon, where immediate pleasures went hand in hand with the search for boyfriends and future husbands. Industrial recreation specialists frequently complained about the low number of "working-girls" who came out for employee or municipal athletics.[45] Even fewer married or older working women participated. They had household responsibilities that prevented them from engaging in public leisure, as did full-time housewives, whose worlds were circumscribed by their labor in the home.[46] However, for the athletically minded single working woman, organized sports provided a novel outlet for her energies and abilities as well as a public arena in which to engage them. Such athletes, along with dancehall girls and flappers, formed part of a generation of women fashioning a new model of womanhood characterized by public activity and a sense of unleashed energy and physicality.

⸺◦◦◦⸺

The rapid growth of female participation in community athletics improved women's skills, stimulated interest in women's sport, and spawned greater opportunities for elite competition. Given the chance to excel, American athletes became a new force in national and international women's sport, competing in established golf and tennis championships and crossing barriers into competitive swimming, skating, and track and field. Top-notch female competitors often gained celebrity status and, from this position, became prototypes of a new, more explicitly sexual style of womanhood.

The escalating demand for women's sports pressed the previously all-male AAU into sponsoring national championships for women. The organization introduced a national swim meet in

1916, a track championship in 1924, and a basketball tournament in 1926. Although unable to match the draw of men's championships, these national meets attracted significant fan interest and media attention. Encouraged by local advertisers and news media, hundreds, and often thousands, of spectators gathered at poolsides, tracks, and basketball arenas to watch women from around the country compete for national titles. The tournament atmosphere combined high-intensity performances by women at the top of their sports with a relaxed, lighthearted atmosphere. Photographs frequently captured athletes hugging, laughing, and lounging about together in the hours before or after competition. A more solemn, ceremonial note was struck by closing rituals in which champions received medals, ribbons, and flowers to commemorate their accomplishments.

National competitions paved the way for American women's increased presence in international sporting events. The United States sent its first women's teams to the Olympic Games in 1920. A few individuals had entered women's tennis, golf, and archery exhibitions in the 1900 and 1904 games, but their participation was not encouraged or well publicized. In 1920 American women competed for medals in Olympic skating and swimming events. Theresa Weld of the Boston Skating Club was a medalist in figure skating. The *New York Times* described Weld (later Theresa Weld Blanchard, winner of nine national women's skating titles and numerous pairs championships) as a stylistic innovator who introduced running steps into skating and who offered brilliant exhibitions "that surpassed even the best performances of the men contestants."[47] Weld's Olympic accomplishment was overshadowed by the stellar performance of the women's swimming team. Led by Ethelda Bleibtrey and Aileen Riggin, U.S. women took four of five gold medals in swimming and diving events. Following their success in 1920, American swimmers continued to dominate at the 1924 and 1928 Olympic Games.[48]

Olympic swimmers built on the accomplishments of earlier stars like Annette Kellermann. In the decade before 1920, Kellermann had helped popularize swimming with her speed and her sleek, streamlined bathing suits—sleeveless, skirtless, form-fitting suits that replaced the bulky, full-length, bloomered costumes of an earlier generation. Spurred on by her success, women began to organize swimming clubs for competitive racing. The most prominent club, the Women's Swimming Association of New York, was founded in 1917 and proceeded to take the swimming world by storm in the 1920s, dominating national championship meets and supplying the majority of the U.S. Olympic swimming team's female members. Another strong club developed under the auspices of the Illinois Women's Athletic Club, and together the two associations trained thousands of swimmers at all levels, including the stars Ethelda Bleibtrey, Helen Wainright, Aileen Riggin, Sybil Bauer, and Gertrude Ederle.[49]

These swimmers burst onto the scene as fresh-faced teenagers, attracting public notice with their amazing ability and girlish charm. The diminutive Riggin won her first Olympic medal in 1920 at the age of thirteen and continued to compete successfully in swimming and diving for more than a decade. In 1922, at the age of sixteen, Helen Wainright captured the AAU all-around swimming title and was celebrated as the "greatest all-around aquatic contestant of her sex the world has ever known."[50] Within two years, however, her star was eclipsed by that of Gertrude Ederle. At seventeen this American-born daughter of a German butcher already held five national titles and ten world records.

As the numbers and accomplishments of women swimmers, skaters, golfers, and tennis players mounted, leading white athletes became overnight sensations, second only to movie stars in national fame.[51] Magazines conveyed their importance with full-length articles and advertisements featuring women athletes. Images of sleek, sophisticated tennis players, dashing automobile drivers, and wholesome, pigtailed basketball players helped sell products from automobiles to breakfast cereals. The media showed special enthusiasm for women in tennis, golf, and swimming, sports with predominantly middle- and upper-class constituencies. A few stars, like Ederle, were second-generation immigrants with working-class roots. But the majority honed their skills at the pools, tennis courts, and golf courses of exclusive athletic associations and country clubs.

These athletes did much more than establish women's place in sport. They helped fashion a new ideal of womanhood by modeling an athletic, energetic femininity with an undertone of explicit, joyful sexuality. In their own public comments, except for predictable responses to questions about current boyfriends and future marriage plans, athletes said little about sexual matters. Yet they seemed to possess a self-awareness as "modern" women pioneering not only athletic achievements but new styles of femininity. Helen Wills wrote in 1932 that, "The feminine mind in sports reflects the general trend of feminine thinking of the day. The ideas and, along with them, the inhibitions imposed upon us by previous generations are being dispelled."[52]

At least some of these inhibitions were sexual. Athletes were clearly perceived and portrayed as attractive, erotic women. Mythological allusions to athletes as goddesses and attractive young "nymphs" combined with a chorus of adjectives like "charming" and "alluring" to alert readers to the sexual attractiveness—and, possibly, the erotic power—of modern female athletes. Swimmers received lavish praise, especially during Olympic years when journalists reported on the "graceful" and "statuesque" young "mermaids" and "Junos" who represented America's Olympic hopes.[53] But day in and day out tennis stars received the greatest media attention, becoming icons of modern athletic womanhood. Three great players of the decade, Molla Mallory, Suzanne Lenglen, and Helen Wills, best exemplify the physicality and implicit sexuality of modern femininity.

While hard work and wholesome life-styles won praise for some athletes, the press heralded Molla Bjurstedt Mallory for her ability to combine a busy nightlife with athletic success. As Molla Bjurstedt, the budding Norwegian athlete emigrated to the United States in 1915 and began to establish herself as a world-class tennis player.[54] She earned celebrity status with her controversial victory over the world's best player, Lenglen (who near the end of the match suddenly claimed an injury and withdrew, apparently to avoid defeat), during the French star's 1921 trip to America. Competing under her married name, Mallory remained among the top female tennis players even as her career ebbed over the decade. Although she never became the media sensation Wills and Lenglen did, she gained a reputation as an exemplar of modernity by sporting a new brand of femininity that combined vigorous physical activity with an active, devil-may-care nightlife. Mallory was reportedly "a lady who can stay up most of the night, smoke cigarettes *ad libitum*, take apparently not the slightest care of her health and yet tirelessly win her way into fame."[55] She disdained rigorous training, explaining to one reporter that "too serious training took more out of a girl nervously than she gained physically."[56]

Local boosters and the national media regularly idealized athletes like Mallory as representatives of vibrant, sexually attractive womanhood. Mallory's ability to combine indulgence with excellence was offered to the public as proof that athletic interest need not interfere with a style of femininity identified with popular nightlife and sex appeal. The ideal woman was encouraged to channel her spirited temper and exuberant energy into interacting with men at cafés, nightclubs, and dancehalls as well as into outdoor sports and recreations.[57]

Suzanne Lenglen enjoyed similar pleasures at her home base on the French Riviera. She endured exhaustive training sessions as a youngster, but in later years preferred drinking, smoking, and dancing to practice. She admitted to sipping alcoholic tonics during matches to prevent fatigue. Though Lenglen toured the United States just twice, she was second only to Wills as a darling of the American press and public. From 1919 to 1927 she ruled the tennis world, tantalizing crowds with her short, gauzy outfits, her personal élan, and her marvelously original, fluid, dancelike style of movement.[58]

Lenglen represented the modern era's reinterpretation of feminine beauty and body type. Earlier associations between beauty and female purity, spirituality, and inner character faded before modern notions that linked beauty to the active, ornamented, external body.[59] Where the Victorian female body was frail, pale, fully covered, and staid, Lenglen's much-worshipped body was tan, lithe, and in constant motion. The crowds that gathered in the thousands to view Lenglen play lauded her great beauty, even though her face was often described as plain or homely. They saw beauty in the way she melded quickness, agility, powerful strokes, and aggressive play with a leaping, pirouetting, apparently effortless style.[60]

As athletes like Lenglen flaunted women's physical freedom, they helped to shape new dress styles and beauty standards based on a more sexualized female body—one appreciated for its sensual physicality and celebrated for its external beauty.[61] Beyond demonstrating the new styles in action, star athletes also took time (and money) to issue advice to admiring followers. Mary K. Browne, Lenglen's opponent in her later professional matches, advised readers on the connections between contemporary fashions, physical fitness, and the modern woman's attractively slim body. In "Fit to Win," Browne noted that fashions of the period featured straight lines; lightweight, loose-fitting garments; slim figures; and "boyish" cuts in clothing and hairstyles. She explained that the new look required exercise: "The slim girl is twice the girl her grandmother was, and half the weight. Keeping fit to-day is more than a necessity to athletic prowess: it is a duty all who seek success in anything must observe."[62] Though Browne did not reveal how exercise led to success outside sport, she implied that by dutifully exercising women could fit themselves for the new fashions, thus opening the door to social as well as athletic success.

Like Browne, Lenglen instructed women on how athletics could help them achieve and display the new "fit" femininity. She wrote popular articles on training methods and tennis techniques.[63] She also tutored through example, playing in make-up, sleeveless blouses or sweaters, her patented bandeau—brightly colored silk cloth woven into a headwrap—and short skirts or silk dancers' gowns that revealed the outlines of her body in the sunlight. The observation of Lenglen's dramatic manner of play and dress gave her followers a lesson in modern styles of uninhibited femininity.

Journalists responded to these qualities by depicting Lenglen in sexual and romantic terms. *Literary Digest* described the "Decidedly Unconquerable" Suzanne as the "best-loved young nymph" of the tennis courts. Her goddesslike gracefulness was

said to be accompanied by an aggressive attack that struck opponents like "an arrow from the bow."[64] Though she never married
and formed her closest relationships with family members and
female companions, Lenglen's appeal lay precisely in the way she
fused athletic ability with heterosexual allure. With her unusual
dress and dancelike movement, she pioneered an ideal of the
female body as physical and actively erotic.

By contrast, Lenglen's nemesis in the mid-twenties, Helen Wills,
struck observers as a wholesome, girlish athlete who combined
old-fashioned female virtues with a new style of athletic, assertive
womanhood. Wills replaced Lenglen as the dominant force in
women's tennis, remaining virtually unbeatable for much of her
career. At her peak the "American Girl" appeared almost daily in
the newspapers and twice on the cover of *Time* magazine.

Although she played the game powerfully, frequently practic-
ing against highly skilled male players and sometimes defeating
them, Wills's long pigtails, schoolgirl costume, and mild temperament reassured observers that an innocent, modest model of
womanhood might win out against the more outrageous, excessive, and worldly flapper. Her sweet face, classical body, and
graceful beauty not only became the subject of artists and poets
but elicited millions of letters from adoring fans. (In later years
Wills's icy "poker face" and unswerving determination struck the
press as disturbingly masculine. But in her 1920s heyday, she
offered a nonthreatening portrait of refined, well-bred, and
charming womanhood that blended modern athleticism with
aspects of conventional femininity.[65]) Wills's distinctive traits
made her a revealing exception to the trend toward a more sexual athletic ideal. Yet the very fact that she was celebrated for
upholding "traditional" virtues—in other words for her lack of
overt sexuality—suggests the pervasiveness of the more eroticized
image of the modern female athlete.

Athletes like Mallory, Lenglen, and Wills announced women's
dynamic entrance into traditionally male realms and their rejection of outmoded, restrictive definitions of femininity. Ironically,
even though working-class and African American athletes were
integral to these dramatic changes, the new feminine norms they
helped to create often failed to include them. The mainstream

press focused on glamour sports and national competitions, ignoring community-based sport and the skilled white and African American athletes who competed in ethnic and working-class settings. The best-known modern athletes typically came from white, well-to-do families and competed in sports that were considered acceptably feminine. Women athletes who did not fit this description received little recognition at the national level. Or, worse, journalists and sports experts referred to them obliquely through unfavorable comparisons of rough, "masculine" athletic types and the charming, feminine stars of popular glamour sports. Celebrities like Wills, Lenglen, and Mallory impressed the public as both cause and symbol of the active, exciting New Woman, while the impact and accomplishments of athletic standouts like Isadore Channels, Ora Washington, and Virginia Willis remained invisible to the dominant culture.

Remembered as a decade of good times in which men and women cast off Victorian formality and became pals, the 1920s were also marked by a new wariness and, at times, a barely suppressed hostility in gender relations. Many wondered when the changes would stop. What lines would demarcate male and female spheres of activity? What boundaries, if any, would remain to differentiate masculinity and femininity? As Americans looked uneasily at sport to understand the dimensions of change, their keen interest in women's athletics made it an important symbolic as well as actual arena of competition.

The assertive, dynamic female athlete of the 1920s posed a clear challenge to men. No longer contained within the narrow confines of a small number of college athletic programs, young women from all social ranks and geographic locations took up community-based sports, the best among them rising to national and international prominence. With unaccustomed boldness, female athletes invaded what had previously been men's exclusive space, claiming "masculine" strength, speed, and power as a right of womanhood.

Consequently both supporters and critics viewed women's athletic achievements as victories in a larger contest between men and women. When Gertrude Ederle swam the English Channel in world-record time, reporters hailed her success as "a battle won for feminism." To former suffrage leader Carrie Chapman Catt, Ederle illustrated the link between political and physical emancipation, proving that "woman's freedom would go hand in hand with her bodily strength." Another observer presented Ederle as "champion extraordinairy [sic] of her sex, and its unanswerable refutation of the masculinist dogma that woman is, in the sense of physical power and efficiency, inferior to man."[66]

An air of jocular sexual rivalry accompanied the media's celebrations of women athletes. Grantland Rice explained that the "alert and aggressive" American girl athlete "is not only getting a finely molded body . . . she is also getting the virility of will to battle against odds." The result was "a new type—a most attractive addition [who] can meet the male upon even terms."[67] Journalists repeatedly alerted readers to the possibility that women would equal or surpass men's athletic feats. Speculating on the coming generations of female athletic success, Rice wondered, "Who will be the weaker sex?" and "Will the men be left behind?"[68]

A tone of hostility and ridicule pervaded less sympathetic media accounts. When Northwestern University swimmer Sybil Bauer broke the men's world record in the backstroke, an editorial in the Nation looked toward a future of mixed-sex competition, asking, "Shall a girl suddenly precipitate herself into a contest of men—and then, conceivably, thrash them?"[69] Similarly, after Ederle's English Channel feat, the press nervously joked that in the future Channel swimming would have "its liveliest interest centered in the gallant and somewhat pathetic efforts of masculine swimmers to equal the feminine record."[70]

Male athletic leaders took steps to insure that men would never be in that position by squelching the few attempts women made to compete directly with men. When Sybil Bauer requested the chance to swim against men in Olympic backstroke competition, Olympic officials quickly turned her down.[71] By the same token, when a teenage baseball player named Margaret Gisolo reached the championship round of the 1928 American Legion

Junior Baseball Tournament, her presence sparked a flurry of criticism, media interest, and official reaction. Gisolo had been accepted by her teammates, local league officials, and hometown fans from the coal-mining town of Blanford, Indiana. But as the team rose through the levels of tournament play, her presence infuriated opponents, made even angrier by losing to a girl. Their vociferous protests attracted national media attention from the *New York Times* and Movietone News. Since league policies did not specify "boys only," Gisolo was allowed to compete in 1928. Immediately afterward, however, American Legion Baseball directors changed the rules to exclude girls explicitly.[72]

These were exceptional cases; women rarely competed directly against men or broke male records. Yet the media persisted in making a leap from athletic competition among women to an antagonistic battle of the sexes that threatened men's reign in sport and, by implication, in society. When observers reported on female-only athletic contests, they frequently transposed the event into a competition between men and women. In "Man's Athletic Crown in Danger," a critic mockingly remarked: "Sundry members of the so-called weaker sex, having obtained the vote and many other things upon which they had set their dear fluttering little hearts, are now out for bigger game." They aimed at "the vaunted superiority of their brothers" in sport: "Not content with competing among themselves . . . many women are actually trying to lower the marks made . . . by men. What is more ominous, from the masculine viewpoint, these women are coming perilously near to achieving this latest desire."[73] The possibility that "the so-called weaker sex" desired not only to excel in sport but to overturn male physical dominance posed a most serious threat to men's "vaunted superiority."

⊂⊃○⊂⊃

To many observers, women's athletic achievements signaled the dawn of a new era. The popularity of sport in the 1920s spanned class, racial, and regional divisions so that a wide array of female athletes came to embody the vibrancy and sexual appeal of modern womanhood. The female athlete seemed to epitomize the "new American girl," but her spark could just as easily kindle cultural fears about women's unceasing demands—their "latest desires"—whether they be economic, political, or sexual.

Women's unapologetic athleticism gave a physical dimension to questions about the proper spheres, qualities, and relative power of women and men. Poised on the edge between the appealing and the threatening aspects of the modern woman's relationship to men, female athletes captivated an intrigued but ambivalent American public struggling to make sense out of contemporary gender arrangements. Media accounts convey a sense of wonder along with the impression of a topsy-turvy world in which the existing social order could be reversed.[74]

Fearing any erosion of patriarchal privilege and resenting female intrusions into a formerly male terrain, men often viewed women's athletic gains as their own loss of a clearly masculine preserve. When defenders of women's sport argued that athletics would not masculinize women, they implicitly raised an alarming flip side—that sport could cease to masculinize men. If not in "manly games," where would men learn masculinity, prove their manhood, and sport their virility? Symbolically, women's sport stood for female advancement and shrinking male hegemony.

# CHAPTER 3

# GAMES OF STRIFE

## *The Battle over Women's Competitive Sport*

In 1929 a director of women's physical education at a Midwestern university witnessed a scene so harrowing she recounted the event to sportswriter John Tunis in hopes that publicity might curb such abuses in the future. Tunis reported that the director had attended a girls' basketball tournament organized by the backers of a local high school team. In the course of the tournament the "utterly exhausted" girls became so fatigued they "were removed from the floor in a fainting and hysterical condition." Yet play continued: "Local patriotism knew no bounds, the audiences grew wilder and wilder, all at the expense of these small groups of girls who became every minute more tense and excited. . . . [T]he game became a wild frenzy. The referee was an ogre and victory was all that mattered."[1] Even more dismaying was the fact that such scenes were not confined to the sport of basketball. "The fact is," Tunis continued, "that the women in many branches of sport have begun to ape the athletics of men."[2]

It seems ironic that by the late 1920s, it was most often women, typically physical educators and recreation leaders, who raised the cry of "masculinization." Women's sport had changed significantly since female physical educators had first developed their philosophy of "moderation." The entrance of working-class women, African American women, and younger students into highly competitive sport, along with celebratory, often sexualized, portrayals of female athletes in the media, violated every tenet of physical educators' belief in female-controlled moderate sport. They looked with horror on male coaches and promoters who encouraged an "excess of zeal" in the "over-athletic" woman of uncertain background.[3]

In 1927 Agnes Wayman, director of physical education at Barnard College, described the situation as "nothing short of criminal."[4] The "crime" was twofold: Female educators saw the increase in male-controlled school and commercial sport as an infringement on their professional turf, a violation of their rightful authority over the young female's physical and moral development. They also understood the growth of popular sport to pose a serious danger to the female athlete. Lacking the firm guidance of wise educators, enthusiastic young women risked being seduced by the glamour and fun of highly competitive sports. The result, according to physical educators, would be a loss of essential "womanly" qualities. Feminine health and reserve would be sacrificed to "masculine" habits, manners, and values.

The profession responded to these perceived dangers with an organized attack against the predominately male leaderships of the AAU, Olympic agencies, and less centralized municipal and industrial sport organizations. Women leaders formed two interlocking organizations that coordinated efforts during the 1920s and 1930s. The Committee on Women's Athletics (CWA, of the APEA) worked within the physical education profession, while the Women's Division of the National Amateur Athletic Federation (NAAF) focused on fighting competitive "evils" at the community level. Their foes—male athletic leaders, coaches, and business sponsors—fought back by either ignoring the criticisms or rebutting them with their own claims of expertise and leadership.

In their attempts to control women's athletics, the two sides quarreled not only over turf but also over competing philosophies of women's sport. At the center of this acrimonious debate lay a fundamental disagreement over the appropriate nature of competition for women. Advocates from all sides accepted that women deserved the right to participate in sport. They differed, however, over the type of sports and the degree of competition suitable for women. Athletic leaders argued furiously over the effects of "games of strife"—highly competitive sports like track and field and basketball—on young women across the nation.[5] The conflict dragged on for four decades, though it was most heated in the 1920s and 1930s. As educators and popular promoters struggled to establish their own brand of sport, they also advanced two competing ideals of athletic womanhood—the "wholesome, modest athlete" and the "athlete as beauty queen"—each designed in its own way to dispel persistent concerns about the "mannish" female athlete.

By 1920 women in physical education had grown confident of their ability to set the athletic course for their female charges. World War I had fostered a sudden national concern with fitness after one-third of U.S. inductees failed the army physical. As a result, a wave of state legislation made P.E. mandatory for elementary through high school students. By 1921 twenty states required physical education in the schools, and other states followed suit in the coming years.[6] School attendance in general rose dramatically in the 1920s as compulsory education laws and protective labor legislation redirected working-class children from factory to school.

As women physical educators began instructing female students in mandatory health and exercise courses, they also oversaw an unprecedented growth of extracurricular athletics at the college level. Female students eagerly joined faculty-sanctioned sorority and dorm leagues, interclass tournaments, and a variety of noncompetitive recreational clubs in such activities as hiking, riflery, and camping. Women physical educators appeared successfully to be implementing their design for a system of separate women's athletics that, while paralleling men's athletics, offered a distinctive brand of female sport under female expertise.

However, international developments were moving in a direction that would soon pit P.E. directors against male sport promoters in a struggle to control and define women's sport. In 1921 French organizer Alice Milliat founded the Fédération Sportive Féminine Internationale (FSFI), which one year later would sponsor the first Women's Olympic Games, held in Paris. Women had competed without controversy in previous international competitions. Physical educators had raised no objections to the much publicized feats of American women swimmers at the Antwerp Olympic Games in 1920 or to the presence of U.S. golfers, tennis players, and archers in earlier games. But the Women's Olympics would focus all eyes on women athletes. And for the first time in international competition, the games would highlight track-and-field athletics.[7]

Women's track featured the "masculine" qualities of strength, speed, and public bodily display that female physical educators found most abhorrent. The profession reacted against the sport's increasingly working-class constituency as well. Katherine Sibley, head of an APEA subcommittee on women's track and field, wrote to colleague Blanche Trilling about the socially less-than-desirable athletes preparing to compete in the Women's Olympics. With dismay she noted how very badly "this Paris meet has appealed to certain classes of women in and about Syracuse. Not college women—and I hear it is true pretty much throughout the state."[8] Trilling, however, was more disturbed by the evident interest of college women in pursuing track and field. She responded, "It is more surprising the apparently nice girls that are planning to go over [to Paris] in August—I can't see it."[9]

Physical educators like Trilling and Sibley believed that the masculine and increasingly working-class sensibility of the sport made it especially hazardous for the "nice girls" they had pledged to protect. They saw danger in both the public exposure and the physical duress of international competitions. In their eyes publicity and large crowds created a disreputable atmosphere in which leering fans and a salacious press would compromise the "nice girl's" modesty and reserve. They feared as well that extreme physical exertion would break down the inner restraints necessary for maintaining female propriety.

Not everyone agreed. Dr. Harry Stewart, a renegade physical educator, formed an organization to coordinate American participation in the Women's Games. After being rebuffed by members of his own profession and the AAU, Stewart organized a National Track Athletic Committee to sponsor U.S. track-and-field athletes in their first international women's meet. Although the American team fared poorly against more experienced European athletes, the Women's Olympics were an undeniable success, attracting 22,000 enthusiastic spectators who viewed women from the United States, France, and several other European nations competing in eleven different events.

The presence of American track women and the overall success of the games rankled leaders of U.S. and European sport, both male and female. International and American athletic organizations condemned the Women's Olympics and attempted to wrest control away from independent actors like Milliat and Stewart. The most vocal critics were women physical educators, but the reaction also involved several men's athletic organizations. Along with women's groups, they entered a complicated and prolonged struggle over who would set the future course of women's athletics. At issue was control over the day-to-day operation of women's sporting activities, but beneath the surface of this dispute lay a more complex question: To what extent should women's sport mirror men's? And who should decide, male athletic officials or trained female professionals? These matters were contested through a series of pitched organizational battles between the men and women who administered women's sport.

⬳◦⬲

Previously content to ignore women's track, male athletic officials expressed a sudden interest in the sport after the conclusion of the 1922 Women's Olympics. The all-male International Olympic Committee (IOC) addressed the issue first, considering women's track and field at its 1923 congress. IOC members agreed that they must regulate women's track to ensure against such "excesses" as the upstart Paris games—a major meet planned by and for women.[10] In this spirit they resolved to assume control of the sport, electing to introduce five women's track-and-field events to the Olympic Games in 1928.

A similar spirit prevailed among members of the International Amateur Athletic Federation (IAAF), the administrative body of European men's track. Two years after the Women's Olympics in Paris, the IAAF decided to draw up rules for managing women's track and field. Although professing a new commitment to

women athletes, IAAF leaders then voted *against* introducing
women's track-and-field events to the International Olympic
Games. The vote, though later reversed, suggests that the IAAF's
primary concern lay not in supporting women's track but in
quashing Milliat and the Women's Olympics, thus maintaining
absolute control in the world of sport. In 1926 the organization
pressured Milliat into adopting IAAF rules and relinquishing the
"Olympic" title in favor of "Women's World Games."[11]

In the United States the AAU also exhibited a newfound interest in women's track and field. AAU President James Sullivan had
announced in 1913 that because he had "no desire to make girls
public characters," he could not support women's athletics.
Sullivan, like others of his day, linked women's public athletic
activity with the negative connotation of "public women", a term
that referred to prostitutes or disreputable women of the streets.[12]
This opinion still predominated in the early twenties, when the
AAU rejected Harry Stewart's request for assistance in organizing
a women's team for the 1922 Paris games. However, realizing
that continued neglect could cut the group out of a major development in international sport, the AAU decided in late 1923 to
offer a women's national track-and-field championship beginning
in 1924. Sullivan's successor, President Prout, announced the new
policy by declaring, "The girls have become athletes. We can't
stop them. We must simply standardize their games."[13]

The sudden interest in women's athletics among leaders of
amateur sport struck women physical educators as rank oppor-
tunism. Even though they refused to sanction Olympic or any
other international or high level competition, they viewed
Stewart's group, the Women's Olympics, the IOC and the AAU as
intruders on their professional turf. Jarred by the challenge to
their authority to determine appropriate venues for women's athletics, women educators and recreation leaders lashed out against
men in sport and vigorously defended their own expertise.
Fearing especially that the AAU would bid for control of all girls'
and women's athletics, physical educators launched a campaign
to reassert their influence in women's sport. Women educators
and recreation leaders formed a steadfast coalition, building
organizational bases from which to oppose all public, highly

competitive sports. Within the profession they acted through the CWA, formed in 1917.[14] As they searched for resources and allies outside the profession, they found that their own concerns overlapped with a new athletic organization recently formed by men, the National Amateur Athletic Federation (NAAF).

The NAAF had been founded in 1922 by collegiate and military sport leaders in an effort to challenge the AAU's domination of amateur sport.[15] They designed the federation as a large umbrella organization of scouting groups, public and semiprivate recreation programs, military athletics, and school sport associations dedicated to ending commercialism and corruption in amateur sport. When women physical educators began their campaign to halt the spread of highly competitive sport, they saw the NAAF as a potential ally and looked to the federation for assistance. In 1923 P.E. leaders joined with women's scouting, recreation, and athletic organizations to form a special Women's Division of the NAAF. Mrs. Lou Hoover, leader of the Girl Scouts of America and wife of Herbert Hoover, headed the group, but women physical educators dominated the committee leadership and active membership roles.

From its founding in 1923 to its collapse in 1940, the Women's Division worked with the CWA (later called the Section on Women's Athletics [1927–31] and then the National Section on Women's Athletics [1932–49]) to forge a united front against all forms of highly competitive sports, which leaders continued to perceive as inherently threatening to the female athlete's moral and physical well-being.[16] The two organizations operated with nearly complete autonomy from their parent organizations, the NAAF and APEA. Through interlocking directorships and overlapping memberships, the groups devised a two-pronged strategy to suppress competitive activities that they believed undermined their authority and the best interests of female athletes. The CWA attempted to set standards for college and high school athletics. The Women's Division extended educators' influence beyond educational circles, reaching out to community sports programs through a variety of public recreation agencies.[17]

Leaders of the Women's Division quickly recruited endorsements from almost 250 school officials, recreational groups, and

athletic associations that supported a program of limited competition supervised by female experts.[18] At its high point in 1932,
the division numbered 481 member organizations.[19] It issued an
official "Platform" that outlined in detail the "Desirable
Practices" it wished to promote in women's athletics. In designing the platform trained educators and recreation specialists
called on the same medical concepts of female weakness and
emotional instability that had informed the profession's earliest
thinking. Pledging "to develop the sport for the girl and not the
girl for the sport," the Women's Division aimed to modify men's
sport to fit the unique capabilities and needs of women.[20]
Through the years the national office distributed more than one
hundred thousand copies of its official platform on girls' and
women's athletics and thousands more of the Women's Division
leaflets *Play for Girls* and *Every Girl in a Sport*. At the national,
state, and local levels, members of the Women's Division pressured education officials, athletic associations, municipal recreation programs, and semiprivate agencies to eliminate state and
regional tournaments and other "hazardous" conditions that
plagued girls' and women's sport.[21]

Why did physical education and recreation leaders object so
strenuously to highly competitive women's sport? What were the
hazardous conditions that so alarmed them? In an article on
"The Athletic Limitations of Women," Sarah Addington succinctly stated the case against high-level competitions: "They're not
good for the girls who participate in them and they're not good
for the girls who don't."[22] In her view the intense competition
endangered the skilled few whose desire to win would inevitably
lead them to exceed recommended restraints on physical exertion. In turn, the emphasis on ability excluded the majority of
less talented girls who preferred to play for fun.

Elaborating on Addington's brief remarks, some reformers reiterated the familiar position that unmodified sport endangered
women's reproductive health. Inconclusive medical evidence
about the effects of rigorous exercise on menstruation forced
women's athletic leaders to admit, "We can't actually put our fin-

ger on the harmful effect of too strenuous athletics on women."[23] Nevertheless they clung to this comfortable and effective argument, long advanced by medical specialists and the earliest proponents of female athletic "moderation." Despite an admitted lack of evidence, they cited the "undeniable" and "profound" influences of menstruation, which, if tampered with, could bring women to "the very borderline of the pathological."[24]

Others spoke to the social effects of highly competitive games. New York State Director of Physical Education Dr. Frederick Rand Rogers believed that boys' rules and state, national, or Olympic competitions were an "unnatural activity for girls" likely "to *distort* their natures." According to this view, girls were naturally less physical, aggressive, competitive, and vocal than boys. Beyond any specifics, what mattered most to critics like Rogers was that, at bottom, the true nature of a girl was to be *not boylike.* He warned that the female tendency to "ape" boys' sport led to competition between the sexes, "a most unsocial condition" that would be "disastrous to the welfare of both men, women, and society."[25]

This position won support from authorities far removed from the world of sport, including the pope. In a letter to the vicar of Rome spelling out his opposition to girls' athletics, Pope Pius XI stated: "If ever women must raise a hand we hope and pray she may do so only in prayer or for acts of charity . . . Everything must be avoided which contrasts with reserve and modesty, which are the ornament and safeguard of virtue."[26] In the absence of reserve and modesty, reformers believed that women would acquire "the inevitable qualities of rowdyism" and other "undesirable" masculine attributes.[27]

Physical educators also believed that the public and commercial elements of sport left female athletes vulnerable to sexual and economic abuses. Having long advocated female privacy and protection alongside exercise, women professionals recoiled at the commercial element introduced by business sponsorship, admission fees, town or school boosterism, and media coverage. They claimed that male coaches, journalists, and promoters depended on a winning team for their livelihood and consequently would necessarily pressure women athletes into overexertion.[28]

Educators described the tragic results, depicting postgame locker-room scenes in which traumatized girls collapsed, "their nervous systems completely broken, and all thoughts of sportsmanship, loyalty, and health thrown to the four winds in the winning or losing of that game."[29]

The profit motive could just as easily lead to the sexual exploitation of female athletes. In the eyes of reformers, the media's focus on physical beauty and promoters' use of "risqué" uniforms with sleeveless tops and short shorts created a danger-ously erotic, carnival atmosphere. Travel and large crowds posed related hazards. Women athletic leaders denounced the "commer-cial interests [which] are luring amateur athletes into their ranks, particularly young girls who travel over the country without proper chaperonage and go in for cocktail and pajama parties."[30] Large crowds ensured that a similar party atmosphere prevailed during the game itself. Women's Division leaders declared that such "exhibitionist type of performances" formed "a case of putting sex into sports, which is the last thing physical educators want."[31]

The belief that commercial, highly competitive sport was inherently undemocratic reinforced such critiques. Women lead-ers condemned the elitist and exclusionary nature of male athletic culture, arguing that varsity teams, tournament play, and interna-tional competitions privileged the talented minority over the neglected majority. Such a system directed harmful publicity toward a few stars while appropriating resources from those who most needed athletic assistance. Reformers did not want such an unhealthy imbalance in women's sport. By the late 1930s they even linked competitive popular sport to the rise of fascism, claiming: "When commercial interests present huge sports pageants and spectacles they are augmenting the ease with which dictators conquer the world."[32] Women wished to stay on the side of democracy, equal access, and sport for the sake of play, not victory.

Women sports leaders reserved their deepest, longest-lasting enmity for the men who coached and sponsored women's sports. Well into the second decade of the conflict, the issue of finding women coaches and officials "roused the usual storm" at a 1935 meeting of the National Recreation Association, one of the NAAF member organizations. "Mrs. R. S. Marshall of Birmingham declared that 90 percent of our difficulties are caused by men coaches and officials, and earned applause."[33] Women reformers looked beyond coaches to criticize the "old boys'" network among school principals, athletic directors, and local chambers of commerce for supporting competitive teams to boost their own towns and schools. Male journalists also earned the wrath of women leaders for their sensationalizing coverage of the "Amazon-type woman . . . whose feminine charms are played above sportsmanship."[34]

The division's critical appraisal of commercialism, sexual exploitation, elitism, and male athletic officials came together in a vehement, all-encompassing attack on male values and power in the world of sport. In her strongly worded "Women's Athletics—All Uses—No Abuses," Agnes Wayman expressed her resentment against men's influence in sport. Noting: "Physical education has too long been in the hands of school men and professional coaches. . . . The men took the tiller—they offered us a tow, and we . . . took it," she went on to list the evils of competition under the male system and concluded with a rousing call to action:

> When we see our adolescent high school girls playing long schedules of outside games, traveling around the country, other groups competing in open meets . . . wearing immodest clothing before mixed audiences, attended by male rubbers, we know that it's time something sane and intelligent was done. [Since] the *men* have decided to take over women's athletics, we can only ejaculate "Heaven help us" and roll up our sleeves.[35]

To counter the male model of sport, the Women's Division and the Committee on Women's Athletics proposed an alternative, more democratic approach. They emphasized the physical development of the "average girl," with special attention to the "motor moron" and the "shy or retarded girl" of "limited organic resources."[36] Under the motto "A Sport for Every Girl, and Every Girl in a Sport," the profession advanced an inclusive vision of sport in which athletic access, resources, and skills would be distributed equitably.

As a model of democratic sport, physical educators instituted "play days," special athletic events at which athletes from several colleges gathered for a day of competition and socializing. Without any practice or preorganization, participants formed mixed teams comprising players from the different schools so that individual institutions would not compete against each other. All interested players could attend, with no special awards for skill or achievement.[37] Following the games, the women mingled socially over tea and snacks in an atmosphere of "jolly sociability."[38] Educators also offered a more competitive alternative— "telegraphic meets" designed to provide "an emotional outlet for those with intercollegiate aspirations."[39] On a given day several schools would set up a series of events for their own students on their home fields. Afterwards the schools would report times, heights, and distances via telegraph to determine winners and losers.

In the 1930s and 1940s "sports days" gradually replaced play days and telegraphic meets. Slightly more competitive than play days, sports days allowed schools to form teams in advance, practice several times, and then gather to compete in a single day or weekend of competition. Some colleges refused to condone these events. Because students competed for preselected teams that practiced prior to the event and then vied against other school teams, cautious administrators judged sports days to be a form of intercollegiate competition. Others argued that by allowing all interested students to join a team and by limiting competition to one day, sports days still offered an inclusive, democratic alternative to elite varsity teams that, by contrast, selected members on the basis of skill and then competed against other schools over a months-long season.

Educators' sincere commitment to expand female athletic experience did not extend to those sports beyond their control, however. CWA and Women's Division leaders viewed the fact that women's athletics "have recently become of general interest" as a problem.[40] They found women's involvement in commercial and industrial sport leagues particularly troubling because, in those settings more than others, male promoters rejected the principles and leadership proffered by female physical educators. In a 1929 essay Ethel Perrin worried that male control of highly competitive athletics would syphon off the most talented women and leave educators with the dregs. Despite the profession's stated interest in mass participation, she complained that "a program which hands over the best athletic material among girls to the men to train and leaves to the women physical educators, the masses, is a poor program."[41]

To guard against such an outcome the profession articulated an adamantly separatist philosophy that insisted on the importance of women coaches, officials, and administrators. From its founding in 1923, the Women's Division operated on the premise that "the welfare, health, and education of women depends upon the women experts on girls and women's athletics organizing themselves as a deliberating and administrative body to deal with the special problems of athletics for girls and women."[42] Women leaders believed that girls and women should play in specially designed female costumes, under a distinct set of women's rules, and before predominantly female audiences. Only through separate organization and supervision could female educators hope to implement their plan for controlled, moderate competition that would protect the safety and preserve the femininity of female athletes.

In hindsight this strategy looks like a rearguard action to conserve professional educators' status and outdated standards of female propriety. Yet the stance was a familiar one among women activists, generations of whom had embraced separatism in order to build solidarity and create a distinctly female public voice. Well into the twentieth century, women active in reform circles, the peace movement, social work, and women's education continued to advance the notion that women's need for protection and their unique public role derived from inherent differences in the biological and social makeup of men and women. Physical educators fashioned policies around these premises, working to unify all women under an athletic umbrella of female supervision and moderate competition.

However, like many other women's organizations of the 1920s

and 1930s, the Women's Division encountered an unexpected problem. Separatism presumed a common female identity; but women could no longer agree on a shared standard of womanhood.[43] By the 1920s working-class and middle-class women alike were abandoning an older model of womanhood based on female weakness, refinement, and propriety for a more energetic, erotic femininity advocated by young working women, feminists, and the new consumer culture. Physical educators, however, clung to notions of sexual difference and female vulnerability—concepts that had been crucial to establishing their professional legitimacy. Not surprisingly, their conservative views met with resistance from inside and outside the profession.

Generated outside leadership circles and silenced by official P.E. publications, opposing perspectives among white physical educators rarely appeared in print. Many dissenters were simply teachers or recreation leaders in small programs or remote areas far removed from the centers of organized professional influence. Some may never have heard of the Women's Division or its officially sanctioned "Desirable Practices." Others, who were acquainted with the official line, probably opted to follow it selectively; as they moved from their professional college training to active work in the field, they preserved what they found useful and discarded the rest. Although these instructors seldom aired their opinions in public forums, evidence from two other groups—African American physical educators and student athletes—clearly reveals procompetition sentiments that cut against the grain of professional orthodoxy.

Black female physical educators were few in number in the first half of this century. In the 1920s many black colleges and normal schools were just beginning to offer P.E. coursework as a required subject. A few instituted degree programs in health and physical education in the late 1920s and 1930s, but as of 1939 only 23 percent of fifty surveyed African American colleges and universities offered P.E. degrees.[44] The college education required for this degree and the graduate training necessary to rise through the ranks discouraged African Americans, as well as women from other racial minorities and economically disadvantaged groups, from entering the profession or assuming positions of leadership in the overwhelmingly white APEA.[45] Yet, however thin in numbers, African American women physical educators and recreation leaders utilized their access to black newspapers, college publications, and education journals to articulate a philosophy independent of dominant professional views.

They differed from white P.E. leaders by stressing issues of community well-being over individual health and by encouraging highly competitive athletics. Usually in cooperation with male colleagues, black women educators geared their programs toward two goals: improving the health of black students and communities in general, and training students to be athletic leaders in their communities. Courses in public health, nutrition, hygiene, and rural sanitation made up a large share of the curriculum. In addition all students studied recreation leadership and coaching techniques. Since few black elementary and high schools had the resources for physical education classes, interscholastic sport was the primary form of exercise provided by schools. P.E. programs saw athletic expertise as an essential skill for male and female majors who, on becoming teachers, would also coach and coordinate interscholastic competition.[46]

African American college administrators held varying positions on the question of female competition. Some educators, like Hampton Institute's Elizabeth Dunham, were content to leave sports to the men. She argued that the physical and mental strain, commercialism, and expense of sport made it "distinctly unwise" for women "who, after all, come to school to study, and not to be members of a traveling troupe of athletic performers."[47] Dunham seemed to represent a viewpoint held by some members of the black middle class. This perspective resembled that of white leaders and determined policy at schools like Howard, Hampton, and Fisk.[48]

However, other black colleges and many normal and industrial schools enthusiastically sponsored interscholastic women's athletics, especially basketball, in the 1920s and 1930s. A study in 1939 found that only 25 percent of black colleges objected to intercollegiate women's sport, compared to a survey of predominantly white institutions that reported 83 percent opposition to women's varsity athletics.[49] Tuskegee Institute took one of the most active stances in favor of women's intercollegiate sport. In 1927, P.E. Director Amelia Roberts wrote a letter to the *Chicago Defender* in which she argued for the importance of women's physical education. She urged the adoption of "girls' rules" in basketball and the hiring of more women as P.E. teachers and athletic coaches. She suggested training women officials, too, because "so many girls are going in for competitive games."[50] Like many of her white peers, Roberts was interested in creating a capable group of women to administer girls' athletics. But she saw no particular danger in "competitive games" and no need to define her agenda in opposition to male or public sport. Instead she accepted women's interest in competitive sport as fact and then proposed that educators should expand their expertise to embrace this development.

Black recreation leader Ruth Arnett, a YWCA Secretary of Girls Work, went even further when she suggested a positive link between competitive sport and womanhood, a position comparable to the AAU's official stance. She rejected curbs on competition and dismissed undue worry about "tomboyish" athletes. In Arnett's view the "real man" desired the vital, vigorous "real woman" who had cultivated these qualities as an athletic tomboy. Employing a concept of womanhood that embraced strength, self-reliance, and competitive spirit, she concluded, "Let's encourage our girls to be 'tomboys.' Let them enter any game of sport and recreation that the boy enters. Let's teach them to be real girls!"[51]

While African American physical educators could express their views in the small number of athletic programs they controlled, female college students—the great majority of whom were white women attending predominately white institutions—found it much more difficult to challenge restrictions on competition. WAAs appeared to fall into line under the guiding hand of faculty advisers. Yet behind students' formal compliance lay a steady stream of resistance.

Athletic directors mentioned that they frequently had to remind students of the reasons for banning varsity competition, reasons many students found unconvincing.[52] In 1924 Wellesley students voted 237 to 33 in favor of intercollegiate sports, with Radcliffe, Mount Holyoke, Wheaton, and Connecticut College also reporting a similar interest.[53] As unswayed P.E. directors continued to forbid intercollegiate competition, some students became more open in expressing their frustration. In 1942 members of the student-run Athletic Federation of College Women (AFCW) complained, "We don't agree, but are being stepped on."[54] A few student organizations managed to circumvent official prohibitions by using "club" teams to keep an informal varsity system alive. In the 1930s Radcliffe sports clubs enjoyed "friendly competition" with Jackson, Pembroke, and Wheaton in field hockey, swimming, basketball, lacrosse, archery, and tennis.[55]

Students could voice their disapproval of restrictive athletic policies only cautiously. But they openly showed their antipathy toward the health-and-hygiene orientation of departments that sought to steer students away from highly competitive sport into mandatory P.E. courses and voluntary intramural activities. Required physical exams and nude posture photos along with a tedious chart system for recording detailed information about weight, diet, sleep, and posture earned the everlasting enmity of many students. One Radcliffe freshman recalled being "thrust into Miss Arrowsmith's class for the overfat and overthin and those of the crooked spines," while another "learned of my insignificance by orders of the Gym department to write my insufficient weight weekly on a horrid tablet that all could view."[56] Even educators admitted that they tired of "the apathy of students in these matters," finding that only a few "[could] work up enthusiasm" for physical improvement.[57]

This realization led a few physical educators to suggest a judicious revision in the profession's stance on competitive sport. In 1931 Ina E. Gittings wrote an article claiming to speak for "a large number of young instructors who are loath to come out flat footed against their directors who may not be in favor of Intercollegiate Competition." Titled "Why Cramp Competition?" the article argued that "varsity competition for college women furnishes the real medium for maximum vigor, skill and joy."[58] Over the course of the decade, a few others chimed in with support for Gittings's view. Some educators worried specifically that by not meeting college women's desire for keener competition, the schools were in fact driving these athletes into the hands of an opposition that offered girls and women the chance to compete in industrial leagues and AAU meets.[59]

⸺◦◦⸺

They were right. The growth of grass-roots sport continued in the late 1920s through the depression and World War II eras, offering a wide range of young athletes, including some college students, an appealing brand of intensely competitive sport. Except for AAU officials, most leaders of industrial- and community-based sport made no attempt to answer the Women's Division or other anticompetition forces; they simply developed competitive sports programs guided by their own values and purposes. AAU leaders, however, confronted their accusers directly.

Made up of prominent businessmen, civic leaders, and former athletes, the AAU's male leadership disavowed physical educators' claims to gender and professional authority. It criticized the entire NAAF as a band of "grouchy reformers" whose federation, by snubbing the AAU, would "continue to be impotent and destined for the scrapheap."[60] In rebuttal to Women's Division accusations of neglect and exploitation, AAU leaders championed their success in bringing athletic opportunity to working-class women. After viewing the first women's national track-and-field championships in 1924, committee chair Fred Steers praised the industrial and business clubs that accounted for most of the participants, expressing the AAU's desire "to encourage athletics among this great class of women."[61] Other officials stressed that the AAU was uniquely situated to create a truly democratic sports culture. Because it extended opportunity and guidance to the majority of youth, who did not complete high school or attend college, the AAU provided athletics to "thousands of young girls of all nationalities, and from all classes of society."[62]

Despite their confident claims, however, AAU leaders felt the sting of physical educators' unrelenting attacks. After nearly a decade of criticism, in 1932 the AAU set up a National Women's Sports Committee to investigate the charges. The committee surveyed 232 top athletes, reporting that nearly every one saw an overall health improvement and suffered no ill effects on menstruation due to competition. Respondents firmly believed that the "competitive spirit" benefited rather than harmed female athletes. While the committee acknowledged a need for greater female leadership and for some minor reforms, it concluded that the AAU was meeting its obligation to protect and guide women athletes.[63] Unfazed by the Women's Division offensive, AAU officials defended the overall excellence of the organization and touted its ability to "guard for our young women their precious heritage of gentleness and feminine charm."[64]

Other evidence suggests that the AAU's commitment to women's sport was more rhetorical than real. When not specifically addressing the topic of women's athletics, president Avery Brundage referred to sport as a "manly" pastime suited to the "virile qualities of strength, courage, initiative, will power and poise."[65] The AAU's promise to develop stronger female leadership also rang false. Only a few women chaired committees or held other leadership positions, and no serious efforts were made to train women as coaches or to expand their numbers and opportunities in the AAU. Male leaders appear to have acted from expedient and self-serving motives, variously ignoring women's sport, assuming a posture of paternalistic guidance, or vigorously defending competition when it served the organization's interests.

Such uneven support did little to create the truly mass-based female athletic constituency of which the AAU boasted. Yet even with its many shortcomings, the organization did effectively expand the institutional base of women's athletics, in 1926 adding a national basketball tournament to its annual national swimming and track championships. Because state and regional AAU chapters could choose to promote or ignore women's sports, national policies often did not translate into full-fledged support at the local level. But for skilled industrial and municipal teams interested in competing beyond their immediate communities, the AAU framework of championship competition offered a structure that ambitious athletes could pursue on their own initiative.

In the process of doing battle, physical educators and promoters of popular sports not only drew on organizational resources, they also called on cultural images that would help them make their case for or against competition. Each side created a model of athletic womanhood designed to dispel the "mannish athlete" stereotype and convert skeptics to their particular brand of women's sport. Not surprisingly the two images were quite different. They reflected the conflicting class and gender sensibilities that underlay the schism between the Women's Division and the AAU.

To women leaders the modern female athlete walked a tightrope, poised between peril and achievement. Overzealous competition could lead to irreparable reproductive damage, sexual exploitation, and selfish elitism. Yet, with proper female supervision, competition could improve reproductive health and instruct girls in cooperation, fair play, and other attributes of good citizenship. Sport could also channel "primitive" physical and emotional desires into wholesome activity, containing sexual urges while imbuing the athletic girl with a vibrancy appealing to the modern man.

The moderate, wholesome athlete idealized by physical educators fused appropriate female athleticism with a middle-class concept of womanhood characterized by refinement, dignity, and self-control. In an address given at the 1930 Women's Division national conference, Carnegie Foundation staff member Howard J. Savage claimed that athletics instilled the "evenness of temper" and "emotional control" that were essential qualities for the modern housewife.[66] Recreation and education experts believed that they could "assist in bringing about the control of emotion, not by repression, but by the utilization of the energy aroused, in healthful activity."[67] While claiming to reject Victorian "repression," the profession retained a middle-class emphasis on self-control and modesty: The ideal athlete would blend earlier bourgeois virtues of control and refinement with contemporary assets of vibrancy and physical competency.

This ongoing emphasis on control and moderation revealed a distinct bias against working-class women—one that came easily to a group of predominantly white, middle-class women who actively promoted their class interests as educated professionals. While urging all young athletes to cultivate emotional and physical control, the Women's Division saw these attributes as especially lacking in women of the working class. Portrayed as coming "from a class where hereditary, unhygienic living and unsanitary environment handicap them in the beginning," poor women were perceived as leading generally unwholesome lives further impaired by "strenuous and unwise recreation."[68]

In her 1932 article "Giving the Girls a Chance," Ethel Bowers incorporated this class distinction into her analysis of women's recreational tendencies. She created two fictional types of female recreation seekers, "Beatrice the Business Girl" and "Ida the Industrial Girl." According to Bowers, "Beatrice enjoys gym classes, games and sports for the fun and the physical benefit she receives, and she takes part in the finer forms of music, dramatics, or handicraft activities because they appeal to her love of the beautiful." Ida, the factory worker, responded to baser appeals, spending "all her play time in one of three ways, movies, cheap dances . . . and automobiling with the subsequent parking and petting." Bored by monotonous work, "She wants strenuous athletics, jazzy music, snappy dramatics or musical comedies, thrilling parties, not for the benefit she will receive, but because she will show off to good advantage before an audience of the opposite sex."[69] Although by the early 1930s it had become more acceptable for young, middle-class "business girls" to work, reformers like Bowers clearly distinguished between the "finer" motives of the middle-class worker and the thrill-seeking, overtly sexual yearnings of her counterpart in the factory.

The assumption that working-class women lacked modesty and self-control went hand in hand with educators' assumptions about the kind of environments likely to cause a loss of control. Leaders attributed athletic "evils" to "the stimulus of large audiences" and accused small-town and big-city crowds of seeking "the emotional satisfaction of a spectacle."[70] Since middle-class school athletics and elite country club sport took place in relative privacy, "the crowd" referred to was predominantly working-class or rural. Boisterous, mixed audiences grated on female educators and recreation leaders who had cultivated their profession-al sensibility in a private, female milieu. They looked aghast at "big unruly crowds" and feared that under pressure from screaming coaches and fans, players swept up in the competitive frenzy would emit shouts of "Atta boy!" and "Come on, gang!" sacrificing the "womanly attributes we admire."[71]

Educators' personal discomfort with working-class styles mixed with professional concern, especially the fear that work-ing-class "mannishness" might infiltrate the ranks of college ath-letics. University of Texas Director of Physical Training Anna Hiss lamented the "semi-professional attitude" that had crept into intercollegiate sport. The term "semi-professional" referred to working-class sport, where industrial and commercial leagues were often called "semipro." To Hiss this attitude led directly to "a swagger and a lack of refinement, a breaking down of reserve, and an inclination toward tomboyishness."[72]

The picture was complicated by the fact that behind the tomboyish athlete often stood respectable middle-class men—the school principals, businessmen, and chamber of commerce offi-cials who promoted popular sport. Unable to challenge them on class grounds, the Women's Division and CWA severely rebuked these pillars of the local community for ignoring the importance of gender differences and female leadership. Women athletic reformers painted themselves as female saviours of misguided young working-class girls in need of protection from unscrupu-lous males.

In their indictment of male sport and the enveloping culture of consumer capitalism, women athletic leaders presented elements of a radical social critique. But their analysis had a highly conser-vative side as well. Although the campaign against competition offered probing insights into the potential for sexual and eco-nomic abuses in highly commercialized women's sport, in the end physical educators struggled to preserve existing class relations and gender differences. They leveled charges against commercial and sexual exploitation in sport, yet neglected to examine either the economic exploitation of working women or their own class and racial biases. Women sport reformers acted, rather, to defend their interests as professional, middle-class women.[73]

Popular promoters of women's sport did not presume to offer a social critique. Where physical educators sniffed danger in every corner, the model of womanhood communicated by popular sport organizations projected a positive sense of excitement and daring. Proponents of competition did not see the zealous athlete as a candidate for salvation but rather as a cause for celebration. And while conceding that unsupervised athletics might sacrifice female health and modesty, AAU and Olympic leaders trusted that their supervision provided adequate protection without elaborate modifications or the total separation of women's sport governance from men's.

AAU officials stressed the positive benefits of competition for American womanhood.[74] In 1929 the AAU's *Amateur Athlete* published a letter from Bernarr MacFadden, an innovator in women's physical culture and advertising, claiming that "strong, vigorous, vital women are badly needed to build up the race." Under the heading "Athletics for Women Will Help Save the Nation," he argued that sport would correct "defective femininity" and create the vital mothers necessary for happy homes and "the future progress of the nation."[75] Fred Steers resorted to similar eugenic and nationalist rationales when defending women's Olympic participation. He reasoned: "As long as there are mothers of statesmen, diplomats, and soldiers, women's participation in the Olympic Games will not be in vain."[76] In this view not only would athletic training in cooperation, teamwork, and loyalty prepare women for their own citizenship, the maternal vigor built through sport would improve the real business at hand—reproducing a stalwart male citizenry.

Popular media accounts made fewer references to political and maternal welfare, looking more often to the matter of sexual attractiveness to explain the value of women's sport. The announced benefits were double-sided: sport would enhance the sexual appeal of young women, at the same time heightening the viewing pleasure of audiences entranced by attractive female competitors.

Journalists likened athletes to chorus girls, movie stars, and beauty queens. The *Baltimore Evening Sun* described a 1925 city-wide track meet attended by more than five thousand girls and seven thousand spectators, stating with delight, "It was a girly show if ever there was one." The reporter described the events and range of body types present, then concluded, "It was a great gathering of budding and full-blooming beauty."[77] In the same vein, a longwinded *Pittsburgh Courier* headline announced, "Washington Pa. Lassies, Famed for Beauty and Ability, Have Been Termed the 'Ziegfield Follies' of the Basketball World by Admirers." The article went on to note that "their beauty, charm, grace, social prestige and that air of friendliness which participation in athletics breeds, have given their home town publicity of the kind which can hardly be reckoned with in terms of dollars and cents."[78] The *Courier* thus praised the very same connections between sport, sexuality, personal fame, and commercial profit that women's sport leaders deplored.

Sports promoters did not stop at simply pointing out likenesses between athletes and sexually attractive dance, stage, and screen performers. They brought sexual entertainment to the sports arena in the form of beauty contests. Beginning in the late 1920s, AAU national basketball tournaments and other independent championships crowned tournament beauty queens. The winners took their place of honor alongside other players selected for all-star teams and most-valuable-player awards.

The image of the athlete as beauty queen emerged in a variety of settings—white working-class and African American sport, smalltown schoolgirl athletics, media coverage of elite sports, and male-dominated athletic organizations like the AAU. For this reason the popular model of athletic womanhood was less coherent than the carefully argued P.E. case for moderation and separatism. Some proponents gravitated toward nationalist and eugenic appeals, others toward sexuality and beauty. Still others saw no need to justify women's sport beyond the obvious pleasure it gave participants and viewers. Yet, however diverse in origin and image, the idealized female athlete shared two characteristics: First, she was linked to other forms of popular culture like dance, movies, and beauty pageants. The connection was achieved symbolically, in media representations, and literally, by combining sporting events with dances or athletic beauty contests. Second, she earned appreciation for her sexual appeal as much as for her athletic ability. Although the popular athlete might display "masculine" athletic ability, she established her femininity through her attractiveness to men.

The depiction of athletes as beauty queens sent physical educators into a rage. Women in sport were regarded as sexual objects, their bodies presented for public consumption, and their achievements coopted by hometown boosters interested in local fame and commercial fortune. But the very aspects of competitive sport that most alarmed physical educators signified success to popular promoters and athletes. Because they lived in a world in which sex, commerce, and sport were frequently integrated, they saw nothing wrong with using commercial and sexual appeals to build the sports they so thoroughly enjoyed.

The competitive ethos and sexualized atmosphere of popular sport remained sharply at odds with physical educators' commitment to limited competition. The Women's Division and the National Section on Women's Athletics (NSWA) continued to struggle for a female-controlled and -defined model of women's sports. By the late 1930s and 1940s, the conflict had reached a stalemate. Neither physical educators nor popular sports promoters could establish complete control over women's athletics or fully discredit their opponents' views.

The tireless efforts of reformers to curb interscholastic and intercollegiate competition succeeded at the college level, where studies conducted in 1936 and 1945 found that only 16–17 percent of colleges had intercollegiate varsity sports for women.[79] At the high school level, a study in the late 1930s found that eighteen states had discontinued state tournaments for girls. Added to those states that had never offered championship play, the total number of states with no tournaments reached thirty-six.[80] Yet among those states, many continued to offer city, district, and regional interscholastic tournaments, and pro-competition sentiment remained even more vital outside the schools.

Demonstrating their continued if tepid support for women's track athletics, American and International Olympic bodies stood firm against Women's Division demands to eliminate Olympic track and field for women.[81] At the local level the phenomenal popularity in the 1930s of two low-budget sports—softball and bowling—allowed popular women's athletics to flourish in spite of cutbacks in industrial and municipal recreation funds. The federal government provided another source of support, sponsoring athletics as an antidote to depression-era unrest and, by the early 1940s, to wartime stress. As part of New Deal deficit spending and emergency relief, such government agencies as the Works Progress Administration (WPA) built playing fields, gymnasiums, swimming pools and playgrounds, providing jobs for some of the unemployed, and creating recreational opportunities for those who remained idle. Although intended to divert unemployed male workers from union activities and political radicalism, New Deal policies had the side effect of opening more recreational doors to working-class women.[82]

Control of competitive sport continued to elude the Women's Division. Problems mounted in the mid-1930s, when the division faced a loss of funds and member organizations. Soon thereafter internal conflicts and severe financial problems led to the group's collapse and its absorption into the APEA's NSWA in 1940.[83] In the 1940s and 1950s, the NSWA (later the Division of Girls' and Women's Sports), continued to provide an effective base for advocates of limited competition. However, a growing number of women from within the ranks began to plead for a loosening of restrictions against interscholastic sport. Gladys Palmer of Ohio State championed the cause of more rigorous competition and in 1941 established the first national women's intercollegiate championship in golf. Although the influence of Palmer and her allies grew very slowly, their actions reopened the issue of intercollegiate sport, in the process gradually shifting the battleground from a rancorous conflict between educators and male sport officials to an internal struggle among women physical educators. Until the late 1950s, however, top-ranking leaders in the profession maintained their stance against highly competitive and male-controlled sport.

On the surface the conflict between women physical educators and popular sports advocates was a straightforward struggle for the right to define and regulate women's athletics. However, at a deeper level, the conflict was not over leadership but over the recurring question of "mannishness." To alter public impressions of the masculine female athlete, physical educators and promoters of popular sport formulated competing concepts of athletic womanhood: the healthy, wholesome athlete of moderate ability and limited activity; and the exuberant, sexy, competitive athlete. Both ideals incorporated athletic enjoyment and competence into notions of femininity. Yet neither fundamentally challenged the commonsense belief that rugged sport and athletic ability were masculine in character.

In voicing their trenchant critique of men's sport and masculinist values, physical educators reinforced the association between vigorous competition and mannishness. They classified the forms of sport most accessible to working-class, rural, and black youth—club, industrial, and semiprofessional athletics—as unladylike and unnatural for women. The effect was to sustain a definition of femininity that excluded the intensely devoted athlete and implicitly left working-class, minority, and poor rural women outside the bounds of respectable womanhood.

Even in their effort to provide a democratic, antielitist athletic experience for every girl and woman, women's sport leaders relied on arguments that actually deepened the divide between the masculine "athletic girl" and the feminine "nonathlete." The Women's Division regarded strenuous competition and femininity as incompatible, thus unintentionally bolstering the belief that feminine girls did not pursue rigorous sports. And by preserving an old-fashioned curriculum dominated by unpleasant health rituals, rules, lectures, and exams, leaders may have ensured the continued alienation of many girls from sport, physical education, and their own bodies.

In popular settings athletic enthusiasts argued that competitive sport would enhance, not sacrifice, womanhood. The model of the athlete as beauty queen appeared to admit energy, vigor and muscle tone into the concept of femininity. However, these were usually presented as benefits accrued toward marriage and motherhood. Women received praise for their physical strength and ability only when it made them better mothers or more attractive mates. The athletic beauty-queen model depended on cultural images and practices *outside* sport—beauty contests, pageantry, sexual appeals—for legitimacy. In the end women athletes found acceptance not simply for their skill but for their usefulness and attractiveness to men.

The unmodified "athlete" remained a male figure. This fact alone kept most girls and women alienated from sports. If not, the lack of opportunity and recognition discouraged many others from competing. Yet in spite of these barriers, a significant number of girls and women did pursue athletic excellence, compelled by their own desire, supportive local communities, and the contagious American enthusiasm for sport.

# CHAPTER 4

# ORDER ON THE COURT

## *The Campaign to Suppress Women's Basketball*

⌐○⌐

"Pretty Virginia Harris Leads Hansell to Iowa Basketball Championship," trumpeted the headline in *Life* magazine's 1940 photo essay on Iowa girls' basketball.[1] The story went on to describe the surprising phenomenon of high school basketball in Iowa, where every year thousands of smalltown students played for one of the state's hundreds of girls' basketball teams, each vying for a berth at the annual state tournament in Des Moines. On its establishment in the early 1920s, the tournament attracted nearly 250 teams. By the 1950s attendance figures for the five-day final event reached 87,000, generating revenues that eventually funded sixteen other girls' interscholastic sports.[2] The number of teams, the extensive involvement of parents and towns-folk, and the level of enthusiasm made Iowa basketball unique in the world of women's sports. Yet in many respects basketball developed in Iowa much as it did in other regions of the country.

Since its invention in 1891, basketball has been the most consistently popular sport among schoolgirls and young women. Originally developed as a settlement-house game, in the 1920s more and more female students and workers took up the sport, accommodated by newly formed interscholastic and industrial leagues. They played a highly competitive, popular brand of basketball that took root outside physical education programs. The aggressive defense, fast-moving offense, cheering crowds, and brightly colored satin uniforms of popular women's basketball challenged the P.E. profession's credo of moderation, modesty, and limited competition. Women educators responded by launching a determined campaign to stamp out the "evils" of interscholastic and industrial basketball.

*Life's* feature essay, which appeared midway in this campaign, reveals the limits of educators' success. The fact that Iowa girls played by the six-player (per side) "girls' rules," rather than the conventional five-player rules, represented a victory for the cause of moderation. However, tournament organizers ran the event as an unabashedly commercial venture, drawing thousands of paying customers who exhibited the kind of zeal that so exasperated women sport reformers. Big crowds attracted media attention, also condemned by educators. *Life* reported that Virginia Harris, the star player for the Hansell, Iowa, team and "just about the prettiest girl in town," was "dated up far ahead"—precisely the kind of sexual commentary that left women sport leaders quaking in anger.[3] Included in *Life's* photo spread was a picture of a partially naked player—undressed from the waist up, but viewed only from the back—undergoing a medical exam for the state tournament's "health contest." The facts that the event was billed as a "health" rather than an AAU-style "beauty" contest, and that a male doctor conducted the exam under the watchful eye of a female nurse, pointed to the moderating influence of physical educators. Yet the profession could hardly fail to notice that commercial photographers had, under the guise of health, cast a voyeuristic gaze on an adolescent female athlete and presented her seminude likeness to a national audience.

Educators found the fully dressed athlete only slightly more tolerable, objecting to the "flashy, too expensive, and too close fitting costumes" worn in tournament play.[4] As an alternative they proposed a distinctively female game of basketball appropriate for the moderate, health-conscious athlete who refrained from overexertion and public display. AAU and semipro officials took a different tack, supporting competition while countering the impression of "masculine" skill with attention to athletes' feminine beauty and sex appeal. Despite the obvious clash in sexual and class sensibilities, the two models of women's basketball shared a common intention to cast off damaging associations between women's sport and masculine athleticism.

The battle over women's basketball reflects not only an organizational dispute over sport governance but, more important, an ongoing effort among educators and popular promoters to make "masculine" sport compatible with womanhood. The resulting stalemate over interscholastic competition, rival forms of "women's" basketball, and contrasting images of "feminine" athleticism wove deeply gendered patterns into the culture and design of sport. Yet the uneven, conflict-ridden history of "women's" basketball also indicates that notions of femininity and masculinity in sport are neither "natural" nor permanently inscribed in cultural practice or belief.

Basketball was invented by YMCA worker James Naismith, who set out to design an inexpensive game that could be played indoors by restless students or recreation seekers during the long winter months. The sport spread rapidly in women's schools and settlement houses where women played the game on small indoor courts, protected from the elements and from public scrutiny. Initially peach buckets served as baskets. The court could be any rectangular space marked off by netting or ropes, thus the nickname "cage game." Although men also took up the game in schools and social agency recreation programs, early observers considered basketball to be a sport appropriate for women, both because they took to it so eagerly and because as an indoor game with limited physical contact and a relatively small playing surface, basketball initially seemed too effete for rugged male athletes.

Despite the game's feminine reputation, the intensity and roughness of women's play alarmed some observers. In 1892 a Massachusetts newspaper described a Smith College match as "a mad game" marred by wild play and riotous cheering. Other editorialists claimed that basketball players tended to "grow bitter in feeling and lose self-control," which "makes the girls rough, loud-voiced and bold."[5] Smith College Athletic Director Senda

Berenson, shocked by both the rough play and the negative publicity it generated, resolved to introduce stricter regulations for women's play. Early organizers of the game had varied the rules to fit immediate conditions and preferences. As many as ten or fifteen players sometimes joined a side, and, depending on space and inclination, players might run the full court or at other times be restricted by as many as nine different divisions of the floor. Berenson hoped to create a single set of rules that would standardize the sport and, more important, define a suitably refined version of the game for women, one in which body contact, physical exertion, and unruly commotion would be minimized.

In 1899 she organized a National Women's Basketball Committee under APEA auspices. Through the Spalding sporting goods company, the committee issued its first official women's rulebook in 1901.[6] The three-court, six-player "girls' rules" sanctioned by Berenson's committee divided the floor into front-, center-, and backcourt regions, with players designated as forwards, centers, or guards correspondingly and confined to their section of the court. The rules allowed players to dribble the ball only one time (later three bounces were allowed) and prohibited physical contact and any effort to hinder the shooter.[7] By contrast, the five-player "boys' rules," played by boys, men, and girls or women who had not encountered the new rules, allowed all players to run the full court and placed fewer restrictions on dribbling or on guarding the offensive player.

The new, more restrictive regulations did nothing to dampen women's enthusiasm. At women's colleges especially, students organized interclass contests that became focal points of college life. Caroline Shaw Sherer recalled turn-of-the-century games at Radcliffe as "great occasions." When "the pale blue of 1901 vied with the red, yellow and green of our sister classes," it formed the "crowning event" of the college calendar.[8] At Smith the "big game" took place every Thanksgiving weekend, with the freshman class challenging the sophomores, coached by juniors and seniors respectively. Class colors, banners, and pranks added to the ritual significance, creating a fervor that spread to the entire student body.

As the new rules took hold, Berenson's Women's Basketball

(ABOVE) At the turn of the century, strict gender conventions confined women to certain sports. Archery was considered a properly refined sport for "ladylike" athletes of the middle and upper classes. (*Chicago Historical Society*)

(LEFT) By 1928, however, "modern" women became a greater presence in sport. This 1928 photo, though clearly in fun, is a reminder of the hostility that many felt toward this new athletic woman who broke with gender conventions. (*Chicago Historical Society*)

(ABOVE) Women's basketball was first popularized in high schools and women's colleges. Here girls from Western High School in Washington, D.C., play a game in 1899. The irregular dimensions of the "court," closed net on basket, bulky uniforms, and teacher/referee's clothing were typical of the game in its early years. (*Library of Congress*)

(ABOVE) By the 1920s, basketball had become popular in working-class settings, especially in city leagues and industrial sports programs such as this 1923 team of textile workers for the Monaghan Plant in Greenville, S.C. (*Library of Congress*)

(LEFT) The sport became a mainstay at African American educational institutions. Students (ca. 1915) from the National Training School for Women and Girls, founded in Washington, D.C., by educator Nannie Helen Burroughs, pose for a team photo. (*Library of Congress*)

(ABOVE) Track-and-field competitions drew heavy criticism on the grounds that they often focused on the athlete's sexual appeal rather than her athletic development. This 1920 photo of a San Francisco track team illustrates the short bloomers, revealing sleeveless tops, and "chorus line" image to which physical educators objected. (*Chicago Historical Society*)

(RIGHT) Objecting to women's high-level strenuous competition as physically and mentally injurious, critics attempted to eliminate track and field from regional and national events as well as from the 1928 and 1932 Olympics. Betty Robinson, a Chicagoan who in 1928 won the first-ever Olympic women's 100-meter sprint, ignored them. As a teenager she trained with the boys' track squad because her high school had no girls' team. (*Library of Congress*)

By the 1930s, it was the "masculine" quality of track and field rather than its effects on women's health that drew the most criticism. Field events like the javelin and shot put were thought to be especially unfeminine. Here, shot putter Lillian Copeland competes in a pre-Olympic meet in early 1930s Los Angeles. (*Library of Congress*)

(ABOVE) Because of its association with genteel leisure, women's tennis was always more acceptable than basketball or track. It first gained popularity during the late nineteenth century as a country club sport played by fashionable women. Gradually, some women began to take the sport more seriously, such as these U.S. players who competed internationally in 1895. (*Library of Congress*)

(OPPOSITE, TOP) By the 1920s and 1930s, women tennis players symbolized the "modern" woman with their energetic athleticism and shorter, fashionable tennis dress. Most popular of all was Helen Wills (Moody), who is shown here (*left*) shaking hands with her defeated opponent, Elizabeth Ryan, after winning her fourth consecutive Wimbledon singles title. (*Library of Congress*)

By the 1930s and 1940s, softball rivaled basketball in popularity among women. Here Evelyn Paeth, third-base player for the 1936 Montgomery Vee-Eights, takes a swing. She has the short haircut, shiny uniform, and short shorts that disturbed female physical educators who sought to dignify and restrict women's industrial sport leagues. While traditionalist critics raised objections, the federal government supported softball during the Depression by building softball diamonds as part of public works projects. (*Chicago Historical Society*)

(TOP) The government also sponsored recreational sports as part of its Depression and wartime social programs. Interned Japanese American women were encouraged to play volleyball and softball during their "free" time at war relocation camps. In this 1942 photo, members of the Los Angeles-based "Chick-a-dee" softball team reconstituted their team at Manzanar, an internment camp in the California desert. (*Library of Congress*)

(BOTTOM) During World War II, sports and fitness training assumed special importance. Encouraged by the U.S. government, educational institutions developed special campaigns to help both female and male students achieve greater fitness as part of wartime preparedness. Here students at Howard University demonstrate Swedish calisthenics in 1943. (*Library of Congress*)

Committee gained permanent status within the APEA. It later evolved into the CWA and then the National Section on Women's Athletics (NSWA),[9] which worked with the NAAF–Women's Division to get these rules accepted wherever basketball was played. Women sport reformers, concerned with halting the spread of all commercialized and interscholastic sport, made basketball the centerpiece of their campaign to safeguard female athletics.

⌐⊃○⊂⊐

Physical educators would not have regarded their mission as one of suppression. They expressed quite the opposite sentiment, demonstrating a genuine interest in making the pleasure of play and its social and physical benefits available to all girls and women. Nonetheless, their actions over the years amounted to a concerted attack on the popular sport of basketball, which seemed to them unfeminine and dangerous when played before raucous mixed-sex crowds and under the influence of male coaches or business interests.

Relying on tested methods of the broader Women's Division campaign against "undesirable" competition, educators formed state and local basketball committees composed of an expanding network of teachers, civic leaders, and recreation workers organized through the Women's Division or the NSWA. The committee system proved to be an effective means of creating coalitions and exerting pressure. A Detroit committee still active in the 1940s, for example, brought P.E. leaders together with representatives from municipal recreation departments, the Catholic Youth Organization, the Jewish Community Center, the United Auto Workers, the Girl Scouts, a private school, the Detroit public schools, and Wayne State University.[10] Coalitions like this one attempted to educate uninformed or indifferent athletic officials about appropriate policies for girls' basketball. Locally committee representatives visited schools to give basketball demonstrations and to offer rules clinics and training sessions for officials. At the state level Women's Division and NSWA leaders helped organize statewide high school Girls' Athletic Associations and urged these groups to substitute play days for interscholastic basketball. The national offices made instructional films, distributed literature, and encouraged members to use the radio and print media to spread the word.

When persuasion failed leaders adopted a more forceful approach. They pressured city officials and local businessmen to stop sponsoring basketball tournaments, often leveling scathing media attacks on male coaches and commercial sponsors. In the late 1920s, the women's coalition went head to head with the AAU, pressuring the city of Wichita to stop hosting the AAU national tournament after its 1926 debut. After a two-year lull, tournament play resumed in 1929, and physical educators never again successfully interrupted the AAU championship. Instead they focused their efforts on limiting competition and improving standards in community, school, and industrial basketball leagues.

A starting point for reducing "unhealthy" competition was to promote the official NSWA rules. Three sets of basketball rules were in use by the early 1930s. The three-court, six-player "girls' rules" sanctioned by the NSWA provided one alternative to the traditional five-player game. Although educators pushed hard for this version, they realized that many athletes preferred the more active, five-player "boys' rules." In 1934 the national chairman of the Women's Basketball Committee confided to the Illinois state chair, "Between you and me and the gatepost, I believe that *nothing* will satisfy the teams which are now playing under boys rules *except* boys rules."[11] AAU leaders also understood the attraction of five-player rules. But pressed by educators to adopt the six-player game, they compromised by inventing a third set of rules—a six-person, two-court game that allowed more movement and active guarding. Women reformers dismissed these rules as unacceptable and, in another strategic move, rebuffed AAU offers to negotiate a single set of women's rules on the grounds that there was no way "two organizations with such totally different objectives and opinions on almost every conceivable subject could possibly live in harmony with each other."[12]

Beyond encouraging the adoption of approved rules and regulations, women reformers also urged community sports officials to hire women referees and coaches. But because their own standards prevented physical educators from actively seeking coaching and administrative positions in competitive leagues, they made little progress in unseating the men. National basketball committee chair Eline von Borries voiced her frustration over the limits of female professionals' power. Referring specifically to the situation in Illinois, she complained to a colleague that, "We have no means at hand through which we could 'control' *any* group, much less the man-coached Chicago crowd."[13]

An alternative to getting women coaches and officials into basketball was to get women athletes out. Sport reformers tried to channel female athletic interest away from basketball into more suitable sports. Oregon leaders spoke quite explicitly about diverting student interest by offering "some pleasing substitute for the school team."[14] Educators suggested that individual sports like golf and tennis made ideal replacements because of their presumed "carry-over value" into adult life. Others looked to supposedly milder team sports like volleyball and a derivative of basketball called captainball, female-dominated sports like field hockey, and social games and dancing as agreeable substitutes. Such alternatives would "counteract some of the intense feeling for girls' interschool basketball" and, in industrial leagues, "redirect interest" among employed women from their "sensational interest in basketball alone to other varied forms of play."[15]

The campaign to suppress interschool basketball succeeded at the college level, where trained physical educators had gained control of athletic programs. Intramural competition became the staple of college athletics, topped off with the occasional play or sports day. Black colleges formed the exception, offering continuous support for intercollegiate basketball even in the face of depression-era budget cuts. By contrast, in primarily white institutions, few major private or public schools still sanctioned intercollegiate women's games by the 1930s.

The profession also extended its influence down to the high school level. School officials cooperated, in part because the growth of boys' sports placed greater demands on athletic facilities and budgets. As schools added freshman, sophomore, and junior varsity teams to their boys' varsity basketball programs, many male administrators happily complied with NSWA requests to eliminate interschool girls' basketball in order to concentrate resources on the boys. At times state athletic associations assumed governance of girls' sport only to discourage its growth. In Wisconsin, for example, the state's Interschool Athletic Association voted 169 to 22 in favor of governing girls' sport but then voted 123 to 80 against actually sponsoring any interschool competition for girls. Physical educators approved of such outcomes, welcoming the chance to develop intramural programs unhampered by the lure of interscholastic contests.[16]

However, though the campaign succeeded in some areas, especially eastern and midwestern states, other regions continued to allow outside competition. A general survey from the mid-1920s found that more than eight hundred of sixteen hundred responding high schools approved of girls' interscholastic basketball, and a 1937 study discovered that more than half of Kansas, West Virginia, and Pennsylvania schools still had girls' varsity basketball programs.[17] In the segregated South, African American colleges actively facilitated interschool competition among black high schools. South Carolina Agricultural and Mechanical College and Alabama State Teachers College hosted state tournaments for high school girls in the 1920s and 1930s. And when Tuskegee Institute hosted the national black high school tournament from 1935 to 1942, a full slate of girls' basketball teams participated.[18] Small high schools in general tended to favor interscholastic sport because low student enrollment precluded viable intramural programs. A 1927 questionnaire found that while the majority of medium- and large-size schools opposed interschool competition, more than 50 percent of small schools desired it and nearly 70 percent of respondents still had varsity teams.[19]

School administrators were caught between NSWA demands to eliminate interscholastic basketball and the widespread popularity of the game among students, parents, and townspeople noted for their "fanatic enthusiasm."[20] A few simply rejected physical educators' warnings outright. In 1926 an irate Wisconsin principal fumed, "Physical weakness, menstrual periods, menopauses, etc. is a lot of cheap talk and poppy cock." He opposed "anything which tends to discourage inter-school competition among high school girls. I am in favor of adequate supervision and regulation, but not of restriction."[21] More often administrators made some attempt to compromise. States such as Florida and Tennessee, for example, dropped their state tournaments but continued to provide a full slate of city and district championships. Rather than ban interscholastic competition altogether, sport officials selectively adopted points of the NSWA platform, incorporating some combination of the proposed girls' rules, approved officials, and required medical exams into their existing competitive program.

In Iowa and Texas, however, small schools resisted attempts to shut down state tournaments. In 1925 the Iowa High School Athletic Association passed a resolution to substitute girls' volleyball for basketball and to end the girls' state tournament despite (or because of) the fact that 250 teams had participated in 1924. Rural school administrators fought back by organizing the first independent girls' state association, the Iowa High School Girls' Athletic Union. Under its sponsorship the tournament became one of the state's biggest sporting events, generating so much enthusiasm that it regularly outdrew the boys' tournament.[22] A similar story unfolded in Texas. After sponsoring a state tournament from 1918 to 1928, the state athletic commission acceded to the demands of women physical educators and agreed to close down the girls' event. However, three rival organizations quickly stepped into the breach and offered their own girls' tournaments. State officials eventually decided that given their failure to eliminate the tournament, they preferred at least to control it. The official Texas state championship resumed in 1951.[23]

By 1940 the two sides had reached a kind of standoff over the issue of school sport. A survey of state departments of education found that sixteen states had no interscholastic girls' basketball, eight or nine states held annual state tournaments, and twenty to twenty-three maintained local or county championships.[24] Despite achieving only partial success, women's organizations gained courage from their victories and continued to press for the elimination of interscholastic competition. They acted out of a deeply held conviction that basketball played under female supervision and restricted to intramural competition would offer the greatest number of girls the best chance to play while protecting them from the perceived moral and physical dangers of inter-scholastic sport. Yet, in imposing these guidelines, NSWA leaders impeded the development of athletic excellence among the most dedicated and talented athletes, many of whom chafed under the restricted brand of play. By discouraging high-level competition and the media attention and popular enthusiasm that usually accompanied it, educators may also have diminished athletic interest among female students and their communities, thus undermining their own stated intention to create a democratic athletic environment in which every girl participated.

⊂◯⊃

Women educators and recreation leaders brought the same ener-gy and dedication to their campaign to modify basketball outside the schools. There they encountered even greater obstacles in the form of community-based basketball leagues sponsored by a vari-ety of public and private interests. Newspapers provided one source of commercial backing. During the early 1930s the *Chicago Evening American* hosted an annual tournament that attracted 240 women's team entries, the great majority of them playing "boys' " rules.[25] A team sponsored by Philadelphia's black newspaper, the *Philadelphia Tribune*, dominated African American women's basketball nationally from 1930 to 1941. In its early years the Tribune Girls competed locally against black schools, recreation centers, and white industrial challengers, receiving excellent press coverage and winning the devotion of many black sport fans. With success they searched outside the area for better competition, playing teams from around the mid-Atlantic states and touring the South to play African American college teams.[26]

More commonly teams were supported through municipal or industrial recreation programs. In the late 1920s and 1930s, city recreation departments shifted their focus from an earlier empha-sis on children's playgrounds toward adult recreation. In Oakland, where eighty plants participated in the city-sponsored Industrial Recreation Association, women's basketball was among the top attractions. During the 1936 season, the league involved 144 players and drew more than four thousand spectators.[27] Chicago was another site of considerable activity. Players could choose from an abundant number of teams in the early 1930s, including a YMCA league of 15 women's teams, 105 Catholic Youth Organization girls' teams, 92 teams in the Chicago American League, and 30 teams sponsored under the Women's Basketball Association.[28] Other cities offered similar, if less plentiful, possibilities. A 1931 Women's Division survey of twenty-five industrial cities discovered that sixty-five different community organizations were providing athletic opportunities for women. The report noted the "appalling fact" that all sixty-five organizations offered basketball, while the second most popular activity, baseball, only had seventeen sponsors.[29]

The popularity of these leagues, whether organized independently by business groups or through public recreation agencies, both helped industrial basketball to survive the depression and left it ripe for wartime expansion. Defense plants were especially strong backers of women's basketball in the early 1940s, as the industry tailored its recreational offerings to its new female labor force.[30] Although the war's end brought the loss of heavy manufacturing jobs for women and a consequent reorientation of industrial recreation around the interests of male employees, commercially backed women's teams held their ground. Some of the best teams nationwide were sponsored by business schools—like the Tulsa "Stenos" of the 1940s and the great Nashville Business College teams of the 1950s and early 1960s.[31] Among manufacturing enterprises, the Midwest remained a stronghold of industrial teams, and southern textile companies actually increased their sponsorship of women's basketball in the postwar era.[32]

The AAU built on the edifice of industrial basketball to offer highly skilled white players the opportunity to compete at the national level. The annual championship tournament began in 1926 and continues to this day, years after the dynamic center of women's basketball has shifted to the college arena. Until the mid-1950s, when an African American team from Philander Smith College of Arkansas entered the tournament, the AAU championship was a segregated event, preventing highly esteemed teams like the Tribune Girls from a chance to try for the national championship.[33] Interested white teams typically competed in industrial or recreation leagues and then moved on to AAU tournaments in late-season competition. The best teams eschewed local leagues in favor of more challenging independent schedules against nationally ranked rivals.[34] From November through March, teams like the Little Rock Flyers, Hanes Hosiery, or the Wayland (Texas) Hutcherson Flying Queens alternated travel weekends with home series, regularly commuting hundreds of miles for a weekend of basketball. Then, in late March or April, they would board trains, station wagons, and (in later years) planes, to attend the national tournament, held for many years in Wichita, Kansas, and then in St. Joseph, Missouri.[35]

Although the AAU coordinated regional and national competitions for top white teams, it never controlled the wide range of five- and six-player basketball played throughout the country.[36] The AAU's expansion efforts were internally hampered by foot-dragging male officials who showed little enthusiasm for the women's game. In 1935, while thirty-five of thirty-nine districts sponsored women's swimming, only six had an organized program for basketball at the district level.[37] Externally the most stubborn opposition came from physical educators and allied professionals. In 1953 AAU women's basketball chair Mrs. Irvin Van Blarcom vented her anger over the unceasing interference of women's P.E. groups, indignantly recalling a quarter-century of being "kicked all over the place by school organizations in most states."[38]

AAU officials were willing to make token accommodations to physical educators' demands but refused to amend the festival atmosphere of AAU tournaments. They understood that their product was rooted in a popular, typically working-class culture that blended public entertainment with sexual sell. Sport formed part of a broader consumer culture in which modern advertising, movies, and other commercial entertainment ventures relied on sexual themes, erotic titillation, or promises of romantic success to stimulate interest and sell products.

Working within this popular milieu, AAU promoters balanced attempts at stricter regulation with the use of beauty pageants and other entertainment forms that, besides appealing to the paying public, might also counteract the mannish image of working-class athletes. Giving literal form to the "athlete as beauty queen" ideal, the AAU selected a tournament beauty queen from among the several hundred players competing at the national championship. Contestants, nominated by their own teammates, paraded before a panel of judges who made the final decision and also named a group of runners-up to serve as the queen's attendants. On announcing the winner, tournament officials bestowed "the queen and her court" with a crown and flowers.

Similar events occurred at other tournaments, with beauty contests forming one part of a larger effort to create a festival atmosphere with basketball at the center. In Florida, for example, the state AAU tournament featured a beauty contest, bus tours, and postgame dances in its promotional package.[39] One annual report explained that the tournament's great success lay in its ability to combine "sportsmanship" with good fun, making the event a veritable "three ring circus [with a] beauty contest, free throw contests, pep contest, sportsmanship trophy, motorboat and air plane rides, sightseeing, free movies for the players, dances."[40] Pageantry and promotional hoopla attracted sponsors, entertained the paying customer, and verified the femininity of athletes.

These types of promotions typified what physical educators loudly condemned as the "popular" influence in women's basketball. Yet there was no single popular culture of women's sport. The great interest in high school basketball in states like Arkansas, Tennessee, Texas, and Iowa made it a community event. Schoolmates and family members packed the gym, often traveling for miles to support their team. In such regions the boosterism surrounding basketball expressed and reinforced a sense of community, especially when it coincided with ethnic identity. Support from local businesses and chambers of commerce added a commercial element, but not the "tawdry" tone objected to by reformers.

Outside the schools most industrial and church leagues contained little of the sexual fanfare—such as beauty pageants, leering crowds, or tight uniforms—that so alarmed physical educators. These teams often played in relative obscurity, watched by only a handful of friends. Their games posed a stark contrast to the atmosphere found in Dallas, Nashville, Little Rock, Chicago, New York, Philadelphia, and Atlanta, venues in which loud cheering, local advertisements, admission charges, public dances, and beauty pageants created a more conspicuously commercial environment.

Though varied, the sensibilities of popular basketball reflected class and sexual styles clearly at odds with the professional ethos of physical educators. Carita Robinson of the University of Illinois explained the split between industrial and school sport: "We have two distinct groups—the educational field and group where basketball is controlled, and the industrial field where the game is not controlled by people with sufficiently high standards."[41] The looming gap between educators and male sport officials was equaled by the social distance between middle-class reformers and working-class athletes, causing professionals to tread softly in industrial circles, where the "very different type of girl will not get the idea right away."[42]

Somewhat fearful of the very working women they intended to protect, physical educators created a discourse pervaded by the language of control. In addition to their concerted efforts to get AAU tournaments and industrial, church, and school leagues "under control," women leaders frequently mentioned the need to bring athletes under "emotional control." In an article supporting the Women's Division platform, John Tunis described the total breakdown of physical and emotional control that occurred in a contest of two industrial basketball teams. Once whipped "to a frenzy of nervous excitement," the girls "pulled hair, hit one another viciously in the ribs with sharp elbows, tripped one another, tore one another's clothing, in fact did everything but play basketball."[43] What players might have experienced as a liberating release from physical inhibitions could become, in the exaggerated rhetoric of sport reformers, a perilous loss of control induced by excessive competition.

⊂◯⊃

Committed as physical educators were to curbing competition, the contrast between their position on basketball and their approach to the sport of field hockey forms something of a paradox. The case of field hockey indicates that it was not competition per se that triggered reformers' anger, but rather breaches of professional control and cultural sensibility.

British physical educator Constance Applebee introduced field hockey to American college women in 1901. It quickly gained popularity, becoming a regular part of high school and college athletic programs, especially in Eastern schools. In 1922, leaders of the sport founded the U.S. Field Hockey Association (USFHA) and a national tournament. Within a decade there were more than four-hundred clubs vying in USFHA competition, with seven regional districts sending two to four teams each to the national tournament.[44]

Even after colleges banned all forms of intercollegiate sport, hockey teams operated as semiautonomous student clubs and continued to compete every weekend against other top-notch collegiate athletes. At the national championships, a selection committee picked an all-star American team to play on European tours and against visiting international teams. During the 1920s and 1930s, while educators attacked women's Olympic participation, they extolled international field hockey competition with such lofty phrases as "hands across the sea." Forgetting their fears of reproductive damage, mannish physiques, and emotional strain, educators praised the strenuous hard play, deep-muscle development, and lean, hard physiques of field hockey players.[45]

Why did field hockey form such a special case? Never popular among American boys or men, it was designated as an exclusively female sport from the beginning. Consequently it remained free from charges of mannishness. Moreover, because of its British roots and its association with elite institutions, it assumed an upper-class aura. Some public high school girls adopted the sport, but high-level competition centered around private eastern schools and their alumnae. A Radcliffe graduate remembered: "On the national level you had to be a debutante—upper crust— to even afford to play hockey after college."[46]

Ironically, highly competitive field hockey flourished at the very eastern women's colleges and midwestern universities that formed the backbone of the campaign to suppress competitive basketball. Because hockey was an elite, all-female sport that operated outside the public view, the same P.E. faculty and under-graduate majors who organized to squelch intercollegiate athlet-ics felt free to join one another in highly competitive weekend hockey matches. Joan Hult, a physical educator and sport histori-an, recalled that in her own student days: "Women said to you Monday morning, 'Do not compete in high level competition.' But on Saturdays and Sundays they all went to a field hockey tournament. And as long as they had tea and crumpets and it was all women, then it was perfectly legitimate."[47] Jeanne Rowlands, a physical educator who attended Ohio State in the late 1940s and early 1950s, remembered that her instructors looked down their noses on students who played in summer industrial softball leagues. In the autumn, however, these students were "the very same people who played field hockey with me, with a kilt on instead of a pair of long pants . . . and everybody thought they were super."[48] Because field hockey fit the class and gender stan-dards of physical educators, it escaped the criticism leveled at other strenuous team sports.

Inconsistent in one sense, their stance reveals the deeper consis-tency of the anticompetition position. Educators sought to con-trol women's sport, to establish professional credibility, and to preserve a middle-class definition of feminine respectability that was personally comfortable and acceptable in educational circles. Field hockey posed no obstacles to these objectives. In fact, the bonds formed among students, teachers, and administrators through the USFHA actually strengthened professional networks and the commitment to a female world of sport.

⸺◦⸺

Compared to field hockey's undisputed status, basketball's more "masculine" reputation presented a problem for women's athletic leaders. As a group they were dedicated to creating distinctively female sport forms that would be impervious to charges of "man-nishness." Believing that basketball, unlike field hockey, required alterations, they set out to create a "female" version of the sport.

The game of basketball has no essential gender attributes; it lacks any natural properties of masculinity or femininity—it is simply a game. Nevertheless, observers commonly remarked on its gender qualities. After first being introduced to women and labeled an appropriately "feminine" game, the sport gained steady popularity with men and became associated with such "masculine" qualities as ruggedness, explosive power, and technical precision. By the 1920s women players, though active in the game since its invention, had come to be viewed as intruders in a male sport. A 1926 article on the problematic participation of women in sports could confidently, if erroneously, describe basketball as "a game which was originally invented as a fighting game for men."[49]

In answer to such concerns, physical educators created an alternative version of the sport. As with "women drivers" or "lady doctors," the distinction took the form of generic (men's) basketball and a special type of "women's basketball." The process of differentiating between male and female versions of the same activity reveals, in a very concrete way, how culturally constructed gender systems have been created and sustained.

In the development of "women's basketball," physical movement, touch, emotion, public space, and dress assumed feminine and masculine forms. Concerns with boundaries and the reduction of physical contact lay at the center of athletic definitions of femininity. In the early 1900s Anne Maud Butner, the director of women's physical education at the University of Minnesota, made the connection explicit when she advocated additional restraints on movement. "Boundaries prevent bunching," said Butner, "and bunching is what causes roughness."[50] J. Anna Norris explained in 1924 that because "woman is not essentially a fighting animal," the "essential feature" of girls' rules was to "discourage personal contact, interference and tussling." In describing the attributes acquired should "tussling" be permitted, Norris hinted that physical touch was in itself masculine. She asserted that allowing the female player more contact would foster "aggressive qualities which seldom add to her charm or usefulness."[51]

Restrictions on space, movement, and touch became codified in NSWA rules. In addition to confining players to sections of the court, the official six-player rules further restricted physical movement by limiting the number of times women could dribble and by barring close guarding of the ball holder. Imposed restrictions on long sprints, aggressive guarding, and physical contact supported the prevailing assumption that men used space freely while women should contain their bodies and limit their movement.

By defining the physical release and emotional intensity of unmodified basketball as suitable only for men, physical educators also suggested that passion, like touch, was essentially masculine. Given the thin line between notions of unrestrained physical expression and sexual desire, depictions of passionate play could acquire sexual overtones. John Tunis, for example, peppered his account of an industrial basketball game with references to "leering eyes," the gym's "sultry atmosphere," and the "taut excitement" of an athlete's "body tightly drawn into a knot."[52] The "aggressive" and "uncharming" woman who pursued highly competitive basketball risked association with sexual as well as athletic deviance.

The fear that insufficient gender distinctions spelled sexual danger underlay reformers efforts to alter the "loud" and "tawdry" uniforms worn by industrial basketball players. Claiming that women's costumes too closely resembled those of men, physical educators railed against the shiny satin, short sleeves, and high-cut pant legs of industrial and AAU attire. While the uniforms were similar in fabric and cut to men's, women's tops featured collars and short sleeves in contrast to the sleeveless, scoop-necked men's. These differences failed to impress women sport reformers, who continued to judge both the uniforms and the women who wore them as undignified and sexually inappropriate.[53]

Under pressure to maintain clear lines of difference in all aspects of men's and women's sport, even structural design and architectural planning for gymnasiums took gender into account. Besides the different floor divisions in men's and women's rules, the length of the women's court did not have to equal the men's regulation length. Anna Hiss is said to have mandated that the women's gymnasium floor at the University of Texas be several inches shorter than the required length for men, shrewdly calculating that this would guarantee women's undisputed access to the gym.[54] On a more conceptual level, a 1950s symposium on gymnasium building carefully distinguished between three differently styled buildings: a men's, a women's, and a coed gymnasium. The men's facility contained several gyms, training rooms, storage areas, and locker rooms. In contrast, the description of the women's facility barely mentioned its single gymnasium, emphasizing instead that "color, harmony, design, femininity, and ease of housekeeping should dominate constructional planning."[55]

Although the opposition to women athletes stemmed from the gendered nature of "masculine" athletics, in creating a female version of basketball, women sport leaders further embedded gender distinctions into the culture of sport. From the rules athletes played to the facilities they occupied and the clothes they wore, notions of "masculinity" and "femininity" became an integral part of the game. The creation of "women's basketball" may have secured women physical educators some degree of respect and autonomy, but it had the additional effect of reinforcing the gendered organization of space in the wider culture. Under prevailing arrangements, bounded space, restricted movement, and a nonphysical nature characterized femininity. Indeed, this description fit the reality of many women who were confined by dress styles, domestic duties, and a lack of leisure time or access to sport. When women athletes attempted to break these binds, concerned officials imposed a new set of restrictions on women's freedom of movement and physical expression.

Although they had little influence on policy, student athletes sometimes expressed their dissatisfaction with the curbs administrators placed on competition. When the Missouri State High School Association voted in 1937 to limit girls to one basketball game a week and eliminate tournament play, a student organization protested the move. Athletes complained that the new restrictions abolished precisely those features of play they found most enjoyable. A protester explained, "One game a week is not enough B/B (basketball) to keep girls interested in the game." She was supported by another, who reasoned: "Most girls play for enjoyment of competing in games and trips that follow going to tournaments. I don't believe it would be worth the hours of practice if all tournaments are removed and games cut to one a week." A third player expressed her outrage that adults should be able to determine her best interests: "I think it is unfair . . . Girls find pleasure in competing against other schools in tournaments. . . . A girl's health is her own—why not let her do with it as she pleases?"[56]

Opinion was not unanimous. Some students, especially P.E. majors, agreed with their professors that women's sport should follow a different path from the flawed model of intercollegiate male athletics. Julia Brown attended New Jersey College for Women in the late 1940s and became a leader of student efforts to clamp down on competition. Brown recalled talking with other students "about the numerous organizations and agencies that sponsored AAU and we talked about the differences because they played men's rules. And again, it was this feeling that we want to be in control." As with her mentors, interest in professional control dovetailed with a personal distaste for the more raucous sensibility of highly competitive athletics. Brown remembered that, while she was a young instructor at Wellesley, she "went out and officiated a high school girls' basketball game which was a curtain raiser for the boys' basketball games. . . . The crowd was enormous—a lot of catcalls and disagreements and that sort of thing. So I found that I didn't enjoy that kind of situation at all."[57] But a growing number of students disagreed. Joan Hult, who grew up in Gary and went to Indiana University as an undergraduate, saw herself as part of a "whole underground of people who in fact wanted high-level competition." She estimated that by the 1950s, more than half the students she knew favored intercollegiate sport.[58]

Hult, along with other students who shared her athletic interests and independent ways, defied professional norms and competed in the prohibited industrial leagues. Most women in industrial leagues, however, were more insulated from professional educators and consequently remained unaffected by their scathing criticisms of popular sport. Former AAU star Alline Banks (Sprouse), touted as the best player in the nation during the 1940s, recalled: "I remember that topic coming up many times, but it didn't bother us in any way because we loved it so much and we were not connected to any college." Asked if the disapproval bothered her, Banks replied, "No, it probably made me strive that much harder."[59] Banks and other players formed their own opinions about what constituted good competition and femininity. Almost point by point they refuted the list of athletic "evils" condemned by physical educators.

Few players were even aware of the controversies over uniforms, rules, or coaches. Without giving much thought to the matter, they simply played in the uniforms they were issued, liking or disliking them on the basis of fit, style, and color. The idea that they were in any way "tawdry" or sexually suggestive did not occur to them. On the contrary, a former Nashville player, Margaret Sexton Gleaves, described the "short shorts" as "really very acceptable." Uniforms were either an unquestioned part of the game or, more positively, a badge that symbolized team membership and advanced skill.

A similar attitude prevailed about rules and coaching. Most players competed (at different times) under five-player rules and one or more versions of the six-player game. Many preferred one version over others, often determined by familiarity. But they seemed unaware that these differences had sparked virulent disagreements among sport administrators. Male coaches, as well, were a given in their sporting experience. Because of the need for seasoned coaching and for business backing to cover travel and other costs, the best industrial teams were usually sponsored, managed, and coached by men with solid business or athletic backgrounds. Few had ever played under a woman coach—a consequence, in part, of physical educators' retreat from highly competitive basketball. Athletes rated their coaches on the basis of personal qualities and coaching ability, paying little attention to gender.[60]

Matters that caused great consternation among reformers were often simply not significant topics of concern to the athletes involved. In other instances, however, ballplayers took issue with, and actively disputed, the views of female educators. For instance, most players found travel an expressly enjoyable, rather than dangerous or exploitative, aspect of their basketball experience. Especially for women who grew up with little money, playing on a team gave them a unique chance to see places and meet people. Some reported taking their first train ride, bus trip, or airplane flight for a tournament. Besides the excitement of traveling to faraway places, players believed that basketball had made them more knowledgeable and worldly. Maxine ("Jimmie") Vaughn Williams described what her life might have been like if basketball had not taken her from rural Tennessee to Nashville and Winston-Salem: "Well, I would have probably gotten a job in a little town, and I'd have probably married there, stayed there, built a house on part of my folks' farm and been there. But when you get a taste of what it's like out of that [place], then I think you want to achieve that for yourself." Athletes found in sport a sense of expanded opportunity, not only in the realm of athletics but in a general sense of extended horizons and wider options in travel, work, residence, and marriage.

Similarly, AAU and industrial league players did not feel they were overtrained and overpublicized. For most female athletes the problem of inadequate gym access made overtraining an impossibility. Women in park programs and industrial leagues might gain the use of a gym twice a week, once for practice and once for games played before near-empty bleachers with little or no media attention. These women athletes were not subject to physical exhaustion or media sensationalism, but rather formed part of an obscure female athletic subculture made up of players, coaches, sponsors, and a few knowledgeable fans.

Even where women's basketball had established a popular tradition and players did receive extensive training and publicity, it does not appear that their careers reduced the chances of less-skilled women to enjoy athletics. Women's Division leaders had often criticized the disproportionate share of resources and attention that highly talented players received. While such athletes did benefit from the chance to play an elite brand of ball, they initially encountered the same set of possibilities and limitations as others with less skill. Some elite athletes came from towns with active sport programs for girls of all ages and abilities, others from areas where opportunities were scarce at all levels. The difference was that extremely dedicated and talented athletes tended to search more doggedly for chances to play, and when they found them continued to play for a longer period of time. For these athletes sustained training and intense game competition became an unqualified source of gratification. The problem lay not in the distribution of resources but in the lack of resources for serious and casual players alike. It was not a case of too much attention to a few athletes, but rather one of societal disregard for all women athletes.

Personal accounts from athletes on the relation of sport to self-esteem contradict the Women's Division claim that competitive sport encouraged skilled athletes to "feel unduly important because of mere physical superiority."[61] Women athletes did enjoy their competence, valuing as well their claim to fame and their unusual success. Few women from rural, small-town and working-class backgrounds had opportunities for recognition from their work, political, or cultural activities. To educators the awards, victory celebrations, and public attention that followed competitive events looked like "sporting athletes gone mad with success."[62] But athletes treasured these times as moments when hours of private training came to public fruition. If players came from supportive families or communities, awards and public acclaim were shared with pleasure by family and townsfolk. For those athletes who faced personal opposition, ridicule, or neglect, public recognition could act as a salve to self-doubt, nourishing identities forged in conflict.

Motivated by a passion for their sport, women basketball players also disagreed with athletic reformers on the question of exploitation, whether economic or sexual. Given the dearth of athletic resources available to women, athletes welcomed industrial sponsorship. Women who played for textile companies, war industries, and business colleges expressed appreciation to companies for offering them employment and athletic opportunity. Yet the frequency with which players quit jobs to join better teams or to follow their friends indicates that they placed their own interests above those of their employers. That athletes were not bound by paternalistic bonds or financial obligation is corroborated by contemporary reports noting that male and female workers typically embraced industrial sports but rejected company-sponsored social and cultural activities.[63] This pattern suggests that workers took advantage of programs that served their own needs while spurning the more intrusive aspects of corporate welfare.

The desire to compete shaped how players viewed the sexual hype surrounding popular sport. Some players thoroughly enjoyed the beauty contests and festive atmosphere. Alline Banks remembered, "I thought it was great. . . . We cheered and carried on as if we were winning a national tournament. . . . The spectators would . . . just roar. It was just like the Miss America Contest." Others remained indifferent. Evelyn ("Eckie") Jordan recalled that "we were always more interested in the free-throw championship. You know, that's part of the game. As far as the beauty contest, that didn't interest us." She felt it was "not necessary, but if they wanted it, O.K."

Most players felt that the publicity and sexual hype were arranged for the audience and had little to do with them as players. They viewed the contest as "just a little something extra I think for the sponsors," or "just something to appease the crowd with."[64] According to this view, if the pageant helped promote the sport, then it served the long-term interests of athletes. Players viewed tournament rituals as either a harmless crowd pleaser or a tolerable sidelight to the real event—the game. The issue faded before their overriding interest in the sport itself: They had come to play ball.

Athletes loved the game. Like Doris Rogers, who grew up playing ball on a dirt court in eastern Tennessee, many had relished the sport from an early age. "I just *loved* to play," recalled Rogers. "It's just the doing, just the joy of playing." And Eckie Jordan explained, "We almost had a teething ring out of a basketball. . . . It was just part of life where I grew up." After high school Jordan moved from her South Carolina mill village to North Carolina to play for the Hanes team because "I wanted to play ball. I had it in my blood."

Players derived joy from physical movement and competition. Maxine Vaughn Williams, who also played for Hanes, loved "the activity, the running, the jumping . . . I guess the competition. And to win gives you a good feeling—to be part of winning."

Like Williams others frequently merged a love of the game with the satisfaction derived from competition. Remarking that "for basketball, I think I would have done most anything," Alline Banks added, "I've always been competitive in life as well as in basketball. To win is a great thing to me." Women athletes saw competition as a healthy exchange with no necessary relation to masculine or feminine qualities, although some pointedly distinguished their concept of competitive spirit from the unfriendly, cutthroat behaviors often associated with masculine competition. In describing their own love for the game, women athletes reclaimed competitiveness as a potentially positive aspect of female experience.

⟞○⟝

Despite the clash of views held by athletes and physical educators, each perspective contained substantial grains of truth. The Women's Division/NSWA critique was not off base, despite its clear prejudices. The commercial, sometimes sexual, element in popular basketball certainly objectified women and diverted attention from their athletic skill. And the dominance of male coaches and officials undoubtedly hindered the development of women in these fields, making it difficult for women coaches or administrators even to get a foot in the door of industrial or AAU basketball. But players approached sport from their own vantage point. Athletes did not see the sexual tone of some sporting events as unusual or especially objectionable. It reinforced everyday sexual realities that women encountered in the nonathletic world as well. Athletes accepted or merely tolerated sexual hype and beauty contests in order to pursue a sport that allowed them to break free from confining forms of femininity. Basketball provided opportunities for skill building, achievement, physical expression, sociability, and public recognition—valued elements of experience that could not be taken for granted in most women's lives.

Women athletes grabbed at the chance to play and made the most of the opportunities they had. The consistent popularity of basketball among young women eventually pushed educators and recreation leaders to reconsider their stance against competition.

However, this occurred only gradually and did not result in any substantial policy changes until the 1960s. Before that time the friction between educators and the AAU continued without abatement and resulted in a stalemate: Intercollegiate competition was rare; high school interscholastic leagues and state tournaments thrived in some regions but were nonexistent in others; and industrial or community-based basketball continued to form a steady but minor strand in the overall fabric of American sporting life.

The significance of the basketball controversy lies less in this outcome than in what it reveals about the ongoing effort to make "masculine" sport and womanhood compatible. The masculine connotation of basketball forced women's basketball officials and players to manage this contradiction. The results challenge the assumption that notions of femininity and masculinity in sport are "natural" or timeless. Rather, these concepts were the outcome of cultural conflicts, organizational politics, and strategic policy-making. While women's organizations tried to feminize basketball by creating a controlled "female" version of a "male" sport, AAU and other popular promoters attempted to feminize athletes by highlighting their beauty and sexual appeal.

These strategies were alike, ironically, in that each ultimately affirmed the widely held notion that "real sport" was a masculine endeavor. The rules advocated by the NSWA and Women's Division dictated that womanly athletes should not "ape" men, implying that only "mannish" or sexually unrespectable women insisted on playing more competitive "masculine" basketball. Popular sport promoters who emphasized the feminine beauty and grace of female athletes also implicitly reinforced the masculinity of sport. AAU officials tried to counter images of "mannish" athleticism through beauty pageants and frequent references to athletes' attractiveness. Yet as long as women's athletic legitimacy rested on beauty and sexual appeal, athletic skill by itself retained a masculine connotation.

In both cases basketball officials strengthened gender distinctions—emphasizing the difference between femininity and masculinity in matters of philosophy and policy, as well as at the more mundane level of rules, court dimensions, uniforms, and gymnasium design. The women who played basketball had fewer opportunities to shape the contours of the game. They did, however, fashion personal meanings from their athletic experiences. Athletes rejected polarized images of the controlled, dispassionate competitor and the athletic beauty queen while savoring the rare opportunity to expand their social and physical horizons.

The strategies and sensibilities of popular promoters, physical educators, and women athletes clashed dramatically, leaving the world of women's sport divided along and across class, race, and gender lines. The persistent tension between athletic skill and femininity found no resolution, and the female ballplayer remained an anomalous figure. Sadly the ongoing conflict between women educators and male sport promoters channeled the energies of basketball advocates into internecine struggles rather than toward outwardly directed efforts to break down opposition to a sport women loved to play.

# CHAPTER 5

# "CINDERELLAS" OF SPORT

## Black Women in Track and Field

⌒○⌒

After World War II forced the cancellation of the 1940 and 1944 Olympic Games, Olympic competition resumed in 1948, hosted by London. Although England remained in a state of grim disrepair, the performance of three female track-and-field athletes shone through the bleakness of the postwar European setting. Francina ("Fanny") Blankers-Koen, competing for the Netherlands, won an astounding four gold medals with victories in the one hundred- and two hundred-meter sprints, the eighty-meter hurdles, and four hundred-meter relay. The Dutch athlete was heralded not only for her medals but for achieving her success as an adult married woman—a full-time housewife and mother of two children. Among Europeans her fame was rivaled by the French athlete Micheline Ostermeyer, winner of gold medals in the shot put and discus and a bronze in the high jump. Ostermeyer, in addition to her athletic excellence, was a concert pianist whose musical ability and middle-class background marked her as a "respectable" woman in a sport many perceived as unwomanly.[1] The third athlete was Alice Coachman, a high jumper from Albany, Georgia. As a track and basketball star for Tuskegee Institute, Coachman had established a reputation as the premier black woman athlete of the 1940s. Her single gold medal in the high jump could not match the totals of Blankers-Koen or Ostermeyer. Nevertheless, it was historically significant, both as the only individual track-and-field medal won by U.S. women and, more important, as the first medal ever received by a woman of African descent.

The superlative performances of these three Olympic champions earned them only momentary glory in the United States. Their names quickly faded from public view, overshadowed by male Olympians and athletes like Barbara Ann Scott, the Canadian Olympic figure-skating champion, whose sport earned far more attention and approval than women's track and field. Track athletics, like basketball, had excited enormous public interest as a women's sport in the 1920s and early 1930s. But even more so than basketball, track had fallen victim to negative media coverage and organized efforts to eliminate it from school and international competition.

By mid-century the sport had a reputation as a "masculine" endeavor unsuited to feminine athletes. Few American women participated, and those who did endured caricatures as amazons and muscle molls. In this climate, despite the temporary enthusiasm inspired by the female champions of 1948, Olympic governing bodies of the 1950s once again considered eliminating several women's track-and-field events from the games because they were "not truly feminine."[2]

In the discussions that followed, Olympic official Norman Cox sarcastically proposed that rather than ban women's events, the IOC should create a special category of competition for the unfairly advantaged "hermaphrodites" who regularly defeated "normal" women, those less-skilled "child-bearing" types with "largish breasts, wide hips, [and] knocked knees."[3] This outrageous but prescient recommendation (the IOC instituted anatomical sex checks in 1967, followed by mandatory chromosome testing of women athletes) placed a new spin on a familiar argument. Cox's assertion that victorious women Olympians were most likely *not* biological females rested on the deep conviction that superior athleticism signified masculine capacities that inhered in the male body.

Among the athletes who withstood this kind of ridicule and continued to compete were African American women, who by mid-century had come to occupy a central position in the sport of track and field. Beginning in the late 1930s, black women stepped into an arena largely abandoned by middle-class white women, who deemed the sport unsuitable, and began to blaze a remarkable trail of national and international excellence. But their preeminent position in the sport had a double edge. On a personal level success meant opportunities for education, travel, upward mobility, and national or even international recognition. The accomplishments of such Olympians as Alice Coachman, Mae Faggs, or Wilma Rudolph also demonstrated to the public that African American women could excel in a nontraditional yet valued arena of American culture. However, viewed through the lens of commonplace racial prejudices, African American women's achievements in a "mannish" sport also reinforced disparaging stereotypes of black women as less womanly or feminine than white women.[4]

Footraces have a long and varied history in world cultures. In the United States the immediate precedent for twentieth-century track athletics was the popular nineteenth-century sport of road racing. Race organizers sponsored long-distance running events with cash prizes. Except for rare instances these races were for men only, and almost exclusively white men. In the early twentieth century, elite urban athletic clubs and northern colleges shifted the focus away from road racing to collegiate track meets. Held in stadiums, these meets treated avid fans to a series of shorter distance races and field events. A few black men entered competitions as members of college track teams, but at top levels the sport remained largely white, elite, and exclusively male.[5]

The growth of popular sport in the 1920s expanded opportunities beyond the rarefied atmosphere of amateur collegiate and club athletics. Industrial sport programs occasionally financed workers' track teams, and urban newspapers sponsored citywide track meets as public relations gestures. Immigrant communities, especially Scots, Germans, and Poles, promoted their own ethnic track clubs. The playground movement created additional openings for working-class youngsters through playground meets and municipal track championships. Some of these opportunities extended to girls, typically through school or city park programs.

With the growth of women's collegiate sport, middle-class women shared in the enthusiasm, competing in intramural track and field meets.

Spurred by the sport's great popularity at the Women's Olympics held in Paris in 1922, American and international sport bodies resolved to begin sponsoring women's track and field.[6] Male athletic officials showed little enthusiasm for women's track but argued that it was better to enter into, and thereby gain control of, the activity than to let a popular sport develop outside their control. In the United States the AAU agreed to offer track-and-field championships for women, beginning in 1924. In a personal letter to Notre Dame football coach Knute Rockne justifying his support for the new policy, AAU president Avery Brundage explained that "regardless of how you and I feel about it," the sheer popularity of women's track and field necessitated AAU sponsorship.[7] After considerable dissension the IOC reached the same conclusion, adding five women's track-and-field events to the 1928 Olympic program.

Organizational support, grudging as it was, helped boost the popularity of women's track and field during the late 1920s and early 1930s, especially among working-class athletes. In 1930 ten thousand spectators crowded the stands to watch fifteen hundred women competing at the Central District AAU meet in Chicago.[8] The sizable number of fans and competitors was not unusual in strongholds like Chicago, where an elaborate system of park district, municipal, and Board of Education playgrounds allowed athletically inclined youth to flourish, even in the absence of extensive press coverage or financial support. Betty Robinson, who in 1928 captured the first Olympic gold medal ever issued in the women's hundred-meter sprint, honed her skills on the playgrounds of Chicago. Following in her footsteps, Tidye Pickett, Annette Rogers, and Ida Meyers ran track in the 1930s on Chicago park district teams. Athletes like these typically made do with a set of loose-fitting running shorts, inexpensive T-shirts, and well-worn spikes, using whatever resources they had at their disposal to pay for transportation to distant meets. Pickett, from a South Side black neighborhood, and Rogers and Meyers, from two of the city's many ethnic white, working-class areas, progressed from neighborhood meets to district meets, city championships, and AAU regional meets. They went on to compete at the national and international levels, Rogers in the 1932 and 1936 Olympics, Pickett in the 1936 games, and Meyers in the 1936 national high-jump finals.[9]

While young athletes like these relished the opportunity to test their skills beyond the schoolyard, the developing network of district, regional, and national competition prompted an altogether different response from P.E. leaders of the interwar era. The Women's Division and the CWA rallied women's organizations into a solid wall of opposition against AAU and Olympic track. They argued vehemently for the elimination of public track-and-field competitions on the grounds that they subjected women to debilitating physical, emotional, and sexual strains.

In the ensuing debate an assortment of critics attacked women's track by raising the specter of the mannish woman. Where sport in general connoted masculinity, track and field had a particularly masculine image. It featured power and speed unmediated by equipment, teamwork, or complicated rules. Thinly clad running, throwing, and jumping athletes appeared to demonstrate "naked" athletic prowess as they exhibited their strained faces and muscles for an audience entranced by elemental human exertion.[10]

Frederick Rand Rogers voiced common objections in a published critique of Olympic track for women. His 1929 article alleged that the brute strength, endurance, and neuromuscular skill required for track-and-field events were "profoundly unnatural" for female athletes. Asserting that the Olympics "are essentially masculine in nature and develop wholly masculine physiques and behavior traits," Rogers claimed that the masculinizing effects of track would make women unfit for motherhood and would sacrifice their "health, physical beauty, and social attractiveness"—costs he deemed "absolutely prohibitive."[11]

In the eyes of her detractors the "wholly masculine" female track athlete became a freak of nature, an object of horror rather than esteem. John Tunis called the Olympics an "animalistic" ordeal for women.[12] And Rogers concluded his discussion of women's Olympic participation with the ominous suggestion: "Manly women . . . may constitute nature's greatest failures, which should perhaps, be corrected by as drastic means as those by which the most hideous deformities are treated."[13]

Educators and their allies did not succeed in halting either the Women's Games or the International Olympics, but they did promulgate a critical standpoint which shaped public perceptions of women's track. In the 1928 Olympics, at the end of the women's eight hundred-meter race, several runners fell to the ground in emotional and physical exhaustion. Although similar dramatics were known to occur in men's races, a tremendous public outcry followed as enraged critics viewed the "collapse" as irrefutable proof that women were constitutionally unfit for such strenuous competition. The opposition drew strength from the incident and succeeded in getting the Olympic Congress to eliminate all medium- and long-distance races and to consider banning women's events completely.

The phenomenal talent of Babe Didrikson, a young, white, working-class track star from Port Arthur, Texas, temporarily revived American enthusiasm for the sport. In the summer of 1932, the eighteen-year-old Didrikson won the AAU national team championship when competing as the sole member of the Dallas-based Employers' Casualty Company "team." Two weeks later she competed at the Los Angeles Olympics, where she proceeded to capture three medals, golds in the javelin and hurdles and a silver in the high jump.

Her astounding feat, along with her quick wit and disarming honesty, made her an instant celebrity among sport journalists and fans. Standing at five foot four and weighing about 110 pounds, she amazed her followers with the strength and skill of her thin, wiry body. Didrikson's blunt, unpolished manner—both in speech and appearance—was also cause for comment. She dressed in loose-fitting sweatsuits, wore her hair in a short, unstyled cut, and addressed the press with plain talk that pulled no punches. Although these features were at times cause for ridicule, they also intrigued reporters and fans who were fascinated by her unapologetic rejection of conventional femininity.

Hearing that in addition to track and field she also played basketball, football, baseball, and numerous other sports, an astonished journalist asked Didrikson, "Is there anything at all you don't play?" Without missing a beat, she reportedly answered, "Yeah, dolls."[14]

In the long run, however, "the Babe's" success did as much to harm as to help the reputation of her sport. Didrikson's disdain for dresses, men, and middle-class etiquette as well as her later involvement with commercial promotions made her the perfect target for horrified foes of track and field. They saw the young athlete's lean physique, short hair, ever-present sweatsuit, and plain, unadorned appearance as evidence that athletic accomplishment did indeed result from or cause masculinity.

Didrikson's immediate successors, Missouri farm girl Helen Stephens and Polish immigrant Stella Walsh, evoked similar reactions. Depictions of the "bobbed-haired, flat-chested, boyishly built" Stephens and the deep-voiced Walsh perpetuated an image of mannishness, unmitigated by Didrikson's popular appeal.[15] From the eight hundred-meter debacle of 1928 to the athletic successes of muscular track stars like Didrikson, Walsh, and Stephens, opponents of women's track and field were confirmed in their image of a masculine sport that elevated "mannish" women into stardom and broke down the feminine health of "normal" women.

The combined impact of organized opposition, media criticism, and depression-era financial woes rapidly undermined women's track and field. While working-class sports like softball and bowling thrived during the depression, interest in women's track declined drastically after the 1932 Los Angeles Olympics. Of twenty-nine AAU districts, only eleven reported holding track championships in 1933 and 1934. The national championship meet of 1935 attracted only several hundred spectators and took a mere three hours from start to finish.[16] Waning attendance led to further reductions in AAU support. One survey found that by 1936 AAU women's track and field no longer existed in most regions of the country.[17] After 1937, unable to find a group to host the indoor national meet, AAU officials canceled the event for several years. They revived it in the 1940s, but as few as

seven clubs participated in some years. Unable to shake its masculine aura, women's track and field by the late 1940s occupied a
marginal, denigrated position within American popular culture.[18]

As white women vacated the sport and amateur athletic organizations withdrew their support, black athletes stepped to the fore
of women's track and field. Along with basketball, boxing, football, and baseball, track was one of the most popular sports in
black communities during the interwar years. African American
men first gained fame as sprinters in the 1920s. Their reputation
grew when Jesse Owens soundly defeated Hitler's vaunted Aryan
superathletes in an astonishing triple-medal performance at the
1936 Berlin Olympics. The success of Owens and other black
Olympians, including Ralph Metcalfe, Archie Williams, and
Cornelius Johnson, challenged assumptions of white superiority
and further popularized track and field among black sport fans
and young athletes, including girls.[19]

Although women's sport had clearly played second fiddle to
men's in black communities, a significant sector of the population
demonstrated interest in women's athletics, whether as fans,
recreation leaders, or athletic sponsors.[20] Additional encouragement came from African American educators and journalists,
who expressed an acceptance of women's sport rare for their day.
In 1939 prominent black physical educator E. B. Henderson
agreed with others in his profession that the first priority of girls
athletics should be health, not competition. But he went on to
criticize "the narrowed limits prescribed for girls and women,"
arguing: "There are girls who ought to display their skill and
national characteristic sport to a wider extent. These national
exponents of women's sport are therefore to be commended for
the prominence they have attained . . . The race of man needs the
inspiration of strong virile womanhood."[21]

Black women's own conception of womanhood, while it may
not actively have encouraged sport, did not preclude it. A heritage of resistance to racial and sexual oppression found African
American women occupying multiple roles as wageworkers,
homemakers, mothers, and community leaders. In these capaci-

ties women earned respect for domestic talents, physical and emotional strengths, and public activism. Denied access to full-time homemaking and sexual protection, African American women did not tie femininity to a specific, limited set of activities and attributes defined as separate and opposite from masculinity. Rather, they created an ideal of womanhood rooted in the positive qualities they cultivated under adverse conditions: struggle, strength, family commitment, community involvement, and moral integrity.[22]

Although these values were most often publicly articulated by women in positions of political and intellectual leadership, they were expressed in more mundane fashion by countless other women who helped build the infrastructure of black churches, community centers, club life, and entertainment—the institutions that sponsored athletic activities for girls and women. The work of earning a living and raising a family, often in near-poverty conditions, prevented the great majority of black women from participating in sport or any other time-consuming leisure activity. Yet by the 1930s and 1940s, as sport became a central component of African American college life and urban community recreation, women were included as minor but nevertheless significant players.[23]

African American interest in track and field and permissive attitudes toward women's athletics set the stage for the emergence of black women's track at the precise moment when the majority of white women and the white public rejected the sport as undignified for women. Tuskegee Institute formed the first highly competitive collegiate women's track team in 1929.[24] The school immediately added women's events to its Tuskegee Relays, the first major track meet sponsored by a black college, and soon thereafter began extending athletic scholarships to promising African American high school girls. Coached by Clive Abbott, Christine Petty, and later Nell Jackson, the Tuskegee team matured into North America's premier women's track club during the 1930s and 1940s, capturing eleven of twelve AAU outdoor championships between 1937 and 1948.[25]

Tuskegee was not alone among black colleges in encouraging women's track and field. Prairie View A & M of Texas added women's events to its annual relays in 1936, followed by Alabama State College. Florida A & M, Alcorn College in Mississippi, and Fort Valley State College of Georgia were among the schools attending early Tuskegee meets. Tennessee A & I (later Tennessee State University, or TSU) first sent participants to the Tuskegee Relays in 1944 and established a permanent program in 1945 under the direction of Jessie Abbott, daughter of Tuskegee athletic director Clive Abbott. Collegiate programs drew primarily from southern high schools. Although travel costs and the scarcity of black high schools prohibited extensive interscholastic competition, high school girls from throughout the South trained hard for annual trips to Tuskegee or another college meet where they competed in special "junior" events organized for high schools from around the region.[26]

In the North independent and municipal track clubs provided initial training and encouragement for black girls interested in the sport. Tidye Pickett and Louise Stokes, a Boston track star, got their start on northern playgrounds and in 1936 became the first African American women to compete on a U.S. Olympic team.[27] In later years, the CYO Comets of Chicago and Police Athletic League of New York produced sprinters like Barbara Jones and Mae Faggs, who both went on to compete for Tennessee State and the U.S. Olympic team.

African American track women compiled their record of excellence while suffering the constraints of racial and gender discrimination. In the late 1940s and early 1950s, efforts to end racial segregation in major league sports like baseball and basketball had made little impact on the extensive segregation in school, municipal, semipro, and minor league sport. The white press gave minimal coverage to black sports and seldom printed photographs of African American athletes. Black women found that sex discrimination, in the form of small athletic budgets, half-hearted backing from black school administrators, and the general absence of support from white-dominated sport organizations, further impeded their development.

The AAU policy of sponsoring white-only meets, where southern state laws permitted, posed another barrier. Southern black women's teams, excluded from regional competitions, were limited to black intercollegiate meets and the AAU national championships. Tuskegee athletes typically competed in only three meets per year—the AAU indoor and outdoor championships and the Tuskegee Relays. Tennessee State University followed a similar pattern until the late 1950s and 1960s, when opportunities increased.[28] En route to these meets, teams faced the additional difficulties of traveling through the segregated South. The shortage of restrooms, restaurants, and motels available to black travelers meant that black athletes had to create makeshift accommodations and endure degrading, exhausting conditions.

Despite these obstacles black women's track survived and even thrived. World War II caused the cancellation of the 1940 and 1944 Olympic Games. In the interlude between 1936 and 1948, African American women became the dominant force in track, a position they would maintain for decades. Commenting on the fact that white women held only two of the eleven slots on the 1948 U.S. national track team, E. B. Henderson surmised that "American [white] women have been so thoroughly licked over so many years by the Booker T. Washington Girls that they have almost given up track and field competition."[29]

African American women had found an athletic niche, and when the Olympic Games resumed in 1948, black sport activists sensed a historic turning point. Fay Young of the *Chicago Defender* announced in bold type: "Negro Women Will Dominate 1948 U.S. Olympic Track Team." Young subtitled his commentary "Negro Womanhood on Parade," suggesting that the black public viewed athletics as a terrain of achievement with import beyond the immediate athletic realm.[30]

But what did it mean when "Negro womanhood" was "on parade" in a controversial, "mannish" sport? Throughout the 1950s African Americans made up more than two-thirds of American women chosen to compete in the track-and-field events of the Pan-American Games, international track meets and the Olympics.[31] Among athletes, amateur track leaders, and the broader public, the achievements of African American women athletes could hold significantly different, even contradictory, meanings. Athletic successes which could, in one context, affirm the dignity and capabilities of African American womanhood, could also appear to confirm derogatory images of both black and athletic women.

⟨○⟩

African American women in their teens and twenties only dimly perceived the historical significance of their athletic achievements. They were far more aware of the personal opportunities and enjoyment they found in track and field. Yet in describing their experiences, athletes commented on the racial and gender barriers they faced, reflecting as well on their knowledge of athletics as a site for personal and social transformation.[32]

Lula Hymes (Glenn) and Leila Perry (Glover) both grew up in Atlanta, Georgia, ran track for Booker T. Washington High School in the 1930s and attended Tuskegee in the late 1930s and early 1940s on college track scholarships. Each won numerous honors in collegiate and AAU competition. Their teammate Alice Coachman (Davis) grew up in Albany, Georgia, and was recruited while still a high school student to attend Tuskegee Institute's secondary school and postsecondary trade school. An extraordinary athlete, Coachman dominated the high jump and sprinting events from 1939 to 1948. Her perseverance paid off in a gold medal for the high jump, the only bright spot for U.S. track women in the 1948 London Olympics.

Shirley Crowder (Meadows), Martha Hudson (Pennyman) and Willye White were part of the next cohort of track women. Crowder and Hudson grew up in Georgia in the 1940s and 1950s, attended Tennessee State University on track scholarships in the late 1950s, and competed in the 1960 Olympics in Rome.[33] Their Olympic teammate White won recognition as a high school sprinter and jumper in her home state of Mississippi. While a member of TSU and Chicago track teams, she competed in five successive Olympic Games from 1956 to 1972.[34]

All six athletes began by running high school track in segregated southern schools. By the 1940s most black high schools offered girls' track and basketball teams, providing at least a modicum of organizational support and coaching for promising young athletes. The women recalled that while it was still unusual for a girl to be heavily involved in sports, they were not lone competitors. Reinforced by teammates and coaches, young athletes also received support from friends and family members.

They were, however, aware that some contemporaries disapproved of female athletes. Willye White learned of these attitudes at an early age, when members of her rural Mississippi community questioned her tomboyish ways. Describing herself as a "tomboy" and an "outcast," she explained, "It was not acceptable in American society." Alice Coachman also met with criticism. Her parents repeatedly tried to prevent her from going to the playground where she played ball and raced with the boys. Coachman recalled that her parents as well as others in the community suspected that athletic girls would suffer injury and poor health: "The general feeling during that time—they just felt that girls were going to break their neck. . . . In my home town, . . . they were always afraid of them getting hurt. . . . They weren't educated about women's track."

Yet, more often than not, athletes found fellow students and community members to be genuinely supportive, especially if they had an interest in sport or personal contact with the women involved. Shirley Crowder described the atmosphere at Tennessee State:

> If the person was not involved with sports as a participant or a spectator . . . they perhaps thought of it as being too masculine— perhaps at that time. Because I've had some people say things like that to me. . . . I just credit it to the fact that some were jealous because we were constantly traveling. I just took it that way. But most of the people who were closer to us appreciated what we were doing.

At Tuskegee athletes rarely encountered criticism. The mannish image of women athletes occupied a remote corner in Leila Perry's mind, since, as she explained: "The people we encountered, you didn't have that kind of a stigma. Like at Tuskegee, everybody was proud of us. Because we were really outstanding. . . . It didn't touch me, because at Tuskegee it wasn't such. They were proud of their athletes."

Insulated from wider cultural criticism by their immediate surroundings, athletes rejected interpretations that conflicted with their own. Lula Hymes reasoned, "They gonna think and talk and say what they want to say anyway, regardless of how you feel about it. I never pay any attention to what people say." Martha Hudson agreed: "I've heard the talk, but it didn't bother me." She explained that her TSU coach and teammates provided a layer of protection: "We were just so prepared for a lot of things—criticism—our coach would talk to us. Things that a lot of people worried about, we didn't. We would discuss it, we would talk about it, but it didn't bother us."

Like Hudson, athletes shielded from public rebuke felt free to participate and enjoy their sport to the fullest. Lula Hymes summarized her experience: "I just wanted to run and win during that time. . . . I was out there just enjoying myself. Because I *liked* it; [it was] something I *wanted* to do!" Similarly Shirley Crowder concluded, "I was just always me. . . . I knew what I had to do and I'd do it regardless." Reflecting on the sheer pleasure of her youthful passion, Alice Coachman commented, "When I look back at it now, I just say, 'Lord, I sure was a running thing!' "

Beyond the elemental joy of competing, athletes also placed high value on the educational and travel opportunities that track and field made available. While several had planned to attend local colleges, athletic scholarships gave them the chance to go away to school and expand their horizons. Hymes, Perry, and Coachman especially appreciated the rich cultural and intellectual life of Tuskegee in the 1930s and 1940s: "They had all kinds of activities around the campus for you. And you just kind of grew as a person. You weren't just involved in athletics, you were involved in the happenings of the world. Because they brought the world to Tuskegee."[35]

Athletes described their travels as a combination of painful and wondrous awakenings. Traveling across the South and into northern cities brought young athletes out of the protective fold of black institutions and communities. They encountered the harsh realities of southern segregation and the more confusing, unwritten rules of northern racism. Growing up in Atlanta's black community, Lula Hymes had not experienced segregation as burdensome or painful. "I wasn't aware until we started traveling," she recalled. On the road she found that "if we wanted to go to the bathroom, we had to stop and go in the woods. We couldn't go in the stores to buy anything. We had to go around. It was really hard, segregated." Alice Coachman described a similar contrast between student life at Tuskegee and traveling with the track team. Remarking on the difficulty of obtaining food, gas, and lodging on the road, she explained that travel with the team brought segregation into full view, especially compared to the relative safety of Tuskegee, where "you had your own little world." Although roadside picnics and stops at black colleges, restaurants, or rooming houses might make for pleasant travel, athletes understood the forces of racism that lay behind those "choices."

Young track women found that travel also offered positive experiences. As high school students spending the summer at Tuskegee's or TSU's junior training program, teenagers gained independence, new friends, and sometimes an escape from difficult work or family situations. After spending her first summer at Tuskegee, Alice Coachman begged her parents to let her return during the school year: "I had gotten a taste of traveling with the girls. . . . You know, going to big cities, and I had never been out of Albany, Georgia. And everybody was nice. I wanted to be with the group—I wanted to be there too!" Willye White saw track as a ticket out of Greenwood, Mississippi. "It was my talent, and my ability. And with that I could do a lot of things. I could get away from my grandparents, I could travel throughout the state. . . . It allowed me freedom of movement." Describing escape from grueling work as her "main motivator," White explained: "I left [Mississippi] every May, and that meant I didn't have to go to the cotton fields and I came back in September. As far as what was traditional and nontraditional, I had no idea. All I knew was it was just an escape for me not to have to go to the cotton fields during the summer."

Travel to AAU and Olympic competitions opened even more vistas. Athletes recalled dancing at the Savoy Ballroom and the Cotton Club in New York City, being taken to historical sites like Mount Vernon, and encountering chop suey and chopsticks for the first time. Top black teams occasionally received celebrity treatment, although it might come with a racist twist. Martha Hudson told of being invited as part of the TSU track team to appear on Dick Clark's "American Bandstand" television program, only to find out afterward that they had been kept off camera nearly the entire show. In a similar vein Leila Perry recalled a ceremony honoring the Tuskegee team at the Atlantic City, New Jersey, city hall. Before being presented with the key to the city, the team was asked to sing for the crowd, because "as always, they think that black folks are supposed to be able to sing."

These racial slights were outweighed by profound moments of racial insight and pride. Recalling her first Olympic journey to Melbourne, Australia, Willye White described a life-altering experience: "That's when I found out there were two worlds— Mississippi and the rest of the world. I found that blacks and whites could eat together, sleep together, play together, do all these things together. And it was just eye opening. Had I not been in the Olympic Games, I could have spent the rest of my life thinking that blacks and whites were separate." For White and other African American athletes, involvement in high-level track and field brought deep satisfactions and worldly knowledge.

Beyond its personal significance to individual athletes, the success of black women in track served as a broader symbol of pride and achievement for black communities. Black colleges and newspapers heralded women's track accomplishments, even when the mainstream press ignored them. When white officials or journalists did occasionally take note of black female athletic accomplishments, their praise represented momentary triumphs in the long struggle against racial oppression. Victorious homecoming ceremonies at which white politicians and reporters showered black Olympians with honors served as a powerful symbolic reversal of racial hierarchy. When the white mayors of Greenwood, Mississippi, and Clarksville, Tennessee, handed Willye White and Wilma Rudolph the keys to their cities, it symbolized a door that could open for all African Americans. It granted due, if temporary, respect and nurtured the hope that racial justice might soon prevail.

⌒○⌒

Paradoxically, while black communities understood the athletic success of African American women to be a measure of black cultural achievement, it held a very different meaning when interpreted through the lens of white America's prevailing racial and sexual beliefs. For the most part black women athletes were simply ignored by the white media and athletic establishment. Figures like Alice Coachman, the first black woman in history to win an Olympic medal, or Mildred McDaniel, the only American woman to win an individual gold medal in the 1956 Olympic track-and-field competition, did not become national celebrities, household names, or even the subject of magazine feature stories. The most striking feature of the historical record on black women athletes is neglect. This pattern is not surprising given the invisibility of minority cultures in mainstream discourse. Yet the historical roots of the silence surrounding black women athletes are complex. They lay deep in the traditions of Western thought, in which women of color have long been viewed as distant but definitive repositories of inferior, unfeminine qualities.

For centuries European and Anglo-American art, science, and popular thought had constructed a normative ideal of white womanhood that relied on an opposing image of black women as the inferior "other." Specifically, images of female sexuality, femininity, and beauty were composed along racially polarized axes. North American and British scientists of the nineteenth century described black sexuality as lascivious and apelike, marked by a "voluptuousness" and "degree of lascivity" unknown in Europe.[36] Citing supposed physical distinctions between African and European women as empirical proof, they contrasted black women's presumed primitive, passionate sexuality to an ideal of asexual purity among highly "civilized" white women. These stereotypes continued to permeate American culture in the early twentieth century. Called "openly licentious" and "morally obtuse," black women posed a negative contrast to the presumed "lily-white" virtue of Anglo-American women.[37]

Theories of sexual inferiority and primitiveness found a corollary in standards of beauty. Early-twentieth-century sexologist Havelock Ellis argued that a scientifically objective chain of beauty ran parallel to the evolutionary chain of being. White European and Anglo-American women occupied the most highly evolved, beautiful end of the scale, while black women were assigned a place at the opposite end.[38] Ellis's "scientific" theory was rooted in popular racial assumptions that found another expression in dominant media standards of beauty. Advertisements, advice columns, and beauty magazines excluded women of color, except for occasional portrayals as dark-skinned exotica from faraway lands.

Racialized notions of sexual virtue and feminine beauty were underpinned by another concept, that of the virile or mannish black female. African American women's work history as slaves, tenant farmers, domestics, and wageworkers disqualified them from standards of femininity defined around the frail or inactive female body. Their very public presence in the labor force exempted African Americans from ideals of womanhood that rested on the presumed refinement and femininity of a privatized domestic arena. Failing to meet these standards, black women were often represented in the dominant culture as masculine females lacking in feminine grace, delicacy, and refinement.

The silence surrounding black athletes reflects the power of these stereotypes to restrict African American women to the margins of cultural life, occupying a status as distant "others." In one sense the invisibility was not specific to athletes. With the exception of a few sensational stage performers like Josephine Baker or Lena Horne, African American women were not generally subjects of white popular interest or adoration. There were, however, more specific causes for the lack of attention to black women's athletic accomplishments, reasons rooted in the striking intersection of racial and gender ideology in sport.

The long exclusion of both African American women and female athletes from categories of acceptable femininity encouraged the development of analogous mythologies. References to imitative "animalistic" behavior had often been used to describe white female athletes, who by "aping" male athletic behavior were suspected of unleashing animal instincts. Charges of mimicry found an even deeper congruence with racist views of African Americans as simian and imitative. Similarly, the charge that sport masculinized women physically and sexually resonated with scientific and popular portrayals of mannishness and sexual pathology among black women. The assertion that sport made women physically unattractive and sexually unappealing found its corollary in views of black women as less attractive and desirable than white women.[39] The correspondence between stereotyped depictions of black womanhood and athletic females was nearly exact, and thus doubly resonant in the case of African American women athletes.

The myth of the "natural" black athlete lent further support to the perception that African American women were biologically suited to masculine sport. Early-twentieth-century education and social science journals, especially in the 1930s, were sprinkled with anthropometric studies of racially determined muscle length, limb size, head shape, and neurological responses. Experts in both science and sport labored to identify genetic factors, including a conditioned "fear-response" and peculiar characteristics of African American hands, tendons, muscles, joints, nerves, blood, thighs, and eye color, which might explain the fact that black athletes sometimes jumped higher or ran faster than whites.[40] This formulation of the "natural" black athlete represented black athletic accomplishment as a by-product of nature rather than as a cultural attainment based on skill and knowledge. By maintaining the myth that people of European descent were cultured, intellectual and civilized, while those of African heritage were uncivilized beings guided by physical and natural impulses, it also converted black achievements into evidence of racial inferiority.[41]

A legacy of racist thought influenced the reception of black women track athletes. This kind of racism was rarely overt and probably not even intended by many sport enthusiasts. It was signaled primarily as an absence—the lack of popular interest, organizational support, media coverage, and public acclaim. White observers may have tacitly dismissed black women's accomplishments as the inevitable result of "natural," "masculine" prowess. By this logic black women's very success could appear to provide further evidence of track and field's unfeminine character. Advocates of women's track may have ignored black athletes because their existence ran contrary to the image of classic (white) femininity that officials so desperately wanted to convey.[42] While racism was only one factor contributing to the poor reputation of women's track and field, the confluence of powerful

racial and athletic stereotypes could only reinforce the stigmatized status of track women in general, and African American
athletes in particular.

⌐○⌐

The influence of these ideas becomes more obvious when track is
compared to swimming, a sport whose development paralleled
that of track and field in important ways. The AAU sponsored
both activities, opening its doors to swimming in 1916 and to
track eight years later. Both sports involved team training and
competition but were primarily individual sports that pitted individual athletes against each other in contests over time and distance. Women and men competed in both sports, so neither activity was logically female or male.

Similarly, in stark contrast to track and field's masculine reputation, from its inception observers deemed swimming appropriate and beneficial for women. The media depicted swimmers as
the ideal "figures" of American womanhood. *New York Times*
columnist Arthur J. Daley praised swimmer Eleanor Holm
(Jarrett) as "perfectly proportioned, right in line for the business
of 'Glorifying the American Girl.' "[43] Beauty, not ugliness, was
the swimmer's hallmark. A 1938 *Amateur Athlete* cover photo
likened AAU swim champs to contestants in a Miss America
pageant, while headlines repeatedly referred to swimmers as
"queens," "beauties," "nymphs," or "pretty plungers" who
could put on a dazzling "show of youth and beauty."[44]

Swimmers, like track athletes, relied on strength, speed, and
technique. Nevertheless commentators saw the two sports as distinctly different. The core concepts used to impugn the gender of
track-and-field athletes—reproductive damage, physical masculinity, and lack of sexual appeal—operated in reverse for swimmers. Motherhood was not an issue in swimming, since as a
water sport it did not involve the high impact or jarring effects
thought to damage female reproductive organs. Contemporary
observers also distinguished between track as an ugly, muscle-
bunching sport and swimming as an attractive, muscle-stretching
one. In direct contrast to track's masculine effects, swimming
purportedly enhanced the feminine physique by keeping it soft

and rounded while building up the chest and developing long, supple leg muscles. The aura of beauty and sexual appeal that surrounded women's swimming was reinforced by popular leisure culture, in which speed swimming shaded into recreational bathing and suntanning. The "swimsuit competition" phase of beauty contests further blurred the lines between competitive sport and beauty culture, as did the entertainment careers of swimming stars like Annette Kellermann, Eleanor Holm, and Esther Williams.[45]

Underneath the association of swimming with beauty lay critical distinctions of class and race. The overwhelming majority of competitive swimmers were white and middle class. Most trained in private swim clubs under salaried coaches. Public pools were uncommon in working-class urban neighborhoods and in rural areas. Where they did exist, legal or de facto segregation and the price of admission prevented most African American, Latino, Indian, Asian American, and white working-class youngsters from attaining basic skills, much less a competitive edge.

For years swimming and track existed side by side as the glamorous and ugly sisters of AAU and Olympic sport.[46] The racial, class, and gender prejudices that informed the distinction operated subtly and remained largely unarticulated. However, the situation changed after World War II, when the global conflict between the United States and the Soviet Union suddenly fixed national and international attention on women's track. As a small band of neglected, undertrained female athletes assumed the weight of the "free world" on their backs, sport advocates and journalists were forced to confront the image of women's track and its leading stars.

⌁◯⌁

Like everything from Third World governments to kitchen appliances, sport became part of a Cold War international contest in which the United States and USSR vied not only for athletic laurels but to prove the superiority of capitalism or communism. Under pressure to triumph over Soviet "slave athletics," the national sports establishment focused unprecedented attention on black and female athletes.

American sport officials paid homage to black competitors, sheepishly admitting, "If it weren't for the sensational performances of the great Negro athletes we wouldn't even be in a secondary position in world athletics today."[47] Furthermore, they relied on African American talent to disprove Soviet charges of pervasive racial discrimination in U.S. society. Claiming that the prominence of black athletes in the United States refuted "Communist ideas about the status of our colored citizens," politicians and sports officials championed black athletic success and the desegregation of major league sports as "an answer to communism."[48] This mind-set filtered into U.S. foreign policy of the late 1950s. The State Department worked with athletic organizations to sponsor international tours featuring African American track and tennis stars. One armchair diplomat boasted that these athletes could do "more to win friends for the United States than formal diplomacy or handouts or economic aid have been able to do."[49]

Though black women were included in the praise for African American athletes, their tribulations as members of the U.S. women's track team caused serious concern. The lack of adequate training and competition left black as well as white women in poor shape for international events. Overall, U.S. women lagged far behind both Western and Eastern European women who received much greater support from their national sport organizations. The deficiencies of women's track and field had been a minor matter in the past. But with the Soviet Union's first Olympic appearance in 1952, these failings posed an acute problem for U.S. politicians, sport leaders, and a patriotic public. The U.S. men's team ranked even with or above the Soviet men, but the Soviet women so overpowered their American counterparts that the United States was in danger of losing the unofficial but highly publicized competition for Olympic gold.

As early as 1946 track insiders warned that without expanded school and college programs, more opportunities to compete, and more official support, U.S. women would fare badly against superior European and Russian teams.[50] The changes were not forthcoming and predictions of dismal international performances came true. The weakness of women's track and field, a sport that most amateur sport leaders had hoped would quietly fade away, now stood out like a sore thumb and threatened American claims that, whether in politics, economics, or athletics, the United States could do it better.

In this climate of controversy Olympic organizers reopened the question of the suitability of women's track and field. In a summary of the 1953 Olympic Congress in Mexico City, IOC President Avery Brundage described the "well-grounded protest against events which are not truly feminine," including field events and long-distance running. He reported that the IOC favored confining women's track-and-field events "to those appropriate to the feminine sex," and noted that despite the 1953 decision to continue women's competition, about one-third of national Olympic committees "would be happier if there were not events for the opposite sex."[51] IOC member Prince Franz Joseph of Liechtenstein remarked that not only would such a reduction solve the problem of Olympic overexpansion, but "we would be spared the unesthetic spectacle of women trying to look and act like men."[52]

The American media expressed similar sentiments. Before the Cold War many journalists who opposed women's track and field just ignored it. But the Soviet threat to American athletic superiority demanded a response. Sportswriters routinely claimed that track and field, especially the strength events like the javelin and and the shot put, unsexed women. In his 1953 New York Times column titled "More Deadly than Male," Arthur Daley described the "grotesque contortions" of track-and-field athletes, noting that "it does something to a guy. And it ain't love, Buster."[53] In a similar vein, in his 1960 article titled "Venus Wasn't a Shot Putter," columnist William Barry Furlong likened patriotic assertions of having the best-muscled girls to claiming the best-looking automobile wreck.[54] According to this view women were a consumer item, "wrecked" for male pleasure by athletic training.

Ironically, the source of the problem—Soviet women's Olympic dominance—provided a partial solution for those officials and journalists who urged support for U.S. women. The American team could shed damning images of unsexed, mannish women by displacing them onto Soviet athletes. Descriptions of "ponderous, peasant-type Russian athletes" and "Amazons from the Russian steppes" created a contrasting "other" whose very presence lent some legitimacy to the less talented U.S. team. These "strong Red ladies" who outshone "frail Red males" shifted the onus away from American athletes onto Soviet women.[55] However, while they could claim to be more feminine than their Russian antagonists, the U.S. team had yet to figure out a way to defeat them.

Concerned observers agreed that to improve women's performance, sport administrators must interest a larger number of girls and women in track and then provide adequate training programs to develop their abilities. The problem was how to popularize a sport deemed by many as unfeminine and undesirable for women. For sport advocates trying to revive popular interest in a dying sport, the commanding position of African-American women in track posed a specially vexing problem. To improve the image of track and field, promoters could either incorporate black track women into approved concepts of athletic womanhood, or they could minimize the presence and contributions of black women in order to create a more respectable image of the sport. Black and white athletic officials approached the dilemma with a variety of strategies.

African American journalists, coaches, and athletic promoters consciously cultivated the feminine image of black women athletes. Tennessee State Coach Edward Temple instituted a dress code and prohibited photographers from taking postrace pictures until after his athletes had retreated to the locker room to touch up their hair and wash their faces. He wanted the visible signs of strain and sweat removed, creating a "public face" of composure. Asked about the masculine image of track athletes, Temple told a reporter, "None of my girls have any trouble getting boyfriends. I tell them that they are young ladies first, track girls second."[56]

Black educator and sports historian E. B. Henderson took pains to establish the femininity of black competitors, asserting in 1948 that "colored girl athletes are as a rule, effeminate. They are normal girls." Contrasting "colored" athletes to those champions who "are more man than woman" (left unnamed, but probably an allusion to Stella Walsh, who was plagued by rumors that she was a genetic male), Henderson assured readers that when African American women won, it would be "as real female women and not as men temporarily masquerading as women."[57] *Ebony* magazine, one of the few national publications to celebrate African American women as the "fastest women in the world," also tried to counter negative stereotypes. A 1955 article explained that girls owed their success to male coaches and that their records never equaled men's. Turning to men for the final stamp of approval, the article concluded that boys, too, were learning "that a girl track star can be as feminine as the china-doll type."[58]

These comments sound identical to other apologetic defenses; the heavy emphasis on *off*-the-field feminine appearance and heterosexual love life accepts that competition endangers femininity, thereby forcing athletes to reestablish their womanhood through nonathletic means. However, underneath the apparent similarities, a distinct African American standpoint took shape. By presenting a public image of well-dressed feminine composure, black sports advocates insisted on integrating African American athletes into standards of athletic femininity. This approach continued a tradition of African American resistance in which generations of black women had defended their femininity and sexual virtue against disparaging stereotypes by asserting their morality and respectability.

Leila Perry explained the importance of creating a decorous public image: "All of us had been taught how to act, how to be graceful, and to be like products of Tuskegee. . . . Now some of us maybe didn't know how to eat and to do things like that. They taught us all of that—when you go out, which way you start with your fork and your knife and what have you. . . . And they always wanted us to look our best." In looking their best, Perry believed that the Tuskegee women demonstrated "that all people are the same. . . . That you are as good as anybody else and you can do what anybody else can do." Tennessee State followed the same policies. Martha Hudson explained, "We knew that we were in the public eye, so . . . our coach at Tennessee State, he demanded that we carry ourselves a certain way." She believed that Coach Temple "wanted to show them that we were ladies—respectable ladies. . . . They said negative things about athletes, about the way they dress and so on and so forth, so he wanted us to try to set an example that athletes were not what some of them thought we were—that we were ladies."

This carefully composed image of athletic womanhood did double duty, debunking myths of the mannish woman athlete and of the natural black athlete. It also raised a wall of defense against misinformed or malicious representations of black women. By publicly asserting their femininity and sexual respectability, black athletes answered tacit denials of their womanhood and demanded inclusion in the realm of culture.[59]

White track-and-field leaders developed similar strategies to deal with the sport's image problem. The most tenacious defenders of women's track and field were the few women who obtained leadership positions within the AAU. In the 1950s two such advocates—former track champions Roxy Andersen and Frances Kaszubski—spearheaded efforts to revive their sport in the face of widespread public apathy or hostility. Andersen and Kaszubski worked tirelessly to establish feminine credentials for track and field, cajoling sports leaders, issuing press releases to city newspapers, and publishing articles in the *Amateur Athlete*. In one media piece titled "Girls Thrive on Sport," Andersen even conceded that several top athletes "were raw-boned, flat-chested and deep-voiced." But she countered that so were some nonathletic girls, and concluded with a standard defense of athletic femininity. Acknowledging that unsightly sweat and dirt were part of the sport, Anderson reminded readers that "a temporarily strained face doesn't permanently destroy beauty, nor does it reduce a woman's social charm or her ability to bake a pie."[60]

In a similar vein Frances Kaszubski issued a glowing report of an appearance on the "Ed Sullivan Show" by the national women's track-and-field team. Playing on references to track and field as the "cinder sport" (because of cinder tracks), Kaszubski described the women as "Modern Cinderellas," kept in the background by the evil stepmother of public apathy and overshadowed by respectable stepsister sports of swimming and tennis. But finally, at the "big ball" of national television, the women found the magic slipper of public approval. Each member of the team rested happily in the knowledge that "at last she was a member of a sport that was being recognized by Prince Charming, Ed Sullivan." To remove any lingering doubts, Kaszubski informed her readers that such "inner happiness only added to the natural beauty and charm that each of the AAU National Champions already possessed."[61]

Fearing that anecdotal evidence alone would not convince a skeptical public, in 1954 the AAU conducted a statistical survey of former athletes to prove that top-notch women were "photogenic and attractively feminine" and, subsequent to competing, were "establishing families in the good old American tradition."[62] Summarizing the "gratifying" results, Andersen explained that under the public spotlight, athletes became even more image conscious and well mannered. As a result, far from becoming "mannish and hardened, . . . sport helped these women win husbands."[63]

While such statements theoretically included a defense of black athletes as well as white, the language and visual imagery of most AAU publicity indicates an effort to put distance between the sport's image and its African American stars. The editors of the AAU publication *Amateur Athlete* rarely printed photos of African American women, choosing no coverage over black representations. The success of black women forced this magazine and other sports media occasionally to give due praise, but the overwhelming emphasis was on white "hopefuls," women who had not yet earned national honors but nevertheless might appeal to the public as promising stars on the rise. Other journalists followed suit. The media regularly described young Olympic hopefuls as cute, blond, little, and fair. Or in a slightly altered version, articles like *Parade* magazine's "Watch this Housewife Jump!" complimented older athletes for their domesticity.[64]

These appeals were implicitly biased against black women. Few had ever had the economic security to combine athletics with full-time housewifery, and none were blond and "fair" skinned. Athletes of all ages and races received the most praise when they met popular ideals of beauty, but mass media beauty standards included black women only insofar as they approached white ideals. The *Amateur Athlete*'s references to fair-skinned blond beauties made the exclusion explicit.

The continued prominence of black women in the sport and the impact of the civil rights movement forced some change in media policy of the early 1960s. African American women were more often featured and photographed. However, the few athletes who attained a visible presence were often treated as exceptional cases. In reporting on Wilma Rudolph's triple-gold-medal performance at the 1960 Rome Olympics, where she won the one hundred- and two hundred-meter sprints and anchored the four hundred-meter relay, *Time* magazine declared: "In a field of female endeavor in which the greatest stars have often been characterized by overdeveloped muscles and underdeveloped glands, Wilma (Skeeter) Rudolph has long, lissome legs and a pert charm."[65] In this view top women track athletes, who in the United States happened to be black, were masculine freaks of nature, and Rudolph was the exception. Even as they applauded her charm and speed, the press resorted to stereotypical images of jungle animals. They nicknamed Rudolph the "black gazelle."[66] Like other black athletes, she was represented as a wild beast, albeit a gentle, attractive creature who could be adopted as a pet of the American public.[67]

With the exception of Rudolph's short-lived popularity, stereotypes of athletic amazons and muscle molls continued to plague track-and-field athletes. In 1962 Frances Kaszubski seemed to accept defeat when she openly admitted that masculine women had an advantage in track and field. She began her article "In Defense of Women Athletes" with the disclaimer, "There is no doubt that certain women reach the summit of the great competitions at the Olympic Games whose morphology, or functional characteristics, are akin to those of men." She insisted, however, that sport did not *create* aberrant females. Rather, "women who are apparently 'virilized' by sport are, in reality, women with android tendencies who succeed in sportive competitions simply by reason of their genetic constitution."[68] Given the admission that the most natural women athletes were in fact the most aberrant females, how were sport advocates to make any headway in popularizing track and field?

A clue lay in the photograph positioned right above Kaszubski's remarks. A young, blond, white gymnast lay with her pelvis delicately balanced on a horizontal bar, arms outstretched and chest thrust forward above the caption, "Doris Fuchs . . . lightness, suppleness, virtuosity and grace."[69] More and more, track-and-field leaders followed a strategy of virtue by association. Rather than credit the achievements of African American athletes who had overcome sexual and racial barriers to excel in their sport, athletic leaders legitimized track and field by treating it as a sister sport to "feminine" and overwhelmingly white sports like gymnastics, swimming, and diving, and the recently adopted sport of synchronized swimming.

⸺◦⸺

Why did the stigma of mannishness prove so intractable? One answer lies in the deeply rooted understanding of track and field as inherently masculine. Given the stifling conservatism of the postwar era, especially with regard to gender norms, this perception was unlikely to be dislodged in the late 1940s and 1950s. But racial issues also played a critical role in reproducing the sport's masculine definition.

Grafted onto the existing image of the mannish female athlete, the figure of the black woman track athlete fused gender and racial stereotypes. When, after decades of media and organizational neglect, American track women suddenly found themselves under the international glare of Cold War athletic rivalries, a complicated matrix of racial and gender issues came to a head. A reservoir of racist beliefs about black women as deficient in femininity buttressed the masculine connotation of track and field. Throughout the Cold War era, the sport was dominated by African American and Soviet women. Thus two symbols of mannishness—black women and Russian "amazons"—stood in the foreground, impeding efforts to overhaul the sport's reputation.

AAU officials and their allies rallied around a feminine ideal rooted in white, middle-class culture. Leaders like Roxy Andersen and Frances Kaszubski did not invent this ideal, nor did they necessarily intend racism. Black athletes along with white benefited from their efforts to advance women's track and field. Nevertheless widespread contempt for women athletes as ugly, unsexed amazons set the terms of public debate. Locked into these terms, defenders of track and field tried to answer criticism with proof that women athletes were indeed pretty, feminine, and sexually normal. To do so they called on historically racist constructions of womanhood that failed to include black athletes within the bounds of athletic femininity.

Constrained by segregation laws, inferior resources, limited competitive opportunities, discriminatory sport agencies, and media "blackouts," African American women athletes faced tremendous barriers to participation. Sadly, when they surmounted these odds, their commanding presence in the "mannish" sport of track and field could appear to verify their absence from "true" (white) womanhood and athletic respectability.

The subtle interplay of racial and gender stereotypes surely did the greatest damage to African American athletes, but it also indirectly constricted the athletic possibilities of other women. Sport advocates who stressed white norms of femininity and attempted to distance the sport from its black stars simply reinforced a definition of femininity that confined women physically, sexually, and athletically. They thereby subverted their own genuine interest in expanding women's athletic freedom. As long as the "mannish amazon" could be represented by the liminal figure of the black female track star, sport would remain an illegitimate activity for all women.

# CHAPTER 6

# NO FREAKS, NO AMAZONS, NO BOYISH BOBS

## The All-American Girls Baseball League

Track and field was already on the wane when a new sport, the game of softball, became the people's choice of the depression and World War II eras. By the mid-1940s an estimated nine million Americans had joined softball teams.[1] When women as well as men flocked to the new game, the media found cause for both praise and ridicule. Journalists described less-skilled female players as "wonderfully erratic" and a "baffling mixture of the Dead End Kids and Sweet Alice."[2] But they also seemed unnerved by the sight of talented women who hit and threw with power, moved with speed and agility, slid hard into bases, and dived for balls with abandon. Highly skilled athletes who could "perform like a reasonable facsimile of the male" evoked the specter of mannishness.[3] When commentators described Olympia Savona, star hitter on the New Orleans Jax team, as a player who "runs bases like a man, slides like a man . . . catches like a man" and is "built like a football halfback," they expressed the familiar tension between athleticism and feminine womanhood.[4]

In the 1940s ambitious sports entrepreneurs tried to capitalize on this tension. Endeavoring to build on the popularity of women's softball while avoiding its mannish taint, Philip K. Wrigley and Arthur Meyerhoff founded the All-American Girls Baseball League (AAGBL).[5] The AAGBL advocated a unique "femininity principle," deliberately contrasting players' amazing "masculine" baseball skills with their "feminine" attractiveness, an appeal accentuated by league-mandated pastel-skirted uniforms, makeup, long hair, and strict standards of off-field dress and behavior. This ingenious strategy worked in the short term; it helps account for the league's twelve-year tenure as a professional women's sport venture. Yet, in the long run, by promoting women's baseball as a spectacle of feminine "nice girls" who could "play like a man," the AAGBL did as much to heighten the cultural dissonance between "masculine" athleticism and "feminine" womanhood as it did to resolve it.

Invented in the early 1900s as a derivative of baseball designed for play indoors or in restricted outdoor space, softball took off as a game of its own in the 1930s.[6] As a relatively inexpensive outdoor sport, it seemed perfectly fitted to depression-era recreational needs. For a minimal admission charge, if any, fans could gather in the twilight of weekday evenings or for long, sunny weekend afternoons and watch friends and neighbors play a modified version of baseball that, with its softer ball and shorter basepaths, seemed more accessible to athletes of modest ability.

The Amateur Softball Association (ASA) was organized in 1934, and after only one year could boast that 950,000 men, women, and young people participated in ASA-sanctioned leagues. The numbers continued to climb as federal New Deal programs like the WPA financed community recreation programs and the building of parks and athletic facilities. The depression-era boom caused the *Christian Science Monitor* to note that softball was fast "becoming a national recreation for the masses."[7] When the war came, softball's popularity continued to soar, so that by the mid-1940s the *New York Times* estimated that 150 million spectators turned out annually to watch the country's six hundred thousand teams at play.[8]

Though softball was popular nationwide, its strongest roots lay on the West Coast and in the Midwest, where cities like Los Angeles and Chicago catered to all ages and abilities through playground, YMCA, church, business, industrial, and municipal leagues. A 1938 survey of the Los Angeles area found that within a one-hundred-mile radius there were nine thousand teams, including nearly one thousand women's teams.[9] The sport attracted wide-ranging interest in these strongholds. White working-class athletes from rural and urban areas formed the bulk of the constituency, but softball also caught on as an industrial sport and playground game in black communities. On the West Coast, Mexican and Asian immigrants took up the sport with help from ethnic businesses, schools, and service agencies. Japanese Americans, for example, organized teams through Japanese-language schools and Buddhist associations.[10]

Girls and women eagerly sought out these opportunities. Compared to baseball's masculine image, softball's use of a larger, "softer" ball, its smaller field dimensions, and early names like "kitten ball" and "mush ball" gave the impression that softball was especially suited to women, youngsters, and those men who lacked the requisite toughness for rugged sports like baseball or football. Although men's growing involvement in softball gradually cast the game in a more masculine light, women's participation remained uncontroversial in working-class and rural settings, where women's softball fit comfortably within community-based gender norms. In contrast to middle-class prescriptions, working-class notions of femininity did not deny women's strength and physicality: The demanding nature of women's domestic, agricultural, and wage labor made physical weakness or delicacy more of a liability than a virtue. Flexible gender definitions, in turn, left space for the "outdoor girl" or "tomboy" with an avid interest in softball. Encouraged by friends, neighbors, family members, and coworkers who gathered to cheer them on, working-class women of the 1930s and 1940s joined softball teams in unprecedented numbers.

Small-town teams like the Syracuse, Nebraska, Bluebirds provided sporting opportunities for young women and a recreational activity for the entire town and surrounding rural community. The Bluebirds formed in 1932 under the sponsorship of local physician W. E. ("Doc") Hillis, a former minor league ballplayer with an avid interest in the new sport of "kittenball." Hillis recruited young women in their teens or early twenties from among Syracuse's nine hundred-odd residents and from the surrounding area, scheduling them to play one or two games per week against teams from elsewhere in Nebraska, Iowa, and Kansas. The Bluebirds' remarkable success quickly distinguished them from other small-town teams. Two winning seasons made it possible for Hillis to attract top-notch athletes from throughout the region. As new recruits moved to town, they gradually replaced some of the original team members who were no longer interested or skilled enough to play at a highly competitive level. By 1935 the Syracuse team had become a regional powerhouse, winning the Nebraska state tournament by defeating Omaha teams that drew from a much larger population base. As state champions for three consecutive years, the team traveled to Chicago in 1935, 1936, and 1937 to play in the national tournament.[11]

Syracuse and its surrounding area supported the Bluebirds with generosity and enthusiasm. Players recalled that people would drive to the ballpark from miles away. They pulled their cars and trucks up in a semicircle around the outfield perimeter, turning bumpers, hoods, and truckbeds into bleachers. Lucille ("Rusty") Hofferber Bateman remembered: "We'd get twelve hundred people out of a town of nine hundred. . . . We could always count on a big crowd at the games. Never, never less than nine hundred." Mildred Emmons Neeman added, "They really turned out. It was something new. There wasn't anything like that before."[12]

Softball held a variety of meanings for the young women who participated. Some women joined teams because softball was a popular sport and one of few available forms of organized recreation. They enjoyed the game but equally valued the recognition and the social life that accompanied it. Several former Bluebirds emphasized the companionship and adventure they experienced as members of the team, fondly recalling train travel, crowded car rides, meals with the Hillis family, or simply meandering about town with teammates. Young players basked in the unexpected attention that success brought. One recalled, "I don't care where you went, you had a bunch of cheerleaders right behind you—and thanking you for everything. Because we put them on the map, really. So it was wonderful."[13] Though they may have played ball for only a few years, former Bluebirds recalled the experience as the highlight of their adolescence or early adulthood.

Several made softball the focus of their young lives, pursuing other teams when the Bluebirds disbanded after the 1937 season, a casualty of the depression and Hillis's personal problems. Myrna Scritchfield Thompson left Manhattan, Kansas, to join the Syracuse team after her junior year of high school, returning home in the fall to complete her education. The following spring she moved full-time to Syracuse in order to play ball, supporting herself by working in a laundry. After the Bluebirds folded, Thompson moved around in Kansas and Missouri to play for several highly competitive, nationally ranked industrial softball teams. Thelma Hirst followed a similar path. In her late teens she found a job in Omaha and began playing city-league basketball with friends from work. Her companions encouraged her to join a softball team during the summer. After playing in Omaha, she joined the Bluebirds, then moved to Missouri, where she played many more years while working in the meat-packing industry. Her friend Nina Korgan moved from Council Bluffs, Iowa, to Syracuse with her family so she and her sister could play for the Bluebirds while they were still in high school. A phenomenal pitcher, Korgan subsequently played in Missouri, Oklahoma, and California before pitching the New Orleans Jax to five national championships in the 1940s.[14] Women like Korgan, Hirst, and Thompson pursued sport with a passion, joining an embryonic women's athletic subculture comprising highly dedicated and skilled athletes. More than a recreational activity, athletics became integral to their identities and their life choices.

Sport offered similar opportunities to women in urban areas in which softball thrived as a city game. During the late 1930s and 1940s, municipal park leagues, manufacturers, and independent sponsors combined to promote amateur and semipro softball. Sponsorship varied, from companies that simply footed the bill for equipment, uniforms, and league fees to those that covered travel expenses and paid players a per-game fee or weekly stipend. At the upper level, semipro teams like Chicago's Rockola Chicks or Music Maids attracted crowds numbering in the several thousands. In 1941, the top four Chicago semipro teams drew a total of 234,000 paying customers.[15]

Many working-class women athletes experienced softball as a

perfectly normal and commonplace activity in their communities. They grew up playing sandlot ball in their neighborhoods and then, typically, joined organized leagues sometime during their teens. It never occurred to Chicagoan Irene Kotowicz that softball, so popular at the time, would later be an unusual activity for women: "That was the thing then—softball. 'Course it was fast pitch, underhand. Oh, they drew like crazy. Filled, packed stadiums all the time. . . . I'm surprised that they don't have that now. . . . Then it was just like it should have been, like girls' softball was always going to be."[16]

As players moved into upper skill levels, they found that beyond mere acceptance, their talents earned public recognition and reward. They particularly relished the large audiences, impressive stadiums, and attendant sense of making it to the "big time." Josephine D'Angelo recalled her softball days in Chicago:

> We had lights, you know, it was a big deal for me. . . . [Shrewbridge Field] was *very* classy. You had dugouts, you had enclosed seating—grandstand seating. We had locker rooms, shower rooms. Before, . . . you'd come right home, just carry your spikes and put on shoes and go home. That was it. So then you got into the big time, it was kind of nice. Crowds of five thousand were nothing at Shrewbridge Field in those days.[17]

Softball players also enjoyed the social life surrounding sport. Though most led busy lives, going to school or working during the day and playing late into the evenings, they still found time to gather at neighborhood bars or restaurants after practices or games. Just as sports like golf and tennis were linked to the upper-class sociability of country clubs, taverns and bars became integral to working-class sports like softball.

In the late 1930s and 1940s, the game's working-class image led to a redefinition of softball as a masculine activity. Women continued as avid participants. But as the sport became more firmly identified with masculine skill, talented female players who demonstrated speed, power, and competitive zeal began to strike critics as peculiarly masculine. Softball's blue-collar reputation only reinforced this connotation. The rugged play, connection to bar life, and the working-class base of softball combined to give the sport a tough, masculine sensibility despite its earlier association with "kittenish" women.

As a result the media lost some of their initial enthusiasm for women's softball. In their 1940 book *Softball! So What*, authors Lowell Thomas and Ted Shane took an apparently positive view, applauding the women's game as an activity that didn't "bunch muscles, give girls a weightlifter's figure, develop varsity-club leg, the usual penalty of fiendish exercise." Yet the authors observed that women often failed to exhibit ladylike manners on the field. Moreover, these "unladylike" athletes resisted "anything effeminate" in the rules, letting out "such a holler as could be heard from Sappho to Amazonia" when men tried to modify the rules for women.[18] Thomas and Shane introduced an element of ridicule by referring to the penalties of "fiendish exercise" and by intimating an association between softball and lesbianism through allusions to Sappho and Amazons.

A double message filtered through to ballplayers. Athletes came to understand that, although the fans loved softball, "There was something wrong with you because you could play ball. You were masculine and all that."[19] This mixed message, and the gender anxieties that infused it, found clear expression in a 1942 *Saturday Evening Post* article on women's softball. Author Robert Yoder granted that "there beats a feminine heart" beneath women ballplayers' sweat-soaked uniforms. But he sounded a note of warning as well, commenting that women "occasionally play like men, and occasionally even look like men." Manly female softball players posed a stark contrast to "the frailest creature on the field [who] is frequently that undeveloped shrimp, the male umpire."[20] By juxtaposing powerful "mannish" women and frail male authority, in the person of the umpire, Yoder expressed the fear that skilled women athletes threatened men's physical prowess and ability to rule.

The fears of male reporters did not dampen popular interest in the game, however. Softball continued to grow in the 1940s as both a spectator and participant sport. Especially during the war years, when most young men vacated the ball fields for military duty, women's softball flourished. With feature articles like "The Batter Half," "Miss Casey at the Bat," and "Queens of

Diamonds," the women's game received unprecedented coverage in nationally prominent publications like *Collier's*, the *Saturday Evening Post*, and the *New York Times Magazine*.[21]

⸺◦◦⸺

The popularity of softball intrigued chewing-gum magnate Philip K. Wrigley. As the owner of the Chicago Cubs major league baseball franchise, Wrigley worried about the wartime depletion of major league baseball. Speculating that a women's league could temporarily replace the men's game, keeping stadiums occupied and fan interest alive, in December 1942 Wrigley hatched a plan for a women's professional baseball league.

The All-American Girls Softball League (changed after two years to "Baseball") began play in 1943. As it became clear that the major league men's game would survive the war, Wrigley lost interest and sold his share of the AAGBL to Arthur Meyerhoff, his close associate and advertising agent. From 1944 through 1950, Meyerhoff's Chicago-based Management Corporation administered the league, with assistance from a board of directors and league commissioner. In 1951 disgruntled team owners in the sponsoring cities bought out Meyerhoff and decentralized the league's organization during its last four seasons.[22]

The AAGBL opened in four midwestern cities, Kenosha and Racine, Wisconsin; South Bend, Indiana; and Rockford, Illinois. After a slow start, attendance climbed steadily, and Wrigley's experiment gained a foothold in the professional sports world. The league later expanded to include teams in Kalamazoo, Grand Rapids, Battle Creek, and Muskegon, Michigan; Fort Wayne, Indiana; and Peoria, Illinois; with short-lived attempts in Chicago, Milwaukee, Minneapolis, as well as Springfield, Illinois. It became much more than a wartime surrogate. It spanned the years 1943–1954 and at its peak operated in ten cities and drew nearly one million fans.

The AAGBL's early success sparked the formation of a rival league in 1944. The National Girls Baseball League (NGBL) initially consisted of four semipro teams that had dominated women's softball in the Chicago area—the Parichy Bloomer Girls, the Music Maids, the Rockola Chicks, and the Match Corp.

Queens. The league expanded to six teams and attracted five hundred thousand annual spectators by the late 1940s. As a Chicago-based venture, the NGBL never attracted the regional support or national publicity that the All-American league did. Nevertheless, it proved to be a constant thorn in the AAGBL's side, leading to salary wars, talent raiding, and an eventual lawsuit.[23]

The rival leagues also developed competing philosophies. NGBL leaders adhered to the formula that had already earned women's softball an enthusiastic following. They did not tamper with the rules, opting to preserve the underhand pitch, larger ball, and shorter basepaths of softball as well as the traditional softball uniforms of shorts or knickers.[24] And while not above printing stylized depictions of shapely, sexy ballplayers on team publicity guides, NGBL officials made little attempt to counter softball's mannish stigma, betting instead on the proven popularity of the women's game to override negative publicity.

Wrigley, who was personally repelled by the "pants-wearing, tough-talking female softballer," devised a different approach, calculated to circumvent the masculine image of women's softball.[25] Insisting that the women adopt the rules of men's baseball, management gradually extended the basepaths and abandoned softball's underhand pitch for a side-arm delivery, eventually switching over entirely to the smaller ball size and overhand pitching of baseball. By introducing baseball to women, Wrigley and Meyerhoff hoped to sustain wartime interest in the sport while putting distance between their women's league and the tarnished reputation of women's softball.

But wouldn't women playing the traditionally male sport of baseball also be perceived as masculine? Wrigley and Meyerhoff decided that instead of suppressing the tension between femininity and male sport, they would accentuate it. They sold the league as a dramatic spectacle of gender contrasts, presenting women's baseball as a unique combination of feminine beauty and masculine athletic skill. Meyerhoff described the game as a "colorful sports show" in which spectators would be awed by the "novelty" of seeing "baseball, traditionally a men's game, played by feminine type girls with masculine skill."[26]

League officials believed that by highlighting this gender contrast they could offer fans an exciting, novel brand of baseball while avoiding the mannish image of softball and other women's sports. First time customers would come to view the "amazing spectacle of beskirted girls throwing, catching, hitting and running like men." As to whether the initial novelty effect might wear off, Meyerhoff supposed that "girls" playing a man's game would remain "a constant source of amazement and wonder to most fans," banking as well on "the fact that the All-American players are 'nice girls' " who would win lasting fan interest and sympathy.[27]

This shrewd approach played on conflicting public sentiments of the 1940s. Plagued by severe labor shortages, wartime government officials called upon women to fill jobs in defense industries and other sectors of the economy. Yet even as government and business leaders praised "Rosie the Riveter" for being willing and able to step into men's shoes, women's massive entrance into manufacturing generated as much anxiety as approbation. Would women doing "men's jobs" lose their femininity? Would the social and economic independence women found during the war permanently alter their relationships with men? And most of all, when men returned, would women relinquish their jobs to male workers?[28] Wrigley and his associates tailored their promotional strategy to address these public concerns.

League officials sought to capitalize on the general support for women stepping into male roles, at the same time reassuring spectators that women playing a "man's game" remained "normal" in every other respect. Thus the AAGBL maintained a clear sense of appropriate divisions between men and women. The league office strongly discouraged the hiring of female coaches. Instead, owners sought credibility and name recognition by hiring ex-major league baseball players and coaches as managers. Speaking from a position of masculine expertise and authority, male AAGBL officials stressed the contrast between masculine sport and the All-American Girls' feminine beauty. Meyerhoff coined the term "femininity principle" to encapsulate the league's commitment to preserving feminine ideals.

In accordance with the femininity principle, management instructed recruiters to weigh both ability and appearance in prospective players. In a section titled "Femininity with Skill," the league handbook reasoned that it was "more dramatic to see a feminine-type girl throw, run and bat than to see a man or boy or masculine-type girl do the same things. *The more feminine the appearance of the performer, the more dramatic the performance.*"[29] The guide further explained that the league's rules must go hand in hand with players' own efforts to project the desired image:

> For the benefit of self and game every player devotes himself [*sic*] to cultivation of both skill and femininity. . . . Masculine appearance or mannerisms produce an impression either of a masculine girl or an effeminate boy, both effects prejudicial to the dramatic contrast of feminine aspect and masculine skill.[30]

Although AAGBL officials absolutely forbade bawdiness or sexual antics reminiscent of barnstorming teams from an earlier era, the carefully crafted impression of femininity included a sexual element. Stressing a kind of respectable femininity, the league boasted that the All-American players were "nice girls" with a "high moral tone," further safeguarded by the watchful eye of a team chaperone. Meyerhoff nevertheless understood that sex appeal would attract customers. By insisting on short skirts, makeup, and physical attractiveness, he pushed an ideal of wholesome, feminine sexuality. A description of the league in the major league *Baseball Blue Book* captured the essence of the ploy, explaining on the one hand that, "The players did not reflect sex-consciousness. On the other hand, if by "sex" is meant the normal appeal of the feminine mode and attitude, then most certainly sex was an important source of interest and a legitimate element of the league's success."[31]

To ensure that players did in fact embody the desired "feminine mode and attitude," the league's first few spring training sessions featured a mandatory evening charm school, which players attended after a long day of tryouts and preseason conditioning. Led one year by beauticians from the Helena Rubinstein salon and another by *Chicago Tribune* beauty editor Eleanor Mangle, the experts coached players on makeup, posture, fashion, table manners, and "graceful social deportment at large."[32] Guidelines on personal appearance accompanied the beauty tips. Reminding players that "boyish bobs and other imitations of masculine style and habit are taboo," management ordered players to keep their hair shoulder length or longer, to wear makeup and nail polish, and never to appear in public wearing shorts, slacks, or jeans.[33]

Although the league dropped the charm school after its value as a public relations stunt ebbed, management's stress on feminine dress and manner never wavered. In fact, as the league's popularity declined after 1948, written dress codes took on a shrill, urgent tone. A 1950 directive from the main office announced: "This league has only two things to sell to the public, baseball and femininity." The memo warned recalcitrant players that they "will feel the sting of a shortened pay check if they don't comply."[34] In 1951 team owners adopted a new constitution that further elaborated dress guidelines:

> *Always appear in feminine attire.* This precludes the use of any wearing attire of masculine nature. MASCULINE HAIR STYLING? SHOES? COATS? SHIRTS? SOCKS, T-SHIRTS ARE BARRED AT ALL TIMES.[35]

To create the desired effect, team owners exercised their right to reject "masculine" players and to fine or release players who violated league rules. Infractions included not only neglecting dress and hair requirements, but "moral lapses" ranging from a bad attitude to negotiations with the NGBL or obvious lesbianism. League officials fired at least one player from the league for her sexual behavior and dismissed another player for her "severe" haircut.[36]

The AAGBL also had an unwritten policy against hiring women of color, though it did employ several light-skinned Cuban players. Not until 1951, five years after the integration of professional men's baseball, did the league openly discuss hiring black women. Torn between the need for skilled players and a desire to promote a particular image of femininity, officials decided against recruiting African Americans "unless they would show promise of exceptional ability."[37] This decision, and the fact that no black players were ever recruited, reflects the pervasive racism in American society during the 1940s and 1950s. But it also can be understood in relation to the league's special emphasis on femininity, an image rooted in white middle-class beliefs about beauty and respectability. This feminine ideal tended to exclude or deprecate black women, making black athletes almost by definition less likely to meet league standards.

Along with strict guidelines on recruiting and dress, the league established a conduct code to monitor players' behavior. The code discouraged public drinking and smoking, required players to obtain prior approval for social engagements and living arrangements, and imposed an evening curfew. To enforce the rules, each team hired a chaperone responsible for reporting violations to the management.[38] Officials hoped that stringent regulations would surround women's baseball "with such safeguards as to warrant public confidence in its integrity and method."[39]

Public relations wizard Meyerhoff also developed several promotional schemes toward this end. He varied spring training sites annually in order to increase media and audience exposure. In later years the league established two touring teams that exhibited the AAGBL's brand of ball to enthusiastic crowds in midwestern, northeastern, and southern states, at the same time functioning as a minor league program to hone the skills of potential league players.[40] Management also courted national media attention. A crew from Movietone News followed the league to its 1947 spring training in Havana, Cuba, where it filmed a preseason game before a crowd of 25,000. Later released as a newsreel called *Diamond Gals*, it exposed millions of moviegoers in theaters around the country to the spectacle of All-American Girls baseball. Meyerhoff's office carefully orchestrated contacts with the media, providing glossy photos of the league's most beautiful players, issuing copies of the league's dress and conduct codes, and emphasizing the difference between baseball and softball. To quiet lingering suspicions about masculinity or lesbianism, AAGBL officials informed the media that league rules allowed "no freaks or Amazons."[41]

While national feature stories in *Collier's*, the *Saturday Evening Post* and *Holiday* highlighted the sex appeal and sensationalism of the league, local promoters stressed their team's contributions to community life and the players' "girl next door" image. AAGBL teams returned a portion of their proceeds to the community by supporting local recreation programs and facility maintenance. Individual players made personal contact with community members by rooming with local families, giving clinics, attending banquets hosted by service organizations like the Elks or the Woman's Club, and making public appearances at community events.

It is difficult to determine whether the league's "femininity concept" was instrumental in a team's success or failure. Many factors contributed to a particular team's fortunes, including financial backing, competition for the entertainment dollar, team strength, and management ability. AAGBL teams fared best in medium-size cities like Rockford and Fort Wayne. Unlike such larger cities as Chicago, Milwaukee, and Minneapolis, where franchises failed, these small industrial centers combined a keen interest in baseball with the absence of other professional sports ventures in competition for the limited market. While crowds may have responded positively to the feminine style and wholesome values projected by the league, good press coverage, skilled play, intense competition, and intercity rivalries proved equally important in courting a solid following.[42] The continued popularity of semipro and amateur softball teams with no special focus on femininity suggests that success did not depend on the "femininity principle." In Peoria, for example, for several seasons the AAGBL Redwings struggled to stay afloat while the powerhouse Peoria Dieselettes softball team remained a popular favorite. And in Chicago the NGBL offered a legitimate and successful alternative to the Wrigley-Meyerhoff brand of "feminine" baseball.

AAGBL officials, however, remained firmly convinced that the contrast between feminine appearance and masculine skill accounted for the league's success. Although financial problems, high manager turnover, and franchise failure plagued the league, teams that survived the initial trial period found a home in medium-size entertainment markets. Fans in these cities exhibited an impressive loyalty to hometown teams with feminized names like the Daisies, Lassies, Peaches, and Belles. In Racine the Belles attracted more spectators than any local men's sports team. And prior to the lean years of the early 1950s, total league attendance for a 120-game schedule averaged between five hundred thousand and one million customers. When these numbers plummeted in the 1950s, the Rockford Peaches were saved from collapse by dedicated fans who raised the money to keep their team afloat. As former Rockford and Kenosha player Mary Pratt remembered, "The fans thought that we were the best thing that ever came down the pike. They really looked up to us."[43] No other women's team sport, before or since, created such a viable professional organization.

⌐○⌐

Recruited from nearly every state and several Canadian provinces, women ballplayers jumped at the opportunity to join the AAGBL. League pay scales ranged from $40 to $85 per week in the early years, climbing up to $125 per week later.[44] To Jean Havlish of the Fort Wayne Daisies, the thrill of playing professionally was "like a dream . . . to get paid for doing something you liked so well." And according to Nora Cross, nothing could top the "incredible" feeling of "getting paid for doing something that was such a joy to do."[45]

Excited and grateful for the chance to play, All-American players accepted the league's "femininity principle," but not without reservations. Many AAGBL members grew up playing ball in supportive communities, little aware of cultural criticisms of women athletes. Eventually, however, athletes encountered the "mannish" stigma surrounding women's sports, softball in particular. They learned that "in the eyes of other people, they think you're a tough when you play baseball and slide and all this stuff."[46] As sensitive as they were to such negative portrayals, All-American players did not necessarily share management's concern with femininity. Interviews with former league members indicate that the concerted attention to gender originated from league directives, not from athletes' own priorities. Players expressed a variety of opinions about AAGBL policies on dress, appearance, and conduct, agreeing only that these issues took a backseat to the much more important matter at hand, the fantastic opportunity to play a game they loved.

Athletes with strong backgrounds in organized softball showed initial dismay at the prospect of playing in a skirt, but they eventually adjusted. "When I first started," recalled the Racine Belles' Anna May Hutchison, "I thought, Gosh, how the heck are we going to play ball in those things? . . . But once you got used to 'em they were just your uniform and that was it."[47] Shirley Jameson described her feelings as "ambivalent," noting that while the uniforms "were very feminine, and you could do the job," because they offered little leg protection, "I spent most of the season with strawberries on both legs" from sliding.[48] Others loved the sharp look of the uniform and spoke of it with pride. Pitcher and second basewoman Nora Cross remembered how "I loved that uniform. . . . When I'd see girls in the softball uniforms, jocks, running around, I didn't like it nearly as much. I was really thankful for the skirt." Individual preferences aside, many players believed that if the uniforms created a good public impression, contributing to the league's survival, they benefited the players regardless of personal taste.

All-American players displayed a similar range of opinion about the dress and conduct codes that regulated off-field behavior. Nora Cross and Jean Havlish found the rules agreeable. They recognized that because of the discredited image of women athletes, "You had to be careful so you wouldn't give someone a bad impression. . . . You had to be . . . above reproach in everything so you wouldn't hurt the image of the league. Because . . . if people didn't want to come out and watch you play ball, then you don't play ball."[49] Phyllis Koehn agreed:

> There were several organized teams in Chicago at that time. . . . And they wore their hair short. I mean they weren't a bit feminine looking. . . . When this league started that was one definite thing that Wrigley said, that the women would have to look like women and act like women. And that's why they put the rules in, which I think was a good thing. It made a real nice image for the league.[50]

Others chafed under the regulations but conformed out of a calculated estimation of the risks. To Delores Moore "It was worth it to abide by it [the dress code] to play on the team. If I bucked them . . . and was too much of a nonconformist I think they would have ousted me." Pepper Paire added, "You have to understand that we'd rather play ball than eat, and where else could we go and get paid $100 a week to play ball? So, if some of the girls liked to wear their hair a little bit short, or liked to run around in jeans, they bent with the rules." Yet Paire also remembered that "there were a few little ways of getting around the rules, as long as you were discreet and didn't flaunt it."[51] Faye Dancer, one of the league's more outspoken and flamboyant players, recounted her own approach to the rules: "I always respected the rules. I *broke* them all, but I respected them."[52]

The charm school was one of the league's most controversial gimmicks. Shirley Jameson conceded that the charm training served a purpose but complained that the charm teachers "didn't seem to be tuned in to what we had to do. Some of it was apropos, but a lot of it you just couldn't use playing baseball."[53] Several players viewed charm training as a "promotional deal" or as a "silly" or "sickening" joke, and they rankled at the implied criticism of women ballplayers. Understanding full well that "they wanted us to be feminine . . . because people thought that probably women in sports were all tomboys," these players laughed at the idea that the league could alter the style of ballplayers.[54] Irene Kotowicz stated the case plainly: "That wasn't for us. . . . We just went out and did our thing. And when they foisted the cosmeticians and the how-to-walk, how-to-this, it was a joke to us—to some of us." Several players realized that the charm school, along with the general emphasis on femininity, was specifically intended to dispel lesbian stereotypes. Even as a young athlete just out of high school, Josephine D'Angelo discerned the league's logic: "I was old enough to understand what they were trying to do. They didn't want to bring a bunch of butchy people or have anybody say—they didn't even use the word 'lesbians' in those days, they just used the word 'queers.' . . . And it was a good move, it was wise. They wanted everybody to look like a girl."

Whether pleased or angered by the league's philosophy, women who wanted more than anything else to play ball recognized that the AAGBL's approach made pragmatic sense. The majority were willing to do whatever they were told in order to protect their chance to play professionally. They viewed the league's regulations as job requirements, which—as in any other job—they must follow or risk dismissal. In an era in which women found few enjoyable, well-paid jobs, Anna May Hutchison never thought about challenging management: "I don't think there was any question about it. I mean, that was our job, and we had to do what they said."[55] Even to players bothered by the restrictions, the chance to play ball professionally was well worth the cost of compliance, especially in light of other work options. Irene Kotowicz spoke for many when she summed up her years in the AAGBL: "We traveled, we saw, we met people. We had fun and we got paid more than we'd ever do working—you know, eight hours every day."

Such sentiments, however, did not prevent players from making fun of the league's hypersensitivity to the issue of femininity. They viewed the subject with humor, using parody and camp to offset the league's deadly serious view of the matter. In 1950, members of the South Bend Blue Sox wrote a skit for their team banquet. The short play featured a locker-room scene involving three players, "Bonnie," "Candy," and "Goo Goo." The characters turn both the stereotype of mannish athletes and the league's concern with femininity into ludicrous nonsense.

The skit opens with the three women suiting up for the evening's ball game. As they dress, Bonnie informs Candy about a recent date, recounting: "So I says to this big lug, 'Don't think just because I catch for the Mishawaka Mudhens that I don't like to be treated like a lady.' . . . He kept getting more and more fresh, so I simply tossed him in the river." Candy replies, "I don't blame you honey. Some guys don't know how to treat a lady." Meanwhile, Goo Goo enters the conversation, asking to borrow Bonnie's razor. She promptly proceeds to lather and shave her face! The activity is not remarked on, and the discussion continues with Candy telling Bonnie about the date she has planned for later that evening. Bonnie encourages her, saying: "Hell, get 'em while you can, I say. . . . Disguise those muscles. Remember once the men find out that you've got more hair on your chest than they have, you're licked." As the three players head for the field, Goo Goo collapses in pain. Candy asks, "What's the matter? Is she having a temperamental fit?" Bonnie replies, "No, but you better call off the game. She's having a baby." And the skit ends.[56]

Its authors turned the league's concern with players' mannish ways, masculine bodies, and possible lesbianism into an absurd scramble of gender and sexual images, including mention of shaving, girdles, bras, jockstraps, fighting, flirting, dating, and pregnancy. In the tangle of images, the players simultaneously affirm their toughness and their womanhood. The themes of dating and pregnancy appear to indicate the authors' wish to establish their heterosexuality, yet the caricatured portrayals serve equally to make fun of the league's concern with sexual reputations. Moreover, Candy, Goo Goo, and Bonnie display an assertive, calculated sexuality that veers away from the "nice girl" image projected by the league. The authors thus inverted and toyed with gender and sexual conventions. They questioned the validity of league policies, at the same time suggesting that their compliance involved an element of playacting.

Although they laughed at management's contorted efforts to defend their femininity, AAGBL players took the "mannish" stereotype seriously, in part because it intruded on their self-interpretations as "normal" women. They denied that either they or their teammates were "mannish" athletes. But ballplayers disagreed over whether the charge of "mannishness" could be accurately applied to other athletes, especially to women in the reputedly more "masculine" NGBL.

To some AAGBL players, the NGBL featured precisely those "mannish" types who damaged softball's reputation. Dottie Green described the league as "beneath us, really. I saw some of the people who came from there, and they weren't number one characters." Phyllis Koehn agreed, adding: "They looked tough to me. . . . They wore regular long pants, you know. And then there'd be beer drinking and things like that on the bench. And after the game . . . they went in their uniforms right into the tavern." Noting their long pants, jackets, short haircuts, and tendency to drink and smoke in public, Dottie Ferguson Key described the NGBL players as "a little more, well, what you'd say tomboy."[57]

Players like Key and Green expressed their gender qualms in terms of class. Key noted, "It hit me right away—it just wasn't our class." Linking "mannish" or tomboy qualities to the working-class environment of the NGBL, Dottie Green explained, "They weren't athletes, they were just tough girls. . . . When you get a team from one metropolis like Chicago, they didn't have much choice to do much else but be rough, tough, and nasty." The class prejudice captured in the distinction between "tough girls" and "athletes" surfaced even among players who came from blue-collar backgrounds. This distinction was a gender-specific version of the historic tension between "rough" and "respectable" working-class styles. Discussed informally by some athletes, it found official expression in the AAGBL's effort to contrast the "mannish" softball tough with the feminine "nice girl" athlete.

Others questioned this distinction, countering with the claim that women ballplayers from both leagues were just that— women and ballplayers—and nothing in their appearance or actions should suggest otherwise. Women who had played in both leagues saw little difference between them. Irene Kotowicz disputed the tough reputation of the NGBL: "I wouldn't say that the girls in the softball league were tougher. I mean, we had some tough ones in the All-American League. . . . To me it was the same." Josephine D'Angelo concurred, stating that there was "no difference whatsoever. Only the costume, and the availability of good supplies [differed]." Delores Moore took personal exception to criticism of the NGBL. Hearing an AAGBL player criticize the National League, she fumed, "I felt like getting up and telling her, 'Look, lady, there's good and bad in everything.' . . . There were nice ladies in the National League just as well as there weren't." Unlike the players who accepted the charge that "tough" women athletes were mannish, NGBL defenders rejected this notion and the idea that displays of femininity made AAGBL players any more "classy" than other athletes. Moore concluded, "The National League didn't have charm school, but they had nice ladies."

Whatever their views on the NGBL, AAGBL players did not experience their own involvement in sport as a masculine endeavor and seem not to have felt a tension between sport and female identity. They uniformly stated that masculinity or femininity had nothing to do with their athletic pursuits. Irene Kotowicz insisted, "We never even though of that! What somebody thought about me, I don't know. . . . We just did our thing. And we didn't think of images, we didn't think of anything."

Rejecting definitions of athletic skill as a masculine attribute, players often described their athletic ability as a natural gift. Phyllis Koehn explained: "We all might have played baseball in our sandlots, but heavenly days, none of us acted like men, I'll tell you that. . . . It's ridiculous. It's something born in you—to be a natural athlete." In contrast to the Wrigley-Meyerhoff concept of the AAGBL as a unique blend of masculinity and femininity, players did not perceive themselves or the league as a dramatic novelty of gender contrast. Rather, they found drama in the thrill of competition and novelty in the rare opportunity to work, travel, and meet people while pursuing their passion for baseball.

By the early 1950s players were in danger of losing this unprecedented opportunity. While the All-American Girls played tirelessly and enthusiastically over the long summer months, the AAGBL management waged a constant battle against financial woes and franchise collapse. With even the most solid teams operating in the red, mainstays like Racine and South Bend withdrew from the league, which shrank to five teams in 1954. By the end of the season, league directors conceded that they could not maintain even this skeleton structure. The board of directors canceled the 1955 season, with the still-unrealized promise to reorganize in the future.

Internal and external problems contributed to the AAGBL's decline. Internally the insistence on baseball rules caused the AAGBL to lose contact with its greatest source of talent, semipro and amateur softball players. After the early years the league fought a constant battle to find quality pitching and young talent. Many of the best softball pitchers were unable or unwilling to make the transition to pitching overhand. Moreover, the league faced a general problem competing for talent with the NGBL and top amateur softball teams. Bidding wars for star players raised salaries and added to the bitterness between the two leagues. Some players jumped leagues or threatened to do so, prompting the owner of the South Bend Blue Sox to complain, "These girls have no idea of loyalty. . . . They are sure a bunch of tough actors and will gouge you regardless."[58] In the end management emphasis on the superiority of women's baseball over softball may have impaired the league's ability to survive.

Ironically, the very popularity of organized baseball may also have created unforeseen problems. Organized leagues tended toward strict gender segregation. Especially with the growth of Little League baseball in the 1950s, fewer girls grew up playing neighborhood baseball on mixed sandlot and playground teams, shrinking the overall talent pool from which great players emerged. League efforts to cultivate young talent through junior leagues and exhibition tours did not produce the hoped-for results, causing league commissioner Fred Leo to lament, "We have too many oldtimers."[59]

Even if the league had overcome such problems, however, developments in postwar American society posed an even greater set of obstacles. As city dwellers joined the suburban exodus and television took the entertainment world by storm, home recreation became the order of the day. Major league spectator sports like football and baseball continued to draw large audiences, but attendance dropped at all other levels. Women's industrial leagues suffered especially. As returning veterans replaced women in the work force, industrial sports as well as jobs once again became the domain of men. Girls' and women's leagues continued to operate, but as very minor programs. And while top-notch amateur and semipro women's softball teams never ceased providing skilled athletes a place to develop and compete, in most communities Little League baseball, men's industrial softball, and minor league baseball commanded the lion's share of funds, facilities, and civic backing.

The presence of women, even "feminine beauties," in "masculine athletics" clashed with the conservative culture of the 1950s. In contrast to the giddy sense of workplace competence and freedom women experienced in the war years, the 1950s witnessed a swift turnabout, propelling women back into domesticity. The emphasis on home, family, and marriage symbolized a return to restrictive definitions of femininity. With baseball firmly reestablished as the national (men's) pastime and femininity once again defined in terms of domestic life, the league's innovative effort to combine sport and femininity and its vigorous affirmation of female athletic ability were at odds with the cultural current.

Virulent homophobia—the fear and hatred of gays and lesbians—accompanied the conservative shift in gender roles. An upsurge of media interest in sex crimes and "perversion" intensified public hostility toward homosexuality. Police raids on gay bars, military purges, and the firing of homosexual government employees under Cold War security policies added to the homosexual panic of the 1950s.[60] In an era of political, legal, and media attacks on homosexuals, the association of women's sport with "mannishness," often a coded reference to lesbianism, jeopardized any attempt to market women's baseball as mass entertainment.

⌐○⌐

AAGBL leaders staked the future of women's baseball on its ability to reassure audiences that women could play baseball with no cost to their womanly charm or baseball's manly reputation. This carefully conceived strategy ultimately blunted the challenge that women's baseball posed to the gender arrangements of American society. By promoting the AAGBL as a spectacle of "feminine-type girls" playing a "man's game," while at the same time condemning the mannishness of female softball players, Wrigley and Meyerhoff effectively reinforced the masculine connotation of both baseball and softball. Far from incorporating athleticism into an expansive femininity, the AAGBL's "femininity principle" advanced a narrow definition of womanhood grounded in restrictive standards of dress, behavior, sexual attractiveness, and "nice girl" respectability.

Leaders of the AAGBL fell into the trap that many other advocates of women's sport have stumbled into—they promoted the very gender distinctions that denied women athletic credibility in the first place. Their efforts to maintain the distinction between feminine appearance and masculine skill existed uneasily alongside the obvious fact that women were indeed crossing boundaries into a male sphere, combining attributes of athletic skill and femininity previously understood as incompatible. By the 1950s this combination seemed more threatening than novel. In a decade that sought security through celebrating the private nuclear family, restoring female domesticity, and championing America's "virile" political might, women's baseball seemed oddly misplaced.

Yet the legacy of women's baseball is a complex one. Although AAGBL policies mandated a concept of femininity consistent with firmly entrenched norms, the existence of highly skilled, well-attended women's softball and baseball leagues subverted the notion that athletic skill belonged in the province of men. Women's leagues provided a once-in-a-lifetime opportunity for female ballplayers to develop their skills and pursue their passion for sport, aided by financial backing, quality coaching, and generous crowds. The players returned the favor, offering delighted spectators the chance to see women playing a brand of competitive, aggressive, superior ball that defied social conventions and athletic traditions. Contrary to official efforts to distinguish between feminine womanhood and masculine ability, women ballplayers offered the public an exciting and expanded sense of female capabilities. Among appreciative fans and players, the "mannish athlete" receded into the shadows of the athletic woman.

CHAPTER 7

# BEAUTY AND THE BUTCH

## *The "Mannish" Athlete and the Lesbian Threat*

⌒○⌒

By mid-century the persistent attempts of women athletes and their advocates to project an image of attractive femininity had failed to sunder the perceived connection between female athleticism and a rough, ill-bred "mannishness."[1] In fact, the task had become doubly difficult in the conservative post–World War II era. During these years women athletes encountered a growing suspicion that they were not only gender anomalies but might be sexual aberrants as well.

Both professional experts and casual observers of the postwar period linked mannish athleticism with lesbianism, sometimes in explicit terms but more typically through indirect reference or veiled suggestion. At a 1956 conference for directors of college women's physical education, guest speaker Dr. Josephine Renshaw warned educators about the danger of same-sex attachments among college female athletes. Her talk, "Activities for Mature Living," advised the audience to do all in their power to encourage heterosexual interest in women athletes because the "muscular Amazon with unkempt hair, clod-hopper shoes, and dowdy clothing" might "revert to friendships with [her] own sex if disappointed in heterosexual attachments."[2]

Given the long association between athleticism and male virility, it was not surprising that there should be speculation about lesbianism among athletes. For decades critics of women's sport had linked "mannishness" to sexual deviance, claiming that mas-

164

culinized female athletes would inevitably acquire masculine sexual characteristics and interests as well. The fear of female sexuality unleashed from feminine modesty and male control runs like a constant thread through the history of women's sport. However, the nature of such fears and the understanding of "mannish" female sexuality had changed significantly between early and mid-century.

Between 1900 and 1930 the sexual debate in sport centered on the problem of unbridled heterosexual desire, the prospect that "masculine" sport might loosen women's inhibitions toward men. But by the 1930s female athletic mannishness began to connote failed (rather than excessive) heterosexuality. Citing expert opinion that intense competition would disfigure the athletic woman and make her unappealing to men, author Fred Wittner asserted in 1934 that as an "inevitable consequence" of athletic training, "girls trained in physical education to-day may find it more difficult to attract the most worthy fathers for their children."[3]

The impression of heterosexual "failure" contained a further possibility as well: The amazonian athlete might be not only unattractive but unattracted to men—she might prefer women. What began as a vague suggestion of lesbianism emerged as a full-blown stereotype of the "mannish lesbian athlete" in the years after World War II. As a stigmatized figure the mannish lesbian functioned as a powerful but unarticulated "bogeywoman" of sport, silently foiling the ongoing efforts of sport advocates to rehabilitate the reputation of women athletes and resolve the cultural contradiction between athletic prowess and femininity.

When American women first entered the sports scene in significant numbers, their detractors insisted that strenuous activity would make the female athlete "mannish." In early-twentieth-century parlance, "mannishness" was an all-encompassing concept signifying female masculinity. But the term contained at least three more-specific charges within the general one: that too much exercise would damage female reproductive capacity; that women athletes would adopt masculine dress, talk, and mannerisms; and that the passion and excitement of sport would lead women to the brink of moral, physical, and emotional breakdown. These claims contained a compelling logic despite their tone, which often bordered on the hysterical. The stated dangers—reproductive incapacity, masculine activities and attributes, and loss of control—contrasted sharply with the maternal, controlled, ultra-feminine image of the Victorian lady. Because fit athletes seemed to violate the cardinal tenets of late-Victorian society, they appeared unfit for womanhood.

Proponents of this idea took it one step further, predicting that "mannish" athletes would also acquire masculine sexual characteristics. But the question remained: Would they simply gain the erotic appetite and sexual aggressiveness of men, or would mannish women also seek out the normative objects of male desire—other women?

Claims linking the mannish female athlete to lesbianism had surfaced in the medical community as early as the 1880s. Because sexologists believed that sexual desire for women was an inherently male trait, they equated female same-sex desire with a total inversion of gender role. Theorists described lesbianism as a symptom and effect of an inverted gender identity, a biological and moral tragedy in which a male soul existed in a female body. Consequently it came as no surprise to find that the mannish "invert" enjoyed masculine sports. In his 1883 article, "Case of Sexual Perversion," P. M. Wise described the "peculiar girlhood" of a lesbian who had "preferred masculine sports and labor; had an aversion to attentions from young men and sought the society of her own sex."[4] Sexologist Havelock Ellis, whose *Studies in the Psychology of Sex* reached a more popular audience than did most scientific works, commented as well that among lesbians "There is often some capacity for athletics."[5]

Outside scientific circles, educators, athletic leaders, journalists, and social critics also contemplated the relationship between athletics and female sexuality. But they departed from scientific concerns by limiting their considerations to sport's impact on the female athlete's heterosexual behavior, never publicly addressing the possibility of lesbianism.[6] The reasons for this focus lie in the

particular anxieties that gripped a society in the throes of transformation from Victorian to modern sexual paradigms.

Early-twentieth-century Americans struggled to come to terms
with dramatic changes in heterosexual behavior. Victorians had
assigned eroticism to men, sexual purity and virtue to women.
However, in the first two decades of the new century even the
staunchest defenders of innate sexual difference had to admit that
a great divide separated social practice from Victorian ideals.
Along with women's entrance into public work and politics, the
assertion of female sexual desire posed one of the most serious
challenges to conventional gender arrangements. The growing
middle-class use of birth control, the explicit sexuality of working-class youth culture, and the sexual freedoms advocated by
radical intellectuals and bohemians caused widespread alarm.

Anxious professionals and social activists made concerted
efforts to shore up traditional values. Sexologists and medical
doctors responded to the social disorder by shining the scrutiniz-
ing light of science on female sexual behavior. At the same time
activists across the political spectrum addressed sexual issues
through social reform campaigns. Middle-class and wealthy conservatives decried the declining birthrate among educated native-
born Americans, looking to eugenics to solve the problem. Other
sexual reformers focused on the movies, penny arcades, cafés,
amusement parks, and street life of modern leisure culture, condemning the world of commercial entertainment and the "new
morality" it celebrated for promoting female sexual exploitation
and immorality.[7]

Until the 1930s the discourse about female sexuality in sport
centered around precisely those issues raised by reformers—
impaired reproductive capacity and incitement to sexual
immorality. Two frightful images hovered around women's
sports: The "damaged mother" warned of the harmful effect of
strenuous athletics on female reproductive health. And the muscular, sexually suspect "muscle moll" sacrificed her physical and
moral control to the "powerful impulses" of sport. Though both
represented femininity gone astray, each corresponded to a particular class-specific image circulating in the broader political dis-

course on female sexuality. The "damaged mother" had to do with fears about the declining middle-class birthrate, while the "muscle moll" reflected anxieties about the sexually active young working woman.

Physical educators and popular sport promoters responded differently to these concerns. When P.E. leaders condemned unregulated competition and public display of the female physique, they stated their allegiance to prevailing middle-class ideals of sexually protected, physically reserved womanhood.[8] AAU leaders countered educators' anticompetition position with the argument that, under proper guidance, strenuous activity would actually strengthen reproductive organs, enabling a vigorous cadre of mothers to produce a generation of stalwart American sons.[9] Commercial promoters took still another tack. By touting events as "feminine attractions," sponsors embraced female eroticism and rendered it reputable through the appealing figure of the sexy, robust athlete.

Within the tangle of competing approaches to sport and female sexuality, there was one note of agreement, however. All sides presumed heterosexuality. Those who feared sport's masculinizing effects warned that women would become more like men sexually—passionate, uncontrolled, assertive—but neither critics nor supporters suggested that "masculine" athleticism might indicate or induce same-sex love. Images of amazonian athletes spoke instead to the fear of heterosexual transgressions. In this view, the physical release of sport might effect a loss of heterosexual control, not inclination. The most frequently used derogatory term for women athletes was "muscle moll." In its only other usages, the word "moll" referred to either the female lovers of male gangsters or to prostitutes. Both represented disreputable, heterosexually deviant womanhood.

Given that medical experts had long associated homosexuality with female athleticism, it is curious that early-twentieth-century sport advocates did not refer to or deny lesbianism when answering charges against the mannish "muscle moll." However, as the origins of the term "moll" indicate, the primary image of deviant sexuality in this period was one of promiscuous working-class sexuality, an image which evoked the even graver danger of prostitution.[10] Moreover, the "mannish lesbian" made little sense in the milieu of popular sports. Mixed-sex crowds, an image of the athlete as beauty queen, and the commercial atmosphere that characterized much of working-class sport ensured that the sexual debate surrounding the modern female athlete would focus on her heterosexual charm, daring, or disrepute. The all-female environment of women's P.E. left educators more vulnerable to insinuations that their profession was populated by "mannish" types who preferred the love of women. However, the feminine respectability and decorum cultivated by the profession provided an initial shield from associations with either the mannish lesbian or her more familiar counterpart, the heterosexual "muscle moll."

In subsequent decades the heterosexual understanding of the "mannish amazon" gave way to a new interpretation. The 1920s and 1930s mark a transition period in which changing sexual practices and beliefs laid the groundwork for later associations between women's athletics and "mannish" lesbianism. A series of related cultural, economic, and intellectual changes form the backdrop to the shifting understanding of mannishness in sport.

Most centrally, by the late 1920s widespread changes in heterosexual behavior and values had weakened perceptions of the female athlete as dangerously erotic or "oversexed." Many "Jazz Age" heterosexuals embraced a modern sexual code that valorized companionship and sexual intimacy between men and women. This new morality recognized female eroticism, granting approval as long as women channeled their desire toward heterosexual romance and eventual marriage. The modern woman, especially as epitomized by the "flapper" of the 1920s, placed sexual vitality at the center of new definitions of femininity.[11]

Changes in the U.S. economy contributed to the emphasis on erotic femininity. The economy increasingly depended on consumer goods like cosmetics, ready-made clothing, and automobiles—products that either promised to enhance sex appeal or utilized sexual imagery in advertising. Moreover, commercial forms of leisure like movies, dancehalls, and amusement parks brought young men and women together in a shared entertainment culture. The central place of sexuality in modern consumer culture and popular leisure situated it at the core of twentieth-century ideas about femininity and personal identity. Assertive heterosexuality, once a sign of sexual deviance, now formed the standard of acceptable femininity. One advertisement stated the case simply: *"The first duty of woman is to attract."*[12]

As new sexual norms affirmed female eroticism, the line dividing acceptable from illicit or deviant sexuality necessarily shifted. Where Victorians had espoused an ideal of the passionless female, by the 1920s sexual advice writers were encouraging female erotic expression in "companionate marriage," a modern marital ideal that stressed friendship and intimacy between spouses. But they validated female passion only conditionally; it had to be directed at and responsive to men. Moreover, men retained their right to initiate and control sexual relations. Under this system the sexy, feminine, and compliant heterosexual became the ideal, while sexual stigmas developed around both the "Victorian prude" and the "mannish lesbian." The latter two represented sexual distance from men, threatening the companionate marriage system and, more generally, men's access to women.[13]

The growing influence of psychology and sexology lent authority to new concepts of sexual deviance. In their classifications of "normal" and "perverse" sexualities, scientists distinguished between heterosexuality and homosexuality as dichotomous sexual identities, marked not only by particular behaviors but by psychic orientations. Medical theories of homosexuality appear to have developed in response to the actual presence of men and women who not only engaged in homosexual practices but came to understand same-sex desire as a defining feature of their identities. Women-loving women of the early twentieth-century found each other in urban bohemian enclaves, education and reform circles, upper-class artistic communities, and working-class rooming-house districts. Some of these women claimed lesbian identities and cultivated a "mannish" style that signified their erotic interest in women.[14]

By the late 1920s and 1930s, the small but noticeable lesbian presence in large cities, together with the popular impact of sexology, led to heightened public awareness and criticism of the "mannish lesbian." Movies, plays, and popular novels with lesbian themes, accompanied in some cases by sensational obscenity trials, made the lesbian an increasingly familiar and detested figure.[15] This attitude reflected, and was fostered by, a more general political and cultural backlash against independent, assertive women. Especially during the hard years of the depression, a hostile public expressed its open contempt for feminists, career women, working wives, and lesbians.[16]

The suspicions of lesbianism that plagued assertive feminists and independent professional women would cut even deeper into the reputation of women athletes. Yet, for a brief period, the line between female sexual liberation and aberration remained blurry.[17] The 1920s and early 1930s stand as an uncertain time when old and new definitions of intimacy and sexuality overlapped, especially in sport. Fears of homosexual deviance, not yet pervasive or fully articulated, coexisted alongside concerns about heterosexual "excess" and more salutary interpretations that accepted same-sex intimacy and a certain amount of "masculine" eroticism as positive benefits of sport.

College yearbooks featured women athletes dressed in shirts, ties, and knickers, often posing together with arms linked or hands grasped. Students cherished the closeness formed in WAAs, unabashedly acknowledging: "One seems to get closer to a person there than in any other group."[18] This closeness could include romantic or sexual love for women. In her autobiography prominent twentieth-century physical educator Mabel Lee commented that early in her career she was quite familiar with the occasional passionate crush between girls.[19] Elizabeth ("Buffy") Dunker, a student at Vassar and Antioch in the 1920s, recalled that crushes among women—especially a younger student for an older student or teacher, "particularly a gym teacher"—were a common, almost required phenomenon in her day. But she explained that such relationships in no way interfered with students' intense, "all-time consuming" interest in dating and marriage.[20] For a brief period romantic same-sex crushes typical of nineteenth-century female culture coexisted with the modern woman's "all-consuming" passion for men.

This ambiguity is illustrated by a set of intriguing comments made by physical educators as they evaluated student majors at the University of Wisconsin. Staff remarks, recorded in faculty-meeting minutes, reveal an increasingly punitive stance toward "mannishness," paired with a remarkably open discussion of students' physical appearance. Wisconsin faculty described students variously as "dirty looking," "too boyish," and having "mannish habits and clothes." Educators clearly wished to avoid the taint of mannishness. However, positive evaluations of students included the following: "exceedingly attractive," "cute," and "good material. Nice body."[21] Such uncensored comments, made during the 1928–29 academic year, reveal a kind of unself-conscious appreciation of women's bodies that would soon be made unspeakable by emerging lesbian taboos.

The first sign of a developing proscription against female intimacy appears in a subsequent faculty discussion at Wisconsin. Contemplating the "crush problem" at a 1932 staff meeting, faculty members were disturbed not so much by the crushes as by the growing suspicion surrounding intimate same-sex relations. Yet the threat was distant enough that although they included the discussion in their minutes, they dismissed the problem on the grounds that "the tendency the last few years has been to exaggerate these things. *Any* attachment which excludes other people is not good."[22] Although physical educators had begun to consider the possible lesbian implications of women's athletic passions, it was not a pressing concern as long as the New Morality's heterosexual emphasis had not yet fully discredited an older pattern of female community, love, and intimacy found in women's educational, athletic, and reform circles.

⌐○⌐

The period of overlap was short-lived. By the mid-1930s, uncensored discussions of harmless "crushes" disappear from the record, pushed underground by the increasingly hostile tone of public discourse on the sexuality of female athletes. Known for their appropriation of "mannish" games and styles, women athletes and physical educators became easy targets for sexual indictment. To the familiar charge that athletic women resembled men, critics added the accusation that sport-induced mannishness disqualified the female athlete as a candidate for heterosexual romance.

An *American Mercury* essay from 1930 set the tone for the coming years. Author George Jean Nathan decried the decline of romantic love, pinning the blame on women who entered sport, business, and politics. Claiming that such women "act like men, talk like men, and think like men," he bemoaned the fact that as "women have come closer and closer to men's level . . . the purple allure of distance has vamoosed."[23] Three years later, the *Ladies Home Journal* advanced a similar position when it printed a "Manual on the More or Less Subtle Art of Getting a Man." The guide listed vitality, gaiety, vivacity, and good sportsmanship—qualities typically associated with women athletes and formerly linked to the flapper's heterosexual appeal—as "the very qualities that are likely to make him consider anything but marriage."[24] Though these comments did not focus exclusively on athletes, they implied that female athleticism was contrary to heterosexual appeal, which appeared to rest on women's difference from and deference to men.

Where earlier references to "amazons" had signaled heterosexual ardor, journalists now used the term to mean unattractive, failed heterosexuals. And contemporary critics made it clear that "failed" heterosexuality referred to, if not an active homosexual interest, at least a lack of heterosexual interest. In 1933, a *Redbook* magazine feature on Babe Didrikson casually mentioned that the track and golf star liked men to just horse around with her and not "make love." Author William Marston then observed that Didrikson's peculiar fondness for her best girlfriends far surpassed her affection for any man.[25] When "virilized" women disdained men, there was always the possibility that they would direct their "mannish" sexual passions toward women.

Overt references to same-sex love were rare; the lesbian connotation of mannishness was forged primarily through indirect links of association. The first indications of an emerging lesbian stereotype surfaced as part of the ongoing debate between opponents and advocates of women's sport over the pros and cons of female athletic participation. In 1934, for example, *Literary Digest* published Fred Wittner's assertion that "worthy fathers" would not find trained women athletes attractive mates. In a printed rebuttal, AAU official Ada Taylor Sackett reassured readers that because athletic muscles resembled "those of women who dance all night," women in sport could no doubt "still attract a worthy mate."[26] When critics maligned athletic femininity, they suggested that athletes were literally unbecoming women: unattractive females who abdicated their womanhood and fell under sexual suspicion. When defenders responded with ardent assertions of heterosexuality, it suggests that they understood "mannish" to mean "not heterosexual."

The separatism and long-standing antagonism of physical educators toward male sport promoters left women in P.E. especially vulnerable to insinuations of lesbianism. After two decades of tolerating or even celebrating the female athlete, college yearbooks of the 1930s began to ridicule P.E. majors and WAA members, portraying them as hefty, disheveled, and ugly. One 1937 yearbook sarcastically titled its WAA section "Over in No Man's Land."[27] The policies that had once protected their heterosexual respectability now cast physical educators as unattractive prudes and perhaps even man-hating lesbians.

Pressed to rebut such assertions, P.E. leaders of the 1930s revised their curriculum to embrace an activist approach toward heterosexuality.[28] Administrators altered coursework to emphasize beauty and social charm over rigorous health and fitness. At Radcliffe, for example, faculty of the 1930s introduced a "social security" plan under which health classes began to include "advice on dress, carriage, hair, skin, voice, or any factor that would tend to improve personal appearance and thus contribute to social and economic success."[29] Other educators recommended that one criterion for acceptance into the P.E. program be whether potential majors "have or possess the possibilities of an attractive personal appearance."[30]

Posture contests, a long-standing ritual of women's P.E. programs, were modified to reflect the new emphasis on beauty and heterosexuality. Formerly student leaders secretly observed their classmates in daily life activities, awarding points for correct sitting, standing, and walking, and then announced the winner at a female-only WAA banquet. This ritual symbolized the female world of P.E., concerned above all with health and propriety but also involving peer approval, ceremony, and intimacy. In the 1930s posture contests became public affairs, designed to resemble beauty contests and showcase the attractiveness of women P.E. students.[31]

The implied connections between beauty, athleticism, and sexual normalcy were further articulated when educators protested the oft-repeated charge that strenuous sport made women look ugly. They conceded that the athlete might momentarily display a strained face and bulging muscles, but declared that yesterday's "mannish, shoulder swinging, shirt-and-tie type of athlete" had been replaced by "lovely, feminine charming girls" whose athletic fitness, suppleness, and grace merely made them "more beautiful on the dance floor that evening."[32] Such defensive efforts to establish women's attractiveness to men and interest in heterosexual activities offer a strong indication that the "mannish lesbian" had supplanted the heterosexual "muscle moll" as the symbol of athletic illegitimacy.

Physical educators, fully grasping this change, altered departmental policies with an eye toward averting charges of homosexual deviance. In a concerted effort to encourage and demonstrate heterosexual interest among student athletes, they began to champion the value of mixed-sex "co-recreation" over single-sex intramural activities. Corecreational bowling, volleyball, swimming, and "fun nights" of table tennis and shuffleboard replaced interclass basketball tournaments and weekend campouts for women. In a related shift, faculty and student leaders deemphasized team sports in favor of individual sports deemed appropriate for postgraduation heterosexual leisure pursuits. They recommended tennis, golf, bowling, horseback riding, and archery as "life-time sports" with "carry-over value."[33] Student leaders of the Athletic Federation of College Women (AFCW) included the following planning goals in their platforms of the 1930s: to "promote those activities which may be adapted to the needs of after college life;" to "promote the sports in which both men and women may participate together;" and to develop an "enlarged sport program to include sports that men and women can enjoy together such as mixed doubles in tennis, mixed foursomes in golf . . . [and] baseball games with men and women on each team."[34]

Programmatic changes reflected a fundamental shift in the philosophical orientation of school sport. WAAs no longer appealed to participants' desire for female companionship, fitness, and fun. Instead they tempted students with promises of greater popularity, trimmer waistlines, slimmer hips, and prettier complexions—the prerequisites of modern heterosexual courtship. Faculty leaders affirmed these objectives. At a 1937 professional meeting of women's P.E. directors, a panel evaluating mixed-sex recreation unanimously approved of corecreation as an "agency for social adjustment" that "provides normal social relationships."[35] Physical educators self-consciously revised their professional philosophy to place heterosexual adjustment at the center of educational objectives.

Despite efforts to keep pace with changing sexual codes, the damning image of the "mannish lesbian" had clearly shaken the confidence of physical educators. Suddenly doubtful of their own expertise on sexual matters, they began to solicit advice from outside authorities. In 1938 the annual meeting of the NAAF's Women's Division invited two psychologists to speak on the subject of sexual development. As experts they warned against the evils of female separatism and sex segregation, linking them to sexual maladjustment. Psychologist Margaret Birdsong described "the different types of people who are unadjusted to heterosexual cooperative activity," including "the arrested development type" and "the domineering type." The second speaker, a male psychologist referred to only as Dr. Pritchard, instructed the audience of physical education and recreation specialists to "sense the enriching values in a democracy and develop cultural prejudice *against* segregation of the sexes."[36]

Attributing sexual maladjustment to the "lack of ability to mix," both speakers associated failed heterosexual development with exclusively female environments. Birdsong and Pritchard went on to warn physical educators that "recreation can either contribute to these negative attitudes or if wisely handled, form the most usable instrument for more constructive social cooperation."[37] Physical educators, who had long advocated female separatism in sport, were thus pressed to promote heterosexuality actively or risk indictment for encouraging undemocratic same-sex association.

⊂○⊃

Tentatively voiced in the 1930s, the stigma of lesbianism became harsher and more explicit under the impact of wartime changes in gender and sexuality and postwar fears of an imagined "homosexual menace." In the conservative Cold War era, a period notably hostile to nontraditional women and to all homosexuals, women in physical education and in working-class popular sports became convenient marks for homophobic invective.

Under the quickening pace of wartime social transformations, embryonic gay and lesbian subcultures blossomed and spread across the mid-century urban landscape. In the early 1940s bars, nightclubs, public male cruising spots, and informal social networks facilitated the development of gay and lesbian enclaves. When the war ended gay communities continued to grow. Cities like Los Angeles, New York, and San Francisco attracted thousands of lesbian and gay migrants, who, after coming out during the war years, chose to settle in urban centers at a safe remove from inquisitive hometown neighbors and family members.

The permissive sexual atmosphere that had nurtured wartime gay communities did not survive the transition to peace. The postwar lesbian and gay presence evoked a hatred and disgust far beyond what one might expect, given the small numbers of identifiable homosexuals. A 1949 *Newsweek* article on sex criminals, entitled "Queer People," warned its readers about the criminal behavior of "sex perverts"—a category that included homosexuals, exhibitionists, and sadists. It went on to accuse social workers of being "foolishly sympathetic" toward homosexuals, warning them to discard this attitude in favor of more punitive approaches.[38]

Postwar government leaders showed no such "foolish" sympathy. At the federal, state, and local levels, officials purged gays and lesbians from government and military posts, initiated legal investigations and prosecutions of gay individuals and institutions, and encouraged the police to crack down on gay bars and street life. The perceived need to safeguard national security and to reestablish gender and sexual order in the wake of wartime disruptions sparked a "homosexual panic" that promoted the fear, loathing, and persecution of homosexuals.[39]

Lesbians suffered condemnation for their violation of gender as well as sexual codes. The tremendous emphasis on "traditional" family, domesticity, and femininity in the late 1940s and 1950s reflected postwar nervousness about reconsolidating a gender system shaken by two decades of depression and war. As symbols of women's refusal to conform, lesbians endured intense scrutiny by scientific and medical experts who regularly focused on their subjects' presumed masculinity.[40]

The most visible examples of lesbian gender transgression were working-class lesbians, who organized their communities around butch-femme styles and roles. Couples composed of a "butch," noted for her masculine dress and manner, and a conventionally feminine "femme" challenged the presumed correlation between gender role and sex. Butches demonstrated that masculinity had no biological basis in the male sex, while femmes proved that femininity had no necessary correspondence to female heterosexuality. Yet, as much as they disrupted commonplace assumptions, butch-femme styles could also confirm popular stereotypes. This was specially true for butches, whose short hair, "tough" posture, and male clothing fueled unsympathetic portrayals of the "mannish" sexual deviant.[41]

Lesbians remained shadowy figures to most Americans, but women athletes—noted for their masculine bodies, interests, and attributes—were visible representatives of the gender inversion often associated with homosexuality. They formed an obvious and accessible target for antihomosexual attacks. College athletes, formerly accused of being unappealing to men, were increasingly charged with being uninterested in them as well. The 1952 University of Minnesota yearbook snidely reported: "Believe it or not, members of the Women's Athletic Association are normal," finding conclusive evidence in the fact that "at least one . . . of WAA's 300 members is engaged."[42]

The stigma of lesbianism quickly spread beyond collegiate circles and began to plague popular athletics, especially working-class sports noted for their masculine toughness. The pall of suspicion did not completely override older associations between mannishness and heterosexual deviance. For example, a 1947 *Collier's* magazine article on the "Red Heads," a barnstorming women's basketball team, exclaimed, "It's basketball—not a strip tease!" This nonsensical comparison (team members were fully clothed) alluded to both the raw sexual appeal and the hint of disrepute associated with working-class women athletes.[43]

But the dominant postwar voice intimated a different type of disrepute. Journalists continued to attack the mannish athlete as ugly and sexually unappealing, possibly deficient. But now more than ever they implied that this image could only be refuted through proof of heterosexual "success." The career of Babe Didrikson, which spanned the 1920s to the 1950s, illustrates the shift. After quitting track in the early 1930s, Didrikson dropped out of the national limelight, married professional wrestler George Zaharias in 1938, and then staged a spectacular athletic comeback as a golfer in the late 1940s and 1950s. Fascinated by her personal transformation and then, in the 1950s, moved by her battle with cancer, journalists gave Didrikson's comeback extensive coverage and helped make her a much-loved popular figure. In reflecting on her success, however, sportswriters spent at least as much time on Didrikson's love life as her golf stroke. They gleefully described how "along came a great big he-man wrestler and the Babe forgot all her man-hating chatter."[44]

Outside the sports media, popular and scientific discourse confirmed the sexual abnormality of "man-hating" athletes, if only through inference. In a 1953 article on seven spinster sisters, *Life* magazine reported that the middle-aged unmarried Texas siblings went to bed at night prattling about their high school athletic feats.[45] Four years later *Science Digest* reported on an American Psychiatric Association study that found that only 14 of 102 gay men had played childhood baseball, compared to 66 percent of other "mentally ill" patients "and perhaps 100 percent of normal American men."[46] Neither article was about women in sport. But the first linked heterosexual failure, in the form of spinsterhood, to sport, and the second brought the weight of science to bear on the equation of sport with "normal" maleness—defined as sexual desire for women. The very strength of the lesbian taboo made direct references to the lesbian athlete rare, but a connection had been made. If sport represented masculinity and sexual desire for women, female athletes might also be mannish types who sexually disdained men and desired women.[47]

Disturbed yet intrigued by this possibility, postwar sportswriters focused inordinate attention on women's sexual as well as their athletic achievements. Journalists investigated the topic from several angles, questioning athletes about their sexual availability and interests while making their own judgments about the sexual desirability of female athletes, both as individuals and as a class. In 1960 a *New York Times Magazine* headline asked, "Do men make passes at athletic lasses?" Columnist William Furlong answered no for most activities, concluding that except for a few "yes" sports like swimming, women athletes, "surrendered" their sex.[48] The challenge, it seems, was not for women athletes to conquer new athletic heights, which would only further reduce their sexual appeal, but to regain their womanhood through sexual surrender to men.

⌒◯⌒

Although national magazines and metropolitan newspapers typically focused on the sexual accomplishments of white female athletes, by the late 1950s the sexuality of African American athletes became a topic of discussion in the black press. Before this time, however, athletic and sexual traditions in African American communities had worked against a homosexual reading of "masculine" female athleticism.[49] Former athletes from Tuskegee Institute's championship track teams of the late 1930s and 1940s noted that while a male student might accuse an athlete of being "funny" if she turned him down for a date, in general lesbianism was not a subject of concern in black sport circles.[50] Even as late as the 1950s and early 1960s, Gloria Wilson found that she encountered far less uneasiness about lesbianism on her black semipro softball team than she did in the predominantly white college P.E. departments she joined later. She explained that the expectation of heterosexuality was ingrained in African American women to the point that "anything outside of that realm is just out of the question." While recalling that her teammates "had no time or patience for 'funnies,' " Wilson noted that the issue rarely came up, in large part because most team members were married and therefore "didn't have to prove it."[51]

Beyond local black communities, however, the perceived link between sport and lesbianism developed at the precise moment when African American athletes were becoming a dominant presence in American sport culture. Mid-century images of sport, blackness, masculinity, and lesbianism revolved in the same orbit. While there was no particular association between black women and lesbianism, the association of each with mannishness potentially linked the two. Sensing the connection, and probably also reflecting the general tone of the times, black sports promoters and journalists of the late 1950s joined others in taking up the issue of sexual "normalcy."

One black newspaper in 1957 described tennis star Althea Gibson as a childhood "tomboy" who "in later life . . . finds herself victimized by complexes."[52] The article did not elaborate on the nature of Gibson's "complex," but the linkage between "tomboys" and psychological illness intimated lesbianism. This connotation found clearer enunciation in the defensive denials issued by supporters of black women's sport, exemplified by *Ebony*'s avowal that "entirely feminine" African American female track stars "like boys, dances and club affairs."[53]

By the 1950s all female athletes and physical educators operated under a cloud of sexual suspicion. The destructive stereotype of the mannish lesbian athlete pressured women in sport to demonstrate their femininity and heterosexuality, viewed as one and the same.[54] Many women adopted an apologetic stance about their athletic skill. Even as they competed to win, they made sure to display outward signs of femininity in dress and demeanor. They took special care in dealing with the media to reveal "feminine" hobbies like cooking and sewing, mention current boyfriends, and discuss future marriage plans.[55]

Leaders of women's sport took the same approach at the institutional level. Physical educators redoubled their efforts to discredit the portrayal of P.E. majors and teachers as social misfits and prudes. In a paper on postwar objectives Mildred Schaeffer explained that P.E. classes should help women "develop an interest in school dances and mixers and *a desire to voluntarily attend them.*"[56] To this end administrators continued to emphasize lifelong sport and daily-life skills (including occasional lessons on how to lift luggage and dodge oncoming automobiles). The idea of "co-recreation" spread from intramural activities to the regular curriculum, where physical educators began designing coeducational classes to foster "broader, keener, more sympathetic understanding of the opposite sex."[57] Lest there be any confusion about the message, in 1956 the University of Texas brought in Dr. Henry Bowman, author of *Marriage for Moderns*, to lecture first-year women's P.E. classes on how "to be gotten."[58]

In conjunction with curricular reform, physical educators launched internal crackdowns on students and faculty who might feed the public image of mannishness. Departments warned against "casual styles" that might "lead us back into some dangerous channels."[59] They implemented dress codes forbidding slacks and men's shirts or socks, adding as well a ban on "boyish haircuts" and unshaven legs.[60] The Ohio P.E. Association left no doubt about the impression it sought to project. Its 1946 brochure for prospective majors flatly stated, "The mannish concept of a physical educator is no longer acceptable." The pamphlet's cover showed a man in a suit and a woman in high heels and a skirt walking hand in hand *away* from a background of athletic fields.[61]

Popular sports promoters adopted similar tactics. Roxy Andersen responded to the implied connection between mannishness and lesbianism by designing AAU promotional campaigns around the assertion of heterosexuality. In her 1945 article "Fashions in Feminine Sport," Andersen created a historical scenario of growing heterosexual appeal and pursuit. She contrasted "prehistoric femmes who developed their speed running AWAY from the men" with "the glamorous girls of this age," who dated six nights a week. The modern athlete's "luscious . . . decorative

. . . long-stem" beauty and frequent dating discredited the "erroneous opinion that men disapprove of women in sport."[62]

Martialing sexual data as if they were athletic statistics, a 1954 AAU poll sought to sway a skeptical public with numerical proof of heterosexuality—the fact that 91 percent of former female athletes surveyed had married.[63] Publicity for the midwestern AAGBL supplemented the usual statistics on total hits, runs, and stolen bases with figures on the total number of married players in the league. In the same vein the professional women's golf tour announced that one-third of its members were married and the rest were on the lookout for attractive marital prospects.[64]

The fear of lesbianism was greatest where a sport had a particularly masculine image and where promoters needed to attract a paying audience. Professional and semipro basketball and softball fit the bill on both counts. Sponsors tried to resolve the problem through beauty contests and other promotional ploys to "prove" the attractive femininity of athletes. While in earlier times such events celebrated the "sexiness" of the emancipated modern woman, in later decades they seemed to serve a more defensive function. Editors of the *Amateur Athlete* made sure that at least one photograph of the national basketball tournament's beauty "queen and her court" accompanied the photo of each year's championship team, as—behind the scenes—teams passed dress and conduct codes designed to allay fears that ball teams attracted "freaks" and "Amazons."[65]

In their efforts to counter pernicious lesbian stereotypes, sports promoters and the media transformed the "unseemly" heterosexual element present in earlier working-class athletics into the basic standard of legitimacy for all women's sport. For decades the overt eroticism of popular sport had sparked internal controversy and external criticism. But by mid-century promoters of a wide variety of women's sports highlighted the female athlete's sexual allure. The most acceptable athletes were the women whose beauty and sex appeal "compensated" for their athletic ability.[66] Those athletes deemed unattractive by virtue of their size, musculature, facial features, or "unfeminine" bearing met with public censure and suspicion of their sexuality.[67]

—⟨○⟩—

In the first half of the twentieth century, a fundamental reorientation of sexual meanings fused notions of femininity, female eroticism, and heterosexual attractiveness into a new ideal of womanhood. Mannishness, once primarily a sign of gender crossing,
assumed a specifically lesbian-sexual connotation in this new
configuration. As a result the strong cultural associations
between sport and masculinity made women's athletics ripe for
emerging lesbian stereotypes. By mid-century the conceptual link
between mannishness and lesbianism meant that to assert athletic
femininity was also an effort to claim heterosexual "normalcy."

Although women's sport advocates did their best to "prove"
heterosexuality and to suppress "mannishness," in the end this
strategy did little to diminish the lesbian stigma of women's sport.
Hostile observers perpetuated lesbian athletic stereotypes through
their unrelenting ridicule of skilled athletes as "grotesque," "ugly,"
"masculine," or "unnatural." Leaders of women's sport unwitting-
ly contributed to the homophobic climate when they began to ori-
ent their programs toward a new feminine heterosexual ideal. As
organizational policies and media campaigns worked to suppress
lesbianism and marginalize athletes who didn't conform to dominant standards of femininity, sport officials incorporated society's
fear and loathing of lesbians into the practice and imagery of sport.
Intentionally or not, policies designed to mollify a homophobic
public merely added to the institutional bulwark that privileged
heterosexuality and condemned lesbianism.

The stigmatized "mannish" lesbian athlete did not disappear
but rather assumed the stature of a negative symbol of female
social and sexual independence. As a powerful representation of
deviance her significance reached far beyond the world of sport.
She announced to all women that competitiveness, strength, independence, aggression, and same-sex physical intimacy were privileged features of manhood or, conversely, the mark of unacceptable womanhood. She represented the border that must not be
crossed, reminding all women to toe the line of heterosexual femininity or risk falling into a despised and liminal category of mannish (not-women) women.

# CHAPTER 8

# "PLAY IT, DON'T SAY IT"

## Lesbian Identity and Community in Women's Sport

—⊃○⊂—

Women's sport sparked public interest, dismay, and controversy because it blurred the sexual and gender categories that governed everyday life. Yet it was precisely this ambiguity that also created space for women to explore unconventional gender and sexual identities. Athletically inclined lesbians, in particular, found that the world of women's sport offered possibilities for self-expression and social life despite the homosexual stigma that beset women's athletics. While the contemptible stereotype of the "mannish lesbian athlete" publicly condemned the female athlete's gender and sexual transgressions, the existence of this caricatured figure did not prevent gay women from generating an alternative set of affirmative meanings and experiences from within the culture of sport. Mid-century lesbian athletes found that athletic life facilitated the individual process of coming to terms with homosexual desires as well as the collective process of forging community ties among gay women.

Josephine D'Angelo, for example, grew up in Chicago during the 1930s and "came out" as a lesbian in the early 1940s. The youngest child of Italian immigrants, she had been raised by an older sister and a hard-drinking, hardworking widowed father who scraped to feed and clothe his family on a laborer's earnings. While still a youngster, D'Angelo found that the athletic program at her neighborhood park offered an escape from family violence and tedious work. "Jo" developed quickly as a softball player,

185

impressing local scouts who granted the young teenager a spot on one of Chicago's highly skilled women's semipro softball teams.

By 1942 wartime opportunities offered some relief from childhood difficulties. D'Angelo graduated from high school that year and took a defense job in a South Side steel mill, working the early shift so she could continue to play ball in the evenings. Although still a teenager, she was supporting herself, saving money for college, playing semipro athletics, and running with a group of "gay girls," or lesbians, she knew through sports. D'Angelo thrived in a working-class sports world that offered the possibility of earning money and public recognition for her athletic skills, at the same time allowing her to forge private social networks with women she described as "people of a kind."

D'Angelo's good fortune increased in 1943 when she attended a tryout session for a new professional baseball venture, the All-American Girls Baseball League (AAGBL), and won a place on the South Bend, Indiana, "Blue Sox" roster. Thrilled by the chance to travel and play baseball full-time, D'Angelo willingly conformed to the league's strict code of conduct—a set of rules designed to create an appealing "feminine" image. She boarded with a local family, dressed in league-mandated attire, and stayed away from the league's "gay crowd."

It therefore came as a jolting surprise when, late in her second season, the team manager approached her in the hotel lobby and told her she had been released. The reason? D'Angelo had gotten a severe or, in her own words, "butchy" haircut. Since the butchy image had been unintended—she had only consented to the haircut after a local hairdresser convinced D'Angelo that her dark, curly locks would look best in a short bob—the dismissal caught her unprepared. With no avenues of appeal the angry, shaken, and embarrassed D'Angelo left the league and returned home to attend college. For several years, however, she continued to play ball and to socialize with lesbians she met in the notoriously "mannish" semipro softball leagues of Chicago.[1]

D'Angelo's story offers a rare and telling glimpse into the usually invisible experience of lesbian athletes; along with other such stories, her account forms an important but neglected chapter in the history of women's sport. Personal narratives from lesbian and heterosexual women active in mid-century athletics confirm that the lesbian reputation of sport was not simply a derogatory stereotype, but had some basis in fact. At least some gay women found sport to be a receptive arena for self-expression and the creation of lesbian social networks. The associations between sport, lesbianism, and "mannishness" were also not unfounded. A masculine or "butchy" style, while not definitive of or exclusive to gay athletes, could facilitate recognition and bonding among lesbians in sport.

But, as D'Angelo's experience painfully reveals, the same signs of "mannishness," whether intended or not, made athletes vulnerable to punitive responses from sport officials and a suspicious public. Given the danger of open declarations, gay women in sport communicated their presence primarily through action, style, and unspoken understandings. They followed a code of "play it, don't say it," in this way ensuring their own survival in a hostile culture while protecting one of the few social spaces that offered a degree of comfort and freedom.[2]

Women involved in highly competitive basketball, softball, track, bowling, and field hockey between the late 1930s and the early 1960s confirm that a significant number of lesbians found sport to be a receptive site for forming relationships and creating a shared culture. Gay and straight athletes alike attested to the lesbian presence in sport.[3]

Knowledge of gay women in sport ranged from a hazy, unarticulated awareness to an informed familiarity or personal involvement. Often an athlete's initial awareness of lesbianism developed from seeing women "pairing off" or getting "very clannish" with each other. On encountering couples she described as "overt," Audrey Goldberg Hull—a Southern California track and softball athlete who would come out as a lesbian years after her playing days were over—became conscious of lesbians in sport: "They'd sit together, be in the same car together, be at the same table after the games together. And then you saw them holding hands once in a while. That's basically how I knew."[4] An Ohio woman who played industrial softball as a teenager in the

1940s recollected a similar experience: "I was a very great gawker and wonderer . . . and it occurred to me that there were some strange sorts of things happening here. And when I got older it became very obvious to me that in that situation there had been some reasonable number of lesbian pairs operating." When she went on to college, she realized that among physical education majors "there were people who appeared to have paired off" as well.[5] Thelma Hirst had witnessed the same phenomenon when playing in Nebraska and Missouri nearly a decade earlier. She recalled that "I've had people say, well, they were running around with this one or that one. . . . They were very close, which didn't make any difference to me."[6]

It apparently did make a difference to some women, who were quite disturbed by what they saw. Describing her years in the AAGBL, Dorothy Ferguson Key recalled, "That's where my eyes opened up. See, I never knew [any]thing like this. But there were girls that came in the league like this. . . . Gay, that's what you'd call 'em." Key added that in addition to attracting lesbians, athletic involvement could apparently transform previously heterosexual women into homosexuals. "I saw things," she explained. "A girl come in, and I mean they just change. . . . When they've been in a year they're completely changed from when they came into the league. . . . They lived together."[7]

Key was at a loss to explain the change, but firsthand testimony from former AAGBL player Nora Cross offers one account of how such a transition might occur: "When I came on the scene I came on cold—I didn't know anything about anything. And I can remember that there was a certain fascination to me when I first discovered that girls like girls. Initially there were quite a few gals from the West Coast. It was my first exposure to gay people. I didn't even know they existed." She recalled making the discovery when "I was pursued by the one I was rooming with. That's how I found out!" Sharing what had become a painful memory, Cross went on to say, "I was involved in a gay life-style for a while as a result of it. . . . There were some absolutely straight people, but there were many who were *not*."[8]

Lesbians in sport formed a circumspect but nevertheless identifiable group. A midwestern softball and baseball player allowed that "I was aware of it. I knew that there were gals that were gay, or lesbians, or whatever you want to call 'em. It happens in any sport." Another ballplayer stressed that public visibility did not mean openness, explaining that lesbians in sport "didn't expound that they were, like they do today on television and all over. It was more of a secretive thing." Nevertheless, she acknowledged that she "had heard some things" about lesbians and concluded: "You'd have to have been pretty naive not to have known. And I *was* naive, too. But not that naive!"

The presence of lesbian athletes attracted lesbian audiences. A Chicago-based ballplayer recalled that after a game, gay ballplayers and spectators would congregate at the same bars: "There were spectators; there were ballplayers, yes. . . . We used to after the game go to a little tavern across the street or something where we always had a few drinks. Well, there were always spectators that would [come]. And they were gay." At least a few of these spectators cared little about sport but attended because they knew that the ball field or the gymnasium was a likely site for meeting other lesbians. In the early 1940s, Lisa Ben, founder of the first known U.S. lesbian magazine *Vice Versa*, moved to Los Angeles thinking she was the only "girl" who preferred to "go out strictly with girls." After meeting several women in her apartment building who admitted to the same desires, she recalled: "Then they took me to a girls' softball game; of course I wasn't the least interested in sports, but it gave me a chance to meet other gay girls."[9]

The fact that Ben went to the ball field to meet other "gay girls" suggests the central role of sport in facilitating the emergence of mid-century lesbian communities. In a day when there were few gay bars or other social institutions, sports opened up a space in which lesbians could gather and begin to forge a collective culture. Athletes recalled that these possibilities were available in a variety of sports, but that softball had the most pronounced lesbian reputation. Lesbian publisher and activist Barbara Grier stated the case for softball succinctly: "It was a place to go where you knew there would be dykes."[10]

The sporting arena not only enabled "dykes" to find other "dykes," it could also play a critical role in the process of *becoming* a lesbian. Athletics provided a point of entry into lesbian culture for young women "coming out" and searching for companionship and community. It proved especially important for athletes who were attracted to other women but who lacked the necessary language and support for articulating and accepting their feelings. Since sport provided public space for lesbian sociability without naming it as such, or excluding women who were not lesbians, women who were unsure about, or just beginning to come to terms with, their sexual identity could explore different social and sexual possibilities without having to make immediate decisions or declarations. Gradually, often relying on unspoken communication, some of these women articulated a lesbian identity and joined in the process of forging broader social networks and a collective lesbian culture.

In relating their coming-out stories, gay women who grew up in the 1930s, 1940s, and 1950s described how frightening and disorienting it was to be a teenager and to realize that one felt sexual or intimate longings for others of her sex. They understood without being told that such feelings were strictly forbidden, and consequently they could not turn to the friends, family members, or mentors from whom they would normally seek advice or reassurance. Explaining that "we didn't have anybody to talk to, we figured it out for ourselves," they pointed to the absence of books, positive media portrayals, or homosexual role models and organizations that could affirm their sense of difference.[11] Under these conditions, coming out as a lesbian often meant fighting an extended battle against loneliness and self-hatred.

Lesbian athletes reported that the sports world was important precisely because it allowed them to pierce the isolation and meet others "of a kind." Ann Maguire, a softball player and top amateur bowler from New England, recalled that as a teenager:

> I had been trying to figure out who I was and couldn't put a name to it. I mean it was very—no gay groups, no literature, no characters on "Dynasty"—I mean there was just nothing at that time.

And trying to put a name to it.... I went to a bowling tournament, met two women there [and] for some reason something clicked, and it clicked in a way that I was not totally aware of.

She introduced herself to the women, who later invited her to a gay bar. Maguire described her experience at age seventeen:

I was being served and I was totally fascinated by the fact that, oh God, here I am being served and I'm not twenty-one. And it didn't occur to me until after a while when I relaxed and started realizing that I was at a gay bar. I just became fascinated. . . . And I was back there the next night. . . . I really felt a sense of knowing who I was and feeling very happy. Very happy that I had been able to through some miracle put this into place.[12]

The social connections and personal clarity Maguire discovered through her introduction to bar culture were reinforced in the world of sport, where she associated with lesbians in bowling, softball, and physical education.

Gloria Wilson had a similar experience, knowing as early as her junior high school years "where my focus was, where I felt I was comfortable. . . . But because of what I heard in the community and in my own family I knew I had to be cautious about revealing my true feelings." Even when she found a school friend who seemed to share the same feelings, Gloria recalled the difficulties. "There weren't any definitions to give to what I knew I was feeling and wanting to be. . . . Neither of us I don't think knew what we were doing, or had words to define it." The isolation and silence ended after high school, when Wilson began playing softball on a team located in a large town some distance from her home community. She found that most of the women she played with were lesbians. The combination of finding a supportive setting in sports and entering into a lesbian relationship ended her isolation and gave her a language with which she could define herself: "I started meeting more and more lesbians. . . . It was talked about. It was very obvious. . . . It wasn't hidden at all."[13]

Wilson's experience points out the importance of some kind of explicit recognition, whether it be verbal or by inclusion in a group. As a teenage athlete, Audrey Goldberg Hull desperately sought the comfort and sense of belonging that this recognition could bring, but in her case it was not forthcoming. She recalled that as a high school student "I already realized that I was gay. . . . But that's something that you try not to deal with. And besides that, I didn't have anyone to talk to [and] there were no reading materials. . . . I didn't know how to deal with it." While still in her mid-teens she began to play on highly competitive softball teams in Southern California. In those leagues she met women in their early twenties who seemed to be somehow like herself. Hull focused on the "more masculine ones" and thought, Wouldn't it be nice to know these girls? Too shy to approach them, she never broached the subject, and they never invited her into their circles, possibly because of her young age. From her softball teammates Hull "knew that it existed and I wasn't totally alone, but I never got that overt validation." Terrified of her own feelings and unable fully to connect with women who she sensed harbored similar desires, the young athlete buried her self-knowledge and sense of difference. While still a teenager she married her male coach, coming out as a lesbian only years later after a long and unfulfilling marriage.

Through postgame socializing and gradual inclusion in private social networks, other lesbians found the support and "overt validation" that Hull had craved. Gloria Wilson described her entry into early 1960s lesbian social circles as a gradual process in which older lesbians slowly opened up their world to her and she grew more sure of her own identity and place in the group:

> A lot was assumed. And I don't think they felt comfortable with me talking until they knew me better. And then I think more was revealed. And we had little beer gatherings after a game at somebody's house. So then it was even more clear who was doing what when. And then I felt more comfortable too, fitting in, talking about my relationship too—and exploring more of the lesbian lifestyle, I guess.[14]

In an era when women did not dare announce their lesbianism in public, the social world of sport allowed women to find each other as teammates, friends, and lovers. Loraine Sumner, a longtime athlete, coach, and referee in the Boston area, explained that in sport she found others like herself. Together they formed teams and joined leagues, so that Sumner estimated that as many as 75 percent of the women she played with were lesbian. In such a setting Sumner grew to accept her own feelings and found others to support her. Using words like "bonding," "unity," and "closeness" to describe the experience, she concluded: "Well, it was very nice because you see you developed your friendships. You didn't have to go out looking for women. They were all right there."[15]

Sport served as a public arena where lesbians could recognize each other, form personal attachments, and construct collective bonds so distinctive that straight as well as gay athletes could discern a lesbian presence. But what exactly was it that people recognized? When athletes examined their own process of recognition, they typically mentioned female intimacy and a "mannish" female style as key cultural indicators.

Both heterosexual and gay athletes often first deduced the presence of lesbians from noticing pairs of athletes who appeared to be in couples. As a method of identification, this seems logical and unremarkable. But it becomes more curious given that lesbians reported that they eschewed verbal revelations or any public sexual expressions.

Athletes described women who sat together, exchanged glances, came and went together, held hands, traded rings, or shared a visibly intimate and affectionate attachment. The fact that these behaviors signaled a lesbian relationship suggests how greatly female intimacy had become circumscribed and sexualized over the first half of the twentieth century. Late-nineteenth-century Americans would have characterized the same behaviors as unexceptional, normal features of women's friendships. The early-twentieth-century redefinition of womanhood around an eroticized heterosexual concept of femininity created a specific taboo against lesbianism; but it also placed a much more general proscription on emotional and physical intimacy between women. By mid-century unusual closeness between women could signal an "improper" intimacy. In the context of sport's reputation for mannishness and lesbianism, such intimacy could be read as a sign of lesbianism.

Far more than they mentioned couples, women athletes consistently explained that the perception of lesbianism in sport derived from the mannish or "butch" style of some athletes. For example, AAU basketball player Margaret Sexton Gleaves recalled a team of lesbians she had encountered at the national tournament. She described the Texas team as having "some outstanding athletes, and some of them were rather boyish-type looking."[16] Nebraska softball player Jessie Rider Steinkuhler suggested that the lesbian image of sportswomen came from the fact that "they tried to act like a man, you know the way they walked, the way they talked, and the things they did."[17]

The distinction between known lesbians and "mannish athletes" who might give the impression of lesbianism was not marked. Even among athletic participants lesbians were assumed to be "mannish," and unusually "mannish" women were assumed to be lesbians. The presumption of lesbian masculinity could even extend beyond dress or mannerism to the body itself. Athletes like Babe Didrikson and Stella Walsh who had the physical build and musculature associated with the male body were rumored to be lesbians. When asked if she had ever heard sport associated with lesbianism, Myrna Scritchfield Thompson answered, "I never heard of it. Well . . . the golfer—Babe Didrikson. That's the first time I ever heard anything about it." Asked what she had heard, Thompson replied, "She's part boy," and added, "I didn't believe it."[18]

Although twentieth-century sexologists had moved away from conceptualizing homosexuality as gender inversion, both scientific and popular images of lesbianism continued to conflate sexual desire for women with a masculine orientation.[19] This was especially true in the context of sports. When athletes attempted to explain the cultural association between lesbianism and athletics, they stated that since most people understand sport to be masculine, they tend to infer the presence of lesbians. None of them went on to say that people also think lesbians are masculine; rather this was assumed, taken for granted. The presumed masculinity of lesbians was the social "fact" on which the connection between lesbianism and sport rested.

How true was this "fact"? When moving beyond the lesbian stigma of sport to describe women they actually knew to be lesbians, athletes also remarked upon hair styles, dress, and an overall mannish appearance. Dottie Green, a former AAGBL player and chaperone, explained: "The lesbians, they dressed like men, with those big pants and big shoes, most of them. . . . Years ago they dressed like that—they had boyish bobs."[20] Dottie Ferguson Key recalled that "tomboyish girls" who "wanted to go with other girls" signaled this "in the shoes they bought. You know, it was how they dressed. . . . In some way you could just tell they were mannish."

Former basketball standout Alline Banks spoke supportively of lesbians in sport, adamantly insisting that gay women's sexuality "is their own right. . . . It is not for me to decide their lifestyle, nor would I criticize them." Yet, like others, Banks relied on gender terminology to denote sexual identity. Avoiding terms like "gay" or "lesbian," she described the women she defended as "more to the masculine side," and referred specifically to an Atlanta team on which she had known some players "who were not as feminine as the others."[21] When Banks and others used terms like "on the masculine side" and "boyish types," they were not necessarily relying on euphemisms, but rather were describing lesbianism as they understood it.[22]

References by heterosexual observers to the mannish walk, talk, and dress of lesbian athletes might merely have indicated the pervasiveness of the *stereotype* of the mannish lesbian athlete. Evidence from lesbian athletes, however, suggests that the connection ran deeper—that at least some lesbians in sport did adopt a style perceived as and probably intended to be "masculine." Describing the lesbian athletes to whom she was drawn, Audrey Hull listed a familiar set of cues: short haircuts, blue jeans, and a particular walk, carriage, and bravado distinctive of "the more masculine girls." "Mannish" posture and dress could simply have been an adolescent or adult continuation of a childhood "tomboy" style, a self-presentation available to lesbians and

straight women alike. But among lesbians mannishness may also
have answered a specific need for an athletic style which could
express their sense of difference. Audrey Hull reasoned that "lesbians want to show sometimes their difference, and that difference carries over into their clothes and the way they behave."

The dress and body language lesbian athletes used to communicate their difference corresponded to the butch style evident in
working-class lesbian subculture of the 1940s and 1950s.
Athletes' "mannish" walk, talk, and dress resembled the dunga-
rees, men's shoes or boots, short "d.a." haircuts, and "tough"
body language typical of "butch" lesbians. As members of a
scorned population, butches announced their existence to the
outside world by presenting themselves as self-consciously defiant
of societal sex and gender conventions. Within lesbian communities, a butch's masculine look and gesture could announce her
erotic desire for other women.[23] In both the bar world and the
sports world, then, "mannish" lesbians embraced similar styles of
self-presentation.[24] Jo D'Angelo recalled that as a lesbian in sport,
"You brought your culture with you. You brought your arm-
swinging or whatever it was, the swagger, the way you tilted or
cocked your head—you brought that with you."

Whether consciously or not, gay athletes drew on a symbolic
language in which masculine gesture and dress indicated lesbianism. One athlete described, quite literally, the sign system among
gay women: "I think that when people were lesbian, or whatever
you want to call them, they wanted short haircuts, they wanted
to wear pants, they wanted to you know, *be* like a boy. . . .
Somebody had a short hair cut then, they might as well [have]
had a sign on their back."[25] Clothes, haircuts, and mannerisms
served as markers which together became the equivalent of wearing "a sign on their back."[26]

Although they spoke of being only vaguely aware of how the
identification process worked, athletes nevertheless discerned the
code. Audrey Hull remarked, "I don't know why, you just could
pick it out." And Loraine Sumner noted that sport was particularly well suited for lesbian recognition: "Well, I shouldn't say
you surmise, but—there's something there that you recognize in
others that are in the same life-style as you. More so than if you

saw a woman walking down the street. Some you can tell and some you can't. But in sports I think there's just a way that you can pick it out." The ability to recognize each other was the first step in building a shared culture among lesbians in sport.

Even as gay athletes acknowledged the presence and described the style of "butchy" lesbians, they were quick to deny any simple equations among lesbianism, sport, and "mannishness." They presented a much more complicated and nuanced explanation of the connections between sport, personal identity, and the behaviors and feelings their society called "masculine." Working within the gendered language and categories of their time, lesbians in sport combined and transformed conventional notions of masculinity and femininity, in the process creating alternative expressions of womanhood that embraced the "mannish" lesbian's unorthodox desires and appearance.

While acknowledging that some lesbians exhibited a masculine manner, gay athletes qualified this by emphasizing that there were heterosexual women who appeared "butchy" and "gay gals" who "were very feminine."[27] Moreover, even among lesbians who did adopt masculine markers, their butch style expressed only some aspects of self. Athletes remarked on the more traditionally feminine qualities of affection and tenderness that lesbian ballplayers shared—an attitude of "caring and sharing" expressed in simple gestures like trading rings, offering rides, sharing meals, or tending to each other's luggage and laundry.[28] Sport allowed women to combine activities and attributes perceived as masculine with more conventionally feminine qualities of friendship, nurturance, and affection.

Personal accounts also suggest the complicated relationship between outward "mannishness" and the interior world of emotion and identity. Although some athletes employed terms like "butch" and "masculine" to describe themselves or other lesbians in sport, no one reported any doubt about her own gender identification as a girl or woman. Women did, however, express frustration with concepts of masculinity and femininity which they found to be artificial, restrictive, and inadequate to describe their own experience.[29] Even so, they themselves could not escape the terms. In mid-century America rigid, polarized notions of masculinity and femininity provided the matrix within which feelings were identified and notions of "self" were formed.

Gender distinctions structure human emotional experience as well as categorize activities and physical traits. Gendered feelings—captured in ordinary expressions which refer to *feeling* "feminine," "manly," or "like a woman"—are typically derived from practices recognized as appropriately female or male. For mid-century lesbian athletes, access to feelings of "womanliness" were complicated by the fact that the wider society defined their very desires as masculine. To know one was a girl or young woman but to have interests, abilities, emotions, and sexual attractions that society perceived as masculine could disrupt any comfortable sense of "fit" between self and gender. For example, Gloria Wilson was a childhood "tomboy" who was also attracted to girls from a young age. The fact that what felt natural to Wilson was seen by others as "different," "queer," or "funny" behavior disturbed her certainty about what it meant to be female. She remembered thinking: "I didn't feel like a boy. And I knew I didn't look like a boy. I didn't want to be a boy. . . . [Yet] there were some phases of my life early on where I can remember thinking things would be better if I'd . . . been a boy." Although secure in their identity as girls or women, Wilson and other gay athletes struggled to make personal sense out of their knowledge that an individual's felt gender identity could conflict with her pursuit of activities and erotic desires that were culturally assigned to the other gender.

"Cross-gender" feelings or traits were in no way specific to lesbians. In fact, many heterosexual athletes described themselves as "tomboys" who rebelled against confining feminine prescriptions. But the experience of feeling "boyish" or outside one's gender was amplified for lesbians. Though they did not necessarily feel "masculine," by virtue of their marginal position they were marked as unfeminine.[30]

Categorized as unwomanly, perverted, failed members of their sex, lesbians had to find new ways of conceiving themselves as authentic individuals and as legitimate women. It was this imperative, and lesbians' creative response to it, that helps explain why sport may have been a particularly inviting cultural realm for lesbians. For despite unyielding barriers to full female participation, modern athletics have been a receptive site for gender innovation. The same blurring of gender lines that made women's participation in sport so controversial also created an ambiguous, fluid space within which lesbians could explore their options and identities.

Lesbian athletes described their feeling of being at home with themselves through the activity and sociability of sport. They thrived in an environment that did not require conformity with restrictive feminine conventions, freeing them to act on feelings or desires which were otherwise discouraged. Audrey Hull's "tomboy" athleticism made her conscious of gender distinctions: "I knew I was called a tomboy, and I knew that was a negative." Yet sport provided the means for transcending or resolving the tension: "It was a way of expressing myself. To me it always seemed positive regardless of what anybody said."

Nurtured by a supportive community, a lesbian's painful sense of difference might even become a source of pride. Loraine Sumner described her childhood sense of difference, which developed first around her love of sports and then around her lesbianism. She reported that, as a youngster, "My mother would make lots of funny remarks over the years about me participating [in sports], about being different, being a tomboy." Sumner's ongoing involvement in sports and the lesbian companionship she found there helped her turn her sense of difference into a badge of defiance: "People used to say something to me—when I wasn't dating or when I'd be going out with the girls and things like this—they'd say something to me and I'd go, "That's the kind of hairpin I am."[31] And I'd laugh and say, 'You gotta be different . . . That's the way I am, if you don't like it don't bother me.' " In athletics women like Sumner found a safe space where people didn't "bother" them. At its best the affirmative atmosphere allowed women to just "be themselves," in what one athlete described as a "comforting" and "comfortable" environment. Their ability to find a viable core, or to express an authentic self, through sport enabled gay athletes to fit in and feel 'right' in a vehemently anti-homosexual society that denied their presence and worth.[32]

—&bigcirc—

The friendship networks, social freedoms, and physical pleasures available through sport appealed to women of all sorts but appear to have exerted an especially strong pull on athletically inclined lesbians. No statistical studies exist to prove or disprove assertions that lesbians were overrepresented in sport—that they formed a higher percentage of female athletes than their percentage among all women. Yet the firsthand reports of both lesbian and heterosexual athletes do suggest that lesbians maintained a greater, or at least more visible, presence in athletics than in most other realms of culture.[33] The relative openness of sport to gender innovation and the shared sensibilities of sport and working-class lesbian culture provide part of the explanation. Additional demographic and cultural factors may also account for the lesbian presence in sport.

Highly competitive athletics, especially adult semipro or professional leagues, with their demanding schedules and frequent road trips, appealed primarily to single working women. Since lesbian women were statistically more likely than heterosexual women to be unmarried, childless, and employed in the work force, they were also more likely to participate in organized athletics.[34]

Furthermore, for most of the twentieth century, unmarried women had few options for socializing outside the home without men. Bars and nightclubs were not "respectable" spaces for women to congregate without a male escort. Outdoor games, however, offered a socially acceptable alternative. More specifically, as a public space for lesbian gathering, sport could provide either a complement or a low-risk alternative to homosexual bar culture. Gay athletes found safety in both the numbers of other lesbians and in the many heterosexual women engaged in the same activities. Unlike the legal and social danger of bar life, where patrons risked arrest and harassment, sports provided a domain of public sociability that was not exclusively lesbian and under no legal cloud.

Even more advantageous was the fact that the athletic setting could transform stigmatized lesbian qualities from vices to virtues.[35] Because aggressiveness, toughness, passionate intensity, strength, physicality, and competitiveness contributed to athletic excellence, "masculine" attributes that might otherwise be viewed as manifestations of sexual deviance were perceived as inherent to sport. "Mannish" athleticism was thus a quality of the activity and the skill, and not necessarily of a stigmatized person. Gloria Wilson commented: "In order to play like a boy, you've got to walk like a boy, throw like a boy, maybe be aggressive like a boy." In sports "mannish" attributes formed valued abilities, not masculine psychological traits of devalued persons.

For this reason a style that would appear masculine in another context could be seen as simply part of the game in an athletic setting. Jo D'Angelo stressed that a boyish style was acceptable in sports: "First thing you did was to kind of imitate the boys because you know, you're not supposed to throw like a girl." The same held true for clothing and appearance. Loraine Sumner remembered that first as an athlete and then as a sports official, she could wear the clothing and hairstyle she preferred without being identifiable as a lesbian:

> I always wore my hair short because I officiated [volleyball and basketball]. Because if not . . . my hair would be in my eyes and you know, of course, you wouldn't want anybody to tell you you were a blind official. . . . So I guess that really saves me from that point of view. And basically I really always dressed in athletic clothes and really never felt as though I really dressed like a man. I always dressed more or less in athletic clothes. And it probably was masculine, but that wouldn't faze me.

Athletes whose rejection of femininity made them conspicuous in other settings found that in sport "it was overlooked, see. You weren't different than the other kids. . . . Same likeness, people of a kind."[36] With masculine skill understood as part of the game, gay athletes gained the freedom to express the full range of their gender sensibilities, turning an isolated sense of difference into a "same likeness."

Beyond permitting unorthodox female behavior, sport also

nourished female intimacy. Women's sport was a same-sex activity that encouraged both physical and emotional intensity among women—qualities at the heart of lesbian relationships. Describing the "natural bonding" that occurred in sport, one athlete and physical educator theorized that lesbian intimacy in sport "was just another bond within a bond," adding that it was "therefore not as discernable" as same-sex bonding in other public arenas.[37] *All* women in sport gained access to female intimacy and to activities and expressive styles labeled masculine by the dominant culture. What is specific to lesbian women is that in the realm of athletics they found a social practice which, while not particular to or discernible as lesbianism, turned stigmatized aspects of homosexuality into quotidian elements of sport.

The same possibilities for female intimacy and gender innovation that drew lesbians to sport most likely drove some conventionally feminine, heterosexual women away. By the 1950s the majority of American women showed little interest in highly competitive sport, in part because of its masculine reputation. The AAGBL collapsed in the early 1950s, the same years in which AAU basketball began to decline. In physical education, recreation, and amateur sport publications, women leaders regularly commented that their task had changed from one of discouraging the competitive zealot to stimulating interest among the majority of nonathletic girls who didn't want to sweat, change clothes, mess up their hair, or, worst of all—be accused of being masculine.

Thus the apparently high percentage of lesbians in sport was probably equally a product of positive appeals to lesbians and negative stigmas that caused nonlesbians to opt out, especially after high school, when the proportion of women in sport has tended to decline.[38] In sports like softball, basketball, field hockey, and golf, athletic culture functioned as a sexual force field—a magnet drawing lesbians in and repelling women who were uninterested in or threatened by the physicality, intimacy, and "masculinity" of sport.

Yet, for all the appeal of athletics, lesbians found sport to be a safe and welcoming environment only if they remained silent about their sexuality. While societal hostility toward homosexuality made lesbianism unspeakable in any realm of culture, the sexual suspicions that surrounded sport made athletics an especially dangerous place in which to speak out. Physical educators and sport officials vigilantly guarded against signs of "mannishness," and teams occasionally expelled women who wore their hair in a "severe" style or engaged in obvious lesbian relationships. Since their safety was contingent on caution, gay athletes avoided naming or verbally acknowledging their sexuality.

Lesbian and heterosexual athletes agreed that they rarely heard or entered into any open discussion of lesbianism. Loraine Sumner explained, "You never talked about it . . . But you knew right darn well that this one was going with that one. But yet it just wasn't a topic of conversation. Never." Nora Cross made the same point, noting that only among "*really* good friends" would the matter come up for discussion, and even then "they were very careful about that, that's a fact." Ann Maguire noted that the same code operated in both physical education and popular sport circles: "It was something that you just sort of never talked about. [There were] lots of unwritten rules." One of the unwritten rules was the avoidance of sexual labeling. The terms "lesbian" or "gay" were rarely used. Instead, through phrases like "this one was going with that one," sexuality was referred to as a relation, not a personal identity.[39]

In some cases caution led women to deny or actively disguise their sexuality. Gloria Wilson recalled that among physical educators especially, suspicions of lesbianism were so strong that "it made you feel that you had to go more into the closet . . . , or to prove on the outside that you weren't a lesbian." Loraine Sumner made the same point about women in semipro and amateur sport, saying that among many of her acquaintances in the 1950s and 1960s, "it was completely denied. Whenever you'd try to talk to somebody on it they would completely deny it—'You can't prove it!' Well, I'm not trying to prove anything. . . . These were friends of mine. But unless you were involved with them you couldn't get them to admit anything. You couldn't have conversations."[40] Though frustrated by the denial, Sumner observed the code and believed strongly that "you don't have to go around broadcasting it and looking for trouble."

Although in hindsight the underground nature of lesbianism in mid-century sport may seem extremely repressive, it may also have had positive dimensions. Unlike the bars, where women's very presence declared their status as sexual outlaws, in sport athletes could enjoy the company of lesbians and retain their membership in local communities where neighbors, kin, and co-workers respected and sometimes even celebrated their athletic abilities.

This opportunity may have been especially important for working-class women, who often remained in their communities of origin and had limited job, travel, and educational opportunities. For them sport was a lifeline, offering the chance to develop talents, win public acclaim, travel, and socialize with other lesbians. Loraine Sumner recalled her own options as an unmarried working-class Catholic in Boston: "Back then you either had to go into the convent or you had to get married and that was about it. Nobody ever thought that there was anything else for women back then. Thank God we had the sports!" Josephine D'Angelo and Ann Maguire also stressed the significance of sport for working-class lesbians:

> I mean if there wasn't sports, I think it really would have cut off a great deal of socializing. . . . If you didn't go to college, and you know some of the women did not go to college, what did that leave?[41]

> With their limited experiences of maybe having a job and that, *period*, and not having traveled and not having gone to the university, . . . where were you going to go?[42]

The unacknowledged, concealed presence of lesbians in sport may also have fostered possibilities for forms of same-sex intimacy that defied the standard, dichotomized definitions of homosexuality and heterosexuality. Even as they started "going around" with other women, some athletes may have participated in lesbian sexual relationships and friendship networks without privately or publicly claiming a lesbian identity.[43] This type of homosexual experience could have been temporary, a brief "phase" passed through on the way to coming out as a lesbian or resuming exclusive heterosexuality. Alternatively, it could have been an extended, yet bounded and thus relatively safe form of sexual experimentation, one confined to the world of sport by women who led otherwise heterosexual lives.

The "play it, don't say it" sexual ethos of sport appears to have sustained a wide range of lesbian experience. Athletic culture provided social space for "gay" women to create clearly delineated and flourishing lesbian identities and communities.[44] At the same time it allowed other women to move along the fringes of this world, operating across sexual and community lines without a firmly differentiated lesbian identity.

The same era that gave rise to the damning stereotype of the "mannish lesbian athlete" also contained the seeds of social and sexual possibility for women. From at least the 1940s on, sport provided space for lesbians to gather and build a shared culture. Lesbians could not publicly claim their identity without risking expulsion, ostracism, and loss of athletic activities and social networks that had become crucial to their sense of well-being. But expressed through a walk, a tone of voice, or a manner of dress, the gay culture of sport was available to women attuned to its physical and emotional cues.

Concealment and secrecy provided a degree of protection and flexibility. But, crucially, this strategy also kept lesbianism underground; the gay culture of sport was rumored but never revealed. Silenced by powerful stigmas against "mannish" athleticism and more general societal taboos against homosexuality, lesbians in sport found it impossible to speak to the wider public. Instead the lesbian culture of sport formed an "open secret" in American society, operating on—but not challenging—the fine line between public knowledge and practiced ignorance.[45]

For this reason the lesbian presence in sport did not lead to a reconsideration of society's heterosexual norms as much as it confirmed them. The image of lesbians in sport was conveyed to the dominant culture primarily as a demeaning stereotype. Presented as a caricature of female masculinity and perversion, the mannish lesbian athlete symbolized the unfeminine "other," the line beyond which "normal" women must not cross.

Yet the paradox of women's sport history is that the mannish lesbian athlete was not simply a homophobic icon; she was a human actor struggling to create new ways of being female in a society profoundly afraid of women's sexual autonomy and collective power. Lesbian athletes used the social and psychic space of sport to create a shared culture and affirmative identity. The pride, pleasure, companionship, and dignity lesbians found in the athletic world helped them survive in a hostile society. The challenge posed by their collective existence and by their refusal of conventional heterosexual femininity formed a precondition for more overt, political challenges to lesbian oppression that have occurred largely outside the realm of sport.

# CHAPTER 9

# WOMEN COMPETING/GENDER CONTESTED

Decades of controversy over female competition, masculinization, and the sexual reputation of women athletes point to an enduring opposition between sport and womanhood. In 1960, after a half-century of women's active involvement in sport, the *New York Times* published a Sunday magazine essay claiming that the great majority of women athletes did not possess "the Image." The "Image," according to author William Furlong, was simply an updated version of what 1930s sportswriter Paul Gallico had called "S.A.," or sex appeal.[1] Furlong approved of sports that enhanced women's "decorative" appeal but condemned any sports that turned women into muscular, unbecoming athletes he called "unwomanly." He was joined by a chorus of others in the media. While journalists praised several 1960 Olympians for their "good looks and charming ways," they ridiculed the "overdeveloped muscles and underdeveloped glands" of competitors who refused the dictum to be "athletes second, girls first."[2]

Why, despite decades of female participation, did the disparaging image of the "mannish" athlete still hold sway in the popular imagination? And why did observers, especially the fraternity of male sportswriters, find it so disturbing when a small group of women placed athletic goals ahead of standard notions of "feminine beauty"? The answer rests in the deeper-seated anxiety that underlay charges of mannishness and ugliness. The presence of powerful women athletes struck at the roots of male dominance in American society—the seemingly natural physical superiority of men. When women "surrendered their sex" to take up masculine sport, might they also be assuming the prerogatives and power of males, threatening what one sportswriter wistfully referred to as "the old male supremacy?"[3]

The resulting sense of gender disorder precipitated a wide array of responses, ranging from those who endorsed women athletes' assertion of power to those who vehemently resisted any change in the status quo. But whether they reacted with amazement, approval, horror, or disdain, twentieth-century observers paid an almost obsessive attention to two issues: the presence or absence of femininity among female athletes, and the comparative capabilities of men and women in sport. In their frequent attempts to address these questions, journalists, educators, sport officials, and social commentators tried to reconcile sport and womanhood and to resolve the nagging question of power that lurked beneath the surface of debate.

Women athletes faced an even more complicated task. In addition to enduring second-class athletic status and finding themselves the focal point of gender controversies, women in sport had to bridge the gulf between societal images of "mannish" athletes and their own positive experience of sport and its compatibility with womanhood. The masculine stigma sometimes hurt, discouraged, or constrained them. Yet they continued to play, relying on athletic peers and supportive families, close friends, or their local communities for reassurance. Most of all, athletes found strength in the actual experience of sport—in the pleasure, knowledge, and opportunities gained through athletic involvement.

Athletes had little control over athletic policies and philosophies that reinforced conventional concepts of masculinity and femininity, weaving these distinctions into the very fabric of sport. Yet they were not powerless to effect changes in their own minds and immediate surroundings. As they played, women athletes developed a kind of double consciousness; while comprehending the cultural interdiction against "mannish" athletic women, they drew on their shared experience as female athletes to generate an expansive definition of womanhood that eliminated, or at least eased, the dissonance between athleticism and femininity.

A sense of threatened manhood lay just beneath the surface of many media portrayals of women's sport. Although nearly all female athletic competition took place in women-only events, male journalists frequently described such events as a contest between women and men.[4] For instance, even in Grantland Rice's laudatory articles on women's athletic achievements in the 1920s and 1930s, a shadowy male opponent seemed to lurk behind competitions that by all appearances involved only women athletes.[5] In articles like "Is There a Weaker Sex?" and "The Slightly Weaker Sex," Rice could not help but compare women's marvelous athletic accomplishments to men's, wondering whether women might someday equal or exceed men's athletic feats. He addressed this theme overtly in "Leading Ladies," concluding his discussion of leading women athletes with an assessment of men's fading athletic superiority.[6] Although Rice determined that men still had a slight edge in strength and stamina, he did not rest secure in this knowledge, ending his poem "Look Out for the Ladies" with the question, "If they keep on getting better / Who will be the weaker sex?"[7]

In the 1920s observers tended to raise these questions in a bemused tone. There was a kind of carnivalesque fascination with women's athletic feats as a symbol of the changing gender order of American society.[8] In its most fantastic form, the image of the female athlete signaled a total inversion of established gender relations, an indication that female dominance might eventually replace men's traditional authority. For example, after Sybil Bauer broke the world record for the backstroke, a 1924 editorial in the *Nation* jokingly predicted that while current female athletic successes amounted to only "a modest invasion of men's rights," in another twenty years sports might be described as "fundamentally feminine pastimes" requiring speed and strength, "not qualities that men should either desire or seek to develop."[9]

In a similar flight of imagination, Grantland Rice fantasized that in the future, in case of shipwreck or other nautical emergency, it would be women, strengthened through sport, who would sound the protective call of men and children overboard.[10]

The fascination with competition faded in the 1930s, probably because both the attention and the opportunities available to women athletes diminished during a decade of financial cutbacks and renewed skepticism toward independent women in traditionally masculine pursuits. When the issue of gender rivalry did surface, however, the lighthearted air was gone. Writers in the early 1930s described female athletic involvement as an uninvited incursion into "man's unassailable domain" and openly declared that women's success in sport and other realms posed a threat to prevailing gender arrangements.[11]

In the few cases in which women directly challenged and defeated men in competition, the threat to male supremacy appeared even more imminent. A 1938 article titled "Foils and Foibles" recounted the story of Helene Mayer's two-day claim to the national fencing title after she unexpectedly defeated the men's champion. The U.S. fencing organization hurriedly imposed a ban on competition between men and women and revoked Mayer's number one status "for chivalry's sake." Officials defended their actions by arguing that men could not fight full force against women because fencing involved physical contact (although only the tip of a foil against a protected body). Faced with the fact that a woman had defeated a man in unrestricted competition, fencing leaders turned the issue upside down, asserting that continued mixed-sex competition "is almost as bad as punching a girl in the eye."[12] This "reasoning" converted a woman's victory over a male champion into an argument for female protection, underlined by a threatening reminder of men's capacity for violence against women.

The Cold War years sparked a recurrence of the symbolism of gender inversion. Fearing that the superiority of women athletes in the Eastern bloc might ruin American chances to win the overall Olympic medal count, the press ridiculed the combination of "strong Red ladies" and "frail Red males." No mixed-sex competition occurred, yet in articles like "The Stronger Soviet Sex," the media responded to the competitive strength of Soviet women by invoking the threat of female athletes competing for gender supremacy.[13]

Given women's "encroachment" into male sport and their sometimes outstanding achievements, contemporary observers asked the question, Who would rule, men or women? In their recurrent comparisons of male and female athletic ability, reporters usually concluded that men would maintain their superiority over women, especially in the realm of sport. But their persistent tendency to interpret women vying against women as women competing with men indicated that their conclusions rested on a foundation of insecurity.

⌐○⌐

Journalists revealed a similar uncertainty as they struggled to apply concepts of masculinity and femininity to successful female athletes whose skills seemed to blur these very distinctions. The surprising abilities exhibited by women athletes induced sportswriters to try to reconcile the "masculine" nature of women's accomplishments with the femininity the public (and they themselves) wanted to see. In describing female athletes' bodies, playing styles, and personalities, the media went to great—sometimes comic—lengths to attribute gender to the anomalous athlete.

To account for women's "masculine" abilities, reporters often described the bodies of female athletes in terms usually reserved for men. For example, "big, splendid, deep-chested" swimmer Gertrude Ederle was a "strapping" girl with a "column-like throat" and "muscles of steel." Yet writers also searched for feminine physical traits that would distinguish the manly female athlete from her male counterpart. One journalist pointed to Ederle's cleft chin as an "odd and alluring contrast to the rest of her . . . so feminine, so sweet, that it makes her all woman despite those iron shoulder muscles that swell beneath her blouse."[14] This journalist had to resort to something that was not there—an empty space in Ederle's chin—to find evidence of physical femininity in a seventeen-year-old athlete whose astounding ten world records signaled masculine physical ability.

Often journalists paired words that suggested masculinity and femininity simultaneously. Tennis and golf star Mary K. Browne had a disarming "sugar-coated truculence."[15] Her tennis rival Helen Wills was described as a "vision of white and pink," with a "chiseled beauty" and arms like "pistoning-columns of white muscle." Obviously, the white of her muscle did not show, but, like the reference to pink, it helped feminize her pistonlike arms. Wills's on-court manner also evoked gendered representation as writers referred to her "meticulous to the point of mincing" pace, her "dainty stateliness," and her "impregnably placid" demeanor.[16] Such contrasts in language revealed observers' struggle to capture the gender ambiguity of athletic womanhood.

There was less ambiguity about successful athletes' skill, which journalists invariably described as masculine. British golfer Enid Wilson, "the girl who hits like a man," reportedly "ripped the ball" with "blasting power." She could "punch out an iron with masculine vigor and hammer a brassie with virile gusto."[17] Tennis players were said to stroke the ball with "machine-like precision" and exhibit "cold, tense, machine-like qualities."[18] In addition to masculine, technological metaphors, journalists depicted female athletic power through sexually evocative images of male aggression. Helen Wills played "without even a pretense of mercy. It was almost as though a man with a rapier were sending home his vital thrusts against a foeman unarmed."[19] Sexual metaphors point to the less conscious connection between sport and male virility, suggesting as well the implicit threat that active, skilled women posed to men's sense of sexual potency.

Losers, by virtue of their lesser skill, were described in more feminine terms. Compared to her victorious opponent Enid Wilson, golfer Leona Cheney struck observers as a "slender, little Los Angeles matron" with a "somewhat frail appearance."[20] Sportswriters commented on the "tow-headed and fluffy helplessness" of defeated athletes and contrasted the "softer" loser of one tennis match to her opponent's "colder mind and . . . hotter vigor."[21] At the 1932 U.S. Open tennis tournament, second-place finisher Carolyn Babcock offered the audience "the smile of a beaten, somewhat bewildered little girl, a pretty girl with white teeth."[22] By reserving the attributes most associated with attractive femininity—those represented by soft, smiling, pretty, slender

white womanhood—for unsuccessful athletes, the media conveyed a powerful message. Femininity presupposed lesser athletic
ability, and athletic success in turn signaled masculine power and
failed femininity.

Yet reporters also sought to restore femininity to the successful athlete, searching for any evidence of feminine activity and
interest that might offset her "masculine" sporting achievements
and stature. Early coverage of Babe Didrikson invariably juxta-
posed her Olympic medals to the blue ribbon she had earned for
sewing or baking (reporters differed on the specifics) at the
Texas State Fair. Similarly, one author assured readers that
Gertrude Ederle sewed her own clothes and, besides swimming,
kept fit through housework.[23] Another reporter noted that
"Queen of the Modern Mermaids" Helene Madison took time
out from swimming to paint her fingernails a brilliant red. He
added, "As a girl Helene liked dolls but never would bother to
sew little garments for them."[24]

Reporters and their contemporaries puzzled over private
details and public personalities in an effort to reconcile a firm
belief in the masculinity of sport with the unsettling fact of
female athletic accomplishment. In his 1933 book *Technics and
Civilization*, Lewis Mumford contemplated the contradiction. To
Mumford the sports hero represented "virility, courage, game-
ness." However, "If the hero is a girl," he reasoned: "her qualities must be Amazonian in character. The sport hero represents
the masculine virtues, the Mars complex, as the popular motion
picture actress or the bathing beauty contest represents Venus."[25]
Journalists and sport promoters resolved the incongruity of a
female Mars by positing an idealized image of the feminine athlete as beauty queen, mermaid, or fashion model. The attempt to
liken athletes to models of womanhood reached the height of
absurdity when John Tunis compared the "galaxy of girl athletes" at the 1929 Wimbledon tennis tournament not to genuine
fashion models but to "a display of mannequins at a fashion
parade."[26] Thus the "Amazonian" female athlete shed the character of Mars and became Venus.

As sportswriters reported the "news" of sports, they also used their stock portrayals of Mars-like "muscle molls" and Venus-like "beauty queens" to create a set of conventional narratives about women in sport. Coverage of women athletes typically conformed to one of two stories, both of which sought to resolve the tension between athleticism and femininity.

In one version the girl or woman athlete assumes a masculine persona while she competes, but after the event drops her "mask" and becomes her true feminine self, illustrated by her overtly feminine demeanor and, in some instances, the search for male love. Helen Wills, for example, was accused of being a "cold, superior, emotionless sphinx" on court. She redeemed herself, occasionally during play but more often off the tennis courts, as she pursued her college degree, art career, and romantic interests. In these settings she tore away the "false, unnatural front that she wore like a cold gray veil" to reveal herself "to be a gay, sprightly, pleasing young girl who could enjoy herself and be gracious in the process."[27]

In a second version a tomboy girl athlete grows up into a champion by honing her "masculine" skills, but along the way trades in her boyish ways for feminine charms. She becomes a champion *woman* athlete. Journalists adopted this narrative to tell the story of Althea Gibson's rise to stardom in the world of tennis. The *Saturday Evening Post* cast Gibson's remarkable achievements as a black Pygmalion story, describing her transformation from a "streetsmart tomboy" to "a little lady." Through the efforts of African American educators, tennis coaches, and society leaders, the "Harlem urchin" had become "America's new Gibson Girl," the esteemed champion of a "game for ladies and gentlemen."[28]

Journalists tried to squeeze their subjects into the mold of these oft-repeated narratives whether they fit or not. Babe Didrikson, whose athletic career spanned the late 1920s to her death in 1957, formed an especially challenging case. Although she observed convention by marrying and donning dresses in her later years, in other ways she defied feminine norms, radiating an independence, bold wit, and athletic virtuosity that struck onlookers as undeniably masculine. Her unconventionality forced

(LEFT) With athletic accomplishments spanning the pre- and postwar decades, Mildred "Babe" Didrikson was the most controversial and popular midcentury American sportswoman. Here she is shown as the sole member of the 1932 Employers' Casualty Company "team," which won the AAU team championship. Didrikson went on to win two golds and a silver medal at the 1932 Los Angeles Olympics. (*Chicago Historical Society*)

(RIGHT) Babe Didrikson fifteen years later in 1947, after leaving track, basketball, and other sports behind for professional golf. Her early reputation for masculine build and bravado faded in the immediate postwar years, as Didrikson took up golf and carefully cultivated a more feminine image. In addition to marrying George Zaharias, she let her hair grow and began wearing makeup and dresses. (*Chicago Historical Society*)

SOPHIE KURYS
Second Base

DOTTIE HA[...]
Shortst[...]

DOTTIE KAMENSHEK
First Base

MARY REYNO[...]
Third Base

1947 A[...]
T[...]

(ABOVE, LEFT) Softball retained its popularity in the 1940s and early 1950s, especially in the Midwest, where paying crowds were entertained by newly organized women's professional leagues. One of the nation's best players was Frieda Savona of the National Girls Baseball League. Her muscled forearms and reputedly "masculine" look and ability made her a controversial figure in the 1940s. (*Chicago Historical Society*)

(ABOVE, RIGHT) It was the "masculine" look that the All-American Girls Baseball League sought to avoid with their pastel, skirted uniforms and attempted "nice girl" image. Here are several members of the 1947 All-Star Team wearing the required uniform. (*Racine County Historical Society and Museum, Inc.*)

Basketball continued to be the favorite sport of many women. The Amateur Athletic Union offered annual championships beginning in the 1920s and continuing to this day. Here members of the 1951 championship team, sponsored by Hanes Hosiery, pose with their trophies and their coach. (*Naismith Memorial Basketball Hall of Fame*)

ANNA MAY HUTCHISON
Pitcher

AUDREY WAGNER
Outfield

RUTH LESSING
Catcher

JO LENARD
Outfield

MILDRED EARP
Pitcher

EDYTHE PERLICK
Outfield

DOTTIE MUELLER
Pitcher

DORIS SAMS
Pitcher & Outfield
Player of the Year

(TOP) In the postwar era, field events continued to draw criticism from within and outside of Olympic agencies. The muscular bulk of athletes like Earline Brown (of Los Angeles and then Tennessee A & I) was considered by some especially "unsightly" or unaesthetic. Here Brown puts the shot during the 1959 Pan-American Games in Chicago. (*National Archives*)

(BOTTOM) In the 1950s and 1960s, Tennessee A & I took the mantle from Tuskegee Institute as the dominant team in women's track. When Tennessee star Wilma Rudolph won three gold medals in the 1960 Rome Olympics she began to win public acclaim for African American female track stars, reversing decades of neglect by the popular white press. (*National Archives*)

(TOP) When women like Althea Gibson and Billie Jean King broke into tennis's top ranks, they challenged the deeply entrenched elitism, racism, and sexism of the tennis world. Shown here competing in the 1956 Wimbledon tournament, Gibson was the first to crash the color line in women's tennis. The reigning American Tennis Association (the black tennis tour) champion made her mark by winning both Wimbledon and the U.S. Open in 1956 and 1957. (*National Archives*)

(BOTTOM) A decade later, Billie Jean King took up where Gibson left off. After establishing herself as a first-rate player in the late 1960s, King earned a reputation for being aggressive off the court as well as on. As an outspoken feminist, during the 1970s she led the charge for equal prize money, an independent women's tour, and improved treatment for women in professional tennis. (*National Archives*)

(ABOVE) In contrast to King, Chris Evert was known for her more traditional baseline game and more "feminine" demeanor (note the ruffled petty pants). The crowd and the press embraced her girlish image and affectionately called her Chrissie. (*National Archives*)

(RIGHT) During the same decade, gymnastics rivaled tennis in popularity. Formerly perceived as a strength sport for muscle-bound male hulks, its image was transformed by agile, petite young stars like 1972 U.S. Olympian Cathy Rigby. Rigby and contemporaries like Olga Korbut and Nadia Comaneci popularized gymnastics as an aesthetic, "feminine" sport, though it continued to demand great strength, control, and explosive power. (*National Archives*)

(ABOVE) The 1980s brought further changes, advances, and controversies in women's sports. Taking the mantle from King and Evert, Martina Navratilova dominated tennis. Her overpowering game led some to suggest that Navratilova was a "bionic" creature whose "masculine" skills gave her an unfair advantage over "normal" women. In the late 1980s and 1990s, Navratilova broke a long-standing athletic taboo by defending gay rights and speaking openly of her own lesbian relationships. (*A. Tannenbaum/Sygma*)

(LEFT) African American women, who had dominated track events since the late 1930s, finally gained public acceptance, acclaim, and, in some cases, stardom in the 1980s. Florence Griffith Joyner (shown competing in the Olympics in Seoul in 1988) and Jackie Joyner-Kersee pioneered a style of self-confident, graceful, but muscular athletic womanhood. Yet they and others were plagued by rumors of steroid use and accusations that their "masculine" skills could have been obtained only by illicit methods. (*P. Perrin/Sygma*)

(RIGHT) Women's body building also met with charges of steroid abuse and "unsightly" masculine appearance. Part beauty contest and part athletic competition, the sport gained rapid popularity in the late 1970s and 1980s. Bikini-clad body builders paraded before a panel of judges who assessed contestants on a combination of extreme musculature and traditionally feminine makeup and costume that mocked and disrupted gender conventions as much as it reinforced them. (*Jean Pierre Fizet/Sygma*)

journalists to work that much harder to insert her into the pre-fabricated narratives they delivered to the public.

Initially reporters found little in Didrikson's appearance or athleticism to reassure them about her femininity. One writer explained: "This chin of the Babe's, the thin, set lips, the straight, sharp profile, the sallow suntan, undisguised by rouge, regarded in connection with her amazing athletic prowess at first acquaintance are likely to do her no justice."[29] Others commented that she had a "button-breasted" figure, a mouth like "a pale slit," and a "door-stop jaw and piano-wire muscles." Her spirit, too, seemed wholly masculine, especially her "Viking capacity for berserk rage" and a "hot resolve and a soaring confidence."[30] Because of her youth and her stated lack of interest in men, reporters in the 1930s focused on her public persona as a masculine tomboy, looking for some "female" interests that might reinstate her as a woman. One reporter insisted: "It's a mistake to think of her talent as 'purely muscular.' " Rather, "The greatest girl athlete in the world just now, with a special liking for men's games, is as feminine as hairpins."[31] He found his proof in the fact that "the Babe can sew, and cook a mean meal. In the wardrobe she brought with her from Dallas is a blue crepe party dress which she made herself."[32]

After quitting track and field and touring for a time as a pitcher on a men's traveling baseball team, Didrikson took up the more socially respectable game of golf. Around the same time she married professional wrestler and promoter George Zaharias, a hirsute, heavy-set man who seemed to exude masculinity from every pore. Whether entered into for love or for convenience, the marriage helped solve the riddle others found in Didrikson's gender, a problem of which she was acutely aware. She had earlier complained about reporters always asking if she would marry, saying, "It gets my goat. They seem to think I'm a strange, unnatural being summed up in the words Muscle Moll."[33] The marriage won her a reprieve from such accusations.[34]

As Didrikson attained prominence as an amateur and then pro golfer, she regained her star status in the late 1940s. But her golfing accomplishments earned scant praise next to her more celebrated achievement—becoming a "real woman" at last. Because she had married, gained weight, and taken up a more "feminine" sport, journalists could now plug her into the tomboy-becomes-real-woman narrative. *Life* magazine trumpeted Didrikson's achievement with the lengthy headline: "Babe Is a Lady Now: The World's Most Amazing Athlete Has Learned to Wear Nylons and Cook for Her Huge Husband." The article left little to the imagination, announcing that the former "Texas tomboy" slept with her husband in an eight-foot-square bed.[35]

In celebrating the transformation reporters remarked that Didrikson's body and her skills, her most noted "masculine" features, had also become more feminine. Pete Martin of the *Saturday Evening Post* wrote that though once rumored really to be a boy, Didrikson now featured big breasts, a small waist, and thirty-seven-inch hips. Frank Fawley, also of the *Post*, lavishly praised the Babe's mastery of "cooking, interior decorating, curtain making, Victory gardening and other housewifely arts." He gushed, "She has evolved from a tomboyish, often blunt-spoken, athlete to a pleasant, mannerly companion." Even one of her harshest critics, Paul Gallico, revised his opinion after seeing the "transition from the man-girl who hated sissies to a feminine woman."[36]

In the rush to establish Didrikson's femininity, her amazing athletic ability nearly got lost in the shuffle. Over the course of her career she starred in basketball, track and field, baseball, and golf. In the 1950s, between bouts of cancer, she became the best U.S. female golfer and helped put the women's pro tour on solid footing. When she died of cancer in 1957 while still in her forties, the press celebrated her less for her athletic accomplishments than for her other "achievement"—femininity. Paul Gallico, who had once ridiculed her "hatchet face," wrote in "Farewell to Babe" that Didrikson would be remembered not only for her amazing athletic feats but "likewise in the hearts of all of us who loved her for what she was, a splendid woman."[37]

The media presented athletes like Didrikson as heroines in a popular success story. But unlike such male heroes as Horatio Alger or Babe Ruth, whose accomplishments in their chosen endeavors enhanced their manhood, women athletes could only achieve a precarious heroic status. It balanced on the tension between "masculine" sporting ability and compensatory efforts to prove their femininity. The tenuous nature of women's athletic heroism found expression in the twin narratives used by sports-writers. In each case, the "masculine-athlete-reveals-true-feminine-self" and the "tomboy-turned-woman" narrative suggested that women's athletic identity was by nature temporary. In this way each scenario admitted women's athleticism without conceding the masculinity of sport or the superiority of men.

A recurring imagery of masks offered further evidence of the ephemeral nature of women's athletic identity. Helen Wills's grim game face was described as a "mask of austerity," while Babe Didrikson's was frozen into a "thin-lipped mask."[38] These descriptions, as well as headlines like "Babe Didrikson Takes Off Her Mask," implied that women athletes assumed a facade, an illegitimate representation of masculinity soon shed for a truer, more rewarding feminine persona.[39] In this view athleticism, was a temporary transgression, rather than a constitutive feature, of true womanhood.

In far more subtle ways the everyday practice of sport mirrored the rhetoric of sport journalism. As particular games, styles of play, and concepts of skill were designated as masculine or feminine, gender differences were woven into the very fabric of sport. The gendered structure of athletics worked to reinforce and naturalize the cultural division between "genuine" male sport and a less legitimate female brand of athleticism.

Women have participated at some point and to some degree in all American sports. Whether a sport became popular among girls and women or attracted a primarily male constituency depended on timing, sponsorship, the interest a sport sparked, and the traditions it developed. However, over time certain sports have been seen as appropriate for one sex only. Currently football and boxing are sports that continue to be viewed as male-only sports, while water ballet and rhythmic gymnastics remain exclusively female. These divisions rest on the assumption that some sports are inherently and incontrovertibly masculine or feminine. For example, IOC members of the 1950s exhibited confidence that they could determine which sports were "essentially feminine" in order to exclude women from those that were not.[40]

What differentiated ordinary "masculine" athletics from "truly feminine" sport? The masculine image of sport cohered around attributes of strength, size, rigorous training, and aggressive competition, which together made up an ideal of athletic virility.[41] The sports onlookers and officials labeled as too masculine for women were usually sports that emphasized these qualities in the extreme. Rugby, ice hockey, and boxing—rough games involving extensive physical contact and aggression—connoted pure masculinity. Sports that demanded sheer strength or arduous training regimens, like shot-putting or long-distance running, also appeared incommensurate with femininity. In addition rugged team sports with a working-class male profile—like baseball and, by the mid-twentieth century, football—evoked a special aura rooted in the popular conception of working-class men as representatives of raw masculinity.[42]

On the other hand, sports that emphasized the aesthetic side of athletics most often received feminine designations.[43] All sports contain an aesthetic dimension as part of their appeal, but in some activities, especially those where violence, aggression, and exhaustion are minimized, the beauty of motion takes precedence in public perceptions. Sports like diving and gymnastics were understood as more feminine, by virtue of their association with beauty. Paul Gallico explained: "It is a lady's business to look beautiful and there are hardly any sports in which she seems able to do it." He admonished women to limit themselves to the beautifying sports of fishing, archery, flying, riding, shooting, swimming backstroke, and speed and figure skating.[44] The appreciation of a feminine aesthetic thus became an injunction to refrain from sports that did not beautify.

Notably Gallico listed only individual sports. The camaraderie, playful roughhousing, and physical intimacy of team play projected a manly image, one jealously guarded by male athletes. Rugged team sport was one of the only social arenas in which male touch did not connote homosexuality but could in fact enhance a man's virile, heterosexual image. If "tainted" by femininity, athletic touch could conceivably intimate homosexuality.[45]

For example, in 1952 a British critic of American men's sport wrote an article titled "American Athletes Are Sissies." As proof of their effeminacy, he pointed out that American men excelled in baseball, basketball, and bowling, sports derived from the British children's games of rounders, netball, and skittles, all played primarily by girls.[46]

The author, however misguided in his assessments, correctly pointed to the fact that even when both sexes participated, individual sports acquired either a masculine or feminine image, sometimes undergoing a "sex change" in the course of development. While basketball and softball originated as "feminine" games and then gradually assumed a masculine gender attribution, the reverse occurred in gymnastics. In the 1950s Soviet women gymnasts dazzled Olympic crowds with their feminine beauty and charm, especially in comparison to Russian women competing in track and field. Hoping to improve American women's Olympic performance, the AAU encouraged female athletes to take up the new "feminine" sport. A *Life* magazine photo essay on gymnastics noted the change. The article contrasted the former image of the sport as "an athletic ritual pursued by crackpots, muscle-bound culturists and misguided persons named Ivan" with the current knowledge "that a gymnast can be as graceful as a ballerina and as appealing as a model in a perfume ad."[47] As the perfumed ballerina replaced the muscular "Ivan," gymnastics attained a feminine status.

A sport's gender theoretically indicated the sex of its main participants. But social class also played an important role in determining the gender reputation of any given sport and of the athletes who played it.[48] The development of bowling illustrates how changes in the class constituency of a sport could also alter its gender designation. The game first gained popularity in the 1890s and early 1900s. In subsequent decades, despite the efforts of amateur leaders to establish it on a wholesome, purely amateur basis, bowling's early links to working-class pool halls, taverns, and gamblers gave it a shady reputation that made it even less respectable for women than for men.

During the depression bowling broadened its appeal, especially among women. Journalists noted the change and engaged in a sometimes comical effort to ascribe gender to the sport and its female participants. While one writer in 1936 praised star bowler Floretta Doty McCutcheon for being a "48 year old matron" whose "refined appearance . . . [was] attracting a high type of women to bowling," another journalist's account of the Women's International Bowling Tournament gleefully described female keglers who swaggered, whooped, downed beer, rode motorcycles, sported black eyes and cowboy hats, and bowled "as well as certain men"—except for the "stenographers and salesgirls who sent ball after ball into the gutters."[49] The "femininity" of bowling remained in doubt, pulled between contrasting images of matronly middle-class refinement and uncouth working-class rowdiness.

Soon the number of positive portrayals outweighed negative ones. When the popularity of bowling soared in the 1940s and 1950s, *Newsweek* attributed the boom to the fact "that Mama has accepted it as a wholesome recreation not only for her husband but for herself and her whole family."[50] Estimates of one million women bowlers in 1936 grew to three million in 1941 and reached six to eight million in the 1950s. As ambitious suburban developers built new bowling alleys to meet the recreational needs of young couples and families living outside the city, efforts to tailor the sport toward women grew more and more elaborate. Bowling establishments built coffee shops, beauty parlors, nurseries, and plush lounges, all designed to attract women customers during the daytime hours, when the regular male clientele was at work. As the sanitized atmosphere of new-style bowling "lanes" replaced the spittoons and smoky bars of old-style bowling "alleys," the reputation of women bowlers improved accordingly.

Through such efforts bowling shed both its disreputable working-class image and its purely masculine reputation. It retained its blue-collar appeal but at the same time gained acceptance as a "feminine" sport by successfully associating itself with notions of middle-class feminine respectability and heterosexual leisure. As one owner put it, bowling had "become the people's country clubs and it's the girls who have made it that way."[51]

The fact that both men and women bowled, golfed, or played tennis could reasonably have led to the disappearance of gender distinctions in sport. This was not the case, however. Instead cross-sex participation typically led to more extensive gender differentiation within a given sport. In softball, tennis, basketball, track, gymnastics, and other sports, athletic administrators devised gender-specific rules to mark women's activities as different from, and usually "less than," men's.[52]

Regulations on the use of space and time in women's sport acted to limit female activity and to create an impression of lesser physical capacity. For example, to compensate for women softball players' presumed lack of arm strength and accuracy, the distance between pitching rubber and home plate—thus, the pitching distance—was shorter for women than for men. In basketball women played for shorter time periods and on a divided court. In tennis, while the court dimensions were the same for men and women, men played five sets and women three for a match. In track and field women threw the shot but not the discus, did not pole-vault, and ran shorter distances than men. In golf the "women's tee" shortened the distance to the cup. The overall effect was to gender space: Women took up less space and time in sport than men did.

Physical touch as well as unrestricted movement acquired masculine associations in sport. Early prohibitions on touch were designed out of concern for female frailty, sexual modesty, and mental health. In 1927 Dr. William Burdick claimed that personal contact in sport could lead to female neuroses. Inadvertent punching or scratching resulted in blemishes and facial disfigurements, which, according to Burdick, would cause not only physical but psychic damage.[53] Although the most exaggerated of these concerns faded with time, restrictions on physical contact continued to distinguish women's play from men's. While "women's rules" minimized physical contact in basketball, "no-slide" rules (which outlawed sliding into bases by base runners) in women's softball leagues effected the same result.[54] These restrictions contained women's athletic exertion and aggressiveness, at the same time making touch among teammates and between opponents a right (and rite) of manhood.

Along with time, space, and touch, athletic clothing also marked gender differences in sport. Often consciously designed to avert accusations of mannishness, most women's athletic dress accented feminine beauty and preserved feminine modesty. Twentieth-century tennis players eventually shed their long skirts but continued to display their femininity and purity in white, wide-skirted, ruffled dresses. Sports in which male and female uniforms differed the least—track and field and softball—were also the least reputable for women, sometimes prompting compensatory strategies like the AAGBL's use of pastel-skirted baseball uniforms.[55] Among commercial promoters concern with modesty and respectability often conflicted with a desire to highlight erotic aspects of femininity. Where sponsors sought to cash in on the sexual appeal of female athletes, they employed short shorts, sleeveless tops, and bright and shiny colors as material signifiers of athletic femininity.[56]

Through athletic policies that regulated space, time, touch, and dress, masculinity and femininity were designated as separate but not equal. Femininity was typically constituted around the edges of sport through references to female beauty and sex appeal. Within sporting activity femininity was defined as "lesser than" (shorter distances, time periods), "different from" (women's rules, special equipment), or "derivative of" ("kitten ball" and "captain ball" as derivatives of baseball and basketball) men's sport. The primary status of male sport found expression in common language, too. Women's presence was signaled with references to "women's basketball" or the "ladies golf tour," while the unmodified "basketball" or "golf" presumed the presence of men. Similarly, by itself the supposedly neutral noun "athlete" was in common usage a male term. Female athleticism found acknowledgement only through the modified term "woman athlete." In language as well as practice, women's sport required modification.

With women's sport defined as the exception to the rule, athletic skill, like the athlete, continued to be construed as essentially and fundamentally masculine. For conclusive proof of the inherent masculinity of athletic skill, conservatives linked their portrait of human athletic performance with evidence from science and the animal world. In 1944 *Time* magazine gave favorable notice to scientists who were paying renewed attention to "natural" sexual differences. Citing scientific experts (but ignoring actual athletic records), the article claimed that "no woman has ever equaled men's records in any athletic activity." For ultimate proof, according to the author, one could look to the animal kingdom, in which "even in horseracing, stallions are faster," demonstrated by the fact that only one mare had won the Kentucky Derby. (Appropriately her name was "Regret.")[57]

The gendered rhetoric and everyday practice of sport reinforced sexual divisions and inequalities in the athletic world. More important, these arrangements shaped the contours of gender relations in the wider society, contributing to notions of "natural" male superiority, immutable sexual differences, and normative concepts of manhood and womanhood.

In modern Western societies the belief that men are superior to women, and its corollary, that men's greater social power flows from their natural superiority, has lost legitimacy. Yet in virtually all realms of society—work, family, politics, academia, the arts—men have retained their advantage in power and prestige. What legitimates their authority? Sport provides one key source of legitimation by giving the impression that, fairness aside, men in fact are biologically superior to women in strength and power. *Time* magazine's 1944 discussion of sex differences in horses and humans went beyond a simple claim for the athletic superiority of talented stallions and men, professing to offer scientific proof that gender differences and men's superior power were artifacts of nature and should therefore be observed and accepted in all realms of society.[58]

There is no logical or necessary connection between biological differences and social and political inequalities; however, the "fit" among supposedly natural inequalities in sport, deep-seated gender traditions, and commonsense beliefs about sexual difference allowed biological "evidence" from sport to authorize male power in other domains. The constant, almost compulsive comparison of male and female athletic performance "proved" the biological basis of gender inequality. Through the "performance gap" in sports, male superiority appeared both normal and just.[59]

Beyond intellectually justifying the power of men, sport has also physically empowered men to maintain their dominance.[60] Through participation in a culturally masculine realm, men have strengthened their bodies and mastered physical force, acquiring both physical power and the permission to express it as masculine prowess. They have accumulated tools—physical strength, training in violence, and permission to use space and touch as they see fit—that have been used to assert male authority outside as well as inside the realm of sport.[61]

Notions of femininity promulgated in sport have had the opposite effect. Athletic participation can potentially strengthen women physically and allow them to gain a knowledge of, appreciation for, and confidence in their bodies. Women athletes have clearly benefited from and enjoyed these aspects of sport. However, when experts and critics consistently emphasized the aesthetic versus strength-related dimension of "feminine" sport, they fortified a set of problematic cultural links between femininity, beauty, and female athleticism.

The belief that femininity is an aesthetic disguises the fact that not just beauty but passivity, submissiveness, frailty, and service—signal features of women's subordination—have also characterized femininity. When women's sport is limited to aesthetically pleasing "feminine" activities, it perpetuates the deceptive emphasis on femininity as beauty, masking its ties to female subordination.[62] For instance, the idea that women should compete primarily in "beauty-producing" sports like swimming, gymnastics, and ice-skating (even though they, in fact, also demand strength and competitive intensity) simply reinforces the belief that muscles, aggressiveness, and competitiveness are neither feminine nor beautiful in a woman. And by barring women from strength-building contact sports like wrestling or football, the sports world reaffirms the expectation of female passivity, submissiveness, and frailty—the demeaning aspects of femininity that underlie the aesthetic.

Cultural characterizations of masculine skill, feminine weakness, and natural male superiority have not gone unchallenged, especially by the many women who have played sports. Yet, as dominant beliefs, these notions have had the power to influence lives, particularly by generating normative and stigmatized conceptions of manhood and womanhood. When boys and men participate in athletics, they are steeped in a culture of masculinity. Their bodies begin to approximate the physical ideal of the manly athlete, and they receive assurance of their manliness by virtue of their interest and participation. But those men who do not like (or excel in) sports are excluded from this path to masculine achievement. As "sissies" they fall into an inferior category of masculinity. Unless they have other means of demonstrating their manhood through political, intellectual, or economic authority, their status as men suffers.[63]

The process has worked in reverse for women's sport, in which the concept of masculinity has fostered a stigmatizing rather than a normative image of the female athlete. For this reason the majority of women have steered clear of competitive sport and the cultural traits associated with it. Yet a minority have chosen to ignore the message and actively pursue "masculine" sport. The censorious figure of the "muscle moll" or "mannish athlete" has captured these activities and presented them through the perspective of a culture that fears women's power and sexual independence.[64]

The stigma of athletic mannishness has spread beyond sport to influence broader cultural values and practices. Conventional beauty standards have equated muscular bulk with ugliness, while scorn has been heaped on aggressive, "ball-busting" women. Beginning in the 1930s the "mannish athlete" even entered the discourse of science. Psychologists Lewis Terman and Catherine Cox Miles developed an extremely influential Attitude Interest Analysis Survey that rated masculinity and femininity. In testing they found that male and female collegiate athletes earned the highest masculine score. Their results confirmed the popular perception that sport masculinized both women and men, codify-ing it as scientifically verified truth. The popular press then reported this result to readers, stating that, according to Terman and Miles, sport was "the most masculine" interest a woman could have.[65]

Terman's student E. Lowell Kelly went on to develop an "inversion scale," which used M/F (masculinity/femininity) rating systems to test for potential homosexuality. Kelly found that his test group of eighteen lesbians scored slightly less masculine than a group of thirty-seven superior women college athletes. The inference that women athletes not only lacked femininity but were similar to, and even more masculine than, lesbians also received scientific verification.[66]

Mid-century popular magazines published the research results of Terman and his colleagues, accompanied by abbreviated M/F surveys for readers.[67] These popularized tests incorporated the internal gender distinctions of sport into the rating mechanism itself. A 1947 magazine quiz to determine "How Masculine or Feminine Are You?" asked readers to choose a word association among options rated along an M/F scale. Under sport they could choose between football, skating, and tennis. On a scale on which higher point totals indicated greater masculinity, readers who chose football earned two points, while those who picked skating and tennis scored zero.[68] The ascribed gender of football, skating, and tennis thus became integrated into scientific mecha-nisms for assessing the gender of the general population.

M/F tests served not only to measure but to instruct, offering the American public a training manual in appropriate gender behavior. In retrospect they also provide a clear illustration of the circular and self-contained logic that formed the rigid cast of mid-century gender prescriptions. In the logic of social science, if a small-town girl grew up coveting the chance to play linebacker for her local football team, experts judged her as deficient in fem-ininity, not questioning whether the flaw might lie in the culture-bound concept of "masculine" sport. Mediated through the authoritative voice of science, gendered notions of sport recon-firmed the idea that sex differences were enduring and indis-putable features of the social landscape.

How, then, did women athletes understand themselves in a society that perceived them as less womanly for their athleticism? Did they accept this idea? Did their sporting involvement cause painful inner turmoil—what social psychologists have called "role conflict"—because their behavior ran contrary to that prescribed by prevailing gender norms? The particular gender distinctions inscribed in the practice and discourse of sport represented the views of powerful forces in American society—middle-class culture, scientists, medical doctors, the national media, male sport leaders, educators, and government officials. Although their views dominated American society and influenced those of ordinary people, women athletes were nevertheless able to ignore, alter, or reject the idea that sport was a manly pursuit. While many might have suffered private doubts, by trusting in their own knowledge and sources of support, athletes somehow managed to disregard those who would ridicule them.

Doris Rogers, for example, grew up in the 1940s and 1950s in an eastern Tennessee mountain community, where she began to play basketball as a second grader when the school team didn't have enough older girls to fill the roster. From that point on Rogers played ball whenever she could—with her siblings, with schoolmates, and by herself on an outdoor dirt court on her family's farm. After excelling in the highly competitive Tennessee high school leagues, she was recruited by Nashville Business College (NBC), the premier women's team of the 1950s and 1960s. Rogers played for NBC from 1961 to 1969 while earning a secretarial degree from NBC and then a bachelor's and master's in physical education from Peabody College. She went on to teach P.E. and coach high school basketball in Nashville while completing a doctorate in physical education.

As she matured and moved away from her basketball-crazed hometown, Rogers learned that "people felt that it wasn't really the feminine thing to do to play basketball." This message was reinforced by her college physical education professors, who strongly disapproved of the kind of competitive sport Rogers engaged in nearly every evening and weekend. Her teachers

formed part of the chorus of educators, sport officials, and journalists who over the course of decades had supported athletic
programs and philosophies that reaffirmed, whether subtly or
blatantly, the concept of sport as an essentially masculine pursuit.
On confronting these views, Doris Rogers doubted the prevailing
wisdom, not herself. She clung to her initial perception that sport
was fun, worthwhile, and perfectly appropriate for women. And
she challenged her critics, wondering "what their expertise was
that they could sit up there and play God."[69]

Rogers was not alone. As an athlete of the 1960s, she represents the last cohort in a long tradition of women who devoted
years to highly competitive amateur, semipro, or professional
sports at a time when women's athletics received little respect,
attention, or institutional support. These athletes were able to
repudiate the powerful messages that emanated from the media
and society's most influential institutions by drawing on personal
insights, friendship networks, and local community traditions to
devise their own standards of judgment for women in sport.

Early childhood experiences of sport as positive and permissible
provided an initial resource against the unflattering image of the
"mannish" female athlete. Successful women athletes who came
of age in mid-twentieth-century America often grew up in working-class or rural enclaves where to be a "tomboy" or "outdoor
girl" made one distinctive but not unacceptable. Neighbors
enthusiastically attended girls' sporting events and honored outstanding female athletes as remarkable, if atypical, members of
the community.[70] Although occasionally teased by peers or discouraged by family members, young athletes on their way up
were generally given a certain amount of freedom and encouragement by their close kin as they ventured into competitive athletics. This support instilled confidence in childhood athletes and
nurtured their sense that sport was both natural and good.

Recalling their early years in sport, women frequently
described themselves as childhood "tomboys." They sketched a
common definition of the activities that invoked the label: rough-
and-tumble outdoor play, a love of sport, athletic ability, and

associating more with boys than with girls. In their understanding "tomboy" generally referred to a girl who was more boyish than girlish, or a girl who was not feminine. Beyond these commonly accepted characteristics, however, the word had held other meanings for women during their childhoods.

"Tomboy" was sometimes perceived as a term of distinction. It recognized an unusual athletic ability and a passion for "boyish" activities. Nora Cross, who went on to play professional baseball in the 1950s, explained that the word "definitely didn't have a negative connotation. There's no question about that. Frankly I think people in the town kind of delighted in it."[71] The local grocer seemed to take special notice, calling Nora by the name "Jimmie" if she appeared in shorts or pants, while returning to her given name when she dressed in skirts. Eunies Futch grew up in Jacksonville, Florida, playing sandlot and organized playground sports. About her tomboy reputation she explained, "No, it wasn't negative. In fact the guys liked it. . . . It didn't bother me and it didn't bother them it seems."[72]

Others stated that "tomboy" was merely a descriptive term used like "blond" or "short," to describe the obvious. Donna Lopiano, a member of the world championship Raybestos Brakettes softball team in the 1960s, recalled that it merely indicated what type of Christmas present was appropriate—that a particular girl should receive a baseball glove rather than a doll.[73] Irene Kotowicz agreed. "I was the tomboy of the neighborhood," she stated. Reflecting on the word's meaning, she explained, "It was descriptive. . . . I just loved sports."[74]

Some athletes had never been called tomboys, either because their activities were not viewed as unusual or because "feminine" activities and attributes insured against a boyish reputation. Maxine Vaughn Williams stated in retrospect that "tomboy" was "a good word" to describe her activities, yet when asked if she heard it growing up said, "No, not that I remember. But then I'd go to church on Sunday and be feminine."[75] Several other women believed that they never encountered the term "tomboy" because their activities were so commonplace that they did not call for a special word. Eckie Jordan grew up in a basketball-crazy textile region of South Carolina. She played sandlot sports with the boys and played on girls' basketball teams from the fifth grade on. To her "That was just part of life where I grew up. . . . I was never considered a tomboy."[76] Mary Pratt remembered that in her childhood those labels simply weren't used, even when they would have been accurate descriptions:

> I don't think anyone ever turned to my mother, or ever said that that was a tomboy. But yet I know it was a remark that was always labeled with girls that liked sports—that they're tomboys. Not till I got older did I realize that people felt that if a boy played with dolls, well "Whoopdeedoo, he's going off in the wrong direction." But we never labeled it.[77]

While women like Pratt remained free of defining labels, others experienced the term "tomboy" as a reproach. Delores Moore grew up playing on the streets of Chicago as a member of a neighborhood gang. In her experience tomboy "was a bad label," indicating sexual promiscuity in rare cases, or more commonly that "a tomboy was a real tough girl."[78] Willye White also experienced the label as a criticism, recalling: "I had a very difficult, challenging childhood in that I was an outcast, I was a tomboy." She spent years running, climbing trees, and playing ball with the boys but grew self-conscious as she learned that "only tomboys participated in activities like that, because little girls didn't. Little girls did not sweat, they just glowed."[79] The term had a more ambiguous meaning for Marcenia ("Toni") Stone Alberga. Growing up in the black community of St. Paul, Minnesota, her avid interest in sports earned her the nickname Tomboy. She recalled that the city's African American "social elites" looked on her as "a disgrace to the human race," yet others applied the name less harshly, using it merely to mark her as different and unique among girls.[80]

Within mid-century American society, and even within particular communities, there was no consensus about appropriate gender behavior for young girls. World War II had opened up new possibilities for women, who through public service and paid labor proved that they could succeed in traditionally male spheres. Those opportunities dried up in the postwar years, when women were dismissed from well-paying industrial jobs and encouraged to return to full-time domestic pursuits. Yet even in the stifling cultural and political climate of the 1950s, new educational opportunities and economic necessity lured women out of the home. While young women pursued higher education in unprecedented numbers, more married women than ever before entered the paid labor force in an effort to maintain or augment their family's income. The shifting, unsettled quality of postwar gender relations affected girls as well as women. Middle-class child-rearing styles typically emphasized physical and emotional restraint for girls, but opinions differed from family to family and across ethnic, regional, and class lines. In this context the word "tomboy," although frequently employed to mark gender variance, could range in meaning from reprimand to compliment. Especially in rural and urban working-class settings, there was often room for the active "tomboy" or "outdoor girl" who might have a passion for sports.

The liberties of girlhood did not survive the transitions to adolescence and adulthood, however. Young women who continued to compete past puberty eventually encountered the harsher image of the "mannish athlete." They realized, as Mary Pratt explained, that there was "some kind of stigma, that if you were too competitive it was wrong."

The belief that women who excelled in sport did so at the expense of their femininity was a source of irritation, anger, and concern among athletes. Yet, few stopped playing sports or dramatically altered their behavior upon realizing that their athletic ability could mark them as deviant. The tensions athletes felt were mitigated by the personal satisfaction and social possibilities they found in sport. Travel, public recognition, and a sense of belonging made athletics a worthwhile endeavor. The opportunities and the affirmation that accompanied their athletic involvement nurtured feelings of confidence and self-worth. These advantages far outweighed any fears they might have harbored about the public image of women in sport. They also provided a resource for women attempting to counter the female athlete's mannish reputation with positive images derived from their own experience.

Growing up on farms, in small towns, or in insular urban neighborhoods, most women athletes had traveled little prior to their involvement in competitive sports. While fondly recalling first train rides, fine hotels, and the wonder of venturing into new worlds, athletes also put their travel experience in a broader framework, explaining that it opened social, economic, and cultural doors that might have remained closed without sports. Phyllis Koehn spoke of baseball as a well-paid, exciting job that allowed her to escape the low-wage, monotonous clerical jobs held by many of her peers: "We were just treated so great, you know. And it was fun to go on these road trips. It was just better than working in an office somewhere I'll tell you. Doing something that you love and getting paid for it."[81] Other AAGBL players agreed. Describing the satisfaction of receiving decent wages for work which allowed her to travel, meet people, and play a sport she loved, Irene Kotowicz declared, "It was just like manna from heaven."[82]

With or without financial compensation, athletic involvement heightened women's sense of independence and expanded their options. Joyce Hill Westerman imagined that without baseball, "I'd have been out on the farm till I got married or something. As we grew up and at that age, girls had to get married. If you weren't married there was something wrong with you by a certain age." Reflecting on the meaning of sport in young women's lives, Westerman concluded, "It made you more independent, and you thought you could get by in life without having to depend on somebody."[83]

Several players specifically referred to their sport experience as "an education." Maxine Vaughn Williams, who left her small Tennessee town to play basketball in Nashville, Atlanta, and Winston-Salem, described her experience: "I think it was an education for most of us that we wouldn't have had. Okay, you graduate from high school. You get a job in a local store. You don't travel—you don't know what goes on out here. [Sport] broadens your thinking, adjusting to different situations."

Sport could provide a racial education as well. Willye White's 1956 Olympic journey to Melbourne, Australia, offered an escape from the segregated South of her childhood and taught her that people of different races and cultures could live together and communicate with each other. Interracial contact proved initially more disturbing than enlightening to Anna May Hutchison, a white athlete raised in Louisville, Kentucky. While still in her teens, Hutchison moved north to join the Racine Belles baseball team. She recalled going to the movies in Racine and being startled to find that "there was a black fellow sitting next to me. Uh! My gosh, I jumped up and got out of there." Over time Hutchison's discomfort eased. She recalled, "Eventually I thought, well, you know, we're all made alike."[84]

Conversely northerners learned about formal segregation when they traveled south to compete. As a member of the AAGBL's Kenosha Comets, Joyce Hill Westerman went south for spring training. Riding the buses in town, she sat in the back rows only to be instructed by other whites that her place was in the front. Another northern ballplayer, Toni Stone, found that her travels through the South of the late 1940s and early 1950s affected her deeply. After growing up in the predominately white state of Minnesota, Stone became the only woman in the semipro and professional Negro baseball leagues. Her southern travels as a member of the San Francisco Sea Lions and Indianapolis Clowns introduced her to both the segregation and the rich African American culture of the South. "I wanted to travel. I wanted to go places," said Stone, who added, "Now, that was my education." She visited black colleges, attended black churches, and learned through her travels of distinguished African American leaders like Mary McLeod Bethune, whom she came to idolize. Stone found her contacts with ordinary African American southerners to be especially gratifying. She relished the long, hot summer evenings when, on front porches throughout the South, she joined her hosts in animated conversation. These encounters made a strong impression. "The things they said, they stayed with you. You couldn't forget them." They endowed Stone with a new sense that "I know who I am and I know how to carry myself accordingly."

Along with horizon-broadening travel, athletes derived keen satisfaction from both the personal pleasure of athletic play and from public recognition of their athletic accomplishments. Nora Cross searched for the right words to convey the happiness and fulfillment she found in sport: "It would be so—what's ethereal mean?—like it's such a joy, it just brought such pleasure to my life to be able to do that. I just enjoyed it so much, that's basically it." Doris Rogers expressed similar sentiments: "It wasn't necessarily the crowds, because I would just go at it in my backyard. Just me and that old lumpy ground—we didn't have asphalt . . . I just *loved* to play, to compete. . . . It's just the doing, just the joy of playing." Beyond this more private enjoyment, adolescent girls and young women found that being noticed, singled out, or appreciated by their community offered another source of gratification. Thelma Hirst and Mildred Emmons Neeman, softball teammates from Syracuse, Nebraska, remembered:

> Whenever you're on a winning team . . . everybody wants to be friends of yours. And it's a good feeling—*I* think anyway. People complimenting us, and speaking to you; it made you feel so much better.[85]

> It kind of made me feel more important. Like at least you could excel in something.[86]

Public affirmation—not to be taken for granted in the lives of most working-class girls and women—combined with the physical and emotional pleasure of competition to place sport at the center of young athletes' lives.

For committed female athletes sport had everything to do not only with what they did, but with who they were. In recalling the physical pleasures and social benefits of sport, many athletes explained that their social worlds and personal identities had become integrally bound up with athletic activity. This kind of personal identification with athletics created a foundation from which to challenge those who doubted their femininity or condemned their athleticism.

In the mill town of Pelzer, South Carolina, Eckie Jordan played basketball with the same girls, including several of her sisters and cousins, from elementary through high school, and then as young adults in the Carolina textile leagues. Noting that family, friends, schooling, work and play came together in her basketball experience, Jordan described the "rightness" of sport in her life with the simple statement: "It was in my blood." Through basketball, she added, "I just felt like I was me."[87]

Others found a sense of belonging at the playground, in high school GAAs, in college P.E. departments, and on industrial teams. They gravitated toward sport as a place where they felt accepted and appreciated in the company of like-minded peers. Loraine Sumner described her envelopment in women's sports: "My whole life has been built on that. . . . It gave me the outlet, it gave me the bonding with other people. I mean, I related everything with sports to my everyday life."[88]

For those athletes who as children were teased or rebuked for tomboy behavior, the satisfaction of sport became a crucial part of identities forged in rebellion against restrictive gender conventions. To Willye White, the very source of her pain also became a source of self-definition and advancement. Describing her staunch devotion to sport, she explained: "When I got into athletics it was something that could not be taken away from me . . . I enjoyed it. I was good and it was an avenue for me to express myself. It was my talent, and my ability, and with that I could do a lot of things."

Pat Stringer and Audrey Goldberg Hull also found that adversity heightened the importance of sport in their young lives. Growing up as an athletic tomboy in a small Minnesota town, Stringer found that her unorthodox interests and comportment cut her off from the shared world of other young girls. After high school she moved to Minneapolis, where in her late teens and twenties she became a star pitcher on the industrial softball circuit. There her athleticism became a source of pride, enabling Stringer to better define and accept herself. She explained that through sports

I felt better about myself. I thought it was the thing I did really well. I was confident, some would argue cocky maybe. I felt there were a lot of rewards . . . a lot of recognition, a lot of personal gratification, because I did it well. And so I guess that was my identity at that time, being very successful at sport.[89]

Audrey Goldberg Hull described the meaning of sport in similar terms. After Audrey's mother ended her daughter's promising track-and-field career at the age of fifteen because she was getting too old for such "unladylike" pursuits, Hull refused to give up sports. She redirected her energies toward softball, which became her new passion and a key to her adolescent identity. She explained that for her, athletics were "a way of expression, I think, that was the main thing. And I knew I was good at it. And when you know you're good at something and you feel good about it, it was a fantastic feeling. It was the best feeling I ever had. . . . That was who I was."[90]

Dedicated athletes like Stringer and Hull continued to pursue highly competitive sports until marriage, injury, aging, or work conflicts gave them reason to stop. Grounded in their own positive experience of sport and bolstered by its social rewards, women involved in high-level competition eventually had to come to terms with the stereotype of the mannish female athlete. From the moment that personal identities and public images clashed, athletes searched for ways to reconcile their positive experiences with the idea "that it wasn't really the feminine thing to do to play [sports], . . . that maybe you had to be a little bit masculine."[91]

Some athletes simply acknowledged that there were competing interpretations, matter-of-factly noting and accepting the discrepancy between disparaging messages from the wider culture and more positive attitudes rooted closer to home. Chicago ballplayer Irene Kotowicz summarized commonly held views of her day: "This is what people think—only men play sports. And if a woman likes sports, there's something wrong with her." Yet in an apparently contradictory statement, she also insisted that in her own community women athletes were completely accepted, so much so that she never thought twice about her intense involvement in sport. "We just did it," she stated, "because gals played ball then. They played softball and everything else, so it wasn't anything."

Athletes like Kotowicz developed a double awareness that allowed them to move skillfully between conflicting systems of meaning. Softball player and physical educator Joan Hult stated clearly: "If you're in sport, you tend to be labeled masculine." But she was able to think outside this framework, dispensing with gender distinctions that ran contrary to her own experience and beliefs. "I always thought everybody else had a conflict, but there was no conflict in my being. I loved sport, and it really had nothing to do with masculinity or femininity."[92] Armed with the knowledge that more positive interpretations were possible, she resourcefully negotiated between dominant, critical views of "mannish" athletes and more sympathetic and permissive understandings of women's sport.

Other women were more troubled by the stereotype of the mannish athlete and tried to resolve the difference between this negative portrait and their own understanding of female athletes as "normal" women. For these athletes maintaining a feminine image carried great importance. They argued in favor of dress codes, public relations stunts like beauty contests, and the suppression of any mention of lesbianism, real or imagined, in sport. Yet in doing so they did not necessarily accept the wider culture's definition of feminine and masculine traits. Instead they subtly reinterpreted femininity, expanding its borders to include the very athletic qualities that many perceived as masculine.

One common approach was for athletes to acknowledge that there were mannish athletic types and to agree that they deserved to be criticized but then insist that they themselves and the women with whom they played were certainly not among them. When Margaret Sexton Gleaves traveled to the national basketball tournament she encountered women who struck her as strangely masculine: "One year we were out there, there was a team out there that was . . . most of 'em looked a little . . . you know . . . weren't quite as feminine as the other players. But that didn't bother me. . . . You know the girls I played with were really feminine, primping, . . . curling their hair, the lipstick and everything." Mannishness, to Gleaves, marked a category of unacceptable females who stood in contrast to the acceptable athletes she knew personally. Yet in presenting this contrast, Gleaves introduced an alternative standard of femininity. She described the women on her *own* team as perfectly feminine, simply by virtue of their familiarity and adherence to minimal standards of femininity. Women who curled their hair, wore lipstick, "primped," or, most important, were known to be "nice" or "decent" individuals qualified as feminine even if they happened to be aggressive, rough, or very muscular.[93]

Eunies Futch and Eckie Jordan employed this standard when describing Lurlyne Greer, a teammate on their Hanes Hosiery basketball team of the early 1950s. They recalled that Greer was a "rough-and-tough" type who "was a real tomboy! She was tough." Yet, they continued, "Talk about tomboys, that's one thing we couldn't look like [if] we wanted. . . . [Hanes] gave us hose and back then you didn't have pants." When discussing the image of women's sport, they contrasted the Hanes team to more masculine teams they encountered from Texas: "Back then, when we went to Texas, I was almost scared of some of those girls. They looked—they were all right, except they looked *tough*! They dressed tough. And you know it wasn't a good image for women's sports." Jordan and Futch described their teammate Greer as a tough tomboy, but because they accepted her as one of their own and because each team member followed the Hanes dress code, they could say with certainty that neither Greer nor any other woman on their team was one of the "tough" types they occasionally encountered at tournaments.

Like Futch and Jordan, some athletes drew the line at wearing pants, labeling those few women who preferred slacks to dresses as "mannish" types who harmed the reputation of women's sports. Yet women who did wear slacks did not see themselves as particularly mannish. Thelma Hirst used the occasion of a trip to Chicago for the 1936 national softball tournament to buy her first suit. She fondly recalled: "I bought a nice little suit, slacks suit, in Chicago the first year I went. And you know, I wore that thing out. It was different. And everybody liked it. And they liked me in it, said I looked nice in it." Hirst agreed that women's sport had an image problem aggravated by "masculine" athletes. But slacks alone did not connote mannishness to her. She attributed the image to a distant "other," those few women who dressed in men's slacks, men's shoes, and even men's underwear.

Hirst, Jordan, Futch, and Gleaves accepted the basic premise of natural gender distinctions to which, in principle, men and women should conform. Yet they also rejected the equation of athleticism with masculinity, employing an elastic definition of femininity based on personal reputation and on compliance with the often more flexible gender standards of local neighborhoods, rural communities, and peer groups. Femininity, by this standard, was an assumed rather than a proven trait, jeopardized only by an exceptionally "mannish" style. In this way women in sport dispensed with the masculine reputation of most female athletes, adroitly deflecting charges of mannishness onto a distant group of unfamiliar, rough-mannered "other" athletes at the margins of their world.

By appearing to accept the boundary between masculine and feminine, but in effect redrawing that line to ensure that most female athletes fell on its respectable side, women in sport distanced themselves from any implied masculine taint. Moreover, as they manipulated the gender norms and concepts of their day, athletes frequently introduced subtle revisions that stretched or even subverted conventional gender distinctions. For example, Tuskegee track star Alice Coachman inverted the aphorism that track was a muscle-bulging sport and swimming a muscle-stretching, beautifying sport. Coachman compared the lean, supple bodies of female track-and-field competitors to the knotty, hardened ones of women swimmers. Stating that swimmers frequently had "legs like baseball bats," she explained that "in track they were trying to get your legs soft so you could run. And swimming was an all-around sport that kind of hardens your muscles."[94] By reversing the media's usual comparison between "pretty plungers" and "android tracksters," she insisted on the femininity of women in a "masculine" sport.

Delores Moore used a similar strategy to reclaim femininity for women baseball players, a group nearly as maligned as track-and-field athletes. In an apparent endorsement of gender orthodoxy, Moore repeated the commonplace admonition that girls must be ladies first, athletes second. Yet when describing the Chicago-based NGBL, referred to by others as a hotbed of rough, rowdy, and mannish athletes, she used the term "nice ladies," especially about the leagues' controversial stars, the Savona sisters: "I played against Frieda and Olympia Savona, very masculine-looking ladies. Forearms, things like this. [She shows large size.] But very nice ladies. And I think you take the niceness and not what they looked like." When asked what it meant to be a lady, she offered an original and defiant definition: "Just being a decent human being. And don't let anybody insult you, put you down, that kind of thing. Or if you're going to play sports, don't worry about what they say. Ignore 'em."

Delores Moore and other athletes accepted the injunction that women in sport must exhibit feminine qualities and consciously create an image beyond reproach. Yet they did not accept dominant definitions of womanhood as they appeared in the national media and commercial culture. Instead women athletes created standards of judgment that balanced received cultural messages with more familiar understandings rooted in personal experience and local cultures. This allowed them to articulate nuanced, complex definitions of womanhood—concepts that went beyond a simple acceptance of the status quo to expand the parameters of womanhood significantly. Delores Moore completed her definition of a "lady" with the comment, "Wear a dress or wear a skirt, like the American league? No, no. I'm saying to be a lady—you think, you feel, you're just as equal as a man."

◦◦◦

In contrast to those who tried to stretch prevailing concepts of gender, some athletes simply ridiculed and rejected imposed standards of femininity. They might adhere to dress and conduct codes rather than lose the opportunity to play, but this in no way implied agreement. Forced to attend the AAGBL's spring charm school, Irene Kotowicz remained absolutely skeptical: "We'd have a couple [of] classes maybe and we'd watch it, and we'd just laugh. I mean, we were what we were. And they weren't going to make us beauty queens! To me that was ludicrous." Josephine

D'Angelo echoed Kotowicz. Describing training sessions in which they were taught proper dress, decorum, and how "to walk like girls," D'Angelo recalled: "They had some professional ladies come in and give us makeup lessons, and how to walk and how to dress and how to talk and how to use a fork and knife and spoon and all that. . . . We thought it was hilarious."[95]

Alline Banks, one of the nation's best basketball players in the 1940s, dismissed the notion that there was anything mannish about sport as absolutely irrelevant and offensive. Noting that "most of the girls on our team were very nice-looking girls and very feminine girls," she quickly added, "but it wouldn't have made any difference if they were not, because that's everybody's own life." When singled out by the media as unusually pretty and feminine for such a talented athlete, Banks stated that far from pleasing her, "it kind of upset me. It implied that all athletes had to be masculine to be successful."[96] Indignant rather than grateful for the compliment, Banks astutely recognized that by focusing on her beauty, the journalist was suggesting that most skilled athletes were unattractive masculine intruders in a male domain.

Rather than untangle the labyrinth of attitudes and values behind this insinuation, many athletes simply claimed that masculinity and femininity were irrelevant to sport. Irene Kotowicz found questions about the image of women athletes exasperating: "At that time we just played. . . . We just had a ball. We played ball, and that was it. There was no image, no nothing. I mean we never even thought of that!" Like Kotowicz a number of women dismissed cultural disputes over gender by insisting on the essential goodness, naturalness, or nongendered character of sport. Myrna Scritchfield Thompson, for instance, turned to the notion of natural talent to counter unsympathetic views of women athletes: "In those days girls weren't supposed to [play sports]. 'It wasn't nice,' I guess they'd say. Well, I couldn't understand it, because if you have talents I think you should get all you can out of them. For your life, and other people enjoy it."

The idea that her involvement in sports, which she had found to be such a thoroughly positive experience, could lead others to criticize her seemed so ridiculous that she rejected it out of hand: "I never thought about it. Because I think if people would think that about you, I don't think they think very much of you, really." She added with emphasis, "It just came naturally for me to play ball!" Jean Havlish agreed, attributing her athletic career to supportive parents and a generous God. "I was good," she recalled. "I mean that's a God-given gift. I think anything is—anything you have a talent for or an ability is a God-given gift."[97]

While Havlish and Thompson accounted for their purported "masculine" athleticism by references to God and nature, Ann Maguire and Audrey Hull offered more complex explanations. They drew a careful distinction between their own sense of athletics as a neutral or nongendered realm and their awareness that the society they lived in attributed an essential masculinity to sport. Recognizing the fact that "there are some women who are more competitive, more aggressive, [and] better skilled," Maguire commented, "we've always assigned the term 'masculine' [to them], and I don't think that's the appropriate term."[98] She expressed her personal belief that sport had no natural gender, but at the same time theorized that sport had become so important in some women's lives precisely because it enabled them to express feelings or interests that *others* labeled boyish, mannish, or deviant.

Audrey Hull's experience bore out Maguire's speculation. Although in retrospect she believed that sport was neither essentially masculine or feminine, as a child Hull's "masculine" athleticism had caused her to feel painfully "wrong" among schoolmates she described as "feminine" types. Her intense alienation from "feminine girls" might have prompted her to give up athletics, but instead Hull clung ever more tightly to sport as the only place where she could express her "true" or "full" self. Athletics became crucial to Hull's identity and self-esteem: "Sports for me was the embodiment of that little girl that could do no wrong. . . . I *was* my sports. I was a full person through what I could do through my sports. This other person went through what was expected of her—going to school, being the princess at the ball with the quivering lip." While athletic critics complained that sport would turn girls and women into a mockery of their sex, Hull appreciated sport for allowing her to be the girl-woman she understood herself to be.

All women in sport had to reckon with the power of the surrounding culture to stigmatize skilled female athletes. Images of mannishness, lesbianism, ugliness, and biological abnormality circulated through society, posing barriers to female athletic participation and placing an especially heavy burden on women whose very excellence evoked the nastiest kinds of accusations. However, this ideology was not monolithic. The majority of women athletes understood that their athletic ability made their femininity suspect. But in various ways they rejected or embraced only selectively the gender norms of mid-twentieth-century America.[99]

This refusal almost never took the form of political action or critique, however.[100] Given public hostility toward aggressive, mannish athletes, many women in sport accommodated, sometimes willingly, to pressures that they demonstrate their femininity and conform to gender conventions inside and outside of sport. Almost none saw themselves as feminist or working-class dissenters in revolt against the tyranny of middle-class gender and sexual codes.[101] Most women simply enjoyed sports and, feeling lucky to have the opportunity to play, spent little time developing a public stance against gender inequality in sport or society.

Yet women athletes demonstrated an independence of thought and action that belied consent. As a group they lacked the social authority to topple the barriers to full female participation in sport or to resolve the cultural contradiction between sport and femininity. But their persistence, their passions, and their skills spoke to the belief that sport and womanhood were not opposed and that sport itself had no necessary gender.

While dominant cultures can circulate ideas with great effectiveness, in the end they cannot tell people what to think. Doris Rogers stated the case eloquently. When asked how the mannish popular image of women athletes affected her, she replied: "It probably hurt my feelings a little bit . . . or maybe it made me mad. But it never made me want to give up sports . . . People that think they know best what's for everybody else—that's kind of irritating, too, sometimes."

—◦—

The end of Doris Rogers's basketball career coincided with the ending of an era. When Rogers retired from active play in 1969 she could look back on decades in which women's sport had captured a relatively small share of athletic resources, media attention, and the public's interest. She could look forward to a future in which, beginning in the late 1960s and early 1970s, women's collegiate athletics breathed new life and women's sport at all levels gained substantial popular, institutional, and legal backing under the influence of a revitalized feminist movement.

The comparative weakness of women's athletic foothold prior to this moment did not, however, signal its cultural insignificance. Between 1900 and the 1960s women's presence and skill in a masculine domain had become integral to the process of making and managing gender in American society. The unsettling effects of women's athletic endeavors revealed the instability of gender and sexual arrangements many people preferred to view as natural and fixed. Women's persistent claims to "masculine" skills and games suggested that gender divisions were malleable cultural constructs and, furthermore, were matters for social and political debate.

As athletes, coaches, administrators, educators, journalists, and casual observers wrestled with women's demands for inclusion and with the negative image of the mannish female athlete, they also confronted deeper issues of gender difference and inequality. Sadly the evolving structure of women's sports and the philosophies advanced by embattled physical educators and popular promoters did little to alter deeply entrenched notions of natural difference and male superiority. The compromises they reached frequently worked to reinforce twin beliefs in the inherent masculinity of sport and innate sexual differences. These compromises similarly failed to undermine related ideas about class, sexual, and racial differences. Strategies devised to break down prejudices against women's full participation in sport, ironically, often reaffirmed the systems of inequality which underlay women's initial exclusion.

But other possibilities remained, possibilities kept alive by sport advocates who maintained their commitment to increasing women's athletic opportunities and by women athletes who asserted not only their right to athletic competence, but their right to define sport and womanhood on their own terms. Together they forged a female athletic tradition that granted at least some women the chance to develop skills and confidence while enjoying the pleasures of physical play. Within this tradition women found space for expressions of female community and identity that stretched beyond restrictive concepts of femininity. It was women's bold insistence on the right to play and their willingness to create and model expansive definitions of womanhood that formed the thread between the early and middle decades of the twentieth century and the dramatic changes of recent years.

# CHAPTER 10

# YOU'VE COME A LONG WAY, MAYBE

## A "Revolution" in Women's Sport?

In the late 1960s and early 1970s, women's sport entered a dramatically new era, a period of tremendous gains and even higher hopes for women athletes. Participation in high school girls' sport increased more than 500 percent between the late 1960s and the early 1980s. At the college level the figures showed an increase of between 300 percent and 500 percent.[1] In international amateur sport, female Olympians attained unprecedented popularity, beginning with sprinter Wilma Rudolph in 1960 and continuing with gymnasts Olga Korbut and Nadia Comaneci in the 1970s. Women's professional sport experienced a similar boom, led by tennis but with significant breakthroughs in golf and team sports as well. The feminist movement of the late 1960s and 1970s, in conjunction with the fitness boom of the 1970s and 1980s had sparked renewed interest in women's sport nationwide. Barriers that had remained unbreakable for most of the century seemed to be rapidly tumbling, creating a new era of excitement and genuine possibility in women's athletics.

Amid the swirl of change, in November 1983 women's sport advocates from around the country assembled for a groundbreaking gathering called "The New Agenda Conference." Subtitled "A Blueprint for the Future of Women's Sports," it reflected the efforts of women's sport leaders to develop strategies and momentum that would allow them to solidify recent gains and set an even brighter course for women's athletics in the coming decades.

Yet the impetus for the conference came not from an envisioned future but rather from immediate setbacks. In what many women viewed as a crushing defeat, the leaders of men's intercollegiate athletics had just completed a successful takeover bid for the right to govern women's collegiate sport, running roughshod over the existing female-headed governing body of women's athletics.[2] Fearing a loss of female autonomy and power in the sports world, concerned women called a national conference where they hoped to take stock of the situation, and from this assessment generate a practical yet visionary plan for the future.[3]

The New Agenda Conference met in Washington, D.C., exactly sixty years and seven months after the first national conference on women's sport had gathered in the same city to found the Women's Division of the NAAF. In 1923, in response to what they understood as hostile attempts by male sport leaders to take over women's athletic activities and impose a dangerous and undemocratic model of sport derived from male athletic culture, women physical educators and recreation leaders had organized to push forward their own new agenda.

Six decades later the issues remained startlingly similar.[4] Angry at being steamrolled by a powerful men's organization, women leaders of the 1980s argued that male-dominated collegiate sport was marred by crass commercialism, corruption, and win-at-all-costs attitudes. They reiterated the well-worn claim that only female leadership could provide an alternative model of women's sport that avoided these pitfalls. And like their predecessors they plotted a strategy for change that combined academic research on female athletes, active promotion of women's sports, and political confrontation with obdurate male sport leaders.

The similarities between the 1923 and 1983 conferences are in one sense predictable, but in another puzzling. Given the long history of men's control of sporting institutions and a pattern of opportunistic involvement in women' sport, it is not surprising that when women's athletics grew in popularity over the 1970s, male-controlled organizations exhibited a sudden interest in managing women's collegiate sport. Contemporary women leaders are grappling with a problem that plagued earlier physical educators: how to press for full inclusion in athletics without being subsumed into a preexisting model of sport viewed by many as fundamentally sexist, elitist, and exploitative.[5]

What is more surprising is that the issues have changed so little when women's athletics have apparently undergone so momentous a change. The transformation begun in the late 1960s has permanently altered the face of athletic culture and provided unprecedented opportunities for the millions of girls and women who have taken up sport in recent years. Yet just beneath the surface strong currents of resistance continue to frustrate women's efforts to achieve full participation and self-determination in athletics. The effect has been successfully to limit the impact of change on established athletic institutions, on each woman's personal sense of possibility, and on the surrounding culture. As in the past the conflict sparked by women's pursuit of athletic access and excellence tells two stories—one about the dynamic interplay of gender and power within the world of sport and the other about the complicated synergy between women's sport and gender relations in the wider society.

The roots of the sea change in women's sports during the 1970s lay in a series of more cautious but important steps taken in the late 1950s and 1960s. After Ohio State University sponsored the first intercollegiate women's golf championship in 1941, the event became an annual one, and by the mid-1950s its backers had succeeded in turning the stubborn disapproval of leading physical educators into a limited endorsement.[6] However, with the exception of golf, leaders of the field remained only minimally receptive to competitive intercollegiate sport.[7] It took the maturation of a younger generation to push for more far-reaching changes, beginning with the founding of the Commission on Intercollegiate Athletics for Women (CIAW) in 1966 to govern and promote major intercollegiate tournaments for women.[8] This group was the direct predecessor of the Association for Intercollegiate Athletics for Women (AIAW), which after its founding in 1971 became the sole sponsor and chief advocate of women's intercollegiate sports during the 1970s.[9]

As an eager young generation of athletes and instructors succeeded in gradually liberalizing the long-standing ban on female varsity competition, their efforts received unanticipated support from forces outside the insular world of women's physical education. The pace of change quickened dramatically when women's sport became swept up in the larger winds of social change that characterized American society of the 1960s and 1970s. By the early 1970s a language of equality, opportunity, and rights fostered by the black civil rights movement, the American Indian and Chicano movements, and the women's and gay liberation movements circulated widely among American citizens who demonstrated a renewed sensitivity to issues of fairness and discrimination. Women in sport could now approach the issue of athletic resources and opportunity from an explicitly political perspective. They were aided by organized feminism. Groups dedicated to women's liberation were increasingly using the courts, the legislature, and organized pressure tactics to address gender discrimination in work, education, and the law.

Beyond formal politics the 1960s and 1970s were also marked by a cultural revolution, expressed most boldly by members of the counterculture and by activists in a "sexual revolution" that advocated a more permissive and experimental approach to sexual expression. Although sport remained peripheral to these developments, the counterculture's emphasis on physical freedom, bodily pleasure, and leisure offered an indirect source of encouragement for women to take up sport and fitness activities as a form of pleasurable recreation. Trends within mainstream commercial culture tendered women another form of inducement. The television era made sports more widely accessible and popular than ever. And in an ever-expanding consumer economy, sport and recreational activities became tied to a multibillion dollar sporting industry that depended on persuading more and more Americans to take up one or more sports and buy the requisite clothing, services, and equipment.

Currents of political reform, women's activism, and cultural innovation fostered a renewed excitement about women's sport and an awareness of its feminist implications, an atmosphere much like that of the post—World War I era. This time, however, the disputed concept of a woman's right to athletic enjoyment became, for the first time, codified in law. When Congress passed the Educational Act of 1972, the legislation included a section addressing the issue of sex discrimination. Title IX of the act stated: "No person in the United States shall, on the basis of sex, be excluded from participation in, be denied the benefits of, or be subjected to discrimination under any educational programs or activities receiving federal financial assistance."[10] Without even mentioning the word "athletics," Title IX ushered in what many believed to be a "revolution" in women's sport. Although it would take years to sort out the law's exact meaning, it indicated that women and men would have to receive equal treatment in both high school and college athletics.

Strictly interpreted, the law might require momentous changes in school sport. Even a relatively lenient interpretation, while not mandating absolute equality, would require that schools offer approximately the same number of sports for women and men, and that athletic department funding be allocated to women's and men's programs in roughly equivalent proportions to the ratio of female to male athletes active in varsity sports. These requirements would begin to redress the egregious inequities discovered in nearly every college athletic budget. At a typical midwestern university in the Big Ten Conference, men's athletics received thirteen hundred dollars for every dollar spent on the women's program. A mid-Atlantic university allocated nineteen hundred dollars for women's sport while granting men's athletics over two million dollars. On the West Coast, Washington State University appropriated less than 1 percent of its two-million-dollar athletic budget for women's sports.[11]

Such extreme disparities characterized women's sport outside the schools as well. In 1970 Billie Jean King became the first professional woman tennis player to exceed the one-hundred-thousand-dollar mark in annual winnings. However, the top male winner of 1970, Rod Laver, raked in nearly three times that amount while winning only one-third as many tournaments as King won. Professional golf presented a similar story. The top female winner of 1972, Kathy Whitworth, played in twenty-nine tournaments and earned $65,000 while top male pro, Jack Nicklaus, earned more than $320,000 in only nineteen tournaments.[12] Pay inequities found their corollary in wildly imbalanced media coverage. Between August 1972 and September 1973, of NBC's 366 hours of televised live sports a mere 1 hour of coverage went to women. CBS devoted ten hours of its 260 hours of athletic coverage to women's events.[13] Altogether, with regard to publicity, funding, coaching, and playing opportunities, the inequities were so glaring that former Olympic sprinter Doris Brown commented that the prospect of being "second-class citizens" seemed to her to be a great leap forward: "Second-class citizenship sounds good when you are accustomed to being regarded as fifth class."[14]

While Title IX would have no official impact beyond federally funded educational institutions, its clearly stated stance against discrimination advanced a principle of equality which women's sport advocates would attempt to apply throughout amateur and professional sport. Even before the passage of Title IX supporters had already begun to pressure athletic officials to remedy the pervasive gender inequities in sport. Lawyers had filed numerous law suits on behalf of female high school athletes seeking access to boys' sports teams in the absence of school teams for girls. Within the Olympic movement steady pressure from women's sport leaders had increased women's representation between 1952 and 1976 from 10 percent to 20.6 percent of Olympic competitors.[15]

In professional sport Billie Jean King led a 1970 boycott to protest pay inequities on the pro tennis tour. Over the next three years she helped launch a separate women's pro circuit sponsored by Virginia Slims, successfully pressured the United States Lawn Tennis Association into equalizing prize money in the U.S. Open, and organized the Women's Tennis Association to represent women on the tour. In September 1973 King won what appeared to be the ultimate victory against sexism in sport when she defeated the fifty-five-year-old former tennis star and self-proclaimed "male chauvinist pig," Bobby Riggs. An estimated forty-eight million television viewers joined more than thirty thousand spectators at the Houston Astrodome to watch a high stakes match that was as much circus as sporting event. After entering the arena on a red-draped divan carried by four men dressed as ancient slaves, King met Riggs—who had rolled onto the scene in a ricksha pulled by five scantily clad women he dubbed "Bobby's bosom buddies"—at center court and proceeded to handily defeat both her opponent and the odds makers, who had not imagined that a woman at the top of her career could defeat an aging male tennis hustler.[16]

King promptly cashed in on her popularity through endorsement earnings, part of which she gave back to women's sports by financing *WomenSports* magazine, a monthly publication for and about women athletes that debuted in 1974. That same year she joined with former Olympic swimmer Donna de Varona and other insiders in the sportsworld in founding the Women's Sports Foundation, an advocacy group that has worked to advance women's opportunities and challenge sexism at all levels of sport.

Although as an athletic superstar King wielded resources and clout unavailable to other advocates of women's sport, she was in no way a lone activist. Rather, she used her position to gain publicity and inroads for a much broader grass-roots movement of women who were determined to break down long-standing barriers to women's access to sport and physical development. Few of these activists laid explicit claim to the word *feminist* or attempted to forge connections with the larger, more politically oriented feminist movement. Nevertheless, women's efforts to attain the right to fully participate in sport, to enhance their strength and coordination, and to compete without psychological or institutional restrictions were consistent with a broad range of feminist activities designed to win for women the right to control and enjoy their own bodies. In this sense, whether they claimed it or not, women's sports advocates shared an agenda and an activist spirit with self-defined feminists involved in reproductive rights campaigns, antirape organizing, women's health clinics, women's self-defense classes, lesbian feminist activism, and self-help efforts that encouraged women to explore their own sexuality.[17]

Infused with the spirit of a broader feminist movement and

inspired by their own early successes, women who played, organized, and wrote about women's sports shared a tremendous excitement and sense of possibility. Perceiving that advancements in women's athletics were directly linked to the improvements in women's condition and the dismantling of sexism within American society, many believed that they were involved in revolutionizing women's lives. A *Ms.* magazine article from 1973, titled "Closing the Muscle Gap," celebrated women's athletic achievements and linked them directly to a revolutionary change in gender relations: "By developing her power to the fullest, any woman, from Olympic star to the weekend tennis player, can be a match for any man she chooses to take on. More importantly, she will inherit the essential source of human self-confidence—pride in and control over a finely tuned body. That alone would be a revolution."[18] Leanne Schreiber, the editor of *WomenSports*, advanced a similar claim, arguing that the systematic discouragement of female physicality served historically to "divorce" women's identities from their bodies. Women, she claimed, "have been divorced from the most basic sense of power and the most basic source of power," experiencing as a result "a very primary disconnection with the world."[19] Sport promised to reconnect women with their bodies and their power.

The sense of revolutionary change spread beyond the confines of feminist sport reformers, capturing the attention of the mainstream sport and news media. In 1973 *Sports Illustrated* published a three-part series on sexism in sport that acknowledged the pressing need for change by presenting an unambiguously feminist indictment of the male-dominated sports world.[20] Five years later *Time* magazine made women's sports its cover story. The article, titled "Comes the Revolution," noted that the female athlete, "whether aged six, sixty or beyond, . . . is running, jumping, hitting and throwing as U.S. women have never done before." The author concluded: "The revolution in women's athletics is at full, running tide, bringing with it a sea change—not just in activities, but in attitudes as well."[21] The article captured the widely shared sentiment that advances in women's sports represented both the personal and collective empowerment of women; confident and strong in their individual bodies, women as a group were mounting an effective challenge to men's athletic monopoly and privileged status in society.

The strong sense of promise that characterized women's sport in the 1970s seemed to be borne out as the decade advanced. By the end of the seventies, the number of women competing in intercollegiate sport had doubled, many of them assisted by athletic scholarships. Participation rates had risen even more dramatically at the high school level. Even team sports, which historically had attracted the least support and the greatest scorn, appeared to be on their way toward full acceptance. Women's basketball, the most popular collegiate sport, received approval as an Olympic sport in 1976, along with women's team handball and, four years later, women's field hockey. At the professional level a women's pro softball league began play in 1976. Although it folded in 1979, that same year saw the launching of the professional Women's Basketball League, which operated for three seasons before going under. The failure to establish a long-running professional team sports venture did not dampen the confident tone that characterized women's sports during most of the 1970s. Advocates saw setbacks such as these as temporary obstacles on a path of irreversible and rapid progress. A hopeful mood prevailed, generating what one report described as an "overall impression of inevitability."[22]

Behind the scenes, however, sports activists were beginning to comprehend the depth and power of the resistance to women's demands for athletic equity. The opposition took several forms. It included a well-organized and financed campaign to reverse Title IX, foot-dragging on the part of officials charged with implementing or enforcing the law and the sports media, which occasionally ridiculed and consistently neglected women's sports.

The strongest opposition to Title IX came from the National Collegiate Athletic Association (NCAA), the governing agency for men's intercollegiate sport. NCAA executive director Walter Byers forcefully denounced the legislation, announcing that Title IX would spell the "possible doom of intercollegiate sports."[23]

Behind this ominous claim lay the belief that men's programs would suffer irreparable damage if forced to endure budget cuts, scholarship reductions, and the loss of other resources that would go toward the support of women's athletics. Under Byers's leadership, the NCAA financed a major lobbying effort aimed at the Department of Health, Education and Welfare (HEW) and Congress. It pressured HEW to excuse athletic departments from compliance regulations, or more generally to interpret the law as applying only to specific programs funded by federal moneys rather than to every program within a federally supported institution. In Congress the NCAA lobbied for the Tower Amendment of 1974, legislation that specifically exempted athletic departments from Title IX requirements.

These efforts failed in the long run, but the intense pressure did succeed in delaying federal action. Officials at HEW did not issue enforcement regulations until 1975, after which schools were given until 1978 to comply. As of 1979, seven years after the act's passage and amid continued shrill cries from male athletic leaders that Title IX presented a crisis "of unprecedented magnitude," not one school had been fined as much as a single dollar for failure to redress gender inequities in school athletics.[24]

Women found their advances blocked on other fronts as well. Some high school athletic administrators matched college officials in their reluctance to comply with Title IX. Jack Short, the director of physical education for the state of Georgia, spoke out against funding girls' interscholastic sport, stating, "I don't think the physical education program on any level should be directed toward making an athlete of a girl."[25] Potential commercial sponsors of professional sport showed a similar reluctance to support women's teams. Despite the significant advances made in women's tennis, the financial base for the women's professional golf tour remained precarious and any attempt to establish professional team sports met with corporate demands that the league promote a "sexy" feminine image.[26] Finally, except for the hoopla surrounding single events like the King-Riggs match, the media continued to neglect women's sports. Both television and print media coverage remained minimal.[27]

When journalists did focus on women, they discovered (or

sometimes revealed their own) lingering cultural suspicions about the validity of women's sport and the femininity of women athletes.[28] The press sometimes intimated that beneath these misgivings lay a more fundamental fear—a concern that the new female athleticism signaled a profound challenge to traditional gender relations. In September 1976 *Time* ran a cover story, called "Sex and Tennis: The New Battleground." Both title and text employed military metaphors of sexual "battles" and "warfare" to describe the tennis craze sweeping America.[29] The image of sport as a battleground in the "war between the sexes" was a recurring one, suggesting that many observers understood women's athletic demands for equality as part of a deeper societal rift over the distribution of power and the definition of masculinity and femininity. Looking back on the changes of the 1970s, a writer for the *New York Times* posed the question forthrightly when he wondered, "How good are women, and how do they compare with men? . . . And incidentally, does any of this have a bearing on the battle between the sexes?"[30]

The rhetorical battle between the sexes became a real one in the early 1980s when the NCAA made its bid to assume leadership of women's intercollegiate athletics. By the end of the 1970s, the NCAA realized that the federal government intended to enforce Title IX and that, consequently, college athletic departments would have to increase their support for women's sports substantially. It was at this point, in 1980, that NCAA leaders decided to offer collegiate championships in a variety of women's sports, even though the AIAW already coordinated 750 state, regional, and national championships for its 970 member institutions. AIAW leaders interpreted the NCAA's offer as an opportunistic, aggressive takeover attempt. The NCAA defended the move as being consistent with its "obligations" under Title IX: If it sponsored men's championships, it must also sponsor women's.[31]

While most women's athletic leaders urged schools to maintain their allegiance to the AIAW, the NCAA offered colleges something that the AIAW could not—money and television exposure. The NCAA promised teams that it would pay travel expenses to championship tournaments and would, in the near future, add women's events to the multi-million-dollar television package the NCAA had arranged with major networks. The AIAW, with a total budget of only two million dollars, could not hope to match the NCAA's financial incentives. Women leaders urged schools to consider whether the financial gains were worth the loss of self-governance under NCAA control. The NCAA countered by offering women 16 percent representation on the NCAA Council and 18–24 percent on other important governance committees.[32]

Most schools judged the incentives too attractive to turn down. When the NCAA sponsored its first set of women's championships in the 1981–82 school year, the vast majority of women's programs switched their affiliation to the NCAA. The AIAW faded quickly from the scene, closing down operations in 1982 and conceding final defeat in 1984 when it lost an antitrust suit against the NCAA, a last-ditch effort to use the courts to halt the takeover.[33]

The antitrust ruling was followed by another, even graver legal setback in 1984. In the early 1980s, under the direction of the Reagan administration, HEW officials had already slackened the pace and rigor of Title IX enforcement. But in 1984 a Supreme Court ruling completely reversed the existing interpretation of the law. In *Grove City College* v. *Bell*, the Court ruled that Title IX applied only to those programs receiving direct federal funds and had no bearing on nonfederally funded programs, even if the sponsoring school received federal support.

In the aftermath of the Grove City ruling, women's sport advocates faced the possibility that more than a decade of anticipated and actual gains might be eradicated. They nervously watched HEW drop more than eight hundred Title IX complaint investigations and compliance reviews.[34] However, the projected disaster did not materialize, prevented in part by subsequent congressional action. Passage of the Civil Rights Restoration Act of 1988 restored the original interpretation of Title IX, once again mandating that schools eliminate gender discrimination in all programs, including athletics.[35]

The tug-of-war between women's sport advocates and the courts, and between the AIAW and the NCAA, was indicative of more general developments in women's sports in the 1980s. The heady enthusiasm and belief in "inevitable" progress that characterized the 1970s was tempered by a new cautiousness and political savvy acquired through years of struggle. The situation in women's sport mirrored that in other feminist-inspired efforts of the 1980s. Women's advocacy groups continued to make headway, often by organizing within, and exerting pressure on, existing institutions. At the same time feminist activists had to weather an antifeminist backlash waged by conservatives of the New Right and supported by a conservative political administration. These crosscurrents were especially strong in the arena of sport. Women continued to work for greater access to and control of sport, while conservatives within sport organizations, media, and corporations dug in their heels trying to preserve sport as they knew it—a profitable industry that, with few exceptions, was governed by men in the interests of men's athletics.

These contending forces produced a complicated outcome. In response to the question of how much has really changed since the early 1960s, and with what implications for women's lives and American gender relations, no simple answer suffices. Women's sport has undergone a genuine and dramatic transformation; girls growing up today have a sense of possibility and entitlement that few girls or women in generations past ever experienced. They can choose from school sports, Little League baseball, youth soccer, and a variety of other activities, some mixed and some for girls only. For this reason talk of discrimination, inequality, and male dominance in sport may seem foreign and oddly irrelevant to them. But not far beneath the surface they will find more disturbing signs of institutional and ideological resistance to women in athletics. Men still receive resources far superior to women's, leaving female athletes little choice but to compete in male-controlled sporting organizations, which are in turn influenced by corporations whose decisions are based on profits, not fairness.

These constraints reveal the limited nature of the changes in athletic culture. The limits, in turn, tell us something about how sport continues to be a bulwark of "old-fashioned" male privilege and at the same time has become instrumental in the development of new, more subtle forms of male domination. A brief exploration of how critical issues from earlier decades have been played out in recent years will suggest both the significance of— and the limits to—the remarkable changes in late-twentieth-century American sport.

—⊂⊃○⊂⊃—

Two central concerns guided the work of early generations of women's sport advocates through most of this century: how to involve more young women in physical activity and how, at the same time, to preserve the leadership of women. Ironically, while physical educators saw these developments as inseparable, in recent decades they seem to be at odds. The most dramatic, yet paradoxical, set of changes in women's sport centers on the tremendous increase in participation and the simultaneous decline of female leadership.

In earlier decades the bulk of female sporting involvement took place in school intramural programs and in community-based recreational sports. While these avenues continue to offer an important athletic resource for women, the dynamic center of women's sport has moved to highly competitive high school and college varsity sports, in which both the sheer numbers and the rate of female participation skyrocketed between 1970 and 1990. At the high school level the number of girls in interscholastic sport climbed from three hundred thousand in 1971 to more than two million in 1992.[36] This number includes the hundreds of female athletes who now wrestle or play ice hockey, baseball, or football on previously all-male teams.[37] In intercollegiate sport, women have increased their numbers from 16,000 in the early 1970s to more than 160,000 by the late 1980s. Currently women make up 34 percent of intercollegiate athletes and receive approximately one-third of college athletic scholarships. Schools that averaged 2.5 women's varsity teams before Title IX now average more than 7.[38]

The increases are equally impressive in nonelite sports, where women make up the majority of new participants in leading fitness and athletic activities like jogging, swimming, and cycling.[39] Women have benefited from new programs that seek to make athletics accessible to people of all ages and ability levels. They participate avidly in masters events organized for older athletes and in sports organized for the physically and mentally disabled, such as wheelchair basketball or the Special Olympics.

Yet as impressive as the numbers appear, women have not come close to parity with men. In high schools and colleges women constitute just over half the student body, yet they make up only slightly more than one-third of varsity athletes, and they receive far less than that in resources. College athletic departments allocate twice as much scholarship money to men than to women and budget three times more in operating funds and five times more in recruiting expenses for men than for women.[40] Despite the rhetoric of progress, after twenty years of Title IX an NCAA committee found that only one of 646 schools actually met its standard for gender equity.[41] Similarly, a study of high school sports reported that despite the advances of the past two decades, girls continue to receive inferior facilities, uniforms, practice schedules, and promotional support.[42] As both high schools and colleges undergo severe budget cuts in a weak economic climate, the strain on resources will increase and women's programs will have to fight to maintain even current levels of support.[43]

These problems pale in comparison to the astounding decline in female leadership which has occurred in the past two decades. As a result of Title IX the vast majority of schools merged their separate women's and men's athletic departments. In almost every case, they named men as department heads and appointed men to most of the administrative positions. Similarly, as the status of women's sports rose and salary levels moved closer to parity with men's, more and more men grew interested in coaching women's sports. As a result women have experienced a severe decline in both coaching and administrative positions.

Before the passage of Title IX, more than 90 percent of women's college teams were coached by women. Today more than 50 percent of these positions go to men, while women receive fewer than 1 percent of the coaching jobs for men's teams. The decline has been even more extensive in athletic administration, in which women used to hold virtually all positions relevant to women's athletics. Today only 17 percent of women's programs are headed by women, and women fill less than 31 percent of all administrative positions in women's college sport. More than 25 percent of women's athletic programs contain *no* female administrators.[44]

The simultaneous increase in participation and decrease in leadership suggests that women have struck an unintended bargain, trading control over sport for greater access to sporting opportunities and resources. The tension between pursuing equal opportunities within an existing system and maintaining a realm of autonomous leadership is not a new one; the bargain struck in the 1970s and 1980s is precisely the trade-off women physical educators warned against in the 1920s and 1930s. The resulting situation, which one contemporary sport advocate described as "perspiration without representation," has allowed a greater number of women to develop athletic skills with fewer restrictions than ever before, but at the same time has meant that women have less ability to influence athletic institutions and chart the course for the future.[45]

Even without a forceful voice in leadership, women's extensive involvement in highly competitive sport is posing a critical challenge to the "maleness" of sport. A strong female presence undermines the assumed masculinity of athletic skill and disrupts the notion that sports "belong" to men. As the deep-seated dissonance between femininity and sport subsides, women are freer than ever to enter the athletic realm without jeopardizing their perceived "normalness" as women. Schoolgirls report that athleticism is a source of popularity and seem unfamiliar with the idea that female athletic ability might carry any sort of stigma. Parents express a similar attitude. A Women's Sports Foundation survey of more than one thousand parents reported that 87 percent stated that sports are as important for daughters as for sons.[46]

However, while the equation of sport with masculinity has been challenged, it has not been permanently eradicated.[47] The associations between masculinity and skill remain especially intense at elite levels of sport where the meaning of excellence remains tightly entwined with concepts of masculine skill and male physiology. Recent controversies surrounding the Winter and Summer Olympics illustrate the persistence of these notions.

As it has in the past, women's athletic success—in mixed or single-sex competitions—is often perceived as a defeat for men and a threat to their masculinity. The discomfort with female excellence surfaced after the 1992 Winter Olympics in Albertville, France, where the U.S. women's team outshone the men's. Although they accounted for only 34 percent of the total U.S. squad, women athletes earned 82 percent of the honors, bringing home nine of the eleven medals won by Americans, including all five American gold medals.[48] The press pounced on the results, writing about the women's success as a defeat for American men. In articles like "An Identity Crisis of Ice and Snow," which recounted how the American women "beat the American men like drums," the media explicitly linked the results to a crisis of masculine identity.[49]

Where women's victorious performance in Albertville report-edly undercut the masculine identity of male competitors, highly successful Summer Olympians have been accused of even graver misconduct. Female athletes suspected of steroid use have been charged with illicitly attempting to acquire a male body. For at least twenty years, rumors have run rampant about the use of performance-enhancing steroids among both male and female Olympians, especially those from the former Soviet-bloc coun-tries. While mandatory testing has confirmed that at least a small number of athletes have used illegal drugs, it is widely accepted that the numbers of undetected steroid users far exceed the num-ber who have been caught. Recently the focus of public scrutiny has shifted from bulky male weightlifters to female sprinters. For example, when Florence Griffith Joyner took the track-and-field world by storm, winning three gold medals at the 1988 Olympics and smashing the world's record for the women's one-hundred-meter dash, critics began charging "Flo Jo" with steroid use almost before the sweat dried. Her accusers pointed to her recently developed musculature, saying that in years past Griffith Joyner was "an extremely feminine person. But today she looks more like a man than a woman."[50]

Whether the charges against Griffith Joyner were true or false, undoubtedly many women in track have opted to take steroids for their strength benefits. The criticism of steroid users has a gender dimension, however. While men are accused of using drugs to gain an unfair advantage, women are attacked for becoming men. Male steroid users are denounced as cheaters, women as gender transgressors; they want to win so badly, they chemically alter their sex to do it.[51] This assertion is an updated, high-tech version of the familiar charge that women athletes must "sacrifice" their sex to succeed in high-level competition. Strength, skill, and victory remain firmly wedded to masculinity, while women athletes, especially in the historically suspect sport of track and field, become subjects of a kind of "witch hunt" in which achievement is tainted by the imputation of an artificially induced sex change.

The Olympic policy of mandatory sex testing rests on similar suspicions. The IOC began genetic testing in the 1968 Olympics, using a procedure called the buccal smear (tissue is scraped from the inside of the athlete's cheek and then analyzed microscopically) to evaluate the chromosomes of female Olympians. Before this, there had been one admitted case of a male competitor passing as a woman, German athlete Hermann Ratjent, who in 1957 revealed that the Nazi party had pressured him to disguise his gender in order to compete as a woman in the Berlin Olympics of 1936. Since that time official testing has not uncovered a single instance of a male athlete attempting to pass as a female.[52]

The tests have, however, turned up several cases in which athletes who have been raised as women and understand themselves to be female are discovered to have irregular chromosome patterns. While some of these instances involve competitors who have ambiguous sex organs, in a number of other cases athletes whose genitalia and other aspects of outward appearance appeared "female" were found to have a Y chromosome.[53] Spanish hurdler Maria Jose Martinez Patino, for instance, was subjected to a lifetime ban from national competition by the Spanish athletic federation after testing revealed an XY chromosome configuration in 1986. Further investigation revealed that a genetic mutation left Martinez Patino unable to process testosterone, so that despite the presence of a Y chromosome, she had developed external female genitalia and secondary sex characteristics.[54] After further review an IOC committee reinstated her, but only after she had suffered two years of inactivity, the withdrawal of her national scholarship and athletic residence, the forced dismissal of her coach, and a painful period of shame and embarrassment in which friends and her boyfriend deserted her.[55]

Because of complicated cases like Martinez Patino's, medical societies like the American College of Physicians and the American College of Obstetricians and Gynecologists have formally denounced Olympic sex testing, claiming that the procedure lacks scientific credibility. They argue that it postulates genetic advantages that have no basis in proven fact, that it leaves no room for frequent instances of ambiguity, and that it equates gender strictly with genetic makeup when, in practice, our society typically determines gender through outward appearance and other factors like hormone levels and psychological orientation.[56]

Aside from its dubious scientific merit, women athletes find the procedure humiliating and intrusive. They resent athletic officials who presume the maleness of men in sport but insist that women competitors have their femaleness documented and then certified on a card that athletes have dubbed their "fem card." The IOC defends the practice by arguing that anatomy is destiny—and moreover, that, male anatomy confers a superior destiny. One IOC spokesman reasoned that since men's records are better than women's, it is obvious that the "difference is due to anatomical differences," specifically the superiority of the "classically male-shaped pelvis and body configuration."[57] Women athletes perceive a more demeaning logic. Olympic heptathlete Jane Frederick explained, "I think they are just saying, 'You are so good, we can't believe you're a woman. So prove it.' "[58]

The dispute over sex testing mirrors the steroid controversy, simply reversing the charges against the highly skilled female athlete. Sex tests examine the athlete not to see if she might be a woman ingesting drugs to become a man, but rather because she might be a biological male trying to pass as a female. In either case the image of the female athlete as imposter and the assumption that athletic superiority is rooted in male biology remain undisturbed.

Very few athletes reach such elite levels of competition that they are forced to verify their anatomical femaleness. However, athletes at all levels of sport experience another version of the tension between femininity and athleticism—the suspicion that athletic ability and interest signals lesbianism. The roots of the stigmatized "mannish" lesbian athlete reach far back into the early and mid-twentieth century, a period in which the constraints on female sexual expression were typically far more stringent than those experienced by women in contemporary American society. Yet, even in an era of relatively greater sexual freedom, the societal taboo on lesbianism remains strong, even more so in the sports world.

Oddly, concerns about lesbianism in sport may even have increased, in inverse relationship to the greater acceptance of women's sport in general. Participating and excelling in sport no longer automatically connote masculinity; an appreciative public generally accepts that a woman can actively pursue athletic excellence with no cost to her "femininity," however one defines it. Yet older associations between masculinity and sport linger on, as do cultural fears about physically strong, sexually independent women.

This creates a peculiar tension: The growing popularity of women's sport hinges on the athlete's success in reassuring the public that, however exceptional her athletic talents, she is in all respects a "normal" woman. The lesbian athlete, with her reputation for masculine style, body type, and desire, represents a refusal to issue this reassurance. Her sexual autonomy and her rejection of conventional femininity—as defined through heterosexuality—make her the locus for enduring fears that women in sport transgress gender lines and disrupt the social order. It is not coincidental that the years in which Martina Navratilova first revealed her bisexuality (later, lesbianism) were also those in which her superlative performance led to assertions that she must be physiologically unlike any other woman on the tennis tour, a bionic marvel to be placed in a unique gender category of not-woman and not-man.

The kind of homophobic responses evoked by Navratilova and other lesbian athletes are most intense when female excellence or demands pose a threat to traditional sources of men's power. This is often the situation with professional sport, collegiate athletics, and women's sport advocacy groups, arenas in which women have commanded attention and demanded equality.

Tennis and golf, two sports with historically white, middle-class constituencies, have typically escaped the masculine stigma that attached to sports like basketball and softball. Yet, as they have professionalized, tennis and golf have become much more vulnerable to sexual disparagement. The success of a professional sports venture depends on attracting sponsors who, in the interest of profit, demand that the sport present an appealing image to the public. This equation leaves no room for lesbianism, which promoters view as a death blow to popular acceptance. When tennis superstars Billie Jean King and Martina Navratilova admitted to lesbian relationships in the 1980s, each lost millions of dollars in endorsement money. More recently, corporate sponsors of women's golf, Lucky Stores and J. M. Smucker, received anonymous threats of a boycott if the two companies did not withdraw their support for a California tournament rumored to include lesbians.[59]

Executives of the Ladies Professional Golf Association (LPGA) decided that to safeguard the tour's image they must take forceful steps to stifle lesbian rumors (the LPGA has been jokingly referred to as the Lesbian Professional Golf Association) and restore the heterosexual credibility of women golfers. In 1989 the LPGA launched a new "sexy" marketing strategy with a photo spread in *Fairways*, the official LPGA publication. The layout, later reprinted in *Sports Illustrated*, featured five "attractive" players modeling bikinis and other "exotic" swimwear on Hawaiian beaches. LPGA officials admitted that they designed this marketing approach in light of the tour's "image problem," hoping it would "remove all the negatives" and squelch the lesbian "whisper campaign."[60]

The lesbian whisper campaign operates with devastating

impact on other levels of sport as well. In college basketball, the discomfort with lesbianism effects hiring, recruiting, and publicity decisions. Women coaches suspect that one reason for the increasing proportion of male coaches is the bias, especially among male administrators, against lesbians in the profession. They admit to choosing dress and hair styles with the intention of deflecting lesbian suspicions; in some cases lesbian coaches have even married men in order to protect their careers.[61]

The issue comes up repeatedly in recruitment as well, with some coaches reassuring parents that they accept only "feminine" players and do not permit lesbians on the team. A recent rumor circulated among coaches that an anonymous person had mailed a list to prospective high school recruits that identified programs as lesbian or straight. The list's existence remains unverified, but regardless of the story's truth, the extent to which the rumor struck fear in the hearts of coaches reveals the powerful effect of lesbian baiting in college sport.[62]

The impulse to deny lesbianism governs publicity as well as recruitment strategy. Pressed to fill the often empty stands at women's events, administrators have attempted to package college athletes as feminine and "sexy." In one of the most ludicrous yet telling expressions of this strategy, Northwestern State University of Louisiana chose a Playboy Bunny theme for the cover photo on its annual women's basketball guidebook. Under the title, "These Girls Can Play, Boy," the guide featured team members posed in basketball uniforms, bunny ears, and fluffy tails.[63]

Feminist advocates for gender equity in sport are among the few groups in a position to understand and combat the fear and hatred of lesbianism in the sports world. Within the last decade, several leaders have spoken out against homophobia. Arguing that the issue has become a "huge lavender elephant" everyone gingerly walks around but no one dares speak about, activists have insisted that the matter will not go away unless directly confronted.[64]

Yet women leaders are not themselves immune from pressure to suppress the issue. At the 1983 New Agenda Conference, organizers agreed to table a resolution that dealt openly with lesbianism when corporate sponsors of the conference threatened to withdraw funding if the word *lesbian* entered into the printed record. Conference members pushed through a resolution about homophobia but consented to withdraw another resolution and delete the word *lesbian* from official conference documents. Caught in a bind, New Agenda leaders were pressed to placate one of the few sources of economic support available to women's athletics. They were similarly reluctant to alienate the media, whose presence they had carefully courted. Realizing the vulnerability of women's athletics to lesbian baiting, women's sport advocates were wary about giving the press corps of predominantly unsympathetic male sports journalists any grist for the rumor mill.[65] While their decision was politically savvy in one respect, it also conformed to the very pattern of lesbian silencing that conference members had hoped to redress.

The fear of lesbianism operates, as it did in this case and has for decades, to police women's behavior within the world of sport. Female athletes and their supporters accurately perceive that acceptance and rewards depend on a willingness to prove their heterosexuality or deny their homosexuality. Whereas in the past, all women athletes were viewed as stepping over a border into masculine terrain, today that boundary line has shifted. Women can compete, even excel, in sports as long as they demonstrate that they are sexually interested in and accessible to men. Anything short of compliance, however, marks an athlete as masculine and sexually aberrant. In contemporary sport lesbianism has come to mark the new line of athletic deviance. The pernicious stereotype of mannish lesbians sustains the masculine symbolism of sport, while within athletic culture lesbian athletes are shunned as secretive figures whose dangerous sexuality could topple all the painstakingly won achievements of women's sport.

Just as antilesbian hostility has not abated in contemporary athletics, the enduring problem of racism in sport continues to diminish the possibilities available to women of color. Although demands for admission and recognition have met with some success, athletes of color still encounter barriers at the level of participation, leadership, and in the media.

Young women of color have benefited along with white women from the significant increase in opportunities to play in school and community-based sports. However, either because they are discouraged from trying other activities or lack the resources to compete in more exclusive sports, minority athletes tend to be disproportionately represented in only a few sports. Hispanic women have been ghettoized in volleyball and softball, while African American women remain concentrated in basketball and track and field.[66]

Exclusion, not skewed representation, characterizes the situation at the upper levels of coaching and sport management. In a ringing indictment of institutional racism and sexism in sport administration, Anita De Frantz, the lone African American woman on the IOC, reported that of the fifty governing bodies of U.S. Olympic sports, not one had appointed an African American female as executive director. At the collegiate level, she noted that a survey of 106 large college athletic programs found only one African American woman in the position of athletic director.[67] That De Frantz and other commentators mention only African American women indicates that other women of color remain equally or even more invisible in leadership positions.

Among women who make it to top levels of competition, pressures to establish an appropriately feminine and heterosexual image may fall especially hard on African American athletes whose accomplishments bring them into the national limelight. On the positive side, persistently high achievement levels, especially in track and field, have finally won for black women a degree of respect and national attention denied them in earlier decades. Yet, a historical legacy of disrespect, distortion, and stereotyping of black womanhood and black female sexuality demands that contemporary African American athletes navigate a complex set of currents.

Beginning with Wilma Rudolph and Wyomia Tyus in the 1960s and more recently with Evelyn Ashford, Florence Griffith Joyner, and Jackie Joyner-Kersee, African American women have gained a celebrity status unknown to their predecessors. As a result of American society's greater acceptance of women's sport in general and of African Americans as cultural heroes, the popular discourse around black female track stars no longer ignores their prominence or denies their femininity. Sport journalists of the 1980s described Olympians like Ashford and Joyner as delicate, ladylike, graceful, and glamorous.[68] The media has begun to do for black women what it has long done for white women—establish their femininity by references to their appearance, off-track interests, and status as wives and mothers.

African American athletes have been far from passive participants in this process. With a refreshing boldness several leading black athletes have utilized their star status and media attention to fashion their own public image, asserting a commanding, energetic personal style that simultaneously demanded recognition of their femininity and their strength. Florence Griffith Joyner, with her long, multicolored fingernails; sleek, one-legged bodysuits; and elaborate hairdos presents the most memorable example. But she was joined by others like Gail Devers, Valerie Brisco, Gwen Torrence, and Jackie Joyner-Kersee, who used various combinations of fashion, flash, and outspokenness to create a portrait of black female athletes as dynamic, self-assured, multifaceted women.

The motives and meanings behind this style of self-presentation appear to be complex. It could indicate a calculated strategy to gain media attention that otherwise would go to white athletes. Even after gaining substantial media recognition, black Olympians who won multiple medals in 1984 and 1988 earned far less in product endorsements, commercial rewards, or lasting popularity than did successful white athletes like gymnast Mary Lou Retton and runner Mary Decker Slaney. On the other hand the glamour and dash of women like Griffith Joyner also suggest a confident form of self-expression, one that is unafraid to display a style of femininity rooted in personal preference and in African American culture. The erotic element of this style—expressed in form-fitting track suits and in the colorful, almost sassy exuberance of off-track appearance—claims for black women a positive, self-defined, and public sexuality that has historically been denied them.

However, athletes who attempt to shape their own image do not ultimately control public representations or interpretations of that image. In popular media coverage of African American female track athletes, an older discourse based on stereotypes of black women as animalistic, hypersexual or inordinately strong continues to flourish. In the flurry of articles published after Florence Griffith Joyner's outstanding performance at the 1988 Olympics, *Time* and *Newsweek* described "Flo Jo" as a "shameless" self-promoter who presented herself as an "erotic alien" in order to "seduce" and "titillate" the public.[69]

Alongside the image of the sexual wanton appeared slightly more subtle references to black women as wild animals in need of taming by strong black men who acted as coach, husband, or both. *Sports Illustrated* reported that under her husband-coach Bob Kersee's direction, "Jackie [Joyner-Kersee] has to be horse-whipped to run any distance," while Florence Griffith Joyner "has to be reined in" by husband-coach Al Joyner.[70] An earlier *Sports Illustrated* piece on Valerie Brisco-Hooks featured the athlete sprawled facedown on the track with coach Kersee looming over her, hands pressed down on her back, with the caption, "It requires a strong hand like Kersee's to keep the stubborn Brisco-Hooks on track."[71] Despite black athletes' attempts to convey an image of confident independence, the popular press seems more interested, at least in these instances, in showing that strong black women remain under the control of male authority.

As athletes attempting to assert some command over their public image and as coaches and administrators seeking entry into positions of authority in the sports world, African American women face overt and subtle forms of discrimination that reinforce their longstanding subordination in athletics and the wider society. For Native American women, Latinas, and Asian American women, the lack of resources or well-traveled avenues into athletic culture has made the sports world even less accessible. These obstacles not only suggest the powerful interconnections of racism and sexism in the history of women's sport but also point to a critical issue for activists concerned with creating a more equitable future.

⎯⊃○⊂⎯

In addition to issues of participation, leadership, sexual stigma, and racial discrimination, two other issues with roots in a more distant era have become of critical importance in the contemporary situation of women athletes. Today matters of money and problems surrounding the control and regulation of the female body have assumed a new prominence in shaping female athletic experience.

For most of women's athletic history, financial matters remained uncomplicated because of the simple fact that there was so little money available. Women's sports took place in schools, community centers, low-budget athletic clubs, and ritzier country clubs in which women's athletic activities received but a small portion of the moneys set aside for athletic activities. Only a few sports promoters attempted to finance professional women's ventures, and those that did tended to sponsor low-budget barnstorming operations like the touring All-American Red Heads basketball team. Small-time professional and semipro women's sports did not differ significantly from many similar ventures in men's athletics.

However, as sports have developed over the last half-century, corporate sponsorship has become central not only to professional sport but to financing amateur events like college athletics and the Olympic Games. Both in the form of direct sponsorship and indirect backing through television and advertising arrangements, private industry makes the wheels spin in the contemporary sports world. More than ever before, decision making in sports revolves around the marketplace: which sports will sell tickets, which activities can attract advertisers, and which marketing strategies enhance a sport's commercial viability.

The priority given to profit making often means that women's events simply do not receive financial support. Professional basketball and softball leagues of the 1970s and early 1980s failed to attract enough paying fans or advertisers to break even, much less turn a profit.[72] When women's events do attract corporate sponsorship, investors concerned with selling their product often decide that what sells the best is not women's athletic ability but their "sex appeal." In 1991 a group of promoters announced the founding of a new league, called the Liberty Basketball Association, in which athletes were "required to be attractive to both in-arena and television viewers." With this in mind players would exchange the "baggy, ugly, grotesque uniforms" worn by college women for a "form-fitting" spandex "unitard."[73]

The need for corporate sponsorship places women's sport advocates in a bind. While they actively solicit the resources business interests can provide, they also chafe under the restrictions corporate funding imposes. In women's tennis, as strong feminists like Billie Jean King and Martina Navratilova worked to gain respect and equality for the women's tour, its primary sponsor, Virginia Slims cigarettes, advertised with the infantilizing slogan, "You've come a long way, baby!" More profoundly the need for corporate funding has restricted the ability of activists to effect either meaningful reform or radical change in the sporting culture in which women compete. Even rather moderate organizations like the AIAW, which attempted to introduce a more democratic structure into intercollegiate sport, crumbled under the weight of the well-financed NCAA. In the absence of the funding and publicity that corporate backing can provide, women who seek to build a cooperative, nonhierarchical model of sport that values participation over victory and emphasizes skill sharing over competitive animosity have not succeeded beyond the local level.[74]

The powerful influence of the multi-billion-dollar sporting industry also bears directly on the more amorphous process of how contemporary society defines and controls the female body. While selling big-time women's sports is of minor concern to most members of the commercialized sporting world, selling sports and fitness to ordinary women has become critical to the industry's financial growth. The fitness boom of the 1970s and 1980s spurred millions of American women to take up jogging, aerobics, walking, weight training, bicycling, swimming, and a variety of team and individual sports in pursuit of better physical and mental health. For the many women who felt nothing but alienation from team and competitive sports, fitness activities like jogging or swimming provided an entrée into physical activity and the pleasures that can accompany it. Aerobics classes—first called "jazzercise"—seemed more like dance than sport, attracting women who were initially more comfortable with a classically "feminine" form of physical exercise. Because classes were scheduled around women's workday, and because they attracted a predominately female clientele, aerobics became a way for busy women to fit exercise into their lives in a comfortable, even social gathering of women.

However, while many women found that exercise contributed to a confident and healthy body, the fitness boom also capitalized on widespread, almost obsessive, anxieties women felt about their body weight. By the 1980s the ideal "look" for women had gone beyond thin to a sculpted, fatless body—a kind of curveless, hard-edged, taut-skinned ideal most women found unattainable. But they didn't stop trying. Diet products and weight-control clinics became a multi-billion-dollar industry; eating disorders reached almost epidemic proportions among young women; and studies found that a majority of girls under ten years old had already begun dieting. As women turned to sport and exercise to shed dreaded pounds, the fitness industry both benefited from and incited women's preoccupation with weight control.

The impulse to use exercise systems to control the body is not new. Early in the twentieth century, physical educators intro-duced European exercise regimens designed to strengthen the bodies of female students while instilling greater physical control over a female body thought to be unpredictable, even hysterical. By contrast today's sporting boom occurred within the context of a popular culture that has emphasized pleasure, release, and the relaxation of controls over mind and body. The concept of libera-tion from coercive controls took on political overtones when sports advocates linked the boom in women's athletics to the freeing of the female body from traditional constraints.

Although many women do indeed experience sport as a form of physical liberation, the all-consuming concern with fitness and thinness forms a distinct countercurrent to that goal. It has evolved into a new form of physical coercion in which the body is no longer controlled by external forms of discipline and supervision but by an internalized surveillance system. Women constantly patrol their own bodies for signs of age, cellulite, and lapses of self-control. Under the rubric of health and physical enjoyment, they endure grueling exercise routines and punishing diets that do not liberate as much as regulate the female body to fit an ideal most women have little voice in creating and little success in attaining.

The tension between physical empowerment and coercive bodily regulation extends to sport as well as fitness activities. Two sports that have gained tremendous popularity since the early 1970s—gymnastics and bodybuilding—illustrate the new athleticism's contradictory influences on the female body.

Since Olga Korbut charmed her way into the public's heart during the 1972 Olympics, gymnastics has been one of the most popular and fastest-growing sports in the United States. The sport's required combination of strength, agility, flexibility, grace, explosive power, and risk enthralls audiences and inspires reverence for its young stars. Yet the daring moves originated by the slight, girlish Korbut and her 1976 successor Nadia Comaneci introduced fundamental changes into gymnastic routines and officiating standards. Judges now place the greatest value on high-risk maneuvers suited to prepubescent girls' highly flexible bodies and low fat ratios.[75] By their late teens most female gymnasts lose this advantage, and their careers go into decline.

That teenage girls have become heroes in a sporting culture that boasts of empowering women contains a certain irony. The 1970s, when gymnastics first burst onto the scene, were years in which a broad-based feminist movement was demanding access to power, in the process threatening the status quo in sports, politics, and business. It was precisely at this moment that the public fastened onto a sport whose heroes were little girls noted for their "tiny" bodies, "cute" looks, and coquettish demeanor. These teenage "pixies" were typically coached by middle-aged adult men who combined the roles of surrogate parent and stern taskmaster. The athletes' childlike bodies and childish relationships to adults seemed to offer some unconscious reassurance to a public who looked with anxiety on the growing power of adult women.[76]

However, as their bodies matured and grew less able to perform the high-risk stunts that won competitions, Korbut, Comaneci, and other young gymnasts fell from grace—figuratively and literally. Comaneci took the logical step of trying to prevent the physical changes that would spell the end of her career; she stopped eating, developing a severe anorexic condition. This phenomenon grew so common among competitive gymnasts that insiders in the sport called it the Nadia syndrome.[77] Eating disorders remain common in gymnastics and have been detected in other sports as well. A 1986 study of female college athletes in the Midwest found that 74 percent of gymnasts—and 33.3 percent of all women athletes—practiced potentially dangerous weight-control methods, including vomiting, laxatives, and diet pills.[78]

As one of the nation's most popular sports, gymnastics illustrates the private and public contradictions of women's athleticism in the late twentieth century. Privately gymnastics can offer great physical confidence and personal satisfaction to a developing athlete, yet the sport all too frequently turns into a nightmare of starvation and self-doubt. To the public it presents at once a virtuoso performance of spectacular athletic beauty and a reassuring picture of the athlete as a tiny, juvenile figure who cloaks her athletic skills in a coy sexuality and girlish cuteness to please her adult coaches, judges, and audience.

Bodybuilding, at first glance, appears to present the exact opposite image. In packed auditoriums women parade their large, well-sculpted muscles before admiring fans who whoop gleefully with every carefully orchestrated pose, each one designed to show off the definition and size of a particular muscle group. By celebrating female bulk and muscularity, bodybuilding rewards women's strength and their ability to take on a look that, until recently, was limited to and definitive of masculine posture. Yet bodybuilding shares with gymnastics many of the same tensions around the control and emancipation of the gendered body.

For years the sport's leaders divided over judging standards, a minority claiming that women should be evaluated by the same criteria used in male competitions, while the majority advanced the familiar athletic double standard that a woman's performance ought to weigh strength and definition alongside evidence of attractive femininity. The emphasis on muscular build without "masculine bulk" has put great pressure on women to reduce fat levels in order to heighten muscle definition.[79] Many female bodybuilders have, consequently, fallen into a dangerous routine of strenuous dieting, exchanging food intake for the consumption of anabolic steroids that aid muscular growth and sharpen definition.[80] The impressive power and bravado of top contenders is the outcome of vigilant, potentially harmful, forms of self-denial and chemical ingestion.

Bodybuilding also encourages women to sculpt their bodies as objects for public display and evaluation. Like Miss America contestants, bikini-clad competitors strut their tanned, hairless bodies before a panel of judges to show off their physical beauty, only in this case they are judged for conventionally masculine attributes rather than classically feminine ones. Yet for all its similarities to entrenched forms of sexual objectification, the exhibitionism of bodybuilding also contains a more subversive element. Where female gymnasts disrupt the traditional opposition between femininity and athletic strength, power, and control, in bodybuilding the combination of traditionally "feminine" ritual and dress with "masculine" muscles and posturing operates as an even-more-daring form of gender provocation. Bodybuilders engage in a playful performance that blends polarities—tiny bikinis and enormous muscles—and transgresses athletic boundaries through a celebration of women inhabiting a "male" sport and posture. In doing so they disturb assumptions about what the culture understands to be masculine and feminine in the human body.

Bodybuilding, gymnastics, and the fitness boom are all elements within a thriving corporate-dominated sport culture that affords women multiple opportunities for physical enjoyment and development. Yet that very culture also serves as a conduit for broader cultural pressures on women continually to shape and monitor their bodies to meet social standards of body size and personal attractiveness. In these activities as in other women's sports, the possibilities for physical pleasure and empowerment compete with entrenched but ever-changing forms of physical constraint that fundamentally undercut women's personal and societal power.

━◦━

In late-twentieth-century America, a skilled adult woman striving for athletic recognition or a young girl just starting out in a local sports program will each find competitive opportunities, athletic resources, and media interest far beyond the typical scenario of earlier times. In all likelihood she will not face the ridicule, rejection, or blatant disregard that earlier women athletes met with time and again.

Yet the path is not clear of obstacles. Even as contemporary definitions of femininity have grown to include athleticism, sporting institutions and resources continue to be dominated by men, while the sports world as a whole continues to reflect a set of deeply inscribed sexist values and meanings which are hostile to women's full participation and enjoyment. Moreover, while women are permitted and even encouraged or pressured to take up sport and fitness activities, sport leaders, corporate sponsors, and the commercial media consistently attempt to regulate women's bodies, their outward appearance, and their sexuality. Sport remains a key cultural location for male dominance, a site where traditional patriarchal values are upheld and transformed in response to changes in the broader society.

Yet, far from being discouraged, women are approaching these barriers with a sense of entitlement, buttressed by the broader inroads of feminism into American society and energized by the personal pleasures and power they experience through their own sporting involvement. It is this sense of entitlement and determination that stamps the recent period of sport history and provides hope for a future in which adequate leisure, athletic pleasures, and physical power are available to all women.

In its fullest expression, the demand for opportunity and equality in the athletic world involves more than asking men to move over and make room for female competitors. It means insisting that men relinquish privilege—most obviously their monopoly on athletic skill and enjoyment. Women's athletic freedom requires that certain attributes long defined as masculine—skill, strength, speed, physical dominance, uninhibited use of space and motion—become human qualities and not those of a particular gender.

This seemingly simple shift would have radical consequences, for the "masculine" attributes of sport are also the very qualities that define manhood in American society. Sport turns boys into men and endows them with the physical strength and social confidence to assume positions of power. The centrality of sport in contemporary culture makes it integral to the way American society organizes and evaluates gender relations—the everyday conventions that govern male and female activities; our images and ideals of masculinity and femininity; and the social hierarchies that have historically granted men greater authority in political, economic, religious, family, and athletic matters.

Ultimately women's efforts to attain meaningful leisure, unrestricted access to sport, and athletic self-determination will be part and parcel of transforming the broader social relations of gender within which sporting life takes place.

# Notes

ABBREVIATIONS USED IN NOTES

## Journals

APER        *American Physical Education Review*
HB          *Harper's Bazar*
JOHPE       *Journal of Health and Physical Education*
JOHPER      *Journal of Health, Physical Education, and
              Recreation*
LHJ         *Ladies Home Journal*

## Research Centers or Libraries

BTHC        Barker Texas History Center
PSUL        Pennsylvania State University Libraries

INTRODUCTION

1. "Martina and Chrissie: At the Top for a Decade," *Ms.* 13 (May 1985), 72.
2. *Sports Illustrated* 59 (September 19, 1983), 29–31; and "The Smartina Show, Or Tennis in a Lethal Vein," *Sports Illustrated* 58 (April 4, 1983), 34.
3. The quote is Navratilova describing her public image. "The Best of All Time?" *Time* 24 (July 16, 1984), 62.
4. "The Smartina Show," 34.
5. Frank Deford, "A Pair Beyond Compare," *Sports Illustrated* 64 (May 26, 1986), 80; and "The Smartina Show," 34. Reference to Navratilova's bisexuality provided an additional clue to her status as a gender transgressor. Media discussions of lesbianism or bisexu-

ality on the women's tennis tour regularly presumed that lesbianism involved masculine qualities or desires. There were also indirect references to Navratilova's lesbianism, even in comments that presumably had nothing to do with sexuality. In *Time* magazine's "The Best of All Time," the reporter concluded that in spite of her reputation, Navratilova "is anything but a diesel truck steaming heedlessly toward immortality" (62). Since tennis has little to do with the business of long-haul trucking and since few diesel trucks make claims on immortality, this can only be read as a coded reference to lesbians as "diesel" dykes.

6. The comment is attributed to Hana Mandlikova, in "The Best of All Time?" 61.
7. This was indeed the case, since within just several years other women on the tour equaled and surpassed Navratilova's skill level.
8. Gary Libman, "Kicking Up a Storm," *Los Angeles Times* (November 8, 1990), E1, 14, 16.
9. Dudley A. Sargent, "Are Athletics Making Girls Masculine? A Practical Answer to a Question Every Girl Asks," *Ladies Home Journal* 29 (March 1913), 11.
10. See *Time* 61 (February 2, 1953), 41; "Farewell to the Babe," *Reader's Digest* 70 (January 1957), 21; Paul Gallico, "Texas Babe," *Houston Post* (March 22, 1960), in which he recalls his impressions from 1932; William Marston, "How Can a Woman Do It?" *Redbook* (September 1933), 60.
11. Frances Kaszubski, "In Defense of Women Athletes—Part II," *Amateur Athlete* 3 (October 1962), 16. Kaszubski was head of the AAU's Women's Track and Field Committee.

## CHAPTER 1    THE NEW TYPE OF ATHLETIC GIRL

1. "The Masculinization of Girls," *Lippincott's Monthly* 88 (October 1911), 565.
2. The "free, vigorous, outdoor girl" was compared to her predecessor, "Lydia Languish," in *Literary Digest* 82 (September 13, 1924), 70. "The Girl and Her Sports," *LHJ* 32 (July 1915), 10.
3. Kathleen E. McCrone makes this point in her study of British girls' sport. She argues that the female athlete stood "at the threshold between definitions of male and female and between women of the past and future." McCrone, "Play Up! Play Up! And Play the Game! Sport at the Late Victorian Girls' Public Schools," in J. A. Mangan and Roberta J. Park, eds., *From "Fair Sex" to Feminism* (London: Frank Cass, 1987), 97–129; quote, 97.

4. "The Masculinization of Girls," *Lippincott's Monthly* 88 (October 1911), 564–65.

5. John Lucas and Ronald Smith, *Saga of American Sport* (Philadelphia: Lea and Febiger, 1978), parts 1 & 2; Benjamin G. Rader, *American Sports: From the Age of Folk Games to the Age of Televised Sports*, 2nd ed. (Englewood Cliffs, N.J.: Prentice Hall, 1990), chaps. 2–5.

6. Rader, *American Sports*, chaps. 2, 4, 6.

7. Ibid., chap. 7; Mabel Lee, *A History of Physical Education and Sports in the U.S.A.* (New York: John Wiley and Sons, 1983), 88–91.

8. In order to compete successfully in AAU events, exclusive athletic clubs grudgingly opened their doors to talented white track men regardless of background, creating a democratizing pressure in elite amateur sport.

9. J. Willis and R. Wettan, "Social Stratification in New York City Athletic Clubs, 1865–1915," *Journal of Sport History* 3 (Spring 1976), 45–63; Lucas and Smith, *Saga of American Sport*, part 2.

10. In contrast the new immigrants and native-born workers who populated America's swelling cities exhibited no such signs of overcivilized effeminacy. Hardened by physical labor and the daily struggle for survival, they impressed anxious observers as having a barely controlled virility. Their physical strength and brawny working-class manner appeared capable of toppling the social hierarchy among men. On masculinity and the late-nineteenth-century sport boom see Michael S. Kimmel, "The Contemporary 'Crisis' of Masculinity in Historical Perspective," in Harry Brod, ed., *The Making of Masculinities* (Boston: Allen & Unwin, 1987), 139–140. See also Peter Filene on masculinity in turn-of-the-century America, *Him/Her/Self* (Baltimore: Johns Hopkins University Press, 1986), especially 71, 75, 95; Daniel T. Rodgers, *The Work Ethic in Industrial America, 1850–1920* (Chicago: University of Chicago Press, 1978); and Roberta J. Park, "Sport, Gender and Society in a Transatlantic Perspective," in Mangan and Park, *From "Fair Sex" to Feminism*, 58–93.

11. Dominick Cavallo, *Muscles and Morals: Organized Playgrounds and Urban Reform, 1880–1920* (Philadelphia: University of Pennsylvania Press, 1981); Cary Goodman, *Choosing Sides* (New York: Schocken Books, 1979); Allen Guttmann, *A Whole New Ball Game* (Chapel Hill: University of North Carolina Press, 1988), 82–100.

12. On the relationship between the medical profession and women's

physical education, see Helen Lenskyj, *Out of Bounds: Women, Sport and Sexuality* (Toronto: Women's Press, 1986), chaps. 1–2; Patricia Vertinsky, "Body Shape: The Role of the Medical Establishment in Informing Female Exercise and Physical Education in Nineteenth-Century America," in Mangan and Park, *From "Fair Sex" to Feminism*, 58–93; Vertinsky, "Exercise, Physical Capability, and the Eternally Wounded Woman in Late Nineteenth-Century North America," *Journal of Sport History* 14 (Spring 1987), 7–27; and Paul Atkinson, "The Feminist Physique: Physical Education and the Medicalization of Women's Education," in Mangan and Park, *From "Fair Sex" to Feminism*, 38–57.

13. Barbara Solomon, *In the Company of Educated Women: A History of Women and Higher Education in America* (New Haven: Yale University Press, 1985), 62.

14. On vitalism, see Cynthia Eagle Russett, *Sexual Science: The Victorian Construction of Womanhood* (Cambridge: Harvard University Press, 1989), 104–29.

15. On the history of women's physical education in the nineteenth century, see Joanna Davenport, "The Eastern Legacy: The Early History of Physical Education for Women," *Quest* 32:2 (1980), 226–36; Lee, *A History of Physical Education*, part 1; Vertinsky, "The Effect of Changing Attitudes toward Sexual Morality upon the Promotion of Physical Education for Women in Nineteenth-Century America," in Reet Howell, ed., *Her Story in Sport* (West Point, N.Y.: Leisure Press, 1982), 165–77; and Roberta J. Park, "The Rise and Development of Women's Concern for the Physical Education of American Women, 1776–1885: From Independence to the Foundation of the American Association for the Advancement of Physical Education," in Howell, *Her Story in Sport*, 44–56.

16. Male and female educators from state schools, women's colleges, and specialized gymnastics institutes joined together in 1885 to found the American Association for the Advancement of Physical Education. Men formed a majority, but from the start a confident female minority participated in the organization, which in 1903 changed its name to the American Physical Education Association (APEA). Women commanded a measure of respect and influence unusual in mixed-sex professional organizations of the period.

17. Allen Guttmann, *Women's Sport: A History* (New York: Columbia University Press, 1991), 103.

18. Ibid., 101.

19. Female footracing, ball games, and pugilism did not begin in the nineteenth century. On earlier women participants, see Guttmann, *Women's Sport*, 71–79; and on the nineteenth century, 96–105. See

also Margery A. Bulger, "American Sportswomen in the 19th Century," in Paul Zingg, ed., *The Sporting Image* (New York: University Press of America, 1988), 89. On prostitution and women in the public sphere, see Mary P. Ryan, *Women in Public: Between Banners and Ballots, 1825–1880* (Baltimore: Johns Hopkins University Press, 1990).

20. On upper-class sport in the nineteenth century, see Cindy Himes, "The Female Athlete in American Society, 1860–1940," (Ph.D. dissertation, University of Pennsylvania, 1986), chap. 1; Roberta J. Park, "Sport, Gender and Society in a Transatlantic Perspective," in Mangan and Park, *From "Fair Sex" to Feminism*, 82–83; Donald J. Mrozek, *Sport and American Mentality, 1880–1910* (Knoxville: University of Tennessee Press, 1983), 103–35; and Karen Kenney, "The Realm of Sports and the Athletic Woman," in Howell, *Her Story in Sport*, 107–40.

21. Bulger, *American Sportswomen*, pp. 90–96; Kenney, "The Realm of Sports," 107–40.

22. Bulger, *American Sportswomen*, p. 92, quoted from Alfred B. Starey, "Lawn Tennis in America," *The Wheelman Illustrated* 2 (September 1883), 467–68.

23. Frances E. Willard, "How I Learned to Ride the Bicycle," in Stephanie Twin, ed., *Out of the Bleachers: Writings on Women and Sport* (Old Westbury, N.Y.: Feminist Press, 1979), 105, 110.

24. On the bicycle craze, see Vertinsky, *The Eternally Wounded Woman: Women, Doctors and Exercise in the Late Nineteenth Century* (New York: Manchester University Press, 1990), 78–79.

25. Kenney, "The Realm of Sports," 107–15.

26. Bertha Damaris Knobe, "Chicago Women's Athletic Club," *HB* 39 (June 1905), 539–46; Ann O'Hagan, "Athletic Girls," *Munsey's Magazine* (August 1901), in Peter Levine, ed., *American Sport: A Documentary History* (Englewood Cliffs, N.J.: Prentice Hall, 1989), 74–75.

27. Lucas and Smith, *Saga of American Sports*, chap. 20; Mary Z. Levy and Barbara Jane Walder, *WomenSports* 1 (June 1974), 31–32; and Guttmann, *Women's Sports*, 126.

28. Cavallo, *Muscles and Morals*, xi, 1, 25–41. Cavallo argues that the organized play movement, attempted to transfer control of children's play from children and families to the state. Through supervised play, reformers believed they could create ideal social personalities and values, reduce the harmful consequences of city life, and decrease ethnic and class conflict. These reforms seem to have been designed around the perceived needs of working-class boys, with girls included as something of an afterthought. Other kinds of

"child-saving" reforms, especially settlement house domestic education and recreation programs, were designed to specifically address the conditions of urban immigrant girls. On athletic programs, see also J. Thomas Jable, "The Public School Athletic League of New York City: Organized Athletics for City School Children, 1903–1914," in Steven A. Riess, ed., *The American Sporting Experience* (Champaign, Il.: Human Kinetics, 1984), 219–38; and William Graebner, *The Engineering of Consent: Democracy and Authority in Twentieth-Century America* (Madison: University of Wisconsin Press, 1987).

29. New York City started a girls' branch of the Public School Athletic League in 1905, two years after opening its boys' program.
30. Barbara Noonkester, "The American Sportswoman from 1900–1920," in Howell, *Her Story in Sport,* 178–222.
31. Scrapbooks of Anne Maude Butner, 1904–5, Butner Papers, University of Minnesota Archives.
32. Radcliffe Yearbooks and Kristen Powell collection on Radcliffe Athletics, Acc. No. R87, Radcliffe College Archives; Mary R. Carson, "Supplementary Notes on 'The History of Physical Education at Smith College,' " student paper, in D. S. Ainsworth Papers, Box 10, #12, and Dorothy S. Ainsworth, "The Sportswoman Prior to 1920," December 1963 speech to NAPECW, in Ainsworth Papers, Box 7—"Notes, Publications, Speeches, Writings," Sophia Smith Collection, Smith College.
33. E. H. Westwood, "Hockey in Women's Colleges," *HB* 39 (July 1902), 655–58.
34. "A Constructive Program of Athletics for School Girls," *APER* 24 (May 1919), 279.
35. This seems to have been part of a transition toward evaluating health by external rather than internal criteria. In the context of consumer society, modern constructions of womanhood emphasized complexion, shape, and physical beauty as "true" signs of good health. This process transformed femininity from a more interior concept, which emphasized traits like piety and purity, to a more exterior set of indicators through which femininity was mapped on the female body.
36. Marie Montaigne, "To Reduce Flesh," *HB* 46 (March 1912), 144.
37. J. Parmley Paret, "Exercise for Women," *HB* 34 (April 6, 1901), 936.
38. Dudley A. Sargent, M.D., "How Can I Have a Graceful Figure?" *LHJ* 29 (February 1912), 15.
39. Helene Saxe MacLaughlin, "Field Hockey—Girls," *APER* 16 (January 1911), 41.

40. "An Appraisal of the Value of Athletic Sports for Girls," *The New York Times* (February 12, 1922), 16; quote from the editor of *Nation's Health*.

41. These conflicts were integrally related to economic and social tensions of the Progressive Era. By 1900 the industrial economy supported the middle class handsomely, affording bourgeois women the time to play a sport, attend school, or enter politics. Their leisure was sustained by the men and women who worked as domestic help or later toiled in the factories that produced time-saving consumer goods for the household. Laborers whose long workdays paid only enough for a bare, miserable subsistence often organized union drives and radical political campaigns to demand a greater share of America's wealth. White, native-born Americans of the middle and upper classes looked uneasily at the social tumult that threatened to bring down their comfortable Victorian world. It was in the context of pre–World War I turbulence, with its conflicting interests and cultural anxieties, that Americans scrutinized the new, unorthodox female athlete.

42. Sargent, "Are Athletics Making Girls Masculine?", 11.

43. G. L. Meylan, "Physical Qualifications of Women," *APER* 10 (June 1905), 156.

44. George Engelmann, "The American Girl of Today: Modern Education and Functional Health," *APER* 6 (March 1901), 60.

45. Inglis, "Physical Culture for Young Girls," *HB* 44 (February 1910), 119.

46. Sargent, "Are Athletics Making Girls Masculine?" 71–73; Inglis, *HB* 44 (March 1910), 183; J. Parmley Paret, "Basket-Ball for Young Women," *HB* 33 (October 20, 1900), 1567.

47. Angenette Parry, M.D., "The Athletic Girls and Motherhood," *HB* 46 (August 1912), 380; and Sarah Addington, "The Athletic Limitations of Women," *LHJ* 40 (June 1923), 147.

48. "Sex O'Clock in America," *Current Opinion* 55 (August 1913), 113–14.

49. The focus on middle-class rather than working-class women's sexuality is most likely due to working-class women's minimal access to sport and the greater concern for protecting the propriety and health of middle-class students. (When working-class women entered sport in greater numbers in the 1920s, the focus shifted to the sexual dynamics of popular sport. This is the subject of chapter 2.) In theory the middle-class Victorian lady was a model of sexual modesty and self-control. Yet underlying late-Victorian notions of feminine refinement and control lurked an older image of unsubdued female passion. This tension became explicit with women's

entrance into sport, an activity that walked a tightrope between "civilized" society and "primitive" emotion. On sexual fears surrounding women's sport, see Donald J. Mrozek, "The 'Amazon' and the American 'Lady': Sexual Fears of Women as Athletes," in Mangan and Park, *From 'Fair Sex' to Feminism*, 282–96; esp. 286.

50. Parry, "The Athletic Girls and Motherhood," 380.

51. Richard Duffy, "Out-Door Women: Their Sports and What They Have Done for Them," *Good Housekeeping* 50 (June 1910), 679–80.

52. Inglis, "Exercise for Girls," *HB* 44 (March 1910), 183.

53. Parry, "The Athletic Girls and Motherhood," 380. While most advocates believed that sport was likely to unleash female sexual desires, a few postulated that athletics could teach girls to control their sexual compulsions. One early advocate turned the belief that girls had "no idea of moderation in things physical" into a pro-sport argument, asserting that, like men, women, too, could sublimate "excessive" sexual passion through sport. See Christine T. Herrick, "Women in Athletics: The Athletic Girl Not Unfeminine," *Outing* 40 (September 1902), 714, 716, 720.

54. For decades women's higher education had endured conservative accusations that educated women were shirking maternal duty in the interest of unnatural intellectual pursuits. Sporting activity seemed to be further evidence of educated women's rejection of their proper feminine sphere.

55. Dorothy Brown, *Setting a Course: American Women in the 1920s* (Boston: Twayne, 1987), 133.

56. John M. Tyler, "The Physical Education of Girls and Women," *APER* 16 (November 1911), 491.

57. In his 1900 presidential address to the American Gynecological Society, Dr. George Engelmann waxed eloquent on the perils of female reproductive development, warning that after the difficult onset of puberty, like a ship navigating a rocky harbor, the adolescent female "may still ground on the ever-recurring shallows of menstruation." Along with other medical and scientific experts, he found a solution in a program of moderate exercise to strengthen the muscles and reduce the cyclical turbulence of females during puberty and young adulthood. A medically sound exercise program, according to Engelmann and many other physicians of his day, could rescue this stranded young woman and allow her to achieve "a healthy approximation to the normal." See Engelmann, "The American Girl of Today," 29–30.

58. For extensive treatment of medical issues and late-nineteenth-centu-

ry exercise prescriptions, see Vertinsky, *The Eternally Wounded Woman*. On female physicians who directed P.E. programs, see especially chap. 5.

59. Grantland Rice, "The Baseball Girl," undated (circa 1905), Grantland Rice Papers, Box 4—folder 2, Vanderbilt Joint University Libraries, Special Collections; Nashville, Tenn.

60. Joan S. Hult, "The Governance of Athletics for Girls and Women: Leadership by Women Physical Educators, 1899–1949," *Research Quarterly for Exercise and Sport*, Special Centennial Issue (April 1985), 64–77; Ellen Gerber, "Chronicle of Participation," in Gerber et al., eds., *The American Woman in Sport* (Reading, Mass.: Addison-Wesley, 1974), 48–85.

61. Physical education records at Smith, Radcliffe, University of Minnesota, University of Wisconsin, University of Texas. See also *APER* articles on measurement, hygiene, and posture (1901–20).

62. Atkinson, "The Feminist Physique," 40–46, 50–53; Vertinsky, *The Eternally Wounded Woman*, 148–49.

63. WAAs had become firmly established student organizations and in 1918 began to coordinate nationally through the Athletic Conference of American College Women. Faculty influenced student policies through their advisory positions on WAA boards and by forming state associations to set athletic policy for high schools.

64. College yearbooks indicate that many student groups continued to select varsity players, usually to honorary clubs that, in the absence of permission for intercollegiate competition, at least symbolically rewarded athletic excellence. Students at the University of Wisconsin stridently opposed an award system that replaced varsity letters and tournament trophies with a point system based on athletic service and attendance. They insisted that points "should be significant of *real athletic ability*." Quote from Margaret J. Swift, "Report of the National Athletic Conference of American College Women," *APER* 26 (June 1921), 306 (emphasis in original).

65. Sheila Fletcher makes this argument convincingly in *Women First: The Female Tradition in English Physical Education, 1880–1980* (London: Athlone Press, 1984), 9–12.

66. Sarah Comstock, "Young Girl at Play," *Good Housekeeping* 64 (February 1917), 23–24, 106–7. Clearly the author did not ask "the laundress" for her opinion on fairness, the benefits of hard work, or the "exhilaration" of backbreaking labor. By implication the laundress and other domestic workers were more "primitive" and "naturally" fit than the leisured modern housewife.

67. Ainsworth Papers, History of P.E. at Smith, 1875–1915, Sophia

Smith Collection, Box 10, #12, Smith College; Blanche Trilling, quote from a "History of Women's Physical Education" (1915), University of Wisconsin Archives.

68. Helen M. McKinstry, "Administration of Physical Education of Girls and Women," *APER* 16 (June 1911), 371.

69. On class- and race-based definitions of womanhood, see Paula Giddings, *When and Where I Enter* (New York: William Morrow, 1984), 31–103; Deborah K. King, "Multiple Jeopardy, Multiple Consciousness," *Signs* 14 (Autumn 1988), 43–72; Bonnie Thornton Dill, "The Dialectics of Black Womanhood," *Signs* 4 (Spring 1979), 543–55. On P.E. class ideology, see Vertinsky, *Eternally Wounded Woman*, 16.

70. Mary Porter Beegle, "Hygiene and Physical Education in Trade Schools for Girls," *APER* 19 (February 1914), 91.

71. Ibid., 77.

72. Ibid.

73. Lenskyj, *Out of Bounds*, chaps. 1–2; Vertinsky, *Eternally Wounded Woman*, chaps. 5–6.

74. Arabella Kenealy, *Feminism and Sex Extinction* (London: T. Fisher Unwin, 1920), 278, quoted in Vertinsky, *Eternally Wounded Woman*, 151–52.

75. Anna de Koven, "The Athletic Woman," *Good Housekeeping* 55 (August 1912), 151, 150.

## CHAPTER 2 GRASS-ROOTS GROWTH AND SEXUAL SENSATION IN THE FLAPPER ERA

1. Larry Engelmann, quoting an unnamed English journalist after 1927 Wimbledon match, in *The Goddess and the American Girl: The Story of Suzanne Lenglen and Helen Wills* (New York: Oxford University Press, 1988), 291.

2. The popularity of girls' and women's sports varied widely, and the meager and scattered nature of the sources for this period make the extent of participation difficult to evaluate. Some communities seem to have developed a strong tradition in women's athletics, often in one particular sport like basketball, while others offered minimal opportunities. Girls' athletics remained a distant second to boys' in most school and playground programs, but even under those conditions managed to thrive in some areas.

3. Helen Wills, *Saturday Evening Post* 202 (August 3, 1929), 6–7ff.

4. Paul Gallico, "Gertrude Ederle," *The Golden People* (New York: Doubleday, 1965), 47–65.

5. Suzanne Lenglen, "Tennis," *Collier's* 66 (July 17, 1920), 16, 41.

6. "Helen Wills as the 'Killer of the Courts,' " *Literary Digest* 102 (September 7, 1929), 61.

7. Paul Gallico, quoted by Engelmann in *The Goddess and the American Girl*, p. 317; "Helen Wills as the 'Killer of the Courts,' " 56, 61; John R. Tunis, "Miss Wills and Mr. Tilden: A Study in Contrast," *Outlook* 153 (September 25, 1929), 198.

8. On popular culture of the period, see Lary May, *Screening Out the Past: The Birth of Mass Culture and the Motion Picture Industry* (New York: Oxford University Press, 1980); Lewis Erenberg, *Steppin' Out: New York Nightlife and the Transformation of American Culture, 1890–1930* (Westport, Conn.: Greenwood Press, 1981); Stuart and Elizabeth Ewen, *Channels of Desire: Mass Images and the Shaping of American Consciousness* (New York: McGraw-Hill, 1982); T. Jackson Lears and Richard W. Fox, eds., *The Culture of Consumption* (New York: Pantheon, 1983); and Richard Butsch, "Introduction," *For Fun and Profit: The Transformation of Leisure into Consumption* (Philadelphia: Temple University Press, 1990), 3–27.

9. Rader, *American Sports*, 131–150; Lucas and Smith, *Saga of American Sport*, 305–72. On a comparison of sport and other forms of popular culture, see Lawrence Levine, *Highbrow/Lowbrow: The Emergence of Cultural Hierarchy in America* (Cambridge, Mass.: Harvard University Press, 1988), 195.

10. See Rob Ruck, *Sandlot Seasons* (Urbana: University of Illinois Press, 1987); Rader, *American Sports*, 114–130.

11. On youth sport and public recreation, see Rader, *American Sports*, 211–34; Jable, "The Public School Athletic League," in Riess, *The American Sporting Experience*, 219–38; Cavallo, *Muscles and Morals*. On industrial sports, see "Athletics in Industry," *Literary Digest* 91 (November 6, 1926), 69–72; "Outdoor Recreation for Industrial Employees," *Monthly Labor Review* 24 (May 1927), 1–16; "Indoor Recreation for Industrial Employees," *Monthly Labor Review* 25 (September 1927); and Monys Ann Hagen, "Industrial Harmony Through Sports: The Industrial Recreation Movement and Women's Sports" (Ph.D. dissertation, University of Wisconsin–Madison, 1990).

12. On the 1920s see Rader, *American Sports*, 131–50; Douglas A. Noverr and Lawrence E. Ziewacz, *The Games They Played: Sports in American History, 1865–1980* (Chicago: Nelson-Hall, 1983), 67–96.

13. The roots of the "New Morality" and the new leisure of the 1920s lay in earlier developments in working-class culture. Turn-of-the-century working-class youth initiated changes in morals and man-

ners by cultivating a streetsmart style and patronizing a world of commercial, mixed-sex amusements. Kathy Peiss has argued that the bold, stylish pre–World War I "working girl" represented an "independent, athletic, sexual and modern" female self who preceded the wealthier flapper. Peiss, *Cheap Amusements: Working Women and Leisure in Turn-of-the-Century New York* (Philadelphia: Temple University Press, 1986), 69.

14. Feminism, too, played a role. Modern feminists broke down barriers to women's political and public activism, demanded the right to female self-development and expression, and questioned commonplace beliefs about sexual difference. Even though the political feminist movement declined in the twenties, it had laid the groundwork for many women to pursue personal fulfillment and nontraditional activities—including sports. On the relationship between modern leisure and new styles of femininity, see Lois Banner, *American Beauty* (Chicago: University of Chicago Press, 1983), 175–201. On feminism and femininity, see Nancy Cott, *The Grounding of Modern Feminism* (New Haven: Yale University Press, 1987), 145–62.

15. *New York News* (August 21, 1919), Tuskegee Institute Archives, News Clippings.

16. In 1925 there were 179 segregated playgrounds for the "exclusive use" of black children, most of them developed through the efforts of the Playground Association of America's Bureau of Colored Work. These playgrounds, along with northern municipal playgrounds which were not officially segregated, held track-and-field competitions for neighborhood children. The winners formed teams that went on to compete against other playground squads citywide.

17. *St. Louis Argus* (September 21, 1923), Tuskegee Institute Archives, News Clippings.

18. *Chicago Defender* (February–October, 1920). On the winning record and eventual disbanding of the Roamer Girls, see the *Defender*, March–April, 1926. The *Defender* reported on the "Roamer Girls," but the team's name also appears in print as the "Romas"; see Arthur R. Ashe, Jr., *A Hard Road to Glory: A History of the African-American Athlete, 1919–1945* (New York: Warner Books, 1988), 45.

19. Little evidence survives to give a more complete picture of black women's basketball in this period. Team names, player names, and scores are available in the black press through box scores and short news items. But these accounts offer almost no information about the athletes, their uniforms, team history, or the players' lives. There is a strong need for ongoing, more-in-depth research, probably at

the level of a community study that could draw from oral histories, local knowledge, and more extensive investigation of community archival sources.

20. Various teams, leagues, and contest results are mentioned on the sporting pages of the *Chicago Defender, Pittsburgh Courier, Atlanta Daily World, Washington* (and) *Baltimore Afro-American,* and *Philadelphia Tribune.*

21. *Chicago Defender* (October 16, 1920) and occasional *Defender* announcements of upcoming or completed Bloomer Girl games, 1919–1921. Black communities throughout the country spawned touring baseball teams, and while most were exclusively male, a few enterprising promoters formed women's teams or even teams like the Missouri Go-Devil Sisters, which featured male and female ballplayers. On the Go-Devil Sisters, see photo in *Washington Afro-American* (September 24, 1932).

22. Edward B. Henderson, *The Negro in Sports*, rev. ed. (Washington, D.C.: Associated Publishers, 1939), 171–80.

23. Rob Ruck makes this argument in his study of semiprofessional and professional black men's sport in Pittsburgh. See *Sandlot Seasons,* 3–6.

24. Henderson, *The Negro in Sport*, 130.

25. African American men and women seemed to have forged an athletic solidarity in the overall interest of advancing the race. Distinguished male athletes like Sol Butler sometimes coached women's teams. After gaining fame in the post–World War I European Inter-Allied Games, Butler went on to star for a Chicago men's basketball team but also found time to coach the Roamer Girls. Companion male and female teams, like the *Philadelphia Tribune* women's and men's squads, played regularly scheduled double bills. In cases in which men and women competed against each other, they vented gender conflict in a lighthearted, playful manner. Madame Caldwell urged fans to attend the Bloomer Girls series against a Chicago Boys' Club with the pronouncement, "We are equal to the men, so let us prove it to them by demonstrating a real ball game" (*Chicago Defender* [October 16, 1920], 6).

26. On the black press's coverage of women's athletics, see Linda D. Williams, "An Analysis of American Sportswomen in Two Negro Newspapers: The *Pittsburgh Courier*, 1924–1948 and the *Chicago Defender*, 1932–1948" (Ph.D. dissertation, Ohio State University, 1987).

27. *Chicago Defender* (June 11, 1927).

28. Ashe, *A Hard Road to Glory*, 60.

29. *Chicago Defender* (January 15, 1927).

30. *Indianapolis Freeman* (May 2, 1914) and *Pittsburgh Courier* (June 1926); in Tuskegee Institute Archives, News Clippings.
31. *Philadelphia Tribune* (March 12, 1931), 11.
32. *Pittsburgh Courier* (February 5, 1927). Ray may never have undertaken the swim. I found no further reference to her or the planned event in the *Courier* or other newspapers.
33. Without public notice their activities presumably did not carry the racial significance that black women's sport did in African American communities, although for the white women involved, interracial or interethnic competition may have been charged with heightened intensity.
34. For a brief description, see Stephanie Twin, "Women and Sport," in Donald Spivey, ed., *Sport in America* (Westport, Conn: Greenwood Press, 1985), 205–7.
35. Ruck, *Sandlot Seasons*, 24.
36. "Industrial Recreation," *Playground* 17 (June 1923), 178.
37. L. C. Gardner, "Community Athletic Recreation for Employees and Their Families," quoted in Ruck, *Sandlot Seasons*, 25–26.
38. Management hoped that by extending industrial sport leagues to the surrounding community, the townspeople who watched and played would associate community pride with the corporation's welfare and in times of labor trouble side with the company. In the process, management also rationalized and brought under corporate control a lively tradition of autonomous sandlot sport. The structure of industrial recreation fostered ideas consistent with the corporate economy: the naturalness of winners and losers, the fairness of competition, and the benefits of submitting to the abstract authority of formal rules and appointed officials. Jacquelyn Dowd Hall et al. make this argument about textile company sport programs in the early twentieth century. See *Like a Family* (Chapel Hill: University of North Carolina Press, 1987), 135–39.
39. Many companies designed recreation programs purely for the benefit of current employees, showing no particular interest in pursuing championships or fame. Others were more ambitious, recruiting talented local athletes, often directly from high school, by offering them well-paid and often undemanding jobs. Athletes employed by the sponsor preserved their amateur standing because they received money as company employees only, not as payment for athletic activity. Women's industrial sport offered opportunities primarily to single white women, typically from lower middle-class or working-class families in which college was not an option.
40. *Travelers Beacon* (March 1922), Travelers Insurance Co. Library, Hartford, Conn.

41. *Amateur Athlete* (June 1930), 3.
42. This plant seems to have had the most advanced program for women. See Ruth Stone, "Recreation for Girls," *Playground* 17 (July 1923), 207–8.
43. The Chicago Brownies took the honors that year and went on to win an interstate tournament, which suggests that states throughout the region offered competitive opportunities. See letter from Shirley J. Schaefer about her mother, Edna Marion Karstens Schaefer, who played for the Jefferson school team, the Chicago Brownies, and the Illinois Athletic Club in the 1920s, in basketball clippings file, Chicago Historical Society.
44. In the early twentieth century, approximately 25 percent of women over the age of fourteen worked in the paid labor force, and by 1930 women workers made up just under 25 percent of all wage laborers. Within the female labor force, married women accounted for 22.8% of women wage workers in 1920 and 28.8% in 1930. Alice Kessler-Harris, *Out to Work: A History of Wage-Earning Women in the United States* (New York: Oxford University Press, 1982), 229.
45. See, for example, Stone, "Recreation for Girls."
46. Rosemary Deem, "Unleisured Lives: Sport in the Context of Women's Leisure," *Women's Studies International Forum* 10:4(1987), 423–32; and C. Griffin, D. Hobson, S. MacIntosh, and T. McCabe, "Women and Leisure," in Jennifer Hargreaves, ed., *Sport, Culture, and Ideology* (London: Routledge & Kegan Paul, 1982), 88–116.
47. *New York Times* (March 21, 1920), 19:3; see also short items on March 22, 1920, 19; April 26, 1920, 15; March 8, 1922, 12; and February 19, 1924, 11.
48. Lucas and Smith, *Saga of American Sport*, 342–72; Stephanie Twin, "Introduction," in Twin, *Out of the Bleachers*, xxvii–xxxiv; Mary Henson Leigh, "The Evolution of Women's Participation in the Summer Olympic Games, 1900–1948" (Ph.D. dissertation, Ohio State University, 1974), 148–51, 220–27.
49. Nancy Doris, "The Swimming Stars," *The Woman Citizen* 11 (June 1926), 19, 40. On women swimmers, see Leigh, "The Evolution of Women's Participation," 300–47; Paula Dee Welch, "The Emergence of American Women in the Summer Olympic Games, 1900–1972," (D. Ed. dissertation, University of North Carolina, Greensboro, 1975), 24–51; and Noonkester, "The American Sportswoman from 1900–1920," in Howell, *Her Story in Sport*, 202–17.
50. *New York Times* (August 14, 1922), 9:2.

51. Banner, *American Beauty*, 271–79.
52. Helen Wills, *Saturday Evening Post* (May 28, 1932), 29.
53. "A Seventeen-Year-Old Mermaid Who Holds Ten World Records," *Literary Digest* 80 (March 8, 1924), 74–76; "'Crawl Stroke' Makes Junos," *Literary Digest* 86 (July 25, 1925), 52–53; "The Swimming Stars," *The Woman Citizen* 11 (June 1926), 19.
54. Paul Gallico, *Farewell to Sport* (New York: Alfred A. Knopf, 1938), 145.
55. "Miss Bjurstedt's Burst into Fame," *Literary Digest* 51 (August 28, 1915), 428.
56. Engelmann, *The Goddess and the American Girl*, 11.
57. On 1920s ideals of womanhood, see Mary P. Ryan, "The Projection of New Womanhood: The Movie Moderns in the 1920s," in J. Friedman and W. Shade, eds., *Our American Sisters* (Lexington, Mass.: D.C. Heath and Co., 1982), 500–518; Brown, *Setting a Course*, 29–47; Banner, *American Beauty*, 249–80. On the relationship between female sexuality, modern femininity, and consumer culture, see Cott, *The Grounding of American Feminisim*, 145–62, and Banner, *American Beauty*, 187–90.
58. For a full-length treatment of both Lenglen and Wills, see Engelmann, *The Goddess and the American Girl*.
59. See Banner, *American Beauty*, 208, and Sandra Lee Bartky, "Foucault, Femininity, and the Modernization of Patriarchal Power," in *Femininity and Domination* (New York: Routledge, 1990) 63–82.
60. According to her biographer Larry Engelmann, Lenglen's use of body and motion characterized a break with nineteenth-century commitments to saving and restraint. Lenglen appeared to many as action epitomized, a human dynamo who freely wasted and never saved energy. See Englemann, *The Goddess and the American Girl*, 279.
61. On fashion, sport, and modern femininity, see Banner, *American Beauty*, 275–77; Barbara A. Schreier, "Sporting Wear," in C. Kidwell and V. Steele, eds., *Men and Women: Dressing the Part* (Washington, D.C.: Smithsonian Institution Press, 1989), 92–123; and Patricia Campbell Warner, "Clothing the American Woman for Sport and Physical Education, 1860 to 1940: Public and Private," (Ph.D. dissertation, University of Minnesota, 1986).
62. M. K. Browne, "Fit to Win," *Collier's* 78 (October 16, 1926), 16.
63. Suzanne Lenglen, "Tennis," *Collier's* (April 10, May 15, May 29, and July 17, 1920).
64. "'Decidedly Unconquerable' is Mlle. Lenglen, Tennis Champion," *Literary Digest* 62 (September 13, 1919), 80. See also Grantland

Rice, "Women with the Wallop," *Collier's* 76 (July 11, 1925), 14, and "The Rival Queens," *Collier's* 77 (January 30, 1926); "Suzanne and Mary K., Pro Tennis Pioneers," *Literary Digest* 90 (September 25, 1926), 50–58.

65. This analysis draws on Engelmann, *The Goddess and the American Girl*, chaps. 2, 8; See also Rice, "The Rival Queens," 14; and for Will's self-presentation, Helen Wills, "Emancipated Legs Mean Better Sports," *LHJ* 44 (April 1927), 33, and Wills's series in the *Saturday Evening Post* (August 3 and November 23, 1929; June 21, 1930; April 4, 1931; May 14 and May 28, 1932).

66. "How a Girl Bear Leander at the Hero Game," *Literary Digest* 90 (August 21, 1926), 52–67; quoted passages from 52, 67.

67. "Our Glorious Sports Girls," *LHJ* 47 (November 1930), 23.

68. "Look Out for the Ladies," *Colliers* 75 (February 21, 1925), 18–19.

69. "Greeks, Girls, and 1944," *The Nation* 118 (February 27, 1924), 222.

70. "How a Girl Beat Leander at the Hero Game," 52.

71. Welch, "The Emergence of American Women," 33.

72. Tony Ladd, "Sexual Discrimination in Youth Sport: The Case of Margaret Gisolo," in Howell, *Her Story in Sport*, 579–89.

73. *Literary Digest* 78 (July 28, 1923), 56–57.

74. Cott also notes the media's "carnivalesque fascination" with women on top in the 1920s, in *The Grounding of Modern Feminism*, 215.

CHAPTER 3   GAMES OF STRIFE

1. John R. Tunis, "Women and the Sport Business," *Harper's Monthly Magazine* 159 (July 1929), 217. The unnamed educator was probably Blanche Trilling at the University of Wisconsin. In her private notes she recorded having discussed these matters with Tunis. Women's P.E. Records, University of Wisconsin Archives.

2. Tunis, "Women and the Sport Business," 213.

3. "Sports Are Not for Women," *New Current Digest* (January 10, 1937), 43.

4. Agnes Wayman, "Play Problems of Girls," *Playground* 20 (January 1927), 548.

5. This term was used by Inglis in "Physical Culture for Young Girls."

6. Himes, "The Female Athlete in American Society," 123.

7. On the Women's Olympics and the International Olympics, see Leigh, "The Evolution of Women's Participation," 155–208; Mary Henson Leigh and Therese Bonin, "The Pioneering Role of Madame Alice Milliat and the FSFI in Establishing International Track and

Field Competition for Women," *Journal of Sport History* 4 (Spring 1977), 72–83; and Welch, "The Emergence of American Women," 40–51.

8. Quoted in Leigh, "The Evolution of Women's Participation," 249.

9. Quoted in ibid., 240–41.

10. Leigh notes the usage of this term and analyzes the IOC debate about "excesses" in "The Evolution of Women's Participation," 155–75.

11. Ibid., 155–208; Leigh and Bonin, "The Pioneering Role of Madame Alice Milliat," 72–83; and Welch, "The Emergence of American Women," 40–51. The Women's World Games were held again in 1926, 1930 and 1934. Conflict continued to mar FSFI-IAAF relations until the FSFI dissolved in 1936, turning over complete control of women's track and field to the IAAF. Although European women continued to participate throughout this period, the games never attracted much interest in America after the initial 1922 Olympics. Leigh claims that the suppression that followed was so successful that many top female track athletes never knew about the succeeding games.

12. *New York Times*, letter (July 13, 1913), 4: 2; quoted in Welch, "The Emergence of American Women," 18.

13. *New York Herald* (April 9, 1922); quoted in Leigh, "The Evolution of Women's Participation," 227. Prout found further justification in Americans' desire to stay atop the world of international sport, explaining that "the women of America should be put upon the same physical basis as the women of other countries. We don't want them to get too far ahead of us."

14. This committee is also sometimes referred to as the Women's Athletic Committee, or WAC. For consistency I will use CWA.

15. Impetus for the group came from two sources. Members of the NCAA, the organizing body of men's intercollegiate sport, feared AAU encroachments on college sport. Also, military leaders wanted to promote physical fitness among future soldiers and to guarantee Olympic representation for military athletes. Historians offer differing interpretations of the founders' precise motives in forming the NAAF. See Himes, "The Female Athlete in American Society," 178; Leigh, "The Evolution of Women's Participation," 220; and Alice A. Sefton, *The Women's Division National Amateur Athletic Federation: Sixteen Years of Progress in Athletics for Girls and Women, 1923–1939* (Stanford, Calif.: Stanford University Press, 1941). Sefton was a leader of the Women's Division and wrote the organization's official history.

16. On this united front, see also Hult, "The Governance of Athletics for Girls," 66.
17. Information on the Women's Division and CWA was regularly reported in *APER* and *JOHPE*. See also Lucas and Smith, *Saga of American Sport*, 342–72; Ellen W. Gerber, "The Controlled Development of Collegiate Sport for Women, 1923–1936," *Journal of Sport History* 2 (Spring 1975), 1–28.
18. Among the original federated organizations were the YMCA, YWCA, Playground and Recreation Association of America, National Lawn Tennis Association, scouting groups, and National Education Association, along with regional and national P.E. organizations such as the APEA, the National Association of Physical Education for College Women, and the Athletic Conference of American College Women.
19. Sefton, *The Women's Division*, 32.
20. Ibid., 7. The Women's Division also attempted to be a clearinghouse and consulting agency for problems reported by its members.
21. Ibid., 34–40.
22. Sarah Addington, "The Athletic Limitations of Women," *LHJ* 40 (June 1923), 38.
23. Elizabeth Burchenal, quoted in ibid., 147.
24. Frances A. Hellerbrandt, "Training Rules and the Athletic Association," *APER* 32 (September 1927), 504–5. The danger lay in competition's capacity to unleash passions and loosen inhibitions. According to Dr. Angenette Parry, the young athlete seduced by "the applause of the multitude, [and] the intoxication of outstripping her competitor" might push beyond the limits imposed by menstruation's "lowered vitality" and "sacrifice what seems like a problematic future evil to the present hour of triumph." Parry was quoted in *LHJ* 40 (June 1923), 147.
25. Frederick Rand Rogers, "Physical Education Programs for Girls," *APER* 33 (May 1928), 354.
26. "Pope States Stand on Girl Athletics," *New York Times* (May 4, 1928), reprinted in R. Lipsyte and G. Brown, eds., *Sports and Society* (New York: New York Times Co./Arno Press, 1980), 245.
27. Mabel Lee, "The Case For and Against Inter-collegiate Competition for Women and the Situation as It Stands Today," *APER* 29 (January 1924), 13.
28. See Helen N. Smith, "Evil of Sports for Women," *JOHPE* 2 (January 1931), 8–9, 50–51.
29. Helen Smith, "Athletic Education," *APER* 32 (October 1927), 608–11.

30. "Exploiting Girls in Sports Decried," *New York Times* (May 4, 1939), article on Women's Division Annual Conference, reprinted in Lipsyte and Brown, *Sports and Society*, 247.

31. "Old Battles Won" (describing the previous decades), Women's Field Report, 1940, National Recreation Association Annual Reports, NRA Papers, Social Welfare History Archives (University of Minnesota, Minneapolis), Box 12, Annual Reports; and "Exploiting Girls in Sports Decried."

32. "Exploiting Girls in Sports Decried."

33. *Recreation* 29 (November 1935), 384.

34. "Exploiting Girls in Sports Decried." Another problem mentioned by physical educators was that by reporting which girls had to sit out for "health reasons," newspapers in effect publicized when individual women had their periods. Players might counter this evil with another one, playing during their periods to avoid either missing the big game or having people know why.

35. *APER* 29 (November 1924), 517, 519. The word "ejaculate" was at that time a perfectly acceptable term for "exclaim," although Wayman's choice of verb may also reveal the troubling sexual nature of her concerns.

36. Sefton, *The Women's Division*, 12; Mabel P. Cummings, "Adaptation of the Physical Education Program for Girls to the Strength and Ability of the Individual," *APER* 30 (June 1925), 327.

37. Gerber, "The Controlled Development of Collegiate Sport for Women," 1–28.

38. Elizabeth Halsey, "The New Sportswoman," *Hygeia* 5 (September 1927), 448.

39. Blanche Trilling, report on University of Wisconsin student athletics, 1902–1946, among Trilling's "reports," in Women's P.E. Records, University of Wisconsin Archives.

40. "Women's Athletic Committee Report," *APER* 28 (February 1923), 68–69.

41. Ethel Perrin, "More Competitive Athletics for Girls—But of the Right Kind," *APER* 34 (October 1929), 473.

42. "Report of the Committee on Organization of the Conference on Athletics and Physical Education for Women and Girls, April 6 and 7, 1923, at Washington, D.C.," *APER* 28 (June 1923), 284.

43. Given regional, race, class, ethnic, and age differences among women, it is doubtful that they have ever shared a common standard of womanhood. But in the dominant culture there has often been the presumption of a common definition. In the early decades of the twentieth century, even the myth of a unified womanhood crumbled.

44. A. W. Ellis, "The Status of Health and Physical Education for Women in Negro Colleges and Universities," *Journal of Negro Education* 8 (January 1939), 58–63.

45. Southern state P.E. associations excluded black teachers. Northern states technically accepted all qualified members, but few African Americans joined, and even fewer received invitations to the conferences and meetings where participants elected leaders and formulated policies. On existing discrimination and efforts to integrate the profession, see Edwin B. Henderson, "Tolerance, An Objective," editorial, *JOHPE* 17 (February 1946), 76.

46. In the mid-1940s Prairie View State College in Texas required that P.E. majors "must at all times be candidates for varsity or intramural sports." Evidence gathered from college bulletins and catalogs of Prairie View State University (BTHC, University of Texas, Austin), Tennessee State University (TSU Special Collections), Hampton College (Hampton University Archives). See also Harry Beamon, "The Rise and Demise of Physical Education at Fisk University: A Historical Analysis" (D. Ed. dissertation, Vanderbilt University, 1979); Joseph D. Simmons, "History of the Development of the Health and Physical Education Program at Tennessee Agricultural and Industrial State University from 1912 to 1952" (M.S. thesis, August 1954, Graduate Research Series #261, TSU Archives).

47. Elizabeth Dunham, "Physical Education of Women at Hampton Institute," *Southern Workman* 53 (April 1924), 167.

48. Beamon, "The Rise and Demise," 18–20.

49. Ellis, "The Status of Health," 58–63; and Gerber, "The Controlled Development of Physical Education for Women," 1–28.

50. *Chicago Defender* (March 12, 1927), 2: 7.

51. Ruth Arnett, "Girls Need Physical Education," *Chicago Defender* (December 10, 1921).

52. See Trilling Papers, including report from Women's Division NAAF eighth Annual Meeting, in Trilling subject files—NAAF, University of Wisconsin Archives; Ainsworth Papers, Sophia Smith Collection, Smith College; and Physical Education Department records at universities of Minnesota and Texas.

53. "Intercollegiate Sports for Women," editorial, *APER* 29 (April 1924), 198–99.

54. Report from the National Conference of the Athletic Federation of College Women, in 1942, in Women's P.E. Records, Trilling subject file—AFCW, 1941–42, University of Wisconsin Archives.

55. Radcliffe Athletics, Official Reports, 1937–38, Kristin Powell Collection on Radcliffe Athletics, Acc. No. R87, Radcliffe College Archives.

56. Radcliffe Student Yearbook, 1936, Radcliffe College Archives.

57. President's Reports, 1920–23, in Powell Collection on Radcliffe Athletics.

58. Ina E. Gittings, "Why Cramp Competition?" *JOHPE* 2 (January 1931), 10–13 ff.; quote from 11.

59. See, for example, Gladys E. Palmer, "Policies in Women's Athletics," *JOHPE* 9 (November 1938), 565–67 ff.; and "'How Do We Do It': We Need Interscholastic Athletics, Too!" *JOHPE* 16 (April 1945), 208.

60. December 1926 address by former AAU President Gustavus T. Kirby to National Amateur Athletic Federation, Box 226, NAAF Folder, Avery Brundage Collection, University of Illinois Archives.

61. AAU Minutes, 1924, 73; quoted in Leigh, "The Evolution of Women's Participation," 268.

62. 1932 Annual Meeting of AAU, Minutes, 109, AAU Archives, Indianapolis, Ind. See also Brundage speech to 1930 AAU Convention, Brundage Collection, Box 251, Annual Convention Speeches, University of Illinois Archives.

63. The report countered the charge of elitism as well, arguing that championship events represented a capstone to a broad edifice of competition at every skill level. The committee did, however, take to heart some of the criticisms leveled by physical educators and agreed to push for greater medical supervision and more women in chaperone, coaching, officiating, and administrative roles. See "National Women's Sports Committee Report," in Minutes of 1932 AAU Annual Meeting, AAU Archives.

64. Avery Brundage, unpublished paper, "The AAU and Women's Athletics," 1928 or 1929 (question mark on document), Box 293, Women in Athletics Folder, Brundage Collection, University of Illinois Archives.

65. Brundage, from his 1930 convention speech and a radio talk (October 31, 1931), in Brundage Collection, Box 251, University of Illinois Archives.

66. Howard J. Savage, "Athletics for Women from a National Point of View," *JOHPE* 1 (June 1930), 13.

67. Report on the Conference on Athletics and Physical Recreation for Women and Girls, April 6–7, 1923, National Archives, Washington D.C.; see R690 PHS, General Records, Venereal Disease Division, 1918–1936, Box 163, 249.1–249.8, folder-lecture 249.212.

68. Beegle, "Hygiene and Physical Education," 76, 91.

69. *Recreation* 26 (April 1932), 15–16.

70. Report on the Conference on Athletics and Physical Recreation for

Women and Girls, April 6–7, 1923; "Everybody Play," *APER* 31 (February 1926), 654–55.

71. Halsey, "The New Sportswoman," 446–48; "Everybody Play."

72. Article from *The Texan* (May 25, 1922), in U.T. Physical Training for Women Collection, Box 3R215, University of Texas, Austin.

73. Himes presents a similar but more detailed analysis of this dynamic in her dissertation, "The Female Athlete in American Society," 188–89. For another analysis of the class and gender politics of the Women's Division, see Karen Epstein, "Sameness or Difference?: Class, Gender, Sport, the WDNAAF and the NCAA/NAAF" (Paper presented at the Nineteenth Annual Convention of the North American Society for Sport History May 27, 1991, Loyola University, Chicago, Ill.).

74. Both AAU officials and women educators championed the benefits of sport and agreed that athletic involvement could enhance motherhood and female citizenship. However, AAU officials tended to utilize eugenic and nationalist rationales, while the Women's Division emphasized individual self-development, "health consciousness," and maternal safety.

75. *Amateur Athlete* 4 (February–July 1929), 7.

76. "Spirit," *Amateur Athlete* (October 1932), 7.

77. AAU *Bulletin*, vol. 2, no. 3 (1925), Box 251, Brundage Collection, University of Illinois Archives.

78. *Pittsburgh Courier* (March 26, 1927), sec. 2.

79. Margaret M. Duncan, "The Status of Intramural Programs for Women," *Research Quarterly* (March 1937), 75–77; and M. Gladys Scott, "Competition for Women in American Colleges and Universities," *Research Quarterly* 16 (March 1945), 49–71.

80. Sefton, *The Women's Division*, 44–45.

81. Women's groups did succeed in removing the women's eight-hundred-meter race from Olympic competition after its 1928 debut, when several women collapsed from exhaustion at the end of the race.

82. William Graebner, *The Engineering of Consent* (Madison: University of Wisconsin Press, 1987), chap. 4; Frederick Cozens and Florence Scovil Stumpf, *Sports in American Life* (Chicago: University of Chicago Press, 1953), 17, 52–60; and Elizabeth Fones-Wolf, "Industrial Recreation, the Second World War, and the Revival of Welfare Capitalism, 1934–1960," *Business History Review* 60 (Summer 1986), 232–57.

83. Hult, "The Governance of Athletics for Girls," 67–69; Sefton, *The Women's Division*, 32–33.

## CHAPTER 4   ORDER ON THE COURT

1. *Life* 8 (April 8, 1940), 41–48.
2. "Hoops, Dear, in Iowa," *Life* 42 (March 4, 1957), 95–96 ff.; Janice A. Beran, "Playing to the Right Drummer: Girls' Basketball in Iowa, 1893–1927," *Research Quarterly for Exercise and Sport*, Special Centennial Issue (1985), 82.
3. *Life* 8 (April 8, 1940), 41.
4. Anna Hiss, 1938 Report of the Women's Advisory Committee of the Texas Amateur Athletic Federation, in NAAF 1936–38 file, University of Texas Women's P.T. Dept. Records, Box 3R 251, BTHC, University of Texas, Austin.
5. Ainsworth Papers, Sophia Smith Collection, Box 10 (File 12— History of P.E. at Smith), Smith College; "No Game for Girls," undated clipping (between 1900 and 1907) from 1900–1912 clippings file of Anne Maud Butner, Butner Papers, University of Minnesota Archives.
6. On the early history of basketball, see Janice Ann Beran, "The Story of Six-player Girls' Basketball in Iowa," in Howell, *Her Story in Sport*, 552–61; Lynne Emery, "The First Intercollegiate Contest for Women: Basketball, April 4, 1896," in Howell, *Her Story in Sport*, 417–23; Beran, "Playing to the Right Drummer," 75–85; Paula Welch, "Interscholastic Basketball: Bane of Collegiate Physical Educators," in Howell, *Her Story in Sport*, 424–31; and Gerber et al., *The American Woman in Sport*, 90–95.
7. Eventually the center region was eliminated and a two-court game replaced the three-court system. The two center-court players became "rovers" who were permitted to run the full length of the court.
8. Quote from Kristin Powell collection on Radcliffe Athletics, Acc. No. R87, Radcliffe College Archives.
9. The name changed during the decades under discussion. The CWA became the Section on Women's Athletics in 1927 and then the National Section on Women's Athletics (NSWA) in 1932. By the 1950s the group was called the Division of Girls' and Women's Sport. To eliminate confusion I will use NSWA even when the time period includes the years before or after this became the official name.
10. *JOHPE* 16 (March 1945), 146.
11. Eline von Borries to Carita Robertson, February 23, 1934, Physical Education for Women, Papers of Laura J. Huelster, Box 2, (Basketball, 4 Div. Folder), University of Illinois Archives, Urbana.
12. Ibid.

13. Ibid. In the early 1930s the committee took a more effective tack by creating a governing body of women's sport officials. This group, the Women's National Official Ratings Committee (WNORC), set standards for referees and tested and rated any official who wanted the WNORC stamp of approval. Women of the NAAF and NSWA pressured school and municipal leagues to employ only rated referees, who in turn encouraged the use of girls' rules and approved standards.

14. Emma Waterman, "A Point System for Girls Athletics in the Oregon High Schools," *APER* 32 (May 1925), 359.

15. *Recreation* 29 (November 1935), 385; *JOHPE* 18 (May 1947), 329; *JOHPE* 1 (December 1930), 45.

16. Blanche Trilling Papers, Dept. of Women's P.E., Athletics for Women File, University of Wisconsin Archives. See also Welch, "Interscholastic Basketball," 424–31.

17. Hult, "The Governance of Athletics for Girls," 72; Alice A. Sefton, *The Women's Division*, 45–49.

18. *Philadelphia Tribune* (March 6, 1930), 10, and (March 24, 1938), 13; Charles H. Thompson, "The History of the National Basketball Tournaments for Black High Schools," (Ph.D. dissertation, Louisiana State Univ., 1980), 53–69. In other years, when the event was held at Hampton and at Tennessee State A & I, the national tourney did not include girls.

19. W. W. Mustaine, "Tabulation of Replies to Questionnaire on Girls' Basket Ball," *APER* 32 (January 1927), 41–45. Of 255 respondents, 174 had interscholastic programs for girls basketball. Studies also found that small schools were the most likely to resist the NSWA rules. By 1955 less than half of small Texas schools played under approved guidelines. See *JOHPE*, 26 (November 1955), 56.

20. *Literary Digest* 89 (April 14, 1926), 74.

21. Trilling Papers, Dept. of Women's P.E., Athletics for Women File, University of Wisconsin Archives.

22. Beran, "Playing to the Right Drummer," 81–82. It isn't clear why the girls' tournament became even more popular than the boys'. Possibly the sense that Iowa girls' basketball was unique helped create its own momentum, drawing more and more spectators and media attention every year. Another factor may be that football, and to a lesser extent baseball, provided other opportunities for sports fans and community members to rally behind boys' athletic championships, while for girls, until recently, high school basketball represented a singular phenomenon.

23. James McLemore, *Texas Schoolgirl Basketball* (UIL: 1976), 1–10, BTHC, University of Texas, Austin.

24. Survey data from University of Texas Women's Physical Training, Box 3R236, Questionnaire Folder, BTHC, University of Texas. Another national survey from the late 1930s found, despite low survey returns, more than 300,000 women playing basketball in high school and colleges. Evelyn Hinton, "Basketball for the Employed Girl," *Recreation* 35 (November 1941), 518. These statistics probably only include information about white school districts. I could find only scattered data on African American interscholastic sport. The evidence suggests that basketball thrived in the segregated black schools of the South, but I found no survey reports on the exact number of participants or tournaments.

25. Carita Robertson to Eline von Borries (March 6, 1934), Physical Education for Women, Papers of Laura J. Huelster, Box 2, (Basketball, 4 Div. Folder), University of Illinois Archives.

26. Though no official national championship existed, the Tribune Girls claimed the title and were generally supported in this claim by the black press. See *Philadelphia Tribune* sports pages, 1930–41.

27. "Industrial Recreation Bulletin" 26 (February 1936), National Recreation Association Papers, Box 63, Social Welfare History Archives (SWHA), University of Minnesota, Minneapolis.

28. Of the total only forty-two played the approved "girls' rules." See Carita Robertson to Eline von Borries (March 6, 1934).

29. "Community Athletics for Girls and Women," in NAAF subject file, no date—but it appears alongside report from 8th Annual Meeting (1931), Trilling Papers, Dept. of P.E., University of Wisconsin Archives.

30. On industrial and union sponsorship, see "Women's Activities," *Recreation* 42 (September 1948), 282; and Hagen, "Industrial Harmony through Sports," chaps. 2, 3, 6.

31. Other nationally known business college teams were those sponsored by the Davenport American Institute of Commerce and the Des Moines American Institute of Business.

32. In addition to supporting women's and men's teams, mills like the Peerless Woolen Mills of Rossville, Georgia, and the Rex Cotton Mills of Gastonia, North Carolina, sponsored grammar school "midget" leagues and high school tournaments for both boys and girls. Greenville, South Carolina, hosted an annual textile tournament that attracted hundreds of teams and thousands of spectators from the Piedmont region. "Industrial Recreation Bulletin," 192 (May 1949) and 204 (December 1949), Box 69, National Recreation Association Papers, SWHA, University of Minnesota.

33. Though the AAU had no stated policy of racial segregation or

exclusion, only white teams competed until 1952, when a collegiate team from Chihuahua, Mexico, entered the tournament (it is possible that highly educated Mexican women were considered "white"). The first American women of color did not participate until several years later, when African American athletes broke the color line. When the tournament moved to Gallup, New Mexico, in the early 1960s, a Native American team from the New Mexico Catholic Indian Center entered. In men's AAU play, southern officials tried to appease black critics by offering a few separate tournaments for black teams, but no record of similar events for women exists.

34. Occasionally the competition extended to games against international rivals. A team from Alberta, the Edmonton Grads, dominated Canadian basketball between 1915 and 1940. On a few occasions they took on American challengers. See John Dewar, "The Edmonton Grads: The Team and Its Social Significance from 1915–1940," in Howell, *Her Story in Sport*, 541–47. In the late 1950s and early 1960s, AAU competitors were also chosen for the Pan American games and a series of games between U.S. and Russian women.

35. There is almost no published historical literature on AAU women's basketball. For dissertations that provide data on particular teams or time periods, see Elva Elizabeth Bishop, "Amateur Athletic Union Women's Basketball, 1950–1971: The Contributions of Hanes Hosiery, Nashville Business College, and Wayland Baptist College" (P.E. master's thesis, University of North Carolina, Chapel Hill, 1984); and Sylvia Faye Nadler, "A Developmental History of the Wayland Hutcherson Flying Queens from 1910 to 1979," (Ed. D. dissertation, East Texas State University, 1980). See also Elva Bishop and Katherine Fulton, "Shooting Stars: The Heyday of Industrial Women's Basketball," *Southern Exposure* 7 (Fall 1979), 50–56.

36. Many teams never considered AAU ball, either because they were unaware of its existence or because they preferred the freedom of movement permitted by five-player rules. Teams like the Rochester Filarets, the *Philadelphia Tribune* Girls, and the Chicago-based Refiners Pride Sugar squad traveled throughout their region and played in national tournaments organized by a network of independent male sport promoters. Independent industrial teams formed a significant but hard to document sector of women's basketball. Data on these teams were gathered from several sources: oral histories with softball players who had also played on highly competitive semipro basketball teams in the Midwest and East; scattered news-

paper articles about leading white industrial teams; and AAU reports of efforts to attract independent teams from non-AAU leagues and tournaments.

37. An AAU president did not attend a national women's tournament until 1944, at which point the visiting dignitary pronounced the high quality of play to be "a revelation." But the enthusiasm was short-lived. In future years President Avery Brundage and his successors regretfully declined requests to attend the event. See 1944 Women's Basketball Committee Report, 56th Annual AAU Meeting, Box 2, Brundage Papers, University of Illinois, and correspondence between Van Blarcom and Brundage, 1946–47, Brundage Papers, University of Illinois.

38. *Amateur Athlete* (May 1953), 14. Frustrated AAU leaders were not above responding with sarcasm. The author of a 1930 committee report mocked P.E. characterizations of strenuous competition, remarking, "I . . . expected to see fainting girls carried away in ambulances, others laced in straight jackets after severe cases of hysteria and some in complete collapse after extreme cases of melancholia."

39. The *Amateur Athlete* covered the beauty pageant as well as the national championship in its yearly article on the tournament. On Florida, see 1936–37 AAU Basketball Rules (New York: Spalding Athletic Library), in AAU Archives, Indianapolis, Ind.

40. 1930 Report of AAU Annual Meeting, Minutes, 195–96, AAU Archives, Indianapolis.

41. Robertson to von Borries (March 6, 1934), Physical Education for Women, Papers of Laura J. Huelster, Box 2 (Basketball, 4 Div. Folder), University of Illinois Archives.

42. 1933 Convention Report, Athletic Federation of College Women (AFCW), Women's Physical Education Papers, AFCW Conference File, University of Wisconsin Archives.

43. Tunis, "Women and the Sport Business," 214.

44. On field hockey see Carol Kane, "Constance M. K. Applebee," *WomenSports* 1 (December 1974), 18, 24; Noonkester, "The American Sportswoman from 1900 to 1920," in *Her Story in Sport*, 194–95.

45. Margaret Wiener, "Hockey Hands Across the Sea," *The Woman Citizen* 10 (October 1925), 20, 44.

46. Radcliffe College Archives, Kristin Powell collection on athletics, Acc. No. R87.

47. Interview, Joan Hult (Greenbelt, Md.), July 19, 1988.

48. Interview, Jeanne Rowlands (Boston, Mass.), February 19, 1988.

49. "Outstanding Problems in Girls' Athletics" *APER* 31 (May 1926), 846.

50. "No Game for Girls," undated clipping (between 1900 and 1907) from 1900–12 clippings file of Anne Maud Butner, Butner Papers, University of Minnesota Archives.

51. J. Anna Norris, "Basketball," in Trilling Papers, General Subject Files—Basketball, Women's Phys. Ed. Papers, University of Wisconsin Archives.

52. Tunis, "Women and the Sport Business," 214.

53. On uniforms, see 1938 Report of the Chairman of the Women's Advisory Committee of the Texas Amateur Athletic Federation, Women's Physical Training (P.T.) Papers, NAAF 1936–38 folder, Box 3R251, University of Texas.

54. Interview, Donna Lopiano, University of Texas (Austin, Tex.), March 21, 1988.

55. Hewitt, Stanley, and Martus, "Building College Gymnasiums," *JOHPER* 27 (January 1956), 15.

56. NAAF Newsletter (December 1, 1938), University of Wisconsin Archives.

57. Interview, Julia Brown (Madison, Wisc.), January 25, 1988.

58. Interview, Hult (Greenbelt, Md.), July 19, 1988. Hult's estimate of one-half the students may even have been low among some student groups. A 1950 report by the Texas Recreation Federation of College Women commented that 100 percent of students supported intercollegiate activities for women. The report noted that, although "frowned upon in the past," a recent trend toward introducing such activities had been "brought about by the demand of the students." See University of Texas Women's P.T. Department Records, TAFCW Folder, Box 3R 236, BTHC, University of Texas, Austin.

59. I spoke with thirteen athletes who played highly competitive recreational, industrial, or AAU basketball during a period from the late 1930s to the late 1960s. All quotes in this section come from the following interviews and will not be referenced with separate endnotes unless the speaker's identity is not clear in the text. The interviews were with Alline Banks Sprouse (Manchester, Tenn.), July 8, 1988; Margaret Sexton Gleaves (Nashville, Tenn.), July 6, 1988; Maxine Vaughn Williams (Winston-Salem, N.C.), July 16, 1988; Evelyn ("Eckie") Jordan (Winston-Salem, N.C.), July 18, 1988; Eunies Futch (Winston-Salem, N.C.), July 18, 1988; Doris Rogers (Nashville, Tenn.), July 7, 1988; Joan Hult (Greenbelt, M.d.), July 19, 1988; Delores Moore (Elmhurst, Ill.), December 17, 1988; Loraine Sumner, (West Roxbury, Mass.), February 18, 1988; Pat

Stringer (White Bear Lake, Minn.), June 2, 1988; Donna Lopiano (Austin, Tex.), March 21, 1988; Thelma Hirst, (Douglas, Nebr.), October 10, 1987; Patricia Brandenburg (Mount Prospect, Ill.), May 29, 1991.

60. Several women who later went into physical education or coaching began to question the dominant role of men in women's sport, but usually in hindsight or out of present frustrations, not from problems they had encountered as players. Interviews with Doris Rogers, Donna Lopiano, and Jeanne Rowlands.

61. NAAF Women's Division Newsletter, 84 (February 1, 1939), AAU Archives (Box: Women's Division of NAAF, 1923–40), Indianapolis.

62. Women's Division Study of "Community Athletics for Girls and Women," report given at the 1932 Women's Division meeting; in Trilling subject files—NAAF, Dept. of P.E. Records, University of Wisconsin.

63. This pattern was noted in occasional updates and articles on industrial recreation, published in *Recreation*, the official publication of the National Recreation Association.

64. Interviews, Maxine Vaughn Williams, Alline Banks.

## CHAPTER 5    "CINDERELLAS" OF SPORT

1. On Blankers-Koen, see Richard Schaap, *An Illustrated History of the Olympics*, 2nd ed. (New York: Alfred A. Knopf, 1967), 241. On Blankers-Koen and Ostermeyer, see Guttmann, *Women's Sports*, 200.

2. Avery Brundage, Brundage Collection, Box 70 (Folder—Circular Letters to IOC's, NOC's, and IF's, 1952–54), University of Illinois Archives.

3. Brundage Collection, Box 115 (Folder—Athletics—Women), "IOC—Quotations for and against women's competition," no date (mid-fifties), University of Illinois Archives.

4. This stereotype has been discussed in much of the historical literature on African American women. See, for example, Giddings, *When and Where I Enter*, chaps. 1, 2, 4; Barbara Hilkert Andolsen, *"Daughters of Jefferson, Daughters of Bootblacks:" Racism and American Feminism* (Macon, Ga.: Mercer University Press, 1986); Patricia Hill Collins, *Black Feminist Thought* (Boston: Unwin Hyman, 1990), chaps. 4, 8.

5. Rader, *American Sports*.

6. For more details see chap. 3. See also Leigh and Bonin, "The Pioneering Role of Madame Alice Milliat," 72–83.

7. Brundage to Knute Rockne, Brundage Papers, Box 8 (AAU—Rockne Folder), University of Illinois Archives.

8. Ibid.

9. Personal communication, Annette Rogers Kelly; interview, Ida Meyers (Glenwood, Ill.), May 28, 1991. Rogers won successive gold medals in the 1932 and 1936 four-hundred-meter relay competition. Meyers narrowly missed making the 1936 Olympic squad, but the same year won the national indoor high-jump championship at the age of seventeen. Pickett qualified for the 1932 Los Angeles Olympic team but was removed from competition by American track officials under circumstances that remain clouded. For a more detailed account of the events surrounding Pickett in 1932, see Michael B. Davis, *Black American Women in Olympic Track and Field* (Jefferson, N.C.: McFarland and Co., 1992), 130–33.

10. Donald J. Mrozek argues that perceptions of women's track and field involved a sexual element as well. Victorian notions of female sexual purity supplanted but did not eliminate older beliefs about uncontrolled female passion. The sensual, physical nature of athletics could signal a loss of self-control and a potential slide into sexual depravity. See "The 'Amazon' and the American 'Lady,' " 282–98.

11. Rogers, "Olympics for Girls?" 190–94.

12. Tunis, "Women and the Sport Business," 213.

13. Rogers, "Olympics for Girls?" 194.

14. This anecdote is retold in Schaap, *An Illustrated History of the Olympics*, 196.

15. "Modern 'Atalantas' at XI Olympiad," *Literary Digest* 122 (August 15, 1936), 32–34.

16. "Women's Sports Committee Report," AAU Annual Meeting Minutes, 1934, AAU Archives, Indianapolis, Ind.; *Amateur Athlete* (October 1935), 12.

17. Charlotte Epstein, chairman of Women's Sports Committee, "Women's Sports," *Amateur Athlete* (January 1936), 5. The American Olympic Committee (AOC) also reduced its support. Ida Meyers recalled that the financially strapped AOC paid for only four members of the women's track team to attend the Berlin Olympics, requiring other qualifiers to raise five hundred dollars for their own transport. (Interview, Ida Meyers, May 28, 1991, Glenwood, Ill.)

18. Leigh, "The Evolution of Women's Participation," 291–94.

19. On Owens, see William J. Baker, *Jesse Owens: An American Life* (New York: Free Press, 1986). On African Americans in track and field, see Ashe, *A Hard Road to Glory*, 73–91.

20. Linda D. Williams's study of the *Chicago Defender* and *Pittsburgh Courier* found that the black press between 1924 and 1948 gave significant and positive coverage to black women athletes. Williams concludes that there was "a more favorable environment for the sportswomen in the black community" and that black women benefitted from a diverse and popular black sports culture during this period. "An Analysis of American Sportswomen," 22, 114.

21. Henderson, *The Negro in Sports*, 218.

22. On black women's construction of womanhood, see Giddings, *When and Where I Enter*, 49, 85–94; King, "Multiple Jeopardy, Multiple Consciousness," 43–72; Dill, "The Dialectics of Black Womanhood," 543–55; Patricia Hill Collins, "Learning from the Outsider Within," *Social Problems* 33 (December 1986) 514–32; and Hazel V. Carby, *Reconstructing Womanhood: The Emergence of the Afro-American Woman Novelist* (New York: Oxford University Press, 1987).

23. There may have been class differences in the degree of support for women's sports. In "Organizing Afro-American Girls' Clubs in Kansas in the 1920s," *Frontiers* 9:2 (1987), 69–72, Marilyn Dell Brady indicates that the largely middle-class National Association of Colored Women sponsored girls' clubs that included athletics among a variety of other cultural activities. But sport was not a major focus of these clubs. While golf and tennis were popular among black country club members, it is not clear whether wealthier African Americans approved of women's involvement in sports like basketball, bowling, or track, which had greater working-class constituencies.

24. *New York Age* (February 16, 1929), 6.

25. See Ashe, *A Hard Road to Glory*, 75–79, and annual reports of AAU track-and-field championships published in the *Amateur Athlete*.

26. On southern high school and collegiate women's track, see *Atlanta Daily World* sports pages from the 1930s and 1940s. On TSU, see Tennessee State University Tigerbelles Clippings Files, Tennessee State University Archives, Nashville, Tenn.; TSU yearbooks; and Fatino Marie Clemons, "A History of the Women's Varsity Track Team at Tennessee State University," MA thesis (April 1975), Graduate Research Number 1766, TSU Archives.

27. On northern track meets, see the *Chicago Defender* and *Pittsburgh Courier* sports pages. Stokes, as well as Pickett, had been deprived of a place on the 1932 Olympic team despite her apparent qualifications. The American Olympic Committee's requirement that most women pay their own travel expenses nearly prevented their partici-

pation in the 1936 Berlin Games, too, until at the last minute money turned up. I was unable to determine how the money was raised, but for a partial explanation, see *Philadelphia Tribune* (August 13, 1936), 14. See also Davis, *Black American Women*, 130–33.

28. Interviews, Lula Hymes Glenn and Alice Coachman Davis (Tuskegee, Ala.), May 7, 1992, Leila Perry Glover (Atlanta, Ga.), May 8, 1992, and Edward Temple (Nashville, Tenn.), July 7, 1988; Clemons, "A History of the Women's Varsity," 22; and TSU clippings files at TSU Archives. In its first three years, TSU competed in only one meet per year, and in fifteen years never entered more than seven meets per year.

29. *Atlanta Daily World* (August 6, 1948).

30. *Chicago Defender* (May 22, 1948).

31. Black track athletes flourished throughout the postwar era. In the mid-1950s, 350 women competed at the Tuskegee Relays. Teams from Xavier, Albany State of Georgia, Alabama State, Prairie View A & M, TSU, Philander Smith of Arkansas, Bethune Cookman, and Chicago's Catholic Youth Organization (CYO) entered the senior division, while high schools from throughout the South sent girls to the junior division meet. During these years the Tennessee Tigerbelle team took the mantle from Tuskegee's fading program. TSU won the Tuskegee Relays in 1953 and began a string of AAU national championships. Between 1948 and 1968 Tennessee athletes claimed twenty-five of the forty Olympic track-and-field medals won by American women. See Ashe, *A Hard Road to Glory*, 73–91; Nolan A. Thaxton, "A Documentary Analysis of Competitive Track and Field for Women at Tuskegee Institute and Tennessee State University" (Thesis, Department of Physical Education, Springfield (Mass.) College, 1970); and news clippings from the *Defender*, Box 401, Claude Barnett Collection, Chicago Historical Society.

32. The following accounts are based on six oral-history interviews with women who competed at Tuskegee or Tennessee State University between the late 1930s and the early 1960s. Interviews with Lula Hymes Glenn (Tuskegee, Ala.) May 7, 1992; Leila Perry Glover (Atlanta, Ga.) May 8, 1992; Alice Coachman Davis (Tuskegee, Ala.) May 7, 1992; Shirley Crowder Meadows (Atlanta, Ga.) December 15, 1991; Martha Hudson Pennyman (Griffin, Ga.) May 8, 1992; and Willye White (Chicago, Il.), February 9, 1988. All the quotes that follow are from these interviews. Individual quotations will be cited only if the speaker is not clearly identifiable from the text.

33. Crowder competed but did not medal in the hurdles. Hudson won a gold medal in the four-hundred-meter relay.

34. White won a silver medal in the long jump in 1956 and a second silver in the four-hundred-meter relay in 1964.

35. Interview, Perry.

36. Sander L. Gilman, "Black Bodies, White Bodies: Toward an Iconography of Female Sexuality in Late Nineteenth-Century Art, Medicine and Literature," in Henry Louis Gates, Jr., ed., *"Race," Writing and Difference* (Chicago: University of Chicago Press, 1986), 223–61.

37. See John D'Emilio and Estelle Freedman, *Intimate Matters* (New York: Harper & Row, 1988), 87–93. Quote from Herbert G. Gutman, *The Black Family in Slavery and Freedom, 1750–1925,* (New York: Pantheon Books, 1976), 536.

38. Gilman, "Black Bodies, White Bodies," 238.

39. Stereotypes about physical beauty and sexuality could be contradictory. Within the dominant white discourse, black women were represented as both unattractive sexual partners and wildly attractive, irresistible seducers of white and black men alike. Similarly, portrayals of the masculinized black woman might endow her body with a kind of virile sexual passion or with a muscular asexuality.

40. Phillip M. Hoose, *Necessities: Racial Barriers in American Sports* (New York: Random House, 1989), 4.

41. This myth had different implications for images of black men and women. While the notion of "natural," "virile" athleticism supported an image of the black man as a supermasculine, sexual, brawny, "stud" or "buck" figure, thus affirming the masculinity (if not the humanity) of black men, the ideology had the reverse effect for women. Notions of the "mannish," "primitive" black female athlete pushed African American women even further outside the parameters of femininity as defined by the dominant culture.

42. Since neither critics nor supporters of women's track and field commented publicly on these omissions, explanations are necessarily based on inference.

43. *New York Times* (April 20, 1931), reprinted in *Amateur Athlete* (June 1931), 8.

44. See *Amateur Athlete* (September 1938), and "A Show of Pretty Plungers," *Life* 46 (May 4, 1959), 65.

45. Kellermann gave popular exhibitions of swimming and diving that were combined fashion, beauty, and skill demonstrations. Holm Jarrett toured with her husband's jazz band and also performed swimming exhibitions. Williams turned her synchronized-swimming skills into a successful movie career.

46. Ironically, the crowning glory of swimming, its supposed femininity, was identified as the problem when, in the mid-1950s, American women lost their number one world position in the sport. Ione Muir, manager of the U.S. women's team, worried that Americans "swim like girls." The challenge for the U.S. team was to find a way that "this femininity in sports may best be overcome." See Muir, "As I See It," *Amateur Athlete* (February 1956), 22.

47. Avery Brundage, speech to National AAU Convention, *Amateur Athlete* (January 1959), 11.

48. George P. Meade, "The Negro in Track Athletics," *Amateur Athlete* (August 1953), 10.

49. Charles Bucher, "Sports Are Color-Blind," *JOHPER* 28 (December 1957), 22.

50. "U.S. Girls Wake Up!" *Amateur Athlete* (December, 1946), 10.

51. Brundage Collection, Box 70 (Folder—circular letters to IOC's, NOC's, and IF's, 1952–54), and Box 54 (Folder—Exeter, Marquess David), University of Illinois Archives.

52. Brundage Collection, Box 115 (Folder—Athletics—Women), "IOC quotes for and against women's competition," no date (mid-1950s), University of Illinois Archives.

53. *New York Times* (February 8, 1953), 5: 25.

54. *New York Times Magazine* (August 29, 1960), 144.

55. *Amateur Athlete* (July 1953), 26, quote from J. Powers of *New York Daily News*; Arthur Daley, *New York Times* (February 8, 1953), 5: 25; "The Stronger Soviet Sex," *Life*, 29 (September 18, 1959), 60–62.

56. *Detroit News* (July 31, 1962), sec. B, 1, in Claude A. Barnett Collection, Box 402, Chicago Historical Society.

57. Edwin B. Henderson, "Sports Comments," *Atlanta Daily World*, (August 4, 1948).

58. *Ebony*, 10 (June 1955), 28, 32.

59. A single, inviolable image of respectability held white observers at a distance, creating a kind of buffer zone between public settings and less public African American environments that may have allowed more personalized, flexible styles of femininity. Darlene Clark Hine makes a similar argument about black women's clubs in the Midwest during the early twentieth century. She argues that African American women developed a "culture of dissemblance" that presented a public face of unimpeachable propriety and apparent openness to counter negative stereotypes, while they hid their inner pain and pleasures under a "self-imposed invisibility" to gain psychic space and freedom from public scrutiny. "Rape and the Inner Lives

of Black Women in the Middle West: Preliminary Thoughts on the Culture of Dissemblance," *Signs* 14 (Summer 1989), 912–20.

60. *Amateur Athlete* (November 1950), 28.

61. *Amateur Athlete* (September 1954), 21.

62. Roxy Andersen, "Girls Thrive on Sport," *Amateur Athlete* (November 1950), 28.

63. Andersen, "Statistical Survey of Former Women Athletes," *Amateur Athlete* (September 1954), 10.

64. *Parade* (March 16, 1952), reprinted in *Amateur Athlete* (April 1952), 22.

65. *Time* 76 (September 19, 1960), 74–75.

66. Guttmann, *Women's Sports*, 204.

67. Patricia Hill Collins has argued that when white culture has accepted African Americans it has often been as "pets" rather than as equals, merely changing the terms of oppression from absolute subordination to subordination with affection. Collins, "Toward a Sexual Politics of Black Womanhood," guest lecture at the University of Minnesota (March 31, 1989). See also Collins, *Black Feminist Thought*, 74.

68. "In Defense of Women Athletes—Part II," 16.

69. Ibid.

CHAPTER 6    NO FREAKS, NO AMAZONS, NO BOYISH BOBS

1. "Queens of Diamonds," *New York Times Magazine* (August 4, 1946), 47.

2. Robert M. Yoder, "Miss Casey at the Bat," *Saturday Evening Post* 215 (August 22, 1942), 17.

3. "Ladies of the Little Diamond," *Time* 41 (June 14, 1943), 73.

4. Yoder, "Miss Casey at the Bat," 48.

5. In its two first years of operation, the league was called the All-American Girls Softball League. It adopted the name All-American Girls Baseball League (AAGBL) in 1945, although the league was also called the All-American Girls Professional Baseball League (AAGPBL). Contemporary and secondary accounts go by either AAGBL or AAGPBL.

6. Most sources claim that softball was invented in Chicago in November 1887 at the Farragut Boat Club. A fire station in Minneapolis also claims to have invented the game in 1912. See Merrie A. Fidler, "The Establishment of Softball as a Sport for American Women," in Howell, *Her Story in Sport*, 527, and Raymond Gathrid, "Softball," *The Digest* 1 (September 11, 1937), 32.

7. Margaret Root Zahler, "Baseball Goes Soft," *Christian Science Monitor Magazine* (December 2, 1938), 4.
8. "Queens of Diamonds," 47.
9. Frank J. Taylor, "Fast and Pretty," *Collier's* (August 20, 1938), 38.
10. Even after wartime incarceration policies wiped out community-based leagues, interned Japanese Americans made softball a part of camp life by organizing recreational teams for all ages. On Japanese American softball, see Sam Regalada, "Incarcerated Sport: Nisei Women within WWII Internment Camps," and Alison Wrynn (paper given with Gwendolyn Captain and Roberta Park), "Methodological and Intellectual Issues in Lesser Researched Areas of Sport History." Both papers were delivered at the North American Society for Sport History (NASSH) Conference, Chicago, May 26, 1991. Valerie Matsumoto mentions interned women's athletic activities in "Japanese American Women During World War II," *Frontiers* 8:1 (1984). While camp leagues could have been part of an imposed Americanization plan, these authors suggest that they were formed at the initiation of incarcerated Japanese Americans. Evidence on black softball was gleaned from the African American press, especially the *Chicago Defender* (1910–50), which reported on softball leagues and posted box scores for industrial, church, and park leagues.
11. Information on the Bluebirds was gathered through interviews with former players and from news clippings they made available to me. Interviewed players were Ruth Andreson (Douglas, Nebr.), October 9, 1987; Lucille Hofferber Bateman (Syracuse, Nebr.), October 9, 1987; Thelma Hirst (Douglas, Nebr.), October 10, 1987; Esther McPherson (Douglas, Nebr.), October 10, 1987; Mildred Emmons Neeman (Syracuse, Nebr.), October 9, 1987; Jessie Rider Steinkuhler (Douglas, Nebr.), October 10, 1987; and Myrna Scritchfield Thompson (Douglas, Nebr.), October 10, 1987.
12. Interviews, Lucille Hofferber Bateman (Syracuse, Nebr.), October 9, 1987, and Mildred Emmons Neeman (Syracuse, Nebr.), October 9, 1987. This chapter draws on a number of oral-history interviews I conducted between 1987 and 1992. The first time a narrator is quoted, I will provide a citation for the interview. Subsequent quotes will not be referenced separately, except where the narrator is not identified in the text.
13. Interview, Thelma Hirst (Douglas, Nebr.), October 10, 1987.
14. Interviews with Thompson and Hirst. Information about Korgan from interviews with teammates and from popular magazine articles. See Aaron Davis, "The Batter Half," *Collier's*, 114 (August 12, 1944), 18–19, and Yoder, "Miss Casey at the Bat," 16–17.

15. Yoder, "Miss Casey at the Bat," 16.

16. Interview, Irene Kotowicz (Elk Grove Village, Ill.), December 20, 1988.

17. Interview, Josephine D'Angelo (Chicago, Ill.), December 21, 1988.

18. Lowell Thomas and Ted Shane, *Softball! So What* (New York: Frederick A. Stokes, 1940), 92, 90.

19. Irene Hickson, quoted in Sharon Roepke, "Diamond Gals: The Story of the All-American Girls Professional Baseball League," (pamphlet published by AAGBL Cards, 1986), 9.

20. Yoder, "Miss Casey at the Bat," 48, 49.

21. Davidson, "The Batter Half"; Yoder, "Miss Casey at the Bat"; "Queens of Diamonds."

22. For histories of the AAGBL, see Fidler, "The All-American Girls' Baseball League, 1943–54," in Howell, *Her Story in Sport*, 590–607; Roepke, "Diamond Gals."

23. The lawsuit was mentioned several times in the AAGBL records, microfilm collection, Pennsylvania State University Libraries. The records do not say whether the suit was ever litigated or resolved.

24. See AAGBL records, microfilm, Pennsylvania State University Libraries; and *National Girl's Baseball League Magazine* 1 (May 1949) and 3 (May–June 1952), along with the "NGBL—Misc." file at the Chicago Historical Society.

25. Quote by Ken Sells, appointed by Wrigley as League president; quoted in Roepke, "Diamond Gals," 8.

26. "Foreword" to *AAGBL Handbook* (AAGBL Management Corp. circa 1945), AAGBL records, PSUL.

27. "Girls' Baseball as a Show," ibid.

28. On the 1940s, see Karen Anderson, *Wartime Women: Sex Roles, Family Relations, and the Status of Women during World War II* (Westport, Conn.: Greenwood Press, 1981); Susan M. Hartmann, *The Homefront and Beyond: American Women in the 1940s* (Boston: Twayne Publishers, 1982); and Leila J. Rupp, *Mobilizing Women for War: German and American Propaganda, 1939–1945* (Princeton, N.J.: Princeton University Press, 1978).

29. "Femininity with Skill," *AAGBL Handbook* (emphasis in original), PSUL.

30. Ibid.

31. Quoted from *Baseball Blue Book*, in ibid.

32. "Making the Show Greater," ibid.

33. "Femininity with Skill," ibid.

34. South Bend Blue Sox records, 1951, in AAGBL records, PSUL.

35. 1951 Constitution, adopted January 31, 1951, AAGBL records (emphasis, capitalization, and punctuation in original), PSUL.

36. Interviews, Dottie Green (Cambridge, Mass.), July 25, 1988, and D'Angelo.
37. November 14, 1951, AAGBL Board Meeting, AAGBL records, PSUL.
38. Evidence on the chaperones' role comes from interviews with former players, including chaperone Dottie Green, and from the *AAGBL Handbook*.
39. 1951 Constitution, AAGBL records, PSUL.
40. The idea grew out of a failed expansion attempt in 1948. To thwart the NGBL's own expansion plans, the AAGBL established a Chicago team to occupy a stadium the NGBL had hoped to use. The team, the Colleens, failed immediately, as did its expansion twin, the Springfield Sallies. To stave off embarrassment and further financial loss, the league used the team names and uniforms to form two traveling squads.
41. Morris Markey, "Hey Ma, You're Out!" undated publication reproduced in 1951 AAGBL records, PSUL; and "Feminine Sluggers," *People and Places* 8: 12, reproduced in 1952 AAGBL records, PSUL.
42. Daily newspapers in league towns provided excellent regular coverage, and in some cities local radio stations broadcast games. In contrast to the national media, the local press rarely resorted to the femininity angle. News coverage adopted a straightforward reporting style that did not refer to gender with modifiers like "pretty blond" shortstop or "Lady" Blue Sox.
43. Interview, Mary Pratt (Cambridge, Mass.), July 25, 1988.
44. During interviews several players indicated that they or other players they knew had received additional "off-the-record" payments to increase their salary without disrupting league pay scales set by the central office.
45. Interviews, Jean Havlish (St. Paul, Min.), June 8, 1988, and Nora Cross (pseudonym).
46. Interview, Delores Moore (Elmhurst, Ill.), December 17, 1988.
47. Interview, Anna May Hutchison (Racine, Wis.), January 3, 1989.
48. Quoted in Jay Feldman, "Perspective," *Sports Illustrated* (June 10, 1985), 98. A "strawberry" was a large, red, scraped area, bruised and scabby from sliding bare-legged.
49. Interview, Havlish.
50. Interview, Phyllis Koehn (Downers Grove, Ill.), December 20, 1988.
51. Quoted in Feldman, "Perspective," 96.
52. Quoted in Sheldon Sunness, "Girls of Summer," *Z Magazine* (May 1988), 74.
53. Quoted in Feldman, "Perspective," 96.

54. Interview, Kotowicz.

55. Compared to other women's jobs, AAGBL salaries usually meant a substantial increase for wageworking young women. Compared to men's professional baseball salaries, AAGBL pay was low, although male salaries were kept down at this time by management's tight control over player contracts. Many major league ballplayers earned less than $3,500 per season in the immediate postwar years. Women making from $50 to $100 per week over a twenty-week season would have been making $1,000 to $2,000 per year. For discussion of male salaries, see Randy Roberts and James S. Olson, *Winning Is the Only Thing: Sports in America since 1945* (Baltimore: Johns Hopkins University Press, 1989), 47–48.

56. This skit, called "On Blue Sox" was written for a banquet at the First Gridiron Club for February 7, 1950, and is reproduced in the records of the Fort Wayne Blue Sox, AAGBL records, PSUL.

57. Interview, Dorothy Ferguson Key (Rockford, Ill.), December 19, 1988.

58. As league finances deteriorated in the 1950s, personnel shortages forced the league into a onetime "amnesty" offer to lure former players back from the NGBL into the AAGBL. Evidence on interleague disputes and quote from South Bend records, 1952, AAGBL records, PSUL.

59. Fred Leo, commissioner's letter, Winter 1950, AAGBL records, PSUL.

60. D'Emilio and Freedman, *Intimate Matters*, 277–95; and John D'Emilio, "The Homosexual Menace: The Politics of Sexuality in Cold War America," in Kathy Peiss and Christina Simmons, eds., *Passion and Power* (Philadelphia: Temple University Press, 1989), 226–40.

## CHAPTER 7   BEAUTY AND THE BUTCH

1. This was not due to a lack of effort. An angry P.E. student at the University of Texas wrote a letter to the editor in response to an article in the school newspaper, the *Texan*, which depicted football-playing P.E. majors as masculine oafs. Claiming, "We are proud of our department," she went on to explain that "the vast majority of physical education majors weigh under 130 pounds, are not bold-mannered, and are shockingly enough downright average sweet pleasant girls." *Texan* (October 28, 1955), Box 3R212, BTHC, University of Texas, Austin.

2. Dr. Josephine Renshaw, M.D., "Activities for Mature Living," workshop report from 1956 NAPECW conference, 56; Box 17 in

Eastern Association of Physical Education for Women (EAPECW) Papers, Sophia Smith Collection, Smith College; and Gertrude Baker et al., "The Physical Education Program for College Women," *JOHPE* 18 (June 1947), 378. The *Texan* used indirection and double entendre to make the same point. A 1955 article on women's touch football established the mannishness of athletic women, comparing the "dainty demure sorority girl" to "gruff . . . heavy set and bold mannered" P.E. majors who stomped, pounced, and bellowed as they played, behaving in a most aggressive, unbecoming manner. One year later the *Texan*'s account of the University of Texas Sports Association (UTSA) women's sports banquet made the link to lesbianism. The article led off with the headline, "UTSA Gives Awards," followed by a subheading, "Gayness Necessary." While appearing to suggest that lesbians had a corner on athletic awards, the article went on to explain that the headline referred to a guest speaker's talk on positive attitudes, entitled "The Importance of Being Debonair." In an age in which homosexual women and men regularly referred to themselves as "gay," the lesbian allusion must have been unmistakable to many readers, even if not recognizable by all. See the *Texan* (May 10, 1956), from the *Texan* scrapbook, Box 3R212, Department of Physical Training for Women Records, BTHC, University of Texas, Austin.

3. Fred Wittner, "Shall the Ladies Join Us?" *Literary Digest* 117 (May 19, 1934), 43.

4. *Alienist and Neurologist* 4 (1883), 88; quoted in George Chauncey, Jr., "From Sexual Inversion to Homosexuality: Medicine and the Changing Conceptualization of Female Deviance," in Peiss and Simmons, *Passion and Power*, 90.

5. Havelock Ellis, *Sexual Inversion*, vol. 2, *Studies in the Psychology of Sex*, 3rd rev. ed. (Philadelphia: F. A. Davis, 1915), 250; quoted in Chauncey, "From Sexual Inversion to Homosexuality," 91.

6. Some historians have argued that sexology strongly influenced popular understandings of sexuality, but others have claimed that at least until the 1920s, medical notions of the homosexual did not significantly alter popular understandings of heterosexual and homosexual behavior. My research seems to support the latter interpretation. For the former, see Jeffrey Weeks, "Movements of Affirmation: Sexual Meanings and Homosexual Identities," *Radical History Review* 20 (Spring/Summer 1979), 164–79, and Lillian Faderman, *Surpassing the Love of Men: Romantic Friendship and Love Between Women from the Renaissance to the Present* (New York: William Morrow, 1981). For the latter, see Chauncey, "From Sexual Inversion to Homosexuality," and "Christian Brotherhood

or Sexual Perversion? Homosexual Identities and the Construction of Sexual Boundaries in the World War One Era," *Journal of Social History* 9 (Winter 1985), 189–211.

7. There is a large literature on sexuality and sexual reform movements in the Progressive Era. For a synthesis see D'Emilio and Freedman, *Intimate Matters*, chaps. 8–10.

8. Parry, "The Athletic Girls and Motherhood," 380.

9. See, for example, "Athletics for Women Will Help Save the Nation," *Amateur Athlete* (February–July 1929), 7; "Spirit," *Amateur Athlete* (October 1932), 7.

10. However, it is possible that the association between "molls" and prostitutes may have included some suggestion of lesbianism. Joan Nestle writes that in both the male imagination and in sexual subcultures, prostitutes and lesbians have been historically connected. There is also the interesting similarity between the terms "moll" and "molly," early slang for homosexual men. See Nestle, "Lesbians and Prostitutes: An Historical Sisterhood," in *A Restricted Country* (Ithaca, N.Y.: Firebrand Books, 1987), 157–77.

11. On the relationships between female sexuality, modern femininity, and consumer culture, see Cott, *The Grounding of Modern Feminism*, 145–62; Banner, *American Beauty*, 175–201; and Brown, *Setting a Course*, 29–47.

12. Quoted in D'Emilio and Freedman, *Intimate Matters*, 278.

13. Christina Simmons, "Modern Sexuality and the Myth of Victorian Repression," in Peiss and Simmons, *Passion and Power*, 157–77.

14. On sexologists, see Jeffrey Weeks, *Sexuality and Its Discontents: Meaning, Myths and Modern Sexualities* (London: Routledge Kegan Paul, 1985); D'Emilio and Freedman, *Intimate Matters*, chap. 10; Chauncey, "From Sexual Inversion to Homosexuality," 87–115; Carroll Smith-Rosenberg, "The New Woman as Androgyne," in *Disorderly Conduct* (New York: Alfred A. Knopf, 1985), 245–96; Jonathan Katz, *Gay/Lesbian Almanac*, part 2, "The Modern United States: The Invention of the Homosexual, 1880–1950" (New York: Harper & Row, 1983). On the mannish woman and early-twentieth-century lesbian subculture, see Chauncey, "From Sexual Inversion to Homosexuality," 87–117; Smith-Rosenberg, "The New Woman as Androgyne," 245–96; Jeffrey Escoffier, "Sexual Revolution and the Politics of Gay Identity," *Socialist Review* 82/83 (1985), 119–53; Eric Garber, "A Spectacle in Color: The Lesbian and Gay Subculture in Jazz Age Harlem," in M. Duberman, M. Vicinus, and G. Chauncey, Jr., eds., *Hidden from History: Reclaiming the Gay and Lesbian Past* (New York: American

Library, 1989), 318–31; and Esther Newton, "The Mythic Mannish Lesbian: Radclyffe Hall and the New Woman," *Signs* 9 (Summer 1984), 557–75. In her study of Radclyffe Hall, Esther Newton argues that "mannishness" offered a way for women to break out of an asexual romantic friendship mode. Through mannishness, women like Hall laid claim to an active, autonomous sexuality using the only existing vocabulary of active sexual desire—masculinity—to make a statement of interest and availability to other women.

15. For analysis and documentary records of gay and lesbian themes in popular drama, fiction, and film, see Katz, *Gay/Lesbian Almanac*, 408–94. On the obscenity litigation in the United States regarding Radclyffe Hall's *The Well of Loneliness* and the theatrical production of "The Captive," see Katz, *Gay American History* (New York: Avon Books, 1976), 128–39, 597–610.

16. Popular magazine articles made subtle references to lesbianism, describing spinsters as disreputable, ridiculous figures "set apart in a queer and inferior stratum of society." ("Queer" was the most commonly used term for homosexuals in this period. Quote from "A Game for Twosomes," *North American Review* 232 [September 1931], 231.) Even sympathetic treatments of female sexuality could unintentionally contribute to the intolerant atmosphere. In her 1929 study, *Factors in the Sex Life of Twenty-Two Hundred Women*, Katherine B. Davis found evidence of frequent lesbian experience among college educated women. Though she presented her findings without judgment, the information merely fueled the suspicions of an intrigued public. One woman interviewed by Davis named lesbianism as "the most serious problem the business or professional woman has to face today," one that caused women to think twice before living together "for fear of the interpretation that may be put upon it." See Katherine B. Davis, *Factors in the Sex Life of Twenty-Two Hundred Women* (New York: Harper & Row, 1929); quoted in Freedman and D'Emilio, 194.

17. The "flapper," as a symbol of the 1920s, captures the sexual and gender ambiguity that marked the decade. The "boyish" flapper charmed men with her slim hips, small breasts, and penchant for smoking and drinking—all qualities identified with masculinity. The flapper, however, was above all *boyish*, not mannish. Her body type resembled an undeveloped male or female, an immaturity that signaled her lack of power and her subordinate status in relation to the fully developed male. Champions of the female athlete saw her as a charming specimen of women's boyish, vivacious, sexual

appeal, akin to that of the flapper. However, her critics believed that the woman athlete overstepped the line between boyish femininity and masculine power.

18. Letter from University of Texas graduate, printed in *Sports Girl*, University of Texas Women's Physical Training, Box 3R247, BTHC, University of Texas, Austin.

19. Interestingly, Lee added with homophobic hindsight that she had "no idea ... I was encountering an extreme problem." Mabel Lee, *Memories of a Bloomer Girl, 1894–1924* (Washington, D.C.: American Association of Health, Physical Education, and Recreation, 1977), 231.

20. Interview, Elizabeth "Buffy" Dunker (Cambridge, Mass.), February 23, 1988.

21. Minutes from 1928–29 (Women's P.E. Staff Meetings 1927–54 File), Dept. of Women's P.E., University of Wisconsin Archives.

22. Minutes (February 25, 1932), (Women's P.E. Staff Meetings 1927–1954 File), Dept. of Women's P.E., University of Wisconsin Archives (emphasis added).

23. George Jean Nathan, "Once There Was a Princess," *American Mercury* 19 (February 1930), 242.

24. "He Hasn't a Chance," *Ladies Home Journal* 51 (December 1934), 12.

25. William Marston, "How Can a Woman Do It?" *Redbook* (September 1933), 60.

26. Wittner, "Shall the Ladies Join Us?" 42; and Ada T. Sackett, "Beauty Survives Sport," *Literary Digest* 117 (May 19, 1934), 43.

27. *Gopher* Yearbook (1937), University of Minnesota Archives. Physical educators and their students regularly bemoaned the "mannish" reputation and consequent dislike of female P.E. majors on campus; drawing on an illness metaphor, they referred to the problem as "majoritis." See 1931 Minutes of Eastern, Western, and Central Sectional Conferences of the AFCW, in University of Wisconsin Women's Physical Education Dept. Records, General Subject Files—AFCW.

28. Those on the margins of the profession—women in black colleges, rural school districts, or city recreation departments—did not necessarily accept the ideas of the leadership. However, the leadership's views shaped the curriculum, policies, and philosophy of physical education programs responsible for training successive generations of P.E. majors. And their perspective went unchallenged in professional journals and organizations.

29. Physical Education Director, Official Reports, Kristin Powell collec-

tion of materials on Radcliffe Athletics, Radcliffe College Archives, Acc. No. R87.

30. Mabel E. Rugen, "Standards for Judging, Selecting and Retaining Professional Physical Education Students" (Paper delivered at the 1933 Midwest Conference of the Association of Physical Education of College Women), EAPECW records (#8—Miscellaneous Research folder), Box 7, Sophia Smith Collection, Smith College.

31. Dept. of Physical Training for Women Records, Box 3R212, BTHC, University of Texas, Austin.

32. Gertrude Mooney, "The Benefits and Dangers of Athletics for the High School Girl," 1937, Dept. of Physical Training for Women Records (Health Ed. Folder), Box 3R251, BTHC, University of Texas, Austin; Alice Allene Sefton, "Must Women in Sports Look Beautiful?" *JOHPE* 8 (October 1937), 481.

33. See 1933 convention report, Athletic Federation of College Women (AFCW), AFCW Conference File, Dept. of Women's P.E., University of Wisconsin Archives. Records from Smith, Radcliffe, and the universities of Minnesota, Wisconsin, and Texas as well as professional journals from the period present consistent evidence of these shifts.

34. 1933 "Platform of the Athletic Federation of College Women." Later platforms retained these objectives, and in 1940 the organization encouraged WAAs to change their names to Women's Recreation Associations to counteract the "all brawn and no brains" connotation of "athletic." See General Subject Files—AFCW, Dept. of Women's P.E. Records, University of Wisconsin Archives.

35. Conference Reports, Box 17, EAPECW, Sophia Smith Collection, Smith College.

36. NAAF—Women's Division, Newsletter #79 (June 1, 1938), from Dept. of Women's P.E., University of Wisconsin Archives.

37. Ibid. Interestingly, the organization considered other viewpoints as well. In 1939 another lecturer, Dr. Laurence K. Frank, addressed the NAPECW convention about the "essential bisexuality of every individual" and the tragic "tyranny of the norm." This more sympathetic view of lesbianism seems to have been ignored, at least with regard to public policymaking.

38. "Queer People," *Newsweek* 34 (October 10, 1949), 52.

39. John D'Emilio, *Sexual Politics, Sexual Communities: The Making of a Homosexual Minority in the United States, 1940–1970* (Chicago: University of Chicago Press, 1983), 9–53; D'Emilio and Freedman, *Intimate Matters*, chap. 12; and Allan Bérubé, *Coming Out Under*

*Fire: The History of Gay Men and Women in World War II* (New York: Free Press, 1990).

40. On the relation between postwar gender dynamics and studies of the "masculine" lesbian, see Donna Penn, "The Meanings of Lesbianism in Post-War America," *Gender and History* 3 (Summer 1991), 190–203. On postwar gender anxieties and social science, see Wini Breines, "The 1950s: Gender and Some Social Science," *Sociological Inquiry* 56 (Winter 1986), 69–92.

41. On butch/femme styles and sexual roles, see Elizabeth Kennedy and Madeline Davis, "The Reproduction of Butch-Fem Roles: A Social Constructionist Approach," in Peiss and Simmons, *Passion and Power*, 241–56.

42. *Gopher* Yearbook (1952), 257, University of Minnesota Archives.

43. John Kord Lagemann, "Red Heads You Kill Me!" *Collier's* 119 (February 8, 1947), 64.

44. Roxy Andersen, "Fashions in Feminine Sport," *Amateur Athlete* (March 1945), 39. For similar remarks, see also Paul Gallico, *Houston Post* (March 22, 1960); Pete Martin, "Babe Didrikson Takes Off Her Mask," *Saturday Evening Post* 220 (September 20, 1947), 26–27; *Life* (June 23, 1947), 90.

45. "*Life* Calls on Seven Spinsters," *Life* 34 (June 8, 1953), 155.

46. *Science Digest* 40 (September 1957), 37.

47. Since the 1930s, psychologists had used surveys of attitudes, interests, and personality traits to measure masculinity and femininity, and then applied these ratings to predict or measure sexual "inversion." Test results from the 1930s found that the only women who rated more masculine than lesbians were a group of thirty-seven superior college athletes. See Henry L. Minton, "Femininity in Men and Masculinity in Women: American Psychiatry and Psychology Portray Homosexuality in the 1930s," *Journal of Homosexuality* 13 (Fall 1986), 1–22; Miriam Lewin, "'Rather Worse than Folly'? Psychology Measures Femininity and Masculinity," 1 and 2, in Lewin, ed., *In the Shadow of the Past* (New York: Columbia University Press, 1984), 155–78, 179–204.

48. William B. Furlong, "Venus Wasn't a Shotputter," *New York Times Magazine* (August 29, 1960), 14 ff.

49. The limited acceptance of homosexuality within some quarters of black society and its concerted rejection in other sectors combined to discourage any initial associations between mannishness, athleticism, and homosexuality. In the street culture of urban African Americans, there is evidence of a history of grudging tolerance, though not approval, of homosexuality. Black autobiographers and songwriters mention "bull dagger" women and effeminate gay men

as a noteworthy but not abhorrent aspect of daily life. Historians have found evidence as well of the significant presence of gay men and women in the early-twentieth-century black art world, ranging from drag queens and cross-dressing musicians to more subtle expressions of gay sensibility in art and literature.

There is contrary evidence, however, pointing to strong anti-homosexual sentiment within black culture, especially from the church. African-American heterosexuals, like many heterosexuals, expressed their homophobia by regarding homosexuals as a distant group of "others," removed from the black community. The idea that "to be lesbian or gay is to be somehow racially denatured," or the view of homosexuality as a "white" phenomenon, made lesbianism less threatening by placing it outside the community. This kind of displacement, in conjunction with the measured tolerance shown homosexuals and women athletes by some African Americans, suggests that the lesbian taboo may have been less associated with sport in black culture than in white, at least at first.

Quote from Jewelle L. Gomez and Barbara Smith, "Taking the HOME out of HOMOPHOBIA: Black Lesbians Look in Their Own Backyards," *Out/Look* 2 (Spring 1990), 37. Essays that deal with black lesbianism and homophobia include Eric Garber, "Gladys Bentley: The Bulldagger Who Sang the Blues," *Out/Look* 1 (Spring 1988), 52–61, and Cheryl Clark, "The Failure to Transform: Homophobia in the Black Community," in Barbara Smith, ed., *Home Girls* (New York: Kitchen Table, 1983), 206. Autobiographical works relevant to this discussion include Anne Moody, *Coming of Age in Mississippi* (New York: Dell, 1968), 169–83; Maya Angelou, *I Know Why the Caged Bird Sings* (New York: Bantam Books, 1973), 232; Jewelle Gomez, "I Lost It at the Movies," *Out/Look* 1 (Spring 1988), 38–41.

50. Interviews with Alice Coachman Davis and Lula Hymes Glenn (Tuskegee, Ala) May 7, 1992, and Leila Perry Glover (Atlanta, Ga.) May 8, 1992.
51. Interview, Gloria Wilson (pseudonym), May 11, 1988.
52. *Baltimore Afro-American* (June 29, 1957), magazine section, p.1.
53. "Fastest Women in the World," *Ebony* 10 (June 1955), 28, 32.
54. This was not necessarily true at the local level. Women who grew up with family and/or community support for their athletic involvement did not feel a conflict between sport and local concepts of appropriate female attributes or activities. More than one cultural construction of womanhood circulated at any given time in U.S. society, offering some girls and women resources with which to challenge the dominant paradigm in which sport and femininity

conflicted. However, even those who felt no initial contradiction eventually became aware of, and had to negotiate, the stereotypes surrounding mannishness in women's sport. For evidence and further discussion of this point, see chapter 9.

55. On the "female apologetic," see Patricia Del Rey, "The Apologetic and Women in Sport," in Carole Oglesby, ed., *Women and Sport* (Philadelphia: Lea and Febiger, 1978), 107–11.

56. Mildred A. Schaeffer, "Desirable Objectives in Post-war Physical Education," *JOHPE* 16 (October 1945), 446–47 (emphasis added).

57. "Coeducational Classes," *JOHPER* 26 (February 1955), 18. For curricular changes, I examined physical education records at the universities of Wisconsin, Texas, and Minnesota; Radcliffe College; Smith College; Tennessee State University; and Hampton University.

58. *Texan* (October 1956); University of Texas Women's P.T. Records, Box 3R212, BTHC, University of Texas, Austin.

59. Dudley Ashton, "Recruiting Future Teachers," *JOHPER* 28 (October 1957), 49.

60. The 1949–50 *Physical Training Staff Handbook* at the University of Texas stated "legs should be kept shaved" (p. 16). Box 3R213 of Dept. of Physical Training for Women Records, BTHC, University of Texas, Austin. Restrictions on hair and dress are spelled out in the staff minutes and P.E. handbooks for majors at the universities of Wisconsin, Texas, and Minnesota.

61. "Physical Education as a Career," Ohio Association of Health, Physical Education and Recreation, 1946; in Trilling Papers (Subject Files—P.E. as a Profession), Dept. of Women's P.E., University of Wisconsin Archives.

62. Andersen, "Fashions in Feminine Sport," 39.

63. Andersen, "Statistical Survey of Former Women Athletes," 10–11.

64. AAGBL records, PSUL; and "Next to Marriage, We'll Take Golf," *Saturday Evening Post* 226 (January 23, 1954), 92.

65. See Markey, "Hey Ma, You're Out!" and "Feminine Sluggers," *People and Places* 8: 12, reproduced in 1952 AAGBL records, PSUL.

66. I want to thank Joan Hult, Professor of Physical Education at University of Maryland, for first pointing this out to me during an interview about her own participation in semipro and collegiate athletics.

67. The emphasis on "feminine attractiveness" compounded the marginal position held by women of color in the sports world. The standards of beauty employed by predominately white media and athletic organizations privileged white skin, light-colored hair, and Caucasian facial features. Though the black press also stressed the

sexual attractiveness and "normalness" of female athletes, the larger mass media's frequent references to "blond beauties"; small, "pert" noses; and "fair" complexions relied on racially specific construc- tions of beauty. These images reinforced racist definitions of black women, and by implication other racial minorities, as less feminine and less attractive than white women, thus deepening the ostracism faced by women of color in sport and society.

CHAPTER 8  "PLAY IT, DON'T SAY IT"

1. Interview, Josephine D'Angelo (Chicago, Il.), December 21, 1988. This chapter draws on a number of oral-history interviews I con- ducted between 1987 and 1992. The first time a narrator is quoted, I will provide a citation for the interview. Subsequent quotes will not be referenced separately, unless the narrator is not identified in the text. In several cases I have left quotes unattributed when I believed they might involve more self-disclosure than the narrator intended.
2. Barbara Smith quotes writer Ann Allen Schockley as using "play it, but don't say it" to describe the attitude toward homosexuality held by many African Americans. This expression aptly captures the atti- tude toward lesbianism I found in discussions with women involved in athletics. See Barbara Smith and Jewelle Gomez, "Taking the HOME Out of HOMOPHOBIA," 33.
3. Only six of forty-four oral-history narrators informed me that they identified as lesbian, the others declaring their heterosexuality or leaving their sexual identity unstated. In addition to the six, several others spoke knowledgeably about gay culture in sport without say- ing whether this was firsthand knowledge. The sample is small and therefore cannot be taken as conclusive or representative of all women's experience in sport. The interviews included women, rang- ing in age from their forties to seventies, who had played a variety of sports in a range of athletic settings in the West, Midwest, Southeast, and Northeast. The majority were white women from working-class or poor rural backgrounds (nine of forty-four athletes were African-American). Because the fear of discussing such a sensi- tive topic made finding openly lesbian narrators extremely difficult, I had to rely on supporting evidence from women who did not claim to be lesbians (though observation and indirect or suggestive comments led me to believe that many of the narrators are or have been lesbian identified but chose not to reveal it explicitly in the interview setting). Except when I knew in advance that the narrator was willing to discuss her lesbian experience, I raised the subject by

asking about lesbian stereotypes in sport. From there many narrators went on to tell me what they knew about actual lesbianism as well. For those who were more reticent, I tried to pose questions that allowed them to discuss the topic as personally or impersonally as they wished. The subject calls for more research, possibly an oral-history project in a single setting where trust and networks could be established over time.

4. Interview, Audrey Goldberg Hull (Santa Cruz, Calif.), November 10, 1988.

5. Anonymous.

6. Interview, Thelma Hirst (Douglas, Nebr.), October 10, 1987.

7. Interview, Dorothy Ferguson Key (Rockford, Ill.), December 19, 1988.

8. Interview, Nora Cross (pseudonym).

9. Lisa Ben, interview in Katz, *Gay/Lesbian Almanac,* 619.

10. Barbara Grier, quoted in Yvonne Zipter, *Diamonds Are a Dyke's Best Friend* (Ithaca, N.Y.: Firebrand Books, 1988), 48.

11. Quote from interview with Loraine Sumner (West Roxbury, Mass.), February 18, 1988; several other narrators also mentioned the lack of resources.

12. Interview, Ann Maguire (Boston, Mass.), February 18, 1988.

13. Interview, Gloria Wilson (pseudonym), May 11, 1988.

14. While some socializing was private, much of it took place in restaurants and bars where lesbian athletes gathered for postgame drinks and food, sometimes joined by spectators. Jo D'Angelo explained that though straight, gay, single, and married teammates "mixed in" and "got along fairly well" when playing together, "after hours the crowds would separate. The gays would go here, and the non-gays would [go elsewhere]."

15. Interview, Loraine Sumner (West Roxbury, Mass.), February 18, 1988.

16. Interview, Margaret Sexton Gleaves (Nashville, Tenn.), July 6, 1988.

17. Interview, Jessie Rider Steinkuhler (Douglas, Nebr.), October 10, 1987.

18. Interview, Myrna Scritchfield Thompson (Douglas, Nebr.), October 10, 1987.

19. On mid-century studies of the "masculine" lesbian, see Penn, "The Meanings of Lesbianism in Post-War America," 190–203.

20. Interview, Dottie Green (Cambridge, Mass.), July 25, 1988.

21. Interview, Alline Banks Sprouse (Manchester, Tenn.), July 7, 1988. At least two Atlanta teams of the 1950s seemed to delight in gender play, calling themselves the Tomboys and the Crewcuts.

22. The word "lesbian" seems to have been used infrequently at this time (one rural woman explained, "We didn't have lesbians back then—just queers, in the countryside") and may have been just as loaded with masculine and pejorative connotations as other terms, like *mannish*. The use of alternative labels may have been a polite attempt to find a "nicer" and more familiar synonym.

23. See Madeline Davis and Elizabeth Lapovsky Kennedy, "Oral History and the Study of Sexuality in the Lesbian Community," *Feminist Studies* 12 (Spring 1986), 7–26; Davis and Kennedy, "The Reproduction of Butch-Fem Roles," in Peiss and Simmons, *Passion and Power* 241–256; Joan Nestle, "Butch-Femme Relationships: Sexual Courage in the 1950s," in Nestle, *A Restricted Country*, 100–109; and Escoffier, "Sexual Revolution and the Politics of Gay Identity," 137–43.

24. Although several narrators mentioned going to gay bars, more research is needed to determine the extent to which lesbian athletes were also participating in the butch-femme world of lesbian bar culture. The personal styles of many gay athletes—whether they were active in the bar scene or not—were fully compatible with the butch sensibility prevalent in working-class lesbian communities.

    One possible difference, however, is that the masculine signifiers in sport were less obvious than in the bar world because they occurred in a realm already equated with masculinity—"masculine" style was a prerequisite for athletic success. Another is that butch styles in sport were not necessarily connected to a specific sexual role or to butch-femme coupling patterns. However, my research does not explore these matters beyond preliminary impressions. Butchy athletes may have been engaging in butch-femme relations in private or through participation in bar culture if not through sport. It is not clear to me whether two "butchy" athletes could "go together." If so, the current understanding of butch-femme eroticism in the 1940s and 1950s would have to be revised.

25. Anonymous.

26. Dennis Altman analyzes how cultural symbols and styles allow people to realize themselves and to find others, fostering "moments of identification," in *The Homosexualization of America, The Americanization of the Homosexual* (New York: St. Martin's Press, 1982), 146–71.

27. Anonymous.

28. This term was used by Jo D'Angelo when describing lesbian friendships and relationships in sport.

29. Ann Maguire, for instance, explained that "a lot of the women playing probably would have been categorized more as being more

butch than more femme. But I think it's for a variety of reasons. Anytime we see a woman who plays aggressively and slides into home plate and runs and throws we think of that as not being feminine." Maguire saw this labeling process as one that "assigned" masculinity to certain behaviors, leading to a "muddling" of personal gender identity and socially imposed definitions.

30. In this sense, "boyishness," "mannishness," or "masculinity" might have entered into lesbian athletic experience at a deeper, more subjective level than that of outwardly manifested gesture and appearance.

31. The term *hairpin* was part of gay slang. Allan Bérubé mentions slang terms that revolved around hair and hairdressing, as in "dropping hairpins" for hinting to another suspected gay person that one was gay, or "letting your hair down." See *Coming Out Under Fire*, 6.

32. The question of lesbian identity raises important theoretical issues relevant to current debates in poststructuralist and social constructionist thought. I find poststructuralist concepts of fragmented, nonunified identities and multiple discourses helpful in understanding how women athletes often felt torn between personal and subcultural knowledges of sport as positive and the dominant cultural view of female athletes as sex/gender deviants. Clearly women had to locate themselves within several interpretations and sources of knowledge, and in this sense their identities were fragmented and unstable. However, evidence from the oral histories convinced me that women went beyond feeling fragmented: Human ability to live with contradiction is crucial here. Athletes negotiated the contradictory messages they encountered, formulating theories of sport and gender that allowed them to place themselves inside the bounds of womanhood. Similarly, while theorists have begun to question the existence of an "authentic," "unified," or "coherent" self, athletes' testimony suggests that while the notions of "self" and individual identity might be products of particular historical conditions and ideologies, a sense of authentic self is both real and necessary to people living within a given context. Women athletes drew on the cultural resources they found within sport and female athletic networks to search for and find a sense of authenticity and coherence in their lives.

33. Narrators disagreed on this point. But so many people spoke of lesbians as being a significant presence in sport that I was convinced there was at least a greater proportion of lesbians in sport than in areas of culture associated with "traditional femininity," such as women's flower-arranging clubs, reading groups, or cooking classes. Even if there were an equal number of lesbians in cultural

spheres like the arts or music, which have no particular lesbian reputation, lesbians were significantly more visible and recognized in sport than in those activities.

34. This analysis draws on ideas developed by Zipter in *Diamonds Are a Dyke's Best Friend,* 47–48.

35. The notion of gay subculture turning stigmatized qualities into valued attributes is discussed by Joseph P. Goodwin in *More Man Than You'll Ever Be!: Gay Folklore and Acculturation in Middle America* (Bloomington: Indiana University Press, 1989), 62. Erving Goffman also provides a useful, more general discussion of stigmas and subcultural responses in *Stigma* (Englewood Cliffs, N.J.: Prentice-Hall, 1963).

36. Interview, D'Angelo.

37. Anonymous.

38. This could be attributed to the lack of post-secondary-school athletic opportunity for women. But gender theorists also point out that while it is somewhat acceptable for younger girls to be "tomboys," during adolescence a narrowing process occurs in which the range of acceptable activities for girls becomes more and more limited.

39. This could suggest that, contrary to historical theories, athletes involved in same-sex relations did not find it important to claim lesbianism as a core aspect of "self" or individual identity. Another interpretation (which seems more likely to me) would be that they did understand themselves as homosexual persons but exercised extreme caution in making this information available to anyone but trusted friends.

40. A similar combination of "masculine" bravado, verbal caution, and attention to "proof" appears in Ma Rainey's 1920s "Prove It on Me Blues," in which the singer brazenly proclaims her mannishness and sexual interest in women and then just as boldly denies that this evidence serves as "proof." Bisexual and homosexual women of the 1920s African American blues scene and lesbian athletes of a later era may have shared a similar ethos around issues of self-presentation and disclosure.

41. Interview, Maguire.

42. Interview, D'Angelo.

43. On twentieth-century lesbian and gay identities, see especially D'Emilio, *Sexual Politics,* 23–39; Katz, *Gay/Lesbian Almanac,* 137–74; and Weeks, "Movements of Affirmation," 164–79.

44. Yet, as much as sport may have facilitated the formation of a collective lesbian culture, it seems not to have generated a collective consciousness in the same way that lesbian bar culture did. The very qualities that made sport comfortable for lesbians—the presumed

"masculinity" and the more concealed and ambiguous presence of lesbians—may also have discouraged the kind of group awareness and defiant political posture that gay women in the bars developed in the post–World War II era. I am grateful to Liz Kennedy for this observation. On lesbian collective culture and consciousness in the bars, see Elizabeth Lapovsky Kennedy and Madeline D. Davis, *Boots of Leather, Slippers of Gold: The History of a Lesbian Community* (New York: Routledge, 1993).

45. Eve Kosofsky Sedgwick develops the concept of the "open secret" in *Epistemology of the Closet* (Berkeley: University of California Press, 1990).

## CHAPTER 9   WOMEN COMPETING/GENDER CONTESTED

1. Gallico, "S.A.," in *Farewell to Sport*, 245–55; Furlong, "Venus Wasn't a Shot Putter," 14ff.

2. Furlong, "Venus Wasn't a Shot Putter"; *Time* 76 (September 19, 1960), 74–75; *Life* 44 (May 4, 1959), 65–66ff.

3. Furlong quotes an Australian athletic expert who claimed that women "cannot hope to keep up [in sport] without surrendering their sex." See, "Venus Wasn't a Shot Putter," 14ff. On the loss of male supremacy, see "The World-Beating Girl Viking of Texas," *Literary Digest* 114 (August 27, 1932), 26.

4. The profession was almost exclusively male. Though I came across only one woman sportswriter and heard of several others, they formed a tiny percentage.

5. Rice, *Collier's* 79 (February 12, 1927) and 82 (September 29, 1928).

6. Rice, "Leading Ladies," *Collier's* 83 (April 6, 1929).

7. Rice, "Look Out for the Ladies," 19.

8. Cott, *The Grounding of Modern Feminism*, 215.

9. "Greeks, Girls and 1944," *The Nation* 118 (February 27, 1924), 222.

10. Rice, "Look Out for the Ladies," 19.

11. Wittner, "Shall the Ladies Join Us?" 42; "The World-Beating Girl Viking of Texas," *Literary Digest* 114 (August 27, 1932), 26. In his 1938 article "Girls Go for Massacres," about women spectators and athletes, boxer Jack Dempsey offered an especially hostile response to women's entrance into sporting arenas, warning readers: "Men will be a doomed breed when women pour out of the stands, roll up their sleeves and join the gladiators in the arena." To Dempsey the battle between male and female "gladiators" was a contest of annihilation men were "doomed" to lose as soon as

women entered, and thereby corrupted, a sacrosanct male realm. See *Collier's* 102 (November 12, 1938), 64.

12. Jean Lyon, *Independent Woman* 17 (January 1938), 12.

13. "The Stronger Soviet Sex," *Life* 29 (September 18, 1950), 60–62.

14. "A Seventeen-Year-Old Mermaid Who Holds Ten World Records," *Literary Digest* 80 (March 8, 1924), 74–76.

15. "Forcing Professionalism of Mary K. Browne," *Literary Digest* 93 (May 7, 1927), 72.

16. John B. Kennedy, "Little Miss Poker Face," *Collier's* 78 (September 18, 1926), 10.

17. "Our Lady Golfers Take the Cup, But Let the British Title Go," *Literary Digest* 113 (June 18, 1932), 34–35.

18. "Little Mo Grows Up," *Time* 60 (July 14, 1952), 44; *Newsweek*, 2 (August 12, 1933), 18.

19. *Literary Digest*, 102 (September 7, 1929), 61.

20. *Literary Digest*, 113 (June 18, 1932), 34–35.

21. "How Molla Mallory Came Back," *Literary Digest* 90 (September 25, 1926), 64.

22. "Helen II, New Queen of the Courts," *Literary Digest* 114 (September 3, 1932), 25–26.

23. "A Seventeen-Year-Old Mermaid Who Holds Ten World Records," 76.

24. "Records Beware!" *Literary Digest* 110 (August 15, 1931), 32.

25. Lewis Mumford, *Technics and Civilization* (1933; New York: Harbinger Books, 1963), quoted in John Hoberman, *Sport and Political Ideology* (Austin: University of Texas Press, 1984), 89.

26. John Tunis, "Pour le Sport: How Tennis Helped the Modern Diana in Shortening Her Skirts," *HB* (July 1929), 113.

27. Gallico, *Farewell to Sport*, 49–50.

28. "America's New Gibson Girl," *Saturday Evening Post* (September 1, 1957), M—5; in Gibson file of Claude A. Barnett Collection (Box 402), Chicago Historical Society.

29. "The World-Beating Girl Viking of Texas," *Literary Digest* 114 (August 27, 1932), 28.

30. Martin, "Babe Didrikson Takes Off Her Mask"; "The World-Beating Girl Viking of Texas," 26.

31. The allusion to hairpins is an interesting one, since by World War II "hairpins" was part of gay slang. The author's choice of words might simply have been a coincidence, but it could have been a clever double entendre whose meaning would be available to those in the know.

32. "The World-Beating Girl Viking of Texas," 28.

33. Didrikson, "I Blow My Own Horn," 103.

34. As in romantic fiction, marriage often formed the narrative climax of these tales. Through marriage, or at least being on the "marriage market," female athletes could repurchase the womanly status they mortgaged to sport. The press did not look kindly on women who refused this transaction. A 1954 *Saturday Evening Post* article on the professional women's golf tour described Patty Berg, an extremely talented but unmarried golfer, as "a tragically lonely individual with no love but golf," making her phenomenal success appear to have come at the expense of love, happiness, and womanly fulfillment. See, "Next to Marriage, We'll Take Golf," *Saturday Evening Post* 226 (January 23, 1954), 92, 94.

35. *Life* (June 23, 1947), 90ff.

36. Martin, "World-Beating Girl Viking," 26–27; Fawley, "Whatever Became of Babe Didrikson," *Saturday Evening Post* 216 (November 20, 1943), 91; Gallico, *Houston Post* (March 22, 1960).

37. Gallico, *Reader's Digest*, 23.

38. "Helen Wills as the 'Killer' of the Courts," 61; *Time* 61 (February 2, 1953), 41.

39. Martin, "Babe Didrikson Takes Off Her Mask."

40. Brundage Collection, Box 115 ("Athletics—Women" Folder); quote by Prince Franz Joseph, Box 70, "Circular Letters to IOCs, NOCs and IFs" (1950s), University of Illinois Archives.

41. See Eric Dunning, "Sports as a Male Preserve: Notes on the Social Sources of Masculine Identity and Its Transformation," in Eric Dunning and Norbert Elias, eds., *Quest for Excitement: Sport and Leisure in the Civilizing Process* (New York: Basil Blackwell, 1986), 267–83; and Charles Critcher, "Women in Sport (1)," *Working Papers in Cultural Studies* 15 (Spring 1973), 9–12.

42. R. W. Connell and John Hargreaves have argued that the maintenance of male power as a legitimate authority depends on cross-class alliances of men in which raw or "essential" masculinity is often associated with categories of men otherwise excluded from power, thus the black superathlete; the muscular, granitelike, working-class laborer; and the rugged, weathered Marlboro man. See, R. W. Connell, *Gender and Power: Society, the Person and Sexual Politics* (Stanford: Stanford University Press, 1987), 109–10; John Hargreaves, *Sport, Power and Culture: A Social and Historical Analysis of Popular Sports in Britain* (New York: St. Martin's Press, 1986), 57–93, 207–10.

43. See Critcher, "Women in Sport (1)," 10–11, and Lenskyj, *Out of Bound*, 143.

44. Gallico, "Women in Sports Should Look Beautiful," *Reader's Digest* 29 (August 1936), 12, 14.
45. Dunning, "Sport as a Male Preserve," 267–83.
46. Don Idden, "American Athletes Are Sissies," *Coronet* 31 (February 1952), 34.
47. "Brace of Balanced Beauties," *Life* 44 (January 13, 1958), 8.
48. For instance, the British author who labeled American athletes "sissies" concluded that British men were superior in sport because in England, "the athlete remains a working bloke." See Idden, "American Athletes Are Sissies," 34.
49. "Lady Bowler," *Literary Digest* 12 (February 21, 1936), 39; *Time* 27 (May 18, 1936), 58–60.
50. "Surging Urge to Bowl and Why," *Newsweek* 52 (September 15, 1958), 96.
51. "The Social Whirl of Ladies' Bowling," *Life* 49 (December 12, 1960), 101.
52. See Mary Jo Kane and Eldon Snyder, "Sport Typing: The Social 'Containment' of Women," *Arena Review* 13 (November 1989), 77–98.
53. William Burdick, M.D., "Safeguarding the Athletic Competition of Girls," *APER* 32 (May 1927), 367.
54. Some leagues had no-slide rules, others continued to permit sliding.
55. Concerns about reputation prompted AAU track officials to dictate a designated length for women's shorts and sleeves. In a similar vein organizers of women's softball and baseball introduced shorts or skirted uniforms intended to convey difference, femininity, and a wholesome image.
56. In basketball the Dallas Employers' Casualty Company team, which competed in the late 1920s and 1930s, was the first to discard bulky bloomers and blouses for streamlined shorts and tops. Coach M. J. McCombs reported that attendance rose from one or two hundred on average to five thousand per night after the switch. While this report might be apocryphal, it is still revealing in that the promoter wanted to give the impression that "sexy" uniforms were attracting customers to women's sports. On McCombs see "The Colonel's Ladies," *Collier's* 97 (May 23, 1936), 28, 60–62.
57. *Time* 44 (October 23, 1944), 55.
58. Ibid.
59. This is not simply because sport seems to demonstrate some natural qualities of gender but because it also portrays women as constantly narrowing the gap and thus approaching equality. The narrative of progress, so basic to American economic and political

mythology, is duplicated in sport as well. The promise of rapid improvement and ever-growing opportunity for women in sport masks power differences, even as those differences are made to seem natural in the athletic arena. This analysis draws on the work of several sports scholars: Lenskyj, *Out of Bounds*; Lois Bryson, "Sport and the Maintenance of Masculine Hegemony," *Women's Studies International Forum* 10:4 (1987), 349–60; Richard Gruneau, *Class, Sports and Social Development* (Amherst: University of Massachusetts Press, 1983); Jennifer Hargreaves, "Theorizing Sport," in Jennifer Hargreaves, ed., *Sport, Culture and Ideology* (London: Routledge & Kegan Paul, 1982), 1–29; Hargreaves, *Sport, Power and Culture*; Hargreaves, "Sport, Culture and Ideology," in Hargreaves, *Sport, Culture and Ideology*, 30–51; Paul Willis, "Women in Sport (2)," *Working Papers in Cultural Studies* 15 (Spring 1973), 23; and Willis, "Women in Sport in Ideology," in Hargreaves, *Sport, Culture and Ideology*, 117–35.

60. Nancy Theberge focuses on the physical aspect of male domination of women in her analysis of male hegemony and sport in "Sport and Women's Empowerment," *Women's Studies International Forum* 10:4 (1987), 388–89.

61. Dunning, "Sports as a Male Preserve," 267–283, and Lenskyj, *Out of Bound*, 11–12.

62. I am drawing on Lenskyj's excellent analysis of femininity. See *Out of Bound*, 13. See also Bartky, "Foucault, Femininity, and the Modernization of Patriarchal Power," 63–82.

63. Connell, *Gender and Power*, 85, 179–85.

64. Some athletes were acutely aware of their liminal status. When called a "muscle moll," Babe Didrikson did not deny her athleticism but rather perceptively noted that "the idea seems to be that Muscle Molls are not people." She understood that the stereotype of mannishness effectively disenfranchised women athletes as people, since people came in only two legitimate forms—feminine women and masculine men. Didrikson's statement reveals the double bind that she and other sports-loving women faced. They could remain on the sidelines of one of the central cultural practices of twentieth-century American society (as do "Monday Night Football widows"), or they could attempt to participate fully and in the process risk being perceived as not fully human, or in Didrikson's words, "not people." See Didrikson, "I Blow My Own Horn," *American Magazine* 121 (June 1936), 103.

65. Jack Pollack, "How Masculine Are You?" *Nation's Business* 38 (June 1950), 49–55.

66. Miriam Lewin, "'Rather Worse than Folly?': Psychology Measures Femininity and Masculinity," part 1, in Lewin, ed., *In the Shadow of the Past* (New York: Columbia Univ. Press, 1984), 155–178.

67. See for example, "A Test for Femininity," *Good Housekeeping* 108 (February 1939), 32–33; "How Masculine Are You?" 49–55.

68. R. B. Amber, *Coronet* 39 (July 1955), 73–75.

69. Interview, Doris Rogers (Nashville, Ten), July 7, 1988. To examine the subjective experience of athletes—the meaning sport held in their lives, their thoughts about gender and sport, and the identities they forged in a society that disparaged women athletes—the rest of this chapter draws on oral histories from forty-four women who played highly competitive sport between 1930 and 1970. Most competed in softball, baseball, basketball, and track, but many were involved in bowling, hockey, golf, and volleyball as well.

70. Of the thirty-five white and nine African American narrators, approximately 75 percent came from either a rural or urban working-class background. Because class categories are vague in both intellectual and popular discourse, it was sometimes hard to determine class, especially in the case of women from rural or small-town backgrounds in which parents farmed or owned small businesses. Also, some parents combined farming with factory or other work, and some family situations changed over time. Based on parental occupations and narrator descriptions of family and neighborhood, I calculated that among the forty-four informants, between thirty and thirty-nine were working class (including farmers who were not well off), and between five and fourteen were middle class.

71. Interview, Nora Cross (pseudonym).

72. Interview, Eunies Futch (Winston-Salem, N.C.), July 18, 1988.

73. Interview, Donna Lopiano (Austin, Tex.), March 21, 1988.

74. Interview, Irene Kotowicz (Elk Grove Village, Ill.), December 20, 1988.

75. Interview, Maxine Vaughn Williams (Winston-Salem, N.C.), July 16, 1988.

76. Interview, Evelyn ("Eckie") Jordan (Winston-Salem, N.C.), July 18, 1988.

77. Interview, Mary Pratt (Cambridge, Mass.), July 25, 1988.

78. Interview, Delores Moore (Elmhurst, Ill.), December 17, 1988.

79. Interview, Willye White (Chicago, Ill.), February 9, 1988.

80. Interview, Marcenia ("Toni") Stone Alberga (Oakland, Calif.), September 15, 1989.

81. Interview, Phyllis Koehn (Downers Grove, Ill.), December 20, 1988.

82. Interview, Irene Kotowicz.

83. Interview, Joyce Hill Westerman (Racine, Wis.), January 3, 1989.

84. Interview, Anna May Hutchison (Racine, Wis.), January 3, 1989.

85. Interview, Thelma Hirst (Douglas, Nebr.), October 10, 1987.

86. Interview, Mildred Emmons Neeman (Syracuse, Nebr.), October 9, 1987.

87. Trying to describe and account for their fervent athletic interest, Jordan and several other women evoked sacred and somatic metaphors to capture their sense that a force beyond their own will—their God, their heart, their blood—had destined them to become athletes. Myrna Scritchfield Thompson commented on her talent: "I think God gave me a good heart. And I loved it—I loved sports." She explained that even though opportunities for advancement had been limited, sport had given her happiness, making her "just happy to be me." From an explanation of her natural "God-given" ability and zeal for sport, Thompson drifted into a statement of identity—that sport was a central and joyous aspect of "being me."

88. Interview, Loraine Sumner (West Roxbury, Mass.), February 18, 1988.

89. Interview, Pat Stringer (White Bear Lake, Min.), June 2, 1988.

90. Interview, Audrey Goldberg Hull (Santa Cruz, Calif.), November 10, 1988.

91. Interview, Doris Rogers.

92. Interview, Joan Hult (Greenbelt, Md.), July 19, 1988.

93. Interestingly, the women they labeled as feminine or ladylike were often precisely the same women stigmatized by the media and other outside observers. Margaret Sexton Gleaves countered the negative image of women basketball players with examples of great beauty among athletes she had known. She pointed especially to Hazel Walker, a longtime star of AAU basketball who went on to form traveling professional teams called the Arkansas Travelers and the All-American Red Heads. In the eyes of physical educators, male sport officials, and the press, traveling troupes of paid women who performed in flashy uniforms before raucous crowds epitomized women's sport at its most outrageous and unacceptable. Yet to Gleaves, Walker's skill, beauty, and reputation as a nice woman ensured her respectability.

94. Interview, Alice Coachman Davis (Tuskegee, Ala.), May 7, 1992.

95. This kind of irreverence may have been especially common among lesbian ballplayers. D'Angelo went on to say that in the joking that went on about charm school, it was "especially all the butchy girls

[who] got teased, poor things—they were just dying." Interview, Josephine D'Angelo (Chicago, Ill.), December 21, 1988.

96. Interview, Alline Banks Sprouse (Manchester, Tenn.), July 8, 1988.

97. Interview, Jean Havlish (St. Paul, Minn.), June 8, 1988.

98. Interview, Ann Maguire (Boston, Mass.), February 18, 1988.

99. The strategies developed by women athletes are a series of "small resistances" nurtured in the culture of everyday life. Athletes challenged the naturalness of a supposedly masculine domain, disrupting commonplace assumptions to reveal the plasticity of gender categories and boundaries. And they used sport to develop broadened definitions of womanhood and to affirm individual feelings of self-worth. In this space women athletes claimed "difference" as a mark of distinction, not deviance. James C. Scott writes about "small resistances" in *Weapons of the Weak: Everyday Forms of Peasant Resistance* (New Haven: Yale University Press, 1985), 255. See 290–300, where he defines the concept of resistance as "*any* act(s) by member(s) of a subordinate class that is or are *intended* either to mitigate or deny claims . . . made on that class by superordinate classes . . . or to advance its own claims vis-a-vis those superordinate classes" (290). See also C. L. R. James, *Beyond a Boundary* (New York: Pantheon, 1983).

100. Important exceptions include the connections between feminism and sport advocacy in the 1910s and 1920s; the small current of feminist analysis that appears unevenly in subsequent decades of public debate; women physical educators' ongoing political critique of male sport; and the efforts of sport activists in the 1960s and early 1970s to raise the issue of equity, paving the way for the passage of Title IX.

101. The few narrators who did adopt this perspective had come to it later in life through political insights and language gained in nonathletic settings.

## CHAPTER 10　YOU'VE COME A LONG WAY, MAYBE

1. "Revolutionizing School and Sports: Ten Years of Title IX," *Ms.* 10 (May 1982), 26. Statistical reports vary in the numbers and percentages they present. See also Guttmann, *Women's Sports*, 213–15; Linda Jean Carpenter, "The Impact of Title IX on Women's Intercollegiate Sports," in Arthur T. Johnson and James H. Frey, eds., *Government and Sport* (Totowa, N.J.: Rowman and Allanheld, 1985), 62–78; and Hult, "Women's Struggle for Governance," in U. S. Amateur Athletics," *International Review for Sociology of Sport*, 24:3 (1989), 249–63.

2. The NCAA wrested control from the Association for Intercollegiate Athletics for Women (AIAW), until that point the strongest independent women's sport organization in the country.

3. The conference was organized and partially funded by the Women's Sports Foundation.

4. Except for some minor changes in terminology, the New Agenda's panels on "Physiological Concerns of Women in Sport," "Promotion and Public Acceptance of Women's Sports," "Athleticism and Sex Role," and "Organization and Regulation of Sport for Women" read like any number of Women's Division or Women's Committee on Athletics meetings of the 1920s and 1930s. New Agenda Conference Program, in possession of Don Sabo, Dept. of Sociology, D'Youville College, Buffalo, N.Y.

5. On the difference between AIAW and NCAA models of sport, see Susan L. Greendorfer, "Women, Sport and Gender: What the 1990s Hold for Post–Title IX Intercollegiate Athletics" (Paper presented to Feminist Scholarship Series, December 6, 1989).

6. The initial tournament was not repeated because of wartime interruptions, but then became an annual event beginning in 1946. The Tripartite Golf Committee received official recognition from women's collegiate sport organizations in 1956, and within two years had expanded beyond golf to form the National Joint Committee on Extra-mural Sports for College Women. The committee was endorsed by the National Section of Women's Athletics, the National Directors of Physical Education, and the Athletic and Recreation Federation of College Women.

7. Women's P.E. organizations did, however, become more sympathetic to competitive sports outside education. In the late 1950s they entered into negotiations with women leaders of the AAU and began to develop more cooperative relations. They also cooperated with U.S. Olympic Committee efforts to improve women's Olympic performances. In the Fall of 1963, the Division for Girls' and Women's Sports (of the American Association of Health, Physical Education, and Recreation) co-sponsored with the Women's Board of the United States Olympic Development Committee its first National Institute on Girls' Sports, designed to encourage women to develop skills in Olympic sports. See *Amateur Athlete* 34 (July 1963), 24.

8. This group was initially called the Commission on Intercollegiate Sports for Women.

9. See Judy Jensen, "Women's Collegiate Athletics: Incidents in the Struggle for Influence and Control," in Richard E. Lapchick, ed.,

*Fractured Focus: Sport as a Reflection of Society* (Lexington, Mass.: D.C. Heath and Co., 1986), 151–61.

10. *Women's Sports and Fitness* 14 (January/February 1992), 28.

11. "College Athletics: Tug of War for the Purse Strings," *Ms.* 3 (September 1974), 114–17; and Bil Gilbert and Nancy Williamson, "Sport Is Unfair to Women," *Sports Illustrated* 38 (May 28, 1973), 90–91.

12. Gilbert and Williamson, "Sport Is Unfair to Women," 90–91.

13. Ibid. 96.

14. Doris Brown, quoted in ibid., 89.

15. Guttmann, *Women's Sports*, 243.

16. This event received extensive media coverage. See, for example, "The Happy Hustler, Bobby Riggs," *Time* 102 (September 10, 1973), 56; "How King Rained on Riggs' Parade," *Time* 102 (October 1, 1973), 110–11; "There She Is, Ms. America," *Sports Illustrated* 39 (October 1, 1973), 30–32ff.

17. Despite this shared agenda, women's sport advocates and feminists typically remained at some distance from one another. Academic feminists tended to ignore the rich potential for feminist analysis and transformation in sport, while women in physical education or athletic administration often shied away from the radicalism of second-wave feminism. Even among liberal feminists, the relationship to women's athletic leaders was typically either nonexistent or strained. For example, the American Association of University Women (AAUW) did not address the question of women's collegiate athletics until 1993, when it held its first-ever conference on gender equity in sport, a regional conference held in Buffalo, New York.

18. Ann Crittenden Scott, "Closing the Muscle Gap," *Ms.* 3 (September 1973), 89.

19. Quoted in Joanna Bunker Rohrbaugh, "Femininity on the Line," *Psychology Today* 13 (August 1979), 41.

20. The series was authored by Bil Gilbert and Nancy Williamson. Articles titled "Sport Is Unfair to Women," "Are You Being Two-Faced?" and "Programmed to Be Losers" ran during the weeks of May 28, June 4, and June 11, 1973.

21. "Comes the Revolution: Joining the Game at Last, Women Are Transforming American Athletics," *Time* 111 (June 26, 1978), 54–60; quotes 54, 59.

22. Bil Gilbert and Nancy Williamson, "Women in Sport: A Progress Report," *Sports Illustrated* 41 (July 29, 1974), 31.

23. Carpenter, "The Impact of Title IX," 63.

24. "An Odd Way to Even Things Up," *Sports Illustrated* 50 (February 5, 1979), 18–19; quote 18. On opposition to Title IX, see also Jensen, "Women's Collegiate Athletics"; Hult, "Women's Struggle for Governance"; and Mary Jo Festle's detailed account in chaps. 9–10 of "Politics and Apologies: Women's Sports in the U.S., 1950–1985" (Ph.D. dissertation, University of North Carolina, Chapel Hill, 1993). In addition, for an excellent primary source, during the 1970s and 1980s the *Chronicle of Higher Education* provided step-by-step coverage of the ongoing conflict over Title IX.

25. Gilbert and Williamson, "Sport Is Unfair to Women," 94. Short's statement was as racially biased as it was sexist, since it erased from memory the fact that African American high school girls from Georgia and surrounding southern states had been competing in interscholastic competitions for decades, suffering no apparent harm.

26. Almost as if time had remained frozen since the days of the AAGBL, during the late 1970s the California Dreams of the professional Women's Basketball League (WBL) required that its players attend charm school for tips on beauty and feminine self-presentation. This is reported by Mariah Burton Nelson, former WBL player, in *Are We Winning Yet? How Women Are Changing Sports and Sports Are Changing Women* (New York: Random House, 1991), 7.

27. One study of *Sports Illustrated* found that in 1976—an Olympic year, which would tend to increase coverage of women—the magazine devoted only 6.9 percent of its articles and 4.3 percent of its overall pages to women's sports. These percentages were almost identical to the figures for 1960.

28. *Sports Illustrated* reporters Bil Gilbert and Nancy Williamson found that the old notion that sport would masculinize female appearance was alive and well, linked to "the even darker insinuation that athletics will masculinize a woman's sexual behavior." They commented perceptively on the "vicious paradox" that still plagued women in sport—the idea that "women athletes are either heterosexual wantons or homosexual perverts or, simultaneously, both." Gilbert and Williamson, "Are You Being Two-Faced?" 47.

29. "Sex and Tennis," *Time* 108 (September 6, 1976), 43.

30. R. S. Wood, "Sex Differences in Sports," *New York Times Magazine* (May 18, 1980), 33.

31. Carpenter, "The Impact of Title IX," 63–66. This was a transparently false claim, since the NCAA itself received no federal funds and had never mentioned this obligation before.

32. Hult, "Women's Struggle for Governance," 255–56; and Donna A. Lopiano, "A Political Analysis of the Possibility of Impact

Alternatives for the Accomplishment of Feminist Objectives Within American Intercollegiate Sport," in Lapchick, *Fractured Focus*, 163–76. These guarantees might have appeased women leaders, but the actual percentages granted them were not sufficient to block the two-thirds' vote needed to approve NCAA decisions. The representation concession in effect became a symbolic gesture, since women remained powerless as a voting bloc within the NCAA.

33. Carpenter, "The Impact of Title IX," 65; and Mary A. Boutilier and Lucinda F. San Giovanni, "Politics, Public Policy and Title IX: Some Limitation of Liberal Feminism," unpublished paper (1989).

34. *Los Angeles Times* (April 5, 1987) 6: 20–21.

35. Guttmann, *Women's Sports*, 220–22.

36. "Shooting for Equality," *Scholastic Update* (teacher's edition) 124 (May 1, 1992), 24–25.

37. *Women's Sports and Fitness* 14 (March 1992), 72; and Burton Nelson, *Are We Winning Yet?* 21–23.

38. See R. Vivian Acosta and Linda J. Carpenter, "Women in Intercollegiate Sport: A Longitudinal Study—Fifteen Year Update, 1977–1992" (copyright 1992, Carpenter/Acosta, Brooklyn College, Brooklyn, NY 11210); *Women's Sports and Fitness* 13 (September 1991) 52, and 14 (January/February 1992), 24–30. The jump in participation has occurred in other elite sports as well. In recent Olympics women made up from 34 to 36 percent of the American team, up from 10 percent in 1952.

39. Burton Nelson, *Are We Winning Yet?* 25–28.

40. *Women's Sports and Fitness* 14 (September 1992), 18.

41. "Report Affirms Women Still Playing Catch-Up," *Washington Post* (March 12, 1992), D8. The school was Washington State University.

42. "Shooting for Equality," 24–26.

43. They will be helped, however, by a recent Supreme Court ruling that allows claimants in Title IX suits to receive monetary compensation if the Court rules in their favor. This should make schools more cautious when deciding to cut women's sports for budgetary reasons.

44. Acosta and Carpenter, "Women in Intercollegiate Sport," 1–6.

45. Quote from Don Sabo, sports sociologist and board member of Women's Sports Foundation (personal communication).

46. "The Wilson Report: Moms, Dads, Daughters and Sports," presented by the Wilson Sporting Goods Co. in cooperation with the Women's Sports Foundation, June 7, 1988. See also Alexander Wolff, "The Slow Track," *Sports Illustrated* 77 (September 28, 1992), 57.

47. An extensive survey funded by Miller Lite (of the Miller brewing company) found that even though women reported no personal concern that athletic activity diminished femininity, they still encountered social pressure to choose between "being athletic and feminine." Respondents added that men seemed particularly threatened by losing to women athletes in mixed competition. If accurate, this suggests that for many men, athletic skills continue to be tied to their sense of manhood; thus, losing to a woman is experienced as a loss of masculinity.

48. E. M. Swift, "Women of Mettle," *Sports Illustrated* 76 (March 2, 1992), 38–39.

49. "An Identity Crisis of Ice and Snow," *U.S. News & World Report* 112 (March 2, 1992), 62. In an amusing reversal of conventional reasoning, U.S. skater Paul Wylie attributed the greater success of women to the fact that, "For the woman Olympian, this is more of a primary thing. It's a career path." He explained that men in amateur sport "feel like they should get real jobs," and thus they are unable to approach the sport with the same concentration that women—who presumably have become athletes but not career women—bring to their training. Pressed to defend his own and his male teammates' manhood, Wylie fell back on an alternate staple of masculinity, the role of provider.

50. "Unfounded Rumors," *Los Angeles Times* (September 29, 1988), 3:3.

51. I am unsure whether to use the term *gender* or *sex* here because it is unclear to me whether the public discussion is about gender or sex. Comments criticizing Joyner's "masculine" build appear to refer to her gender—the socially ascribed attributes we assign to each sex; yet the charge also implies a fundamental physiological change and thus seems to be referring to the alteration of biological sex, not social gender.

52. Alison Carlson, "Chromosome Count," *Ms.* 17 (October 1988), 40–44.

53. About twelve women have been eliminated from Olympic competition based on their test results. They were not, however, "men" trying to masquerade as "women." Some women born with XY chromosomes, because of genetic mutations, do not produce or respond to testosterone and therefore do not develop a penis, testes, or male secondary sex characteristics. Ironically these athletes face disqualification from competition despite the fact that they receive no genetic "benefit" from male hormones because of their inability to process them. Other women athletes, if they chose to take steroids,

could even gain an advantage because of their capacity to respond to hormones that the XY athlete's body rejects.

54. Internally she developed no uterus and had testes, which, in the absence of testosterone, never descended and eventually atrophied.
55. Alison Carlson, "When Is a Woman Not a Woman?" *Women's Sports and Fitness* 13 (March 1991), 24–29.
56. Ibid., 26–27. Based on the rationale of eliminating unfair genetic advantages, the IOC could just as easily be disqualifying athletes on the basis of larger bone structure, greater oxygen capacity, or a number of other genetically related physical characteristics.
57. Carlson, "When Is a Woman Not a Woman?" 28.
58. Carlson, "Chromosome Count," 44.
59. "Lesbian Issue Stirs Discussion," *Los Angeles Times* (April 6, 1992), C12. Figures on lost endorsements are difficult to calculate, but *Sports Illustrated* (July 12, 1982, 22) cited a figure of 1.5 million dollars in estimating the loss of off-court income for King after her relationship with Marilyn Barnett became public.
60. Jaime Diaz, "Find the Golf Here?" *Sports Illustrated*, (February 13, 1989), 58–64.
61. This claim is reported in the *Los Angeles Times* (April 6, 1992) and in "Out of the Closet," *Women's Sports and Fitness* 14 (September 1992), 62. These pressures affect women in athletic administration as well. The *Los Angeles Times* also reported that in a survey of female administrators, over 50 percent of respondents believed that their involvement in sports led others to assume that they were lesbian.
62. On homophobia and recruitment, see "Out of the Closet," 60–63; Robert Lipsyte, *New York Times* (June 21, 1991), B13; Alisa Solomon, "Passing Game: How Lesbians Are Being Purged from Women's College Hoops," *Village Voice* (March 26, 1991), reprinted in *Women's Sports Pages* (March 1991), 8, 13; "Lesbian Issue Stirs Discussion," *Los Angeles Times*, C1, C12; and "The 'Huge Lavender Elephant' of Women's Athletics: Homophobia's Contribution to the Decline of Women Coaches," *Equal Time* (April 12–26, 1991), 8.
63. Solomon, "Passing Game," 8.
64. The phrase comes from Pat Griffin, quoted in "The 'Huge Lavender Elephant,' " 8. See also Donna Lopiano, "How Should We Handle the Lesbian "Problem" in Women's Sports?" *The Advocate* (September 8, 1992), 96.
65. New Agenda Conference proceedings; Burton Nelson, *Are We Winning Yet?* 138; and Don Sabo, personal communication. The

decision made by conference members can, on the one hand, be understood as caving in to corporate and media pressure. On the other hand, it can be understood as a politically savvy, strategic decision based on a calculated assessment of corporate and media power to use lesbian baiting and homophobia to damage women's sport. This is precisely the bind in which feminist sport advocates committed to working within the system regularly find themselves: They can ask for and often win a bigger piece of the athletic pie but risk losing these gains whenever they attempt to reveal the underlying sexism and homophobia of the existing system.

66. "White Girls Can't Jump," *Women's Sports and Fitness* 14 (October 1992), 62.
67. Anita De Frantz, "We've Got to Be Strong," *Sports Illustrated* 75 (August 12, 1991), 77.
68. See "The Lady Vanquishes," *Sports Illustrated* 54 (September 21, 1981), 41–42; "Life in the Fast Lane," *Essence* 19 (March 1989), 48–50, and "The Best and the Brightest," *Newsweek* 112 (September 19, 1988), 54–57.
69. "For Speed and Style, Flo With the Go," *Time* 132 (September 19, 1988), 52; and "The Best and the Brightest," *Newsweek* 112 (September 19, 1988), 54–57.
70. "Flo-Jo and Jackie," *Sports Illustrated* 69 (October 10, 1988), 46, 48. It is interesting that African American men are put in the position of holding the whip/reins, when cultural stereotypes abound about strong black women and absent, emasculated black men.
71. "After the Gold, Some Glitter," *Sports Illustrated* 62 (June 3, 1985), 46.
72. Low levels of support then justify television executives in their decisions to ignore women's events. Knowing that corporations will not buy advertising time when viewing audiences are small, television programmers play it safe by sticking to popular men's sports. Similar concerns about ratings and advertising budgets govern news telecasts. A 1990 study conducted by the Amateur Athletic Federation of Los Angeles found that over a six-week period, the city's NBC affiliate devoted 92 percent of its news sportscasts to men's athletics, 5 percent to women's, and 3 percent to gender-neutral or mixed activities. Reported in *Women's Sports Pages* 4 (January/February 1992), 10–11.
73. *Women's Sports Pages* (March 1991), 4.
74. Burton Nelson envisions a sporting culture based on the partnership model rather than the current "military model" of men's and some women's sport; see *Are We Winning Yet?* For feminist discussions of alternative models of sport, see also Lopiano, "A Political

Analysis," 163–76; Boutilier and San Giovanni, "Politics, Public Policy and Title IX;" and Helen Lenskyj, "A New Ball Game: Historical and Contemporary Women-Centered Models of Sport and Physical Activity," paper presented at the Canadian Leisure Congress, University of Waterloo (May 11, 1990).

75. The fatty tissues that gradually alter the balance points and strength-to-weight ratios of the mature female body form a liability that seems to outweigh the potential advantages of experience and maturity.

76. Adrienne Blue makes this point persuasively in *Faster, Higher, Further: Women's Triumphs and Disasters at the Olympics* (London: Virago, 1988), 79–88. Blue's analysis has influenced my own thinking about gymnastics.

77. Ibid., 84.

78. The study was conducted at Michigan State University by Dr. Lionel W. Rosen and reported in the *Chicago Tribune* (May 4, 1986), 6:6.

79. The emphasis on fat reduction is true for men as well as women. But because men begin with a lower percentage of body fat and because in men's competition bulking up continues to receive more emphasis than dieting, the pressures on women to achieve definition through dieting exceed those faced by men.

80. Burton Nelson, *Are We Winning Yet?* 97–116.

# INDEX